The
Incarnation
as God's
First Intention

"Edwin van Driel is an exemplary scholar. His philosophical argumentation is delicious in its meticulousness and rigor. The Christology for which he contends in this book reaches back before the foundation of the world and thus has transformative ramifications for fundamental commitments in theology. He presents a truly theocentric vision of the gospel that is far more exciting than the lame, anthropocentric versions the church has propagated for centuries. This is the best kind of theology—the kind that brings us to praise the living God more profoundly and humbly than we did before we read it."

—**Samuel Wells**, King's College London

"In this wide-ranging study, Edwin van Driel not only makes his case for a radically supralapsarian Christology; he also works out its implications for topics ranging from the Trinity and creation to missions and everlasting life. Shaped by the conviction that, rather than being just a means to an end, the incarnation is itself the goal of God's works, *The Incarnation as God's First Intention* offers a powerful vision of what it means to confess Jesus as Emmanuel—God with us."

—**Ian A. McFarland**, Candler School of Theology

"In this engaging book, Edwin Chr. van Driel reassesses the meaning of classical Christian doctrine in light of the premise that God's first intention was to embrace human nature as a good in itself—irrespective of humanity's fall into sin—and through the incarnation to be with humanity throughout creation's history and eschatological destiny. In fluid prose and cogent argumentation, the author extolls this beautiful christological idea on every page and shows how this minority tradition can reshape our understanding of the scriptural narrative, as well as Christian belief and practice."

—**John E. Thiel**, Fairfield University (emeritus)

"Christian doctrines seek to go on talking about God as the Bible does to answer the questions it raises. The most famous of those may be, Would Jesus have come if we hadn't sinned? Implied in this are the most intimate questions about what God must desire, if the biblical stories hang together. Theologians like Van Driel make careful distinctions and seem to know more about God than is quite decent. The best book about election I know of, after Wyschogrod and Barth."

—**Eugene F. Rogers Jr.**, University of North Carolina at Greensboro (emeritus)

"In this courageous, exegetically driven, and historically informed analysis Van Driel considers what it means to rethink Christian doctrine by placing Jesus Christ at the center of the theological task. The result is a trinitarian interpretation of God and creation that not only elevates God's covenantal and koinonial purposes but provides profound insight into the account of the atonement and the vision of participation at the heart of the New Testament. A brilliant and timely study!"

—**Alan J. Torrance**, University of St. Andrews (emeritus)

The Incarnation *as* God's First Intention

Supralapsarian Christology *for* Faith and Practice

Edwin Chr. van Driel

© 2025 by Edwin Chr. van Driel

Published by Baker Academic
a division of Baker Publishing Group
Grand Rapids, Michigan
BakerAcademic.com

Printed in the United States of America

All rights reserved. No part of this publication may be reproduced, stored in a retrieval system, or transmitted in any form or by any means—for example, electronic, photocopy, recording—without the prior written permission of the publisher. The only exception is brief quotations in printed reviews.

Library of Congress Cataloging-in-Publication Control Number: 2025018048
ISBN 9781540969477 (paper)
ISBN 9781540969675 (casebound)
ISBN 9781493452057 (ebook)
ISBN 9781493452064 (pdf)

Unless otherwise indicated, Scripture quotations are from the New Revised Standard Version Bible, copyright © 1989 National Council of the Churches of Christ in the United States of America. Used by permission. All rights reserved worldwide.

Baker Publishing Group publications use paper produced from sustainable forestry practices and postconsumer waste whenever possible.

25 26 27 28 29 30 31   7 6 5 4 3 2 1

CONTENTS

Preface ix

Introduction: *The Firstborn of All Creation* 1

PART 1 • Historical Explorations 15

1. God and God's Beloved: *A Constructive Rereading of Scotus's Supralapsarian Christological Argument* 17

2. "To Know Nothing . . . Except Jesus Christ, and Him Crucified": *Supralapsarian Christology and a Theology of the Cross* 33

3. "Too Lowly . . . to Reach God Without a Mediator": *John Calvin's Supralapsarian Eschatological Narrative* 51

4. "His Death Manifested Its Power and Efficacy in Us": *The Role of Christ's Resurrection in John Calvin's Theology* 73

5. Sharing in Nature or Encountering a Person: *A Tale of Two Different Supralapsarian Strategies* 91

6. All Things Summed Up in Christ: *Reading Lesslie Newbigin's Missional-Ecumenical Project in a Supralapsarian Key* 109

PART 2 • Constructive Explorations ... 129

7. "All Things Have Been Created ... for Him":
   On Christ, Election, and Creation ... 131

8. "So That He Might Be the Firstborn Within a Large Family":
   On Supralapsarian Christology and Israel's Election ... 153

9. "In Him All the Fullness of God Was Pleased to Dwell":
   On Trinitarian Theology and Supralapsarian Christology ... 173

10. "In Him All Things Hold Together":
    Supralapsarian Christology and Astrotheology ... 203

11. "By Making Peace Through the Blood of His Cross":
    Supralapsarian Christology and Atonement ... 225

12. "First Place in Everything":
    Supralapsarian Christology and Eschatological Expectation ... 251

13. On *Being With* and Resonance:
    Supralapsarian Christology for a New Missional Era ... 277

Conclusion: *The Promise of Supralapsarian Christology* ... 299

Credits   303

Index   305

PREFACE

What would it look like to think about Jesus as the center of the universe? How would it be if everything that God has done, is doing, and will do were embedded in God's decision to take on human flesh? What difference does it make to think about everything and everyone around us, our family and friends, and those who are not so much our friends, as created for Jesus—not simply the second person of the Trinity, but Jesus, incarnate God and son of Mary? And what would it do to us, to our sense of identity and meaning making, if we were to think about ourselves not just as people created by God but as people called into existence to be part of Jesus's family?

These ideas and questions go to the heart of supralapsarian Christology. On this approach, Jesus did not come for the sake of us, but we exist for the sake of him. The incarnation is not God's response to sin, but the very first of God's intentions. Christ is not the means to a larger goal; Christ is the goal.

This book offers explorations in supralapsarian Christology. *Explorations* because it is not a full-blown Christological design. Rather, it is an interim report on the way to such a design, offering six in-depth analyses of voices past and present that help us put together the conceptual tools for such an account and seven constructive explorations of the implications of a supralapsarian Christological approach for a variety of related theological topics.

About half of this book's chapters go back to earlier essays and articles, published in a variety of journals and essay collections. While I did not write these with an eye to making them into a book, it was in conversation with Samuel Wells that I realized they actually do form the backbone of a coherent argument. I thank Sam for the inspiration. For the sake of this book, I edited the existing material to form a smooth, connected whole, and I wrote six more chapters that, together with the previously published material, explore the vast theological terrain and fresh insights and vistas that open up to us when we embrace a supralapsarian Christological approach. This book builds on my earlier book *Incarnation Anyway*, which mapped the variety of supralapsarian Christological approaches and points the way to what I hope will be a future, multivolume account of the incarnation from a supralapsarian perspective.

I would like to thank all those who supported the genesis of this book. My family—Kimberly, Christiaan, and Claudia—created the space at home for me to work. Pittsburgh Theological Seminary provided a sabbatical that allowed me to put the book together. Both my wife, Kimberly, and the PTS Center for Writing and Learning Support—Dan Fryer Griggs and Rebecca Konegen—worked on editing out the Dutchisms from my prose. Dustyn Keepers and Alexander DeMarco saw the book through the editorial process at Baker Academic, and both offered very helpful feedback on the text. Numerous publishers, named separately in the credits, allowed for reuse of earlier writings. I am deeply grateful to all of these persons and institutions.

Edwin Chr. van Driel

Introduction

The Firstborn of All Creation

The very first thing God decides is to be Jesus Christ. That is, God's first intention with regard to what is not God is to be a God with others, to give Godself to what is not God, to become incarnate. All other divine intentions *ad extra* are embedded in and shaped by this fundamental commitment. Everything else is called into being for the sake of this act of divine self-giving. As Colossians says, "All things have been created . . . for him" (Col. 1:16). The purpose of this book is to explore this central intuition.

And there is a lot to explore. If God's first intention is to be Jesus Christ, and if all of creation is called into being for him, then this fundamentally determines the way we tell the history of God and what is not God. It means that, in Jesus Christ, God does not become human because we are human but, rather, the other way around: our human existence reflects the existence God intended for Jesus Christ and is fashioned so that we might commune with him, be engaged with him, and be his friends and family. Jesus does not exist for the sake of the created cosmos; rather, creation is called into existence for him, as the theater in which the history of God's created and embodied being with God's creatures unfolds. History, including the history told in the Scriptures, is a history that has its focus and fulfillment in Jesus.

What would it look like to rethink our understanding of the biblical narratives, and the theological *loci* that are built on them, in this light? What if sin is resistance to a God whom we feel comes too close by taking on human existence itself, rather than the thing that prompts God to become incarnate to reconcile us? What if Israel is not God's plan B—called to serve God and embody God's will where Adam failed and humanity wandered off—but, rather, the people elected to be the family of God and the recipients of God's foundational gift: God's own self? What if the church, the body of Christ, is the community for which we were originally created? What if we think about the *missio Dei* as, in the words of Ephesians, the divine plan from before the foundation of the world to draw all things up into Christ? And what if the eschaton is the ongoing celebration and fulfillment of this primordial divine determination of God to come as close to God's creatures as possible by taking on a human nature, so that God can be seen, touched, and heard, so that God can sit down with us, look us in the eyes, have a meal with us? What if all of Christian theology, spirituality, and practice were rethought in this light? This book is here to wrestle with the answers to these questions.

Supralapsarian and Infralapsarian Christology

The line of thought explored in this book is an example of what is called *supralapsarian Christology*: the idea that the divine intention to become incarnate precedes (*supra*, before) the divine intention to allow for sin (*lapsus*, fall). This can be contrasted with *infralapsarian Christology*, according to which the divine intention to become incarnate logically follows (*infra*, after) the intention to allow for sin.[1] To put it differently, infralapsarian Christology holds that the incarnation is contingent upon sin; supralapsarian Christology holds that it is not.

There are various ways to explicate further the differences between these two approaches. As my language suggests, one way is to think about them in terms of a different ordering of divine intentions. Classical theology, to which I am sympathetic, holds that God's will is not subject to time. God does not deliberate God's decisions; God wills all things all at once. But this does not exclude an ordering in God's intentions. One can think about it in terms of goals and means: one might be committed to various things at the same time, but one is committed to some things not as goals in themselves but, rather, as means to accomplish other things. Or consider a mathematical formula: all parts of a formula are true at once, but the truth of things on

---

1. The terms *infralapsarian* and *supralapsarian* were originally situated in Reformed discussions about the doctrine of election. It was, however, the Roman Catholic theologian Karl Rahner who, at least in German- and English-language literature, first applied these terms to Christology. See Karl Rahner, "Grace," in *Sacramentum Mundi: An Encyclopedia of Theology*, ed. Karl Rahner et al., vol. 2, *Contrition to Grace and Freedom* (Herder & Herder, 1968), 422. See also Edwin Chr. van Driel, *Incarnation Anyway: Arguments for Supralapsarian Christology* (Oxford University Press, 2008), 5n2.

one side of the equation supports the truth of things on the other side of the equation. In the same way, we might think about different intentions within the one divine will—all these intentions are true at once, but they are distinct nonetheless; and God is committed to some for their own sakes, while others serve as means.

If one were to accept this picture of the ordering of divine intentions, even simply as a heuristic device, one could think about the difference between infralapsarian and supralapsarian Christology according to the following outlines:

Infralapsarian Christology	Supralapsarian Christology
God intends to call forth creation.	God intends to become incarnate and to call forth creation.
God intends to allow for the fall.	God intends to allow for the fall.
God intends to solve the sin problem.	God intends to solve the sin problem.
God intends to become incarnate in order to solve the sin problem.	God intends to solve the sin problem through the incarnate One.

Three things should be said to unpack these schemas further. First, the infralapsarian story is embraced by most Christian theological traditions, which hold that the incarnation is motivated by God's desire to deal with sin and evil. But these traditions nonetheless differ greatly among themselves in conceiving of how exactly God does this. *Infralapsarian Christology* is itself a family name, referring to a variety of Christological narratives falling along a wide spectrum of theological convictions. An evangelical may tell a story of Christ coming to take the punishment of sin in our stead and setting free those who accept him as their Lord and Savior. A liberation theologian may tell a story of Jesus as the one who embodies freedom for the oppressed, the one in whom God expresses solidarity with the poor. A North American mainline pastor may preach a gospel of the embrace of justice and peace, of Jesus inviting us to build God's kingdom on earth. But in each of these ways of telling the Christian story, God's presence with us in Jesus Christ is perceived against the background of, and as a response to, a problem: that of creation's brokenness and of human sin and alienation from God. For all of these ways of telling the story, the incarnation is itself embedded in a larger, already established history of God and creation.

Second, supralapsarian Christology, by contrast, embeds the story of sin and its divine response in the context of a larger narrative about Jesus. Supralapsarian Christology does not deny that in Christ God takes care of the problems of sin and evil. In fact, a supralapsarian might tell the very same story about the ways in which God in Christ counters sin and evil as the aforementioned evangelical, liberation theologian, or North American mainline pastor. But for the supralapsarian, this story is incorporated into a much larger, Christologically determined narrative that encompasses the whole story of what is not God.

Third, supralapsarian Christology itself is also a family name; it, too, refers to a variety of accounts of the incarnation and the difference they make. These accounts all hold that the incarnation is not contingent upon sin, but they differ on their understandings of why this is the case. One area of difference concerns the first step of the supralapsarian ordering of the divine will: God's intention to allow for sin is logically posterior to God's intention to become incarnate. This makes a Christological position supralapsarian. Where supralapsarians differ is in answering the question, How does the divine intention to become incarnate relate to God's intention to call into existence the rest of creation? If the incarnation is not contingent upon sin, is it nonetheless contingent upon creation? Or is the incarnation God's very first intention *ad extra*, logically preceding even God's commitment to creation?

Different Kinds of Supralapsarian Christology

There is a long tradition of portraying supralapsarian Christology as simply being concerned with a counterfactual: Would God have become incarnate had human beings not sinned?[2] Presented in this way, it can easily be dismissed as nothing but speculation. After all, human beings *have* sinned, and sin and evil shape the lives of creation in innumerable ways. What God might have done had things turned out otherwise seems to have little bearing on reality as we know it.

The best representatives of a supralapsarian Christological approach, however, do not consider the issue as concerned with a different possible world. The issue concerns *this* world and *this* incarnation. Is the event of divine self-giving, as embodied in the actual person of Jesus Christ, contingent upon sin? Is Jesus accidental to the structures of creation and eschatological consummation as we know it? Is Jesus human because we are human, or is our humanity Christologically determined, such that we are human because he is? These are the questions at hand.

---

2. This is exactly the way Thomas Aquinas presents the matter in his *Summa Theologiae* III.1.5.

Nevertheless, there are a variety of ways in which one might argue for a Christologically determined understanding of the overall story of God and what is not God. In an earlier work, I argued that one way to map the various branches of the supralapsarian Christological family tree is to focus on the three ways in which, according to the biblical story, God relates to what is not God: in creation, in eschatological consummation, and in reconciliation. That is, one can account for each of these three ways of divine relating in such a way that they give rise to a supralapsarian understanding of the motives for incarnation.[3] For example, the nineteenth-century Lutheran theologian Isaak Dorner developed a supralapsarian Christological argument rooted in his understanding of God's act of creation. He argued that God is a lover of love. In creating what is not God, God aims at aggrandizing the life of love—a twofold surrender, of God to human beings and of human beings to God. This twofold surrender is embodied in religion. The divine contribution to religion is revelation. The consummation of revelation—and thereby of religion and, ultimately, creation—is the incarnation. Twentieth-century Reformed theologian Karl Barth offered an approach that is rooted in eschatological consummation. Barth anchored his Christology in the notion of election, but election is really an eschatological category: it is the determination of the final outcome of someone's history. Barth argued that in electing creatures, God determines not only their fate but

---

3. For what follows, see Van Driel, *Incarnation Anyway*. I wrote this book partly out of frustration about the ways in which, at the time, various dogmatic handbooks would deal with supralapsarian Christology in a few simplistic paragraphs, with curiosity, and maybe with sympathy, but without seriously considering it as an alternative tradition. Since the appearance of *Incarnation Anyway*, several excellent in-depth studies of instances of supralapsarian Christology have appeared: Justus H. Hunter, *If Adam Had Not Sinned: The Reason for the Incarnation from Anselm to Scotus* (Catholic University of America Press, 2020); Dylan Schrader, *A Thomistic Christocentrism: Recovering the Carmelites of Salamanca on the Logic of the Incarnation* (Catholic University of America Press, 2021); and Phillip A. Hussey, *Supralapsarianism Reconsidered: Jonathan Edwards and the Reformed Tradition* (T&T Clark, 2024). Two Anglican theologians published major supralapsarian Christological proposals: Kathryn Tanner, *Christ the Key* (Cambridge University Press, 2010); and Samuel Wells, *Constructing an Incarnational Theology: A Christocentric View of God's Purpose* (Cambridge University Press, 2024). Theologians from a variety of backgrounds have expressed their adherence to a supralapsarian Christology: Ian A. McFarland, *The Word Made Flesh: A Theology of the Incarnation* (Westminster John Knox, 2019), 11–12; Oliver D. Crisp, *Analyzing Doctrine: Toward a Systematic Theology* (Baylor University Press, 2019), 121–38; Eugene F. Rogers Jr., *Elements of Christian Thought: A Basic Course in Christianese* (Fortress, 2021), 57–62; and David Bentley Hart, *You Are Gods: On Nature and Supernature* (University of Notre Dame Press, 2022), 112. Several New Testament scholars have since argued that Paul also adheres to a supralapsarian Christological logic. See N. T. Wright, *Paul and the Faithfulness of God* (SPCK, 2013), 1210–11; and Douglas A. Campbell, *Pauline Dogmatics: The Triumph of God's Love* (Eerdmans, 2020), 572–93. On this, see also Edwin Chr. van Driel, *Rethinking Paul: Protestant Theology and Pauline Exegesis* (Cambridge University Press, 2021), 254–84.

also God's own eschatological life. Election is a determination toward eternal life with God; but therefore, and first of all, it is also the determination of the divine life as being with God's creatures. The fullest expression of this divine intention to be God with others is Jesus Christ. Finally, Friedrich Schleiermacher illustrates that even the doctrine of redemption can give rise to a supralapsarian Christological argument. His supralapsarianism was based on his doctrine of absolute dependence and divine causality. Because absolute dependence of humans on God implies a nonreciprocal relationship between God and creation, the incarnation cannot be conceived as a divine response to human sin. And since everything falls within the scope of divine causality, including sin, Schleiermacher did not construe sin as opposition to the divine initiative, but as part of it. Sin and redemption are means through which God connects all humankind to Christ, through whom the divine impartation enters the world.

This schema, however, does not yet get at the issue identified earlier: In the ordering of divine decisions, should we think about creation or incarnation as having first priority? For many supralapsarian Christological approaches, incarnation stands in the service not of sin but of creation. For both Dorner and Schleiermacher, the incarnation is still a means to a larger end: to consummate creation and to impart Godself to the world. Similarly, analytic theologian Oliver D. Crisp recently proposed participation in the divine life to be the goal of creation. God therefore calls into being creatures who are ideally suited for that kind of relationship with the divine. In order to accommodate this participation, God unites "with one of these creaturely natures, assuming it and thereby generating an interface between divinity and humanity so that human beings may have a conduit by means of which they may be united to God."[4] On this understanding, God "intends the incarnation as a fitting means to [the] final end in creation," and as such, the incarnation is located in the ordering of divine intentions in a supralapsarian manner.[5]

But is the incarnation indeed a means to a goal? Is the incarnation contingent upon creation? Interestingly, Crisp supports his proposal with a quotation from Colossians. In the hymn in Colossians 1:15–18a, Christ is said to be much more than simply the Redeemer, Crisp points out; he is also the one "*for whom* all things are created."[6] But this is not what Crisp's own argument amounts to. On his proposal, Christ is not the one for whom all things were created. He is the means to a larger end, the conduit through which

---

4. Crisp, *Analyzing Doctrine*, 125.

5. Crisp, *Analyzing Doctrine*, 127. Crisp's approach is in some ways very similar to David Bentley Hart's. Hart also thinks about the incarnation as the supralapsarian means to the divinization of humanity (see his *You Are Gods*, 112).

6. Crisp, *Analyzing Doctrine*, 135 (emphasis original).

creation might reach its goal; and while he does not come for the sake of sin, he nonetheless comes for the sake of creation.

Why Supralapsarian?

Why might one embrace a supralapsarian reading of Scripture? And in particular, why might one embrace a reading that denies, not only that Christ is contingent upon sin, but also that he is contingent upon creation? Why say that the very first divine determination *ad extra* is to be Jesus Christ?

Rowan Williams likens the theologian's reading of the Scriptures to a medical doctor who, before the time of X-rays, might gain knowledge of a human body by very carefully tracing their hands over the skin, feeling what lies hidden under the surface. What is the layout of the bone structures, and how are the ligaments connected? What are the muscles that make the body move? Where are organs located, and what can one say about their size and health by paying close attention to what one can feel through the skin? Likewise, the theologian carefully moves their hands over the surface of Scripture, feeling for what lies hidden. What is this text's narrative substructure? How do the parts join together? In what direction does the movement go? And how does this order and movement compare to the order and movement discernable from a similar examination of a theological narrative or a constructive theological proposal?

One strategy to support a supralapsarian Christological reading of Scripture is to show how the alternative simply does not hold up to the pressures exerted by the biblical narrative. For example, the Scriptures tell us that the eschaton is intimately bound up with the person of Christ. Not only are human beings eschatologically modeled after him; the eschaton is also an eternally being with him. Moreover, in this, creation is changed for the better. Eschatologically, human beings will no longer sin exactly because they will be like Christ. They will enjoy a closeness with God that goes beyond what they have ever received before; and the key to this is the centrality of the incarnate One. On an infralapsarian reading of things, Christ is not part of God's original eschatological intentions for creation. If the eschaton is better than the proton because of Christ, and Christ's presence in creation is contingent upon sin, then sin makes the eschaton better than originally intended. Human beings end up closer to God because of sin. This seems, however, theologically incongruent—or, as Albert the Great said, "*valde improprie*" (very improper).[7]

---

7. As reported by his student Thomas Aquinas. See Aquinas, *Summa Theologiae* III.1.3 ad. 3. For a much more detailed version of this argument see "Incarnation Anyway," in chap. 2, below, 36; and Van Driel, *Incarnation Anyway*, 150–55.

However, there are also places in the Scriptures where the supralapsarian logic does not stay hidden under the surface but directs the logic of the text in unmistakable ways. One such place is the already-referenced hymn in Colossians 1. What is striking in this hymn is not just its supralapsarian Christological character but also that it implies the absolute priority of Christ. Speaking about the incarnate Son, the one in whom the invisible God has become visible (1:15), the hymn claims that "in him all things in heaven and on earth were created"—that is, "all things have been created through him and for him" (1:16). Infralapsarian Christology cannot make sense of this claim. On the logic of the infralapsarian story, all things have not been created for the incarnate One; rather, the incarnate One was fashioned a human nature for the sake of all things. Further, if all things were created for Christ, then before God intended to create all things, God intended to be Jesus. The hymn then goes on to say, reflecting the schema outlined above, that once creation wanders away from God it is also the incarnate One through whom "God was pleased to reconcile to himself all things" (1:20). Jesus is not just the firstborn of creation; he is also the firstborn from the dead, "so that he might come to have first place in everything" (1:18). The hymn is governed by the logic of Christ's absolute priority.[8]

Once we notice the idea of Christ's priority appearing on the surface of Scripture in a place like Colossians 1, we can also detect it in other places. For instance, scholars often assume that the Colossians and Ephesians letters are closely related. The Ephesians letter is shaped by a Christological narrative that speaks of a plan that God had from "before the foundation of the world" (1:4) to "gather up all things" in Christ (1:10). One might debate where one should locate this divine determination. Does "before the foundation of the world" refer to a divine foreknowledge of sin, because of which God determined to save creation through Christ? An infralapsarian reading of the text has to suppose so. However, it is not clear that such a determination truly can be said to be "before the foundation of the world." It seems that, on such a reading, the world was founded at least in God's intentionality before God intended Christ: God determined to call forth creation, foresaw human sin, and subsequently determined the plan of salvation. Read through the lens of Colossians, we can give full weight to the Ephesian "before": before God determined there would be any world at all, God already elected God's beloved in Christ.

A similar lens can be used to read Paul's rhapsody in Romans 8. He there claims that the predestined will be "conformed to the image of his Son, in

---

8. For an extensive exegetical discussion of the Colossians hymn, see "The Firstborn of All Creation," in chap. 7, below, 133–37.

order that he might be the firstborn within a large family" (Rom. 8:29). Again, Paul is most likely speaking here of the incarnate Christ, not just the second person of the Trinity. It is only as the incarnate One that Christ is "the firstborn." But on infralapsarian logic, Christ is actually *not* the firstborn; he is the lastborn. Or, to put it differently, on such a reading, Christ is born for the sake of the human family. According to Paul's claim though, humanity is elected and refashioned for the sake of the incarnate One. That fits the idea of the absolute priority of Christ.[9]

Finally, the whole prologue to John's Gospel can be read quite coherently and revealingly from a supralapsarian Christological perspective. The prologue can be read as telling the story of a world that is created with an eye to the Word's incarnation and his taking up residence in creation. Beginning the narration even before the "in the beginning" of Genesis 1, it starts with a moment when there is only God and the Word. This Word starts to speak, and his speech is life, and this life is the light, the light that is the presence of himself, a light that seems to come closer and closer until it becomes visible to all as the Word steps onto the world scene on Christmas night. "The true light, which enlightens everyone, was coming into the world" (v. 9). This in turn expresses something about the nature of this creation. "He was in the world, and the world came into being through him. . . . He came to what was his own" (vv. 10, 11). This world is not strange to the Word. It is the place he calls his own. It is a place created to host the Word—it is supposed to be the Word's home. This world nonetheless resists the coming of the Word. John has no qualms pointing this out, either. "He came to what was his own, and his own people did not accept him" (v. 11). But John also makes clear that the resistance against the Word does not have the last word: "The light shines in the darkness, and the darkness did not overcome it" (v. 5). The deepest word about this world is not that it is dark; the deepest word about this world is that it was made by, and for, the Word.

The Road Ahead

This book does not present a fully developed supralapsarian Christological account. Rather, it explores a set of historical debates, conceptual distinctions, and lines of thought that will hopefully stimulate further thinking and conversation about a supralapsarian Christological approach and its consequences for Christian theology and practice. As such, it is also an interim

---

9. See also "*Being With*," in chap. 7, below, 138–39.

report on the way to a complete account of Christ's being and work from a supralapsarian perspective.

The first half of the book contains in-depth analyses of several key figures and concepts that help us along the way.[10] The second half consists of constructive explorations of the ways in which the central intuition of this book—God's first intention is to be Jesus Christ—shapes the way we tell the Christian story and live the Christian life.

The medieval theologian John Duns Scotus is usually seen as one of the key figures in the development of supralapsarian Christology. It is therefore proper to start with an exploration of his thought. In the first chapter, I lay out Scotus's supralapsarian argument and contrast it with the earlier, less felicitous, approaches of his medieval predecessors. I also argue that, Scotus's reputation for clarity and precision notwithstanding, his key argument has been read in several ways, all of which lead to theological problems. I therefore suggest a different interpretation—one that, while not consistent with the letter of Scotus's argument, I believe is nonetheless consistent with its spirit. This interpretation of Scotus's argument will feed into my own constructive explorations.

In the second chapter, I turn to what can easily be seen as the exact opposite of supralapsarian Christology: a theology of the cross. Supralapsarian Christology decenters the cross in the overall story of God and creation. But, as I noted above, it does not deny the centrality of the incarnate One for reconciliation and atonement. Nonetheless, what does a supralapsarian Christology make of Martin Luther's claim that the only one who "deserves to be called a theologian" is the one "who comprehends the visible and manifest things of God seen through suffering and the cross"?[11] Engaging various versions of a *theologia crucis*, including Luther's classic statement in his Heidelberg Disputation, I show that my preferred version of supralapsarian Christology does not contradict the theological intuitions undergirding a Lutheran cross theology and that such theology can actually form the basis for another supralapsarian Christological argument.

Moving from one Reformer to another, in the third and fourth chapters I focus on the thought of John Calvin. Though Calvin has previously been seen

---

10. As I mentioned in the acknowledgments, these chapters go back to previously published book chapters and journal essays. Several of them have already found their way into wider theological discussions. I have edited them only lightly for this volume. Therefore, readers who come to these essays looking for the content of the earlier versions will find no change. Readers who are new to this material will hopefully experience these chapters as a coherent set of explorations.

11. Martin Luther, Heidelberg Disputation, *Luther's Works*, vol. 31, *Career of the Reformer I*, ed. Harold J. Grimm (Fortress, 1957), 40.

as an avid infralapsarian, recently some bold proposals have argued that a supralapsarian Christological approach is actually embedded in his thought. I show that this reading is mistaken but that it nonetheless puts us on track to surface something previously not discovered: While Calvin does not have a supralapsarian Christology, he does have a strong supralapsarian eschatology that shapes his thought in deep and complicated ways. This implicit supralapsarian eschatological through line needs to be distinguished from his explicit infralapsarian account of traditional eschatological notions such as resurrection and the last judgment. Making these distinctions both allows us to solve some theological conundrums regarding Calvin's own thought and also introduces the constructive idea that, in addition to Christology, one might entertain supralapsarian accounts of other key parts of the Christian story. In the second part of this book, I will explore examples of these accounts, such as God's love for Israel and the formation of the church.

In the fifth chapter, I move to more contemporary representatives of supralapsarian Christological thought. The works of Anglican theologians Kathryn Tanner and Sam Wells include a supralapsarian understanding of the incarnation and the difference it makes. They conceive of this difference in very dissimilar ways, though. Tanner thinks of the difference the incarnation makes in terms of ontological transformation; Wells thinks of it in terms of closer interpersonal engagement. Analyzing this difference invites a closer examination of the ontological claims about the incarnation embedded in the ecumenical creeds. I argue for the superiority of the Christological approach represented by Wells and will draw on this argument in later, constructive chapters of this book.

In the sixth and last analytic chapter, I turn to the work of the ecumenist and missiologist Lesslie Newbigin. I read his work as offering one of the first postcolonial ecclesiologies, drawing us into the experiences and theological thought of the Church of South India, in which Newbigin served as a bishop. In this chapter, I analyze Newbigin's fresh and original accounts of the doctrines of election, salvation, and the church. Newbigin's thoughts about these doctrines developed from his time in South India to his work, in retirement, on ecclesial life in a post-Christian European world. I show how a yet-undetected through line in all this is formed by an appeal to the Ephesians image of all things being gathered into Christ. I argue that this theme is best read in a supralapsarian Christological key. As such, Newbigin's work offers an entryway into a supralapsarian Christological retelling of the Christian story for a new missional era.

In the seventh chapter, I turn to further constructive explorations of the implications of the absolute priority of Christ for the ways in which we unpack

Christian doctrine and practice. These constructive chapters are not meant as a consecutive argument but, rather, as explorations in multiple directions, all fueled by the same, central, theological intuition. I imagine them as spokes of a wheel, held together by the one idea of the absolute priority of Christ. I begin with a rereading of the doctrine of election. When John Duns Scotus transformed medieval supralapsarian Christological thinking, he did so by offering an argument about the predestination of Christ. A similar thing can be said about Karl Barth's Christocentric turn in his *Church Dogmatics*. This book's central intuition can likewise be read as an argument about election. If election is a determination of one's eschatological goal, then God's first intention *ad extra*—to become incarnate—is a form of election. God determines to be a God *with* others and to call others into existence *to be with* God. In this programmatic and constructive chapter, I explore how the whole of the unfolding of the relationship between God and God's creatures can subsequently be read in this light.

In the eighth chapter, I continue the previous discussion about election, but now focused on the election of Israel. The notion that the Creator of all would elect a particular people is still a theological stumbling block for many. I argue that supralapsarian Christology offers a novel way to negotiate the tension between universality and particularity. God determines to be a God with others, and as such becomes Creator and Consummator of all. At the same time, and primordially, God determines to be so as a particular human being: Jesus Christ, Mary's son. Embedded in this determination to be a particular human being is also the election of a particular family, a particular tribe, and a particular place and time as the family, tribe, and location of this human being. This chapter offers a reading of Israel's election through this lens.

The seventh and eighth chapters are thus supralapsarian Christological explorations downstream from God's commitment to become incarnate and create. In the ninth chapter, I ask whether a commitment to this kind of Christology also has consequences upstream: What does it mean for our understanding of God-in-Godself, the triune nature of God, and how we conceive of the relationship of the triune God to what is not God? Supralapsarian Christology invites us to read differently some of the New Testament passages that concern the second trinitarian person's involvement with the origins of creation. Since, on an infralapsarian Christology, the incarnate One comes only late to God's relating to what is not God, in this tradition these texts are usually read as concerning the non-incarnate divine Word. They are understood as telling us something about the personal properties of the second person and his particular role within the taxis of the Trinity. But once one embraces a supralapsarian Christology, another reading becomes possible:

These texts can be understood to be speaking about the *logos incarnandus*, about the God who is committed to be Jesus Christ. By reading closely sections from Thomas Aquinas and engaging current Roman Catholic theology, I draw out the consequences of this rereading for an alternative approach to the doctrine of the Trinity.

In the tenth chapter, I add a little science (fiction) to this book's theological explorations. In current conversations, supralapsarian Christology intersects with arguments about theology, astrobiology, and extraterrestrial life. Some theologians hold that supralapsarian theology creates the logical space for the notion of multiple incarnations throughout the cosmos. In this chapter, I explore the implications of my constructive supralapsarian Christological approach for this conversation and what light my approach may be able to shed on the question of how to conceive of the relationship between Christ and the cosmos as a whole.

In the eleventh chapter, I return to a question raised at the beginning of this book: What does a supralapsarian approach to the incarnation make of the cross? In this chapter, I focus on the doctrine of atonement. The chapter has a twofold aim. First, I wish to disillusion those who think that supralapsarian Christology is meant as an alternative to particular readings of the cross that are deeply embedded in Protestant traditions, such as the notion of penal substitution. Using Anselm of Canterbury's mapping of the different ways in which God might have dealt with the sin problem—through simply offering forgiveness, obtaining payment, or executing punishment—I show that each of these approaches can be, and has been, combined with a supralapsarian understanding of the incarnation. Second, I unpack what the particular theological commitments that give rise to this book's constructive supralapsarian approach imply for the ways one might want to think about the difference the cross makes.

In the twelfth chapter, I turn to eschatology. This book is driven by a supralapsarian Christological argument that results in an eschatological vision that is particular and universal, communal and personal, participatory but not divinizing. In this last chapter, I show how this approach offers new trajectories for contemporary conversations on eschatological remembering and forgetting, deification, and the ultimate vision of God.

Finally, in the thirteenth chapter, I return to the promise embedded in my earlier discussion of the work of Lesslie Newbigin: Supralapsarian Christology might offer a retelling of the Christian story that is particularly fruitful for a new missional era. In this chapter, I make my case in conversation with the North American theologian Andrew Root and the German sociologist and philosopher Hartmut Rosa. Root has drawn significant attention with a series of books about Christian ministry in a secular age. In his cultural analysis, Root draws heavily on Rosa's work, which makes the case, in several highly influential studies, that the alienation many in the West experience is the result of a lack of resonance. Human beings need experiences of resonance, Rosa argues, in order to find meaning in their lives. Root takes up this insight by arguing that in the Christian faith such experiences of resonance are found in cruciform encounters with God and others. Delving into Rosa's argument, I argue that Root is mistaken. What Rosa observes is much better understood in the context of a supralapsarian Christological understanding of creation—that is, we are called into being to *be with* and, as such, to experience resonance with the incarnate God and with one another. I explore the implications of this for the ways we think about church, mission, and the life of the Christian community.

PART 1

Historical Explorations

Though supralapsarian Christology may be a minority tradition within Christian theology, it can boast a venerable history. Some detect the first, implicit building blocks for a supralapsarian Christological account already in the church fathers' understandings of redemption.[1] The first time the idea that the incarnation might not be contingent upon sin explicitly entered the theological discussion was in the work of the early medieval writer Rupert of Deutz (ca. 1075–1129/30). Since then, one can detect a continuing supralapsarian Christological tradition, carried by medieval luminaries such as Robert Grosseteste, Alexander of Hales, Albert the Great, and John Duns Scotus; controversial Reformation voices such as Andreas Osiander and Michael Servetus; venerable Puritan divines such as Thomas Goodwin and Jonathan Edwards; and an explosion of supralapsarian Christological thought in the nineteenth century, spanning Roman Catholic, Lutheran, Anglican, and Reformed traditions.[2]

---

1. See Samuel Wells, *Constructing an Incarnational Theology: A Christocentric View of God's Purpose* (Cambridge University Press, 2025), chap. 4.

2. I offer a sketch of the genealogy of Christological supralapsarianism in Edwin Chr. van Driel, *Incarnation Anyway: Arguments for Supralapsarian Christology* (Oxford University Press, 2008), 171–75.

We sorely need a history of supralapsarian Christology to trace these names and the historical and conceptual ties that bind them together. This, however, is not such a book. The next six chapters offer soundings of several historical figures and theological notions and ideas. They are chronologically ordered, beginning with the medieval theologian John Duns Scotus and ending with the twentieth-century missionary and ecumenicist Lesslie Newbigin. They are selected not for the sake of narrating a historical story but because of the ways in which these figures and ideas may contribute to advancing the construal of a particular supralapsarian Christological argument. Some, such as John Duns Scotus and Samuel Wells, serve as inspirational and congenial conversation partners for the approach I take in this book. Others, such as John Calvin and the theologians representing forms of a *theologia crucis*, help illuminate my case by serving as contrasting figures. The missional thinking of Lesslie Newbigin opens up the potential of a supralapsarian Christological narrative for a missional age. All together, these chapters provide building blocks for the constructive explorations in the second part of the book.

1

God and God's Beloved

A Constructive Rereading of Scotus's Supralapsarian Christological Argument

John Duns Scotus is usually seen as a decisive contributor to theological reflections on the primacy of Christ.[1] His thinking therefore seems an appropriate place to start the explorations of this book. But while this characterization is certainly deserved, the burden of this chapter is to draw attention to a complication in Scotus's Christological theological heritage, as well as to suggest a constructive way forward. Scotus's work contains two different arguments about the supralapsarian nature of the incarnation. The most extensive, and the one that has generated the most attention, is an argument about an ordering within God's will. The second argument is found in only one part of Scotus's writings and consists of a description of the ordering of God's love. I begin this chapter with an analysis of Scotus's first argument and the ways in which Scotus's approach differs from his supralapsarian predecessors. This is ground covered many times over in the literature, and I do not pretend to offer any new insights. A good grip on the nature of Scotus's first argument serves two

---

1. See, e.g., Francis Xavier Pancheri, *The Universal Primacy of Christ*, trans. Juniper B. Carol (Christendom, 1984), 31; and Ilia Delio, "Revisiting the Franciscan Doctrine of Christ," *Theological Studies* 64 (2003): 3–23. See also the multiple studies on Christ's primacy that enthusiastically present the idea as "the Scotistic viewpoint" or an expression of "the Scotistic school": Michael D. Meilach, *The Primacy of Christ: In Doctrine and Life* (Franciscan Herald, 1964); Jean-François Bonnefoy, *Christ and the Cosmos* (St. Anthony Guild, 1965); Juniper B. Carol, *Why Jesus Christ? Thomistic, Scotistic and Conciliary Perspectives* (Trinity Communications, 1986).

goals, however: It allows me to show how Scotus's second argument is different, and it clarifies some parameters for my intended constructive rereading. As I will argue, Scotus's first argument tells us only that incarnation is first in the order of divine willing, but it does not tell us anything about the divine intentions in becoming incarnate. It is a formal argument without material theological content. Scotus's second argument is the place to go to learn more about God's intentions in becoming human. However, as has almost never been observed in the secondary literature, the most natural reading of Scotus's second argument is inconsistent with Scotus's own account of the metaphysics of the incarnation. This is the point that I would like to invite further conversation about. To start this conversation, in the second part of this chapter I offer an alternative approach to the primacy of Christ that, while not consistent with the letter of Scotus's arguments, I believe nonetheless to be consistent with their spirit.

Incarnation and Election

The Shape of the First Argument

Scotus locates his first supralapsarian argument in an observation going back to Saint Augustine, that incarnation is a form of election. In the incarnation, God takes a particular human nature to be God's own. This nature is in no respect different from any other human nature; in other words, all human natures are assumable. In assuming this particular nature, God therefore elects it for this particular goal.[2]

To this observation, Scotus adds his own argument regarding the supralapsarian nature of election. Scotus premises this on the idea that every purposefully acting person sets a goal before deciding on the means to achieve the goal. The goal of election is eschatological bliss—"the enjoyment of God." The means by which God draws people to eschatological bliss are acts of their will: faith and love. As a most-ordered decider, God predestines people before God considers the right use of their will. The order is reversed when it comes to condemnation. A righteous God cannot condemn unless there is cause for condemnation—the wrong use of the will: sin. The upshot of this argument is that the object of election is just a creature; the object of rejection is, however, a sinner as well as a creature. Condemnation is infralapsarian; predestination is supralapsarian.[3]

---

2. See Augustine, *The Predestination of the Saints* 15.30–31; and Augustine, *The Gift of Perseverance* 24.67.

3. See, e.g., John Duns Scotus, *Lectura* 1.41, in *Duns Scotus on Divine Love: Texts and Commentary on Goodness and Freedom, God and Humans*, ed. A. Vos, H. Veldhuis, E. Dekker,

Putting these two positions together, Scotus observes that incarnation is not just a form of election but the predestination of a particular human nature to bliss, to be hypostatically united with the divine Word. Since predestination is supralapsarian, so is the predestination of the human nature of Christ. Moreover, to be made the very human nature of God is the highest form of enjoyment of God a nature could experience. A most-ordered decider will not only determine a purpose before the means but will also decide on the most central object of the purpose before deciding on those who are included in the purpose at a greater distance. Christ's human nature therefore must have been predestined first. The incarnation is not only supralapsarian; it also has priority over everything else.[4]

The Advantages of Scotus's Argumentative Strategy

Scotus was not the first to advance an explicitly supralapsarian Christological strategy. Since Rupert of Deutz in the eleventh century, a number of theologians had argued that the incarnation is not contingent upon sin.[5] Compared to the approaches of his predecessors, the nature of Scotus's argument has at least three theological advantages.

First, Scotus's predecessors tend to appeal to the principle of plenitude, according to which the highest being, God, as perfectly good, is maximally self-giving.[6] From this, someone like Robert Grosseteste concludes that, given God's nature, incarnation must happen and would have happened even if humans had not sinned: "Goodness exerts itself, insofar as it can, for the benefit of all. . . . The universe is capable of this good, namely, that it have a part of itself as the God-man. . . . It is capable of this good, and was not made capable of this good by the fall of man. . . . So then, even if man had not fallen, the universe would not lack so great a good."[7] The problem with this line of

---

N. W. den Bok, A. J. Beck (Ashgate, 2003), 146–64. See also Dolf te Velde, "Verkiezing en verwerping bij Johannes Duns Scotus: Een analyse van Ordinatio 1.41," *Kerk en Theologie* 65 (2014): 233–48.

4. See John Duns Scotus, *Ordinatio* 3.7.3, in *Franciscan Christology: Selected Texts, Translations and Introductory Essays*, ed. Damian McElrath (Franciscan Institute, 1980), 146–53. For a collection of Latin texts and translations, see Maximilian Mary Dean, *A Primer on the Absolute Primacy of Christ* (Academy of the Immaculate, 2006), 125–30, 33–43. I am bracketing here the ongoing conversation about the authenticity of some, or any, of these texts.

5. For a recent analysis of this history, see Justus H. Hunter, *If Adam Had Not Sinned: The Reason for the Incarnation from Anselm to Scotus* (Catholic University of America Press, 2020).

6. On the principle of plenitude, see the classic study by Arthur Lovejoy, *The Great Chain of Being: A Study of the History of an Idea* (Harvard University Press, 1971).

7. Robert Grosseteste, *On the Cessation of the Laws*, trans. Stephen M. Hildebrand (Catholic University of America Press, 2012), 3.1.3. For recent studies of Grosseteste's arguments, see Dominic Unger, "Robert Grosseteste, Bishop of Lincoln (1235–1253) on the Reasons for

argument is that it necessitates both that God incarnates and that God creates. If God is necessarily and perfectly good, and it is an essential feature of the good to share of itself, then God's actions of creation and incarnation are not contingent but necessary implications of God's being. This contradicts the Christian understanding of creation as a free act of God. Scotus's argument carefully avoids appealing to the principle of plenitude; his argument, rather, starts from the otherwise contingent acts of divine election and incarnation *as they happened* and reflects on the logical ordering of these acts in the light of God's perfections.[8] Scotus's argument does not oblige God to do anything; rather, it takes God's free acts of creation, election, and incarnation as given and discerns their internal logic in the light of God's perfection.

Second, in taking his starting point in history as it actually unfolded, Scotus distances himself from an argumentative strategy that casts supralapsarian

---

the Incarnation," *Franciscan Studies* 16, no. 1 (1956): 26–54; James McEvoy, "The Absolute Predestination of Christ in the Theology of Robert Grosseteste," in *Sapientiae Doctrina: Mélanges de théologie et de littérature médiévales offerts à Dom Hildebrand Bascour O.S.B* (Abbaye du Mont César, 1980), 212–30; James McEvoy, *Robert Grosseteste* (Oxford University Press, 2000), 127–30; James R. Ginther, *Master of the Sacred Page: A Study of the Theology of Robert Grosseteste, ca. 1229/30–1235* (Ashgate, 2004), 121–12; and Hunter, *If Adam Had Not Sinned*, 71–110.

For an argument identical to Grosseteste's, see Thomas Aquinas's teacher Albertus Magnus, who a century later would write, "Good is diffusive of itself, as is being: therefore it belongs to the best, in the best manner that it can, to diffuse itself: but the good cannot diffuse itself better among us, than by incarnating: therefore it seems that there would have been incarnation even if there were no sin." Quoted in Brendan Case, "'More Splendid than the Sun': Christ's Flesh Among the Reasons for the Incarnation," *Modern Theology* 36, no. 4 (2020): 762n19. See also Hunter, *If Adam Had Not Sinned*, 167–69.

8. That Scotus avoids the principle of plenitude should be no surprise, since an account of the contingency and freedom of God's actions in relation to what is not God is an essential part of his theological outlook. See John Duns Scotus, *Freedom and Contingency: Lectura I.39*, trans. and ed. A. Vos Jacz., H. Veldhuis, A. H. Looman-Graaskamp, E. Dekker, and N. W. den Bok (Kluwer, 1992). For a study of Scotus's supralapsarian argument in the light of his predecessors' adherence to the principle of plenitude, see Nico den Bok, "Geven om de ander: Scotus' visie op God's liefde, verkiezing en menswording als moment in de geschiedenis van het volheidsbeginsel," *Bijdragen* 60, no. 1 (1999): 25–53.

Hunter rightly chides Carol, Pancheri, and Horan for not clearly observing the structuring difference between Grosseteste's and Scotus's argumentative strategies. See Hunter, *If Adam Had Not Sinned*, 26; Carol, *Why Jesus Christ?*; Pancheri, *Universal Primacy of Christ*; and Daniel P. Horan, "How Original Was Scotus on the Incarnation? Reconsidering the History of the Absolute Predestination of Christ in Light of Robert Grosseteste," *Heythrop Journal* 52, no. 3 (2011): 374–91.

Scotus's strategy should also alleviate the concerns of his predecessor Saint Bonaventure, who, even while the structure of his theology seems to bend inevitably toward a supralapsarian Christology, resists this move on grounds of the freedom of God, fearing that it "in a certain manner encloses God with the perfection of the universe, and imposes a certain necessity on him, since it says that otherwise his works could not be brought to perfection." Bonaventure, *III Sent.* 1.2.2.concl., quoted in Case, "'More Splendid than the Sun,'" 771.

Christology in terms of counterfactuals. As illustrated by Grosseteste's formulations, before Scotus the issue of supralapsarian Christology was framed as a debate about whether God would have become incarnate had humanity not sinned. This leaves supralapsarians open to the charge of being involved in a speculative exercise. The Reformer John Calvin, an avid infralapsarian, would later speak of "vague speculations that captivate the frivolous and the seekers after novelty."[9] In fact, he says, whoever engages these kinds of questions "shows that he is not even content with the very Christ who was given to us."[10] To this, Scotus would have a simple answer. His account is not an exercise in speculation about a counterfactual situation but an investigation into the very Christ who was given to us. His point is that the claims of the biblical narrative about God's character and God's relationship to the world as it is suggest a richness to the act of incarnation that goes beyond a divine measure to counter sin.

Third, Scotus's argument allows one to give full weight to the *priority* of Christ in God's relating to that which is not God. This is not the case with many of the arguments Scotus's predecessors developed to argue for Christological supralapsarianism. As noted above, one of their preferred argumentative strategies was premised on the necessary self-diffusing goodness of God. The other, maybe even more popular, avenue was to argue for the incarnation as the necessary means to perfect creation. For example, Grosseteste argues that without the incarnation creation would have no coherence because it would be missing a center. As Grosseteste aims to illustrate in multiple examples, the human family and the church would be missing a head that draws all other members together.[11] Both these lines of argument advanced by Scotus's predecessors support supralapsarianism. As I noted above, the problem with the first line of argument is its necessitarianism. The problem with the second line of argument is that it puts the incarnation in the service of another, larger good. While the argument entails that the incarnation is not contingent upon sin, the incarnation is still contingent upon a prior goal in the ordering of divine determinations. This approach contrasts with a Christological supralapsarianism based on a text like Colossians 1, a favorite of many contemporary Scotists.[12] On this text, the incarnation does not happen for the sake of something else; rather, all things exist for the sake of the

---

9. John Calvin, *Institutes of the Christian Religion*, ed. John T. McNeill, trans. Ford Lewis Battles, 2 vols. (Westminster, 1960), 2.7.4.

10. Calvin, 2.7.5. On the thought that Calvin's own Christology has supralapsarian tendencies, see chap. 3, below.

11. Grosseteste, *On the Cessation of the Laws*, 3.1.10–29.

12. See, e.g., Meilach, *Primacy of Christ*, 66–76; Bonnefoy, *Christ and the Cosmos*, 134–214; Carol, *Why Jesus Christ?*, 155–60; and Dean, *Absolute Primacy of Christ*, 67–90. I myself explore this text as a starting point for Christological supralapsarianism in chap. 7 of this book,

incarnate One. "All things have been created . . . for him" (Col. 1:16). This calls for an ordering of God's determinations in which the incarnation has absolute priority. If all things were created for him, before God determined to call forth anything else at all, God already had determined to be Jesus Christ. This is not the case in an argument that sees the incarnation as a means to perfect creation. But it is the case in Scotus's supralapsarian argument.

What the Argument Does Not Deliver

Scotus's argumentative strategy thus has significant advantages over the ones employed by his supralapsarian predecessors. Nonetheless, it is important to observe what his argument does not deliver. Scotus's argument is only formal, not material. It is an argument about what, given divine perfection, can be said about the ordering of God's determinations. It offers no material suggestions about the intention behind God's decision. The argument concludes with the absolute priority of the incarnate One; it has nothing to say about why there is an incarnation in the first place. As such, the argument offers very little to shape our theological imagination. It knows that Christ undergirds God's relationship with all that is not God, but it offers us nothing with which to step beyond this.[13] For this, we need a differently shaped argument.

However, in order to stay true to the argumentative strategy Scotus has chosen, whatever we say materially beyond this point should not lean on the principle of plenitude but should do right by the contingency and freedom of God's relationships to what is not God; it should avoid speculation about counterfactual realities and instead discern the intentionality of and within salvation history as it has been unfolding; and it should allow us to say not only that the incarnation is not contingent upon sin but that the incarnation is the very first thing God determined as God decided there would be anything beyond God at all.

Incarnation and Love

The Shape of the Second Argument

Scotus's second argument is significantly less prominent in his writings; it can be found in only one location. However, from a constructive theological

---

as well as in Edwin Chr. van Driel, *Rethinking Paul: Protestant Theology and Pauline Exegesis* (Cambridge University Press, 2021), 276–84.

13. It is thus surprising that Richard Cross presents this argument under the heading "The Motive for the Incarnation," since what is conspicuously absent from the argument is any discussion of the motive for the incarnation. See Richard Cross, *Duns Scotus* (Oxford University Press, 1999), 127.

point of view, it is crucial, as it offers the material content lacking in Scotus's formal supralapsarian stance: "At the first moment, God loves himself; at the second moment, God loves himself for others, and this love is a pure love; at the third moment, God wills that he is loved by him who can love him above all, speaking of love from someone extrinsic; and, at the fourth moment, he foresaw the union of that nature which ought to love him above all, although nobody had fallen.... At the fifth moment, God saw that the coming mediator would suffer and would redeem his people."[14]

Love motivates incarnation. Scotus distinguishes five instances, or "moments," of divine loving. In identifying these instances, Scotus suggests not a chronological structure but an intentional ordering within God's single, indivisible will.[15] According to the first structural moment, every other movement of the divine willing is embedded in God's love for Godself. God is the best possible person, and as such the most lovable. As the best possible person, God loves that which is most lovable above all else. In the second instance, this God then also "loves himself for others." This instance still expresses a desire God has for Godself, but it is distinct and independent from the first instance of divine self-love. In the first instance, God loves Godself for God's own sake; in the second instance, God loves Godself for the sake of others. God determines to step outside of Godself, to be a God for that which is not God. It is a "pure love" (*amor castus*), Scotus asserts. Commentators have wrestled with what this means.[16] I will return to it in due course. This divine loving of God for the sake of others is followed by the third structural moment, in which Scotus names the incarnate One: "him who can love [God] above all." In the fourth moment, God foresees uniting Godself with this human nature. As God foresees this union before sin obtains, it is a supralapsarian union.

In what follows, I will focus on the third instance: "God wills that he is loved by him who can love him above all." Whereas the fourth instance identifies the act of incarnation, this third instance names the divine intentionality

---

14. John Duns Scotus, *Reportatio Parisiensis* 3.7.4 (my trans.). Latin: "Primo Deus diligent se, secundo diligent se aliis, et iste est amor castus; tertio vult se diligi ab illo qui potest eum summe diligere, loquendo de amore alicuius extrinseci; et quarto praevidit unionem illius naturae, quae debet eum summe diligere etsi nullus cecidisset . . . et ideo in quinto instanti vidit Deus mediatorem venientem passurum, redempturum populum suum." In C. Barlic, *Ioannis Duns Scoti, Doctoris Mariani Theologiae Marianae Elementa* (Sibenik, 1933), 14–15.

15. See Bonnefoy, *Christ and the Cosmos*, 11–14; Carol, *Why Jesus Christ?*, 135–39; and Antonie Vos, *The Theology of John Duns Scotus* (Brill, 2018), 110–11.

16. See Vos, *Theology of John Duns Scotus*, 112; and Nico den Bok, "Liefde op zoek naar een geliefde: Over person-zijn in Augustijns-Franciscaanse zin, belicht vanuit christologie en verkiezingsleer," *Kerk en Theologie* 50 (1998): 187.

behind the incarnation.[17] I offer three possible ways to further unpack this instance. I argue that the first, most natural and standard interpretation runs afoul of the Chalcedonian Christology Scotus adheres to. A second, minority view is also untenable in the wider context of Scotus's theological commitments. I therefore offer a third way of reading, one that entails a conscious reconstruction of Scotus's position that, while rejecting the letter of Scotus's argument, nonetheless adheres to its spirit.

A First Interpretation: To Be Loved by Another

A first interpretation offers what seems to be the most natural reading and the one Scotus most likely intended. In the third and fourth instance, God (who has committed Godself, in the second instance, to be a God in relationship to others) now desires that, at the very core of this relationship, there be one who will love God above all other things, and thereby do right by God's character as the most lovable person. To accomplish this, God will assume this one to be God's very own, a nature elected to be hypostatically united to Godself. God's self-love thus finds a reflection in the realm of creation. Within Godself, God is loved above all else by Godself; within the realm of creation, of that which is other than God, God is loved above all else by one who belongs to that which is other than God.[18]

The problem with this interpretation is twofold. First, read in this way, it is unclear what the relationship is between God's intentions in becoming incarnate and the creation of everything else. In the third instance, God wills to create one who can love God above else; in the fourth instance, God wills to accomplish this by hypostatically uniting with a human nature. Nothing in these intentions leads to the creation of other humans, let alone the rest of creation. In fact, elsewhere Scotus underscores that even if God had

---

17. In later traditions, it became suspect to speak of the *motives* for the incarnation, since that language would suggest that the divine will is moved by something beyond it, which a classical doctrine of God denies. To sidestep this discussion, I will speak of the intentionality of the incarnation. See Bonnefoy, *Christ and the Cosmos*, 6; and Pancheri, *Universal Primacy of Christ*, 50. Cf. The Salmanticenses, *On the Motive of the Incarnation*, trans. Dylan Schrader (Catholic University of America Press, 2019), xxiv.

18. See, e.g., Karl M. Balic: "Was ist der Beweggrund der Inkarnation nach den Reportationen? . . . Der Beweggrund der Inkarnation ist: Gott wollte geliebt warden von irgendeinem ausser ihm selbst Existierenden, und zwar 'summe'!" Balic, "Duns Skotus' Lehre über Christ predestination im Lichte der neuesten Forschungen," *Wissenschaft und Weisheit* 3 (1936): 25. Pancheri suggests "the most sublime product of God's love *ad extra* is necessarily a lofty Lover, one who is capable of loving God in a perfect manner. Corresponding to God's creative love (the ultimate and dominating reason of his *ad extra* communication) we have Christ Jesus (the most perfect of all works *ad extra*) embodying the supreme response to God's love." Pancheri, *Universal Primacy of Christ*, 36.

not created others, God still would have become incarnate.[19] Incarnation is focused solely on the one who is to be loved: God. It has no intrinsic relationship to anything beyond the incarnate One. Nonetheless, much Scotian theology likes to read Scotus as if there were such an intrinsic relationship.[20] Scotus himself may even invite such an impression by introducing "[God's] people" in the fifth instance of his argument. But he does not mention any inclusion of God's people within the relationship between God and the incarnate One. His argument about the incarnation neither expresses nor needs an expanding circle of divine love. This should caution us. On the interpretation offered, Scotus's account of the divine loves is, internally, not as tightly woven together as one might like and, externally, not as comprehensive as one might want.

A second problem with this reading of Scotus's argument is that on the logic of the very Chalcedonian Christology that Scotus employs to describe the incarnation, the incarnate One is not another; the incarnate One is Godself. Likewise, the incarnate One's love is not the love of someone different from God; it is God's love, even while expressed through a created nature. On Chalcedonian logic, in the incarnation the person of the divine Word assumes a human nature. The divine Word thereby becomes the supposit, or the ontological subject, of all the properties, powers, and actions of the human nature.[21] To put it differently, person and natures relate to each other as *who* relates to *what*. When we meet the incarnate One, we meet a human *what*, and the one we engage is a divine *who*. If this is the case, though, then the love of the incarnate One may be a human love, a love offered by a human nature, but the One who is loving is divine. And as such, when this love is turned toward Godself, God is not loved by *another*, but God is humanly loved by Godself.

---

19. "In fact, even if no human being or angel had fallen, nor any human being but Christ were to be created, Christ would still have been predestined in this way." Scotus, *Reportatio Parisiensis* 3.7.4 (my trans.). Latin: "Immo etsi nec homo nec angelus fuisset lapsus, nec plires homines creandi quam solus Christus, adhuc fuisset Christus predestinatus sic." In C. Barlic, *Ioannis Duns Scoti*, 13.

20. See, e.g., Agathon Kandler, "Die Heilsdynamik im Christusbild des Johannes Duns Scotus," *Wissenschaft und Weisheit* 27 (1964): 175–96 and *Wissenschaft und Weisheit* 28 (1965) 1–14; Johannes Schlageter, "Das Menschsein Jesu Christi in seiner zentralen Bedeutung für Schöpfung und Geschichte bei Johannes Duns Scotus und heute," *Wissenschaft und Weisheit* 47 (1984): 23–36; Giovanni Iammarrone, "Wert und Grenzen der Christologie des Johannes Duns Scotus in heutiger Zeit," *Wissenschaft und Weisheit* 52 (1989): 1–20; and Henri Veldhuis, "De hermeneutische betekenis van de supralapsarische Christologie van Johannes Duns Scotus," *Bijdragen* 61 (2000): 152–74.

21. I offer a short account of the medieval understanding of assumption, persons, and natures, particularly in Scotus, in Edwin Chr. van Driel, "The Logic of Assumption," in *Exploring Kenotic Christology*, ed. C. Stephen Evans (Oxford University Press, 2006), 265–90.

In defense of Scotus, one might appeal to the ways, in his metaphysics of the incarnation, he relates Christ's human nature and actions. According to Scotus, it is a general rule that a nature is the causal originator of its own actions. This also holds for Christ's human nature, even when this nature is assumed by the second person of the Trinity, and therefore the nature's agency is predicated of the Word. Scotus rejects an alternative account on which for the Word to assume a nature is for that nature to become an instrument of that person.[22] It is not unlikely that Scotus worked with this analysis of Christ's willing when he formulated his supralapsarian argument. On this account, when Jesus loves God, this love originates in the human powers of Jesus's human nature, not in the divine powers of his divine nature. However, even on this analysis, the person who is said to be the lover is the divine Word. The *what* that is doing the loving is the human nature, and the *who* that is doing the loving is the second person of the Trinity.[23] And this means that Christ's love for the Godhead is a form of divine self-love, even while it is a love enacted through the Word's human nature.[24]

22. For instance, "The [human] will in Christ has dominion over its own acts to the same extent as in any other man, for the will in Christ does not cause in any other way [than in any other substance], and the Trinity permits the human will to elicit its acts in the same way as it permits other wills to elicit their [acts]." Scotus, *Reportatio Parisiensis* 3.17.1–2, n. 4, quoted in Richard Cross, *The Metaphysics of the Incarnation: Thomas Aquinas to Duns Scotus* (Oxford University Press, 2002), 221. For an extensive analysis of this point, see Cross, *Metaphysics of the Incarnation*, 218–29. Thomas Aquinas takes the alternative position and holds that "the human will in Christ had a certain determinate mode from the fact that it was in the divine hypostasis: namely that it was moved always according to the nod of the divine will." Aquinas, *Summa Theologiae* III.18.1 ad. 4, quoted in Cross, *Metaphysics of the Incarnation*, 220n6. If one were attracted to Aquinas's, rather than Scotus's, understanding of Christ's human willing, this would also bring home the point more forcefully. If Christ's human will is to be seen both as terminating in a divine person and as an instrument of the divine will, then indeed there is no ground to deny that Christ's human loving of God is nothing but an expression of divine self-love.

23. If Scotus were to analyze things differently, it is hard to see how he could avoid the often-expressed accusation of Nestorianism. See Cross, *Metaphysics of the Incarnation*, 190–92.

24. A very similar point is made by Nico den Bok, "Geven om de ander," 35–40. For an in-depth contemporary discussion of these matters, see Adonis Vidu, *The Same God Who Works All Things: Inseparable Operations in Trinitarian Theology* (Eerdmans, 2021), 158–216.

One might continue a defense of Scotus's position by pointing out that even if this criticism is on target, the divine self-love expressed by the incarnate One is different from the necessary, internal self-love of God. The latter is enacted by the divine nature and has all three trinitarian persons as term. The former is enacted by the human nature and has only the person of the divine Word as term. In becoming incarnate, God thus really gains the ability to love Godself in a different way. While this is correct, I believe two observations should be made: First, even on this further refinement of the account of the incarnate One's love, we are still not dealing with the love of another. The whole point of the divine Word being the term of his human nature is that in this nature Godself is present and at work in our midst. Second, it is a mistake to characterize God's will to be loved and the incarnate One's love of God as the interplay between

A Second Interpretation: To Be in Love with Another

If on the first interpretation the focus of the incarnation is still directed at God—God becomes human because God wishes to be loved by another—in a second interpretation, proposed by Marilyn McCord Adams, the focus turns toward humanity. God comes to love the human nature of Christ so much, the argument goes, that

> (i) God first loves Godself above all with friendship love (*amor amicitiae*) that values the love-object for its own sake and not merely as a means to something else. (ii) Since friendship is non-possessive, it partly expresses itself in the will that others should value the love-object the same way. The persons of the Trinity love another with such friendship love. (iii) That this love should be shared by others, the soul of Christ preeminent among them, is, for Scotus, God's *principal end in creation*. Scotus says that God so loved the rational soul of Christ that God wanted to create and be loved by it whether or not any other creatures existed. In fact, God has willed that Christ should be the head of many co-lovers, including both angels and other human souls.[25]

Because these are God's intentions, Adams exegetes Scotus: "(iv) Next, God wills the *proximate* means to that end. . . . The human soul of Christ is hypostatically united to the Divine Word, so that it may be fittingly infused with fullness of grace, maximal human knowledge, and impeccability of will. Other human and angelic co-lovers are supplied with graces in lesser degree." And "(v) next, God wills the *remote means* to his end by creating other things naturally suited to human souls. Thus, God wills to create the material world, so that human souls may be united to human bodies and function accordingly."[26]

Adams thus interprets the divine self-love from which Scotus starts as an inner-trinitarian love in which the persons of the Trinity relate to one another in friendship. In the incarnation, the three persons widen this friendship circle

---

Father and Son (as does, for example, Pancheri, *Universal Primacy of Christ*, 36). Scotus says that it is *God* whose aim it is in the incarnation to be loved—that is, the triune God, not just the Father, is the subject and object of Scotus's argument.

25. Marilyn McCord Adams, *Christ and Horrors: The Coherence of Christology* (Cambridge University Press, 2006), 181. A possible early instantiation of this line of interpretation is offered by Dominic Unger when, having referred to the text of the *Reportatio*, he states the issue thus: "Whether God willed the incarnation for the glory of Christ; i.e., for Christ's own excellence, to love him most of all and to receive the greatest love in return; to favor him with the greatest grace and glory possible." Dominic Unger, "Franciscan Christology: Absolute and Universal Primacy of Christ," *Franciscan Studies* 2, no. 4 (1942): 432. Unger, however, does not explore the interpretative difficulties I am trying to surface in this chapter.

26. Adams, *Christ and Horrors*, 182.

and share their love with Christ's human nature. Scotus's own text, however, gives no reason to import such an account. The divine self-love is not cast in trinitarian terms. Moreover, Adams's social trinitarian language does not fit Scotus's trinitarian theology, according to which the divine self-love is a loving of the divine essence in which all three persons share, not a mutual loving among the persons in their distinctiveness.[27]

Bracketing the social-trinitarian aspect of Adams' interpretation, what should one think of the understanding of the incarnation as an expression of God's love for the human nature that is being assumed? On this line of thought, the intentional focus of the incarnation turns from God to humanity. God "so loved the rational soul of Christ that God wanted to create and be loved by it."[28]

On this, I would like to make three observations: First, this line of thought suggests that God's decision to create and to incarnate is moved by something outside of God—that is, the rational soul that will be Christ's evokes such love in God that it motivates God to assume it in incarnation. This is inconsistent with the general position of scholastic theologians, including Scotus, that God's will is not motivated by anything outside of God.[29] Second, even if we were to allow for the idea that God's love is moved by that which exists outside of God, it is nonetheless the case that before God calls forth anything that is not God, there is nothing yet to love apart from Godself. Before the act of creation, Jesus's human soul is nothing but an idea produced by God's own mind.[30] It is hard to see how we could speak in any meaningful way about the preexisting human nature of Christ as that which called forth God's love, and that in calling forth God's love, motivated God's decision to create it and be loved by it. The most one might say is that God loved the idea of being loved by this potential human nature and therefore created it, but this would bring us back to the first interpretation of Scotus's series of instances. It would be an expression of divine self-love, not love for this human nature. Third,

27. See Richard Cross, *Duns Scotus on God* (Ashgate, 2005), 218–19.
28. For a somewhat similar line of thought, see Ilia Delio: "For Scotus . . . the incarnation represents not a divine response to a human need for salvation but instead the divine intention from all eternity to raise the human nature to the highest point of glory by uniting it with the divine nature." Delio, "Franciscan Doctrine of Christ," 9.
29. See chap. 1, note 17 (above).
30. An alternative interpretation would be a Molinist understanding of the incarnation, according to which God, via middle knowledge, knows the lovable ways in which the human nature of Christ would freely live its life and therefore love it. To this one might respond by wondering whether there only would be one human nature that would live its life in the lovable ways that would attract God's attention; and, if not, why this would result in the singular choice for this particular nature. For explorations in Molinist Christology, see, in particular, the work by Thomas P. Flint.

if God united Godself to this human nature out of love for this particular human nature and then elected others as co-lovers under God, the election of this particular nature would be accidental to the election of others, and the election of others would be accidental to the election of this one. This leads us back to a problem noted about the first interpretation of Scotus's argument. Adams rightly refers to Scotus's earlier statement that God would have elected the human nature of Christ whether or not others were to be created. This suggests that the divine choice for incarnation has no intrinsic relationship to God's choice for the rest of creation. This observation is strengthened, though, by Adams's reading of the incarnation as motivated by God's love for this particular human nature. Such love has in and of itself no intrinsic concern for others who are not loved. But then one wonders why God, in the last instance, would decide that, through the one who is beloved, God would bring salvation to a fallen creation. This assumes a relationship between incarnation and creation for which Adams's interpretation does not account. This should, once again, be cause for caution.

A Third Interpretation: To Embody Love for Another

In light of the difficulty of interpreting Scotus's series of instances coherently, I offer a third approach that amounts to a constructive rereading of his argument.

I wish to return to the difficult-to-interpret second moment of divine loving: "God loves himself for others, and this love is *castus* [pure]." Only God exists by necessity; everything else is contingent. If God regards others as objects of an act of love, this act therefore has to be contingent. If it were otherwise, and this act of loving others were necessary in the way God's act of loving Godself is necessary, the objects of this divine love would themselves be necessary. However, if God's act of loving others is contingent, this act has to go back to a decision. The content of this decision is for God "[to love] himself for others." The divine self-love for others is therefore different from God's act of loving God for Godself. The latter is a necessary act. By contrast, God's act of loving Godself for others is a contingent, accidental act of the divine will. This is why Scotus makes a distinction between the first and second structural moments. At the same time, this being only the second structural moment of divine willing, and only the very first moment in which God's willing is directed at anything but Godself, this is also the first moment when that which is not God enters reality. And notice how it does: as the recipients of God's decision to love Godself for others. I propose that Scotus's moment in which God loves Godself "for others" is best interpreted as God's self-determination to be a God-with-others.³¹ This is God's first act of relating to anything that is not God, and the essential nature of this act is *to love*—to love that which is not God by God's loving the divine self-commitment to that which is not God. Moreover, this love is *castus* (pure). It is a love not mixed up with ulterior motives. It does not come forth out of a divine lack or need. It is not even the result of a necessary urge for divine self-expression. It is a free, contingent act of the divine will purely focused on the ones who, in this divine turn outward, are established as recipients of God's creative love.³²

What shape does this divine self-determination to be a God-with-others, this divine turning outward, take? I suggest that the solution to the difficulty of offering a coherent reading of Scotus's instances lies in switching around the third and fourth instances of divine willing. The shape of God's loving Godself for others is incarnation. The divine being a God-with-others is God's union with that which is not God. The embodiment of God's self-giving is Jesus. That is, the incarnate One is not so much the one who is to receive and reciprocate the divine love as the one who expresses it. He is the embodiment of the divine self-giving to which God commits Godself in the very first moment when God's will turns to that which is not God.

Everything else that is not God is now established within the context of this first divine decision to be a God-with-others and this decision's expression in the incarnate One. That is, everything that is not God is determined as the recipient of and respondent to this act of divine self-giving. Therefore, in a fourth structural moment "God wills that he is loved by him who can love him above all." Having decided to be Jesus, God wills to create fellow human beings. They are called into being by a God who already has determined to love them in ultimate self-giving, and they are invited to love "him" in return—"him," that is, the God who has a human face and a human life, the face and life of Jesus.³³

---

31. Consider this in connection with Karl Barth, according to whom God's act of election is first and foremost an act of self-determination: "God in his love elects another to fellowship with himself. First and foremost this means that God makes a self-election in favour of this other. He ordains that he should not be entirely self-sufficient as he might be. He determines for himself that overflowing, that movement, that condescension. He constitutes himself as benefit or favour. And in so doing he elects another as the object of his love." Karl Barth, *Church Dogmatics* II/2, trans. G. W. Bromiley (T&T Clark, 1957), 10. My constructive rereading of Scotus suggests significant structural parallels between Scotus's and Barth's approaches.

32. See den Bok, "Liefde Op Zoek," 187.

33. One might wonder whether this line of interpretation, including the connection with Karl Barth, was not anticipated by Francis Xavier Pancheri. See Pancheri, *Universal Primacy of Christ*, 35–38.

Like I do in my constructive rereading of Scotus's argument, Pancheri calls for a picture in which "Christ is not the 'crown' and the 'zenith' of the universe, but rather its root, its end, its

Read in this way, Scotus's argument becomes consistent with his own account of the incarnation's ontology. The argument rests in the Chalcedonian stipulation that while in meeting the incarnate One we see and experience a human nature, the *who* we engage is the divine Word. Moreover, while my reading of the argument demands its reconstruction, in its new form it lives up to the stipulations that flow out of Scotus's first supralapsarian argumentative strategy. Scotus's reconstructed second argument underscores the freedom and contingency of God's relating to what is not God. It is an argument about how all of created reality is embedded in God's decision to give Godself to what is not God in incarnation; it is not an argument about a counterfactual reality. And, finally, it not only advances supralapsarianism; it expresses the primacy of Christ. On the reconstructed argument, it truly can be said that "all things have been created . . . for him" (Col. 1:16) and, as such, he is to be "the firstborn within a large family" (Rom. 8:29). Thus, my reconstruction establishes an intrinsic relationship between incarnation and the creation of all other human beings. As I observed above, on the alternative readings of Scotus's argument, this is challenging.

Conclusion

According to Scotus, God becomes incarnate for the sake of love. The Scotist tradition has rightly focused in on this argument as an extraordinarily important claim. If God becomes incarnate for the sake of love, and to become incarnate is first in God's intentions vis-à-vis that which is not God, love is at the center of the universe. At the same time, this love has a human face: Christ.

The *direction* of this love is, however, unclear in Scotus's argument. Scotus seems to be saying that God becomes incarnate so that, in addition to being loved by Godself, God may be loved by another. This would be inconsistent with the logic of Chalcedonian Christology, according to which the supposit

---

raison d'être. . . . God freely and gratuitously willed all things to have their center and foundation *in Christo Jesu*." Pancheri, *Universal Primacy of Christ*, 37. But Pancheri does not register the interpretative difficulties that have to be teased out regarding Scotus's text, nor does he note that one can come to his particular position only by a *reconstruction* of Scotus's argument. Pancheri thus happily ascribes positions to Scotus that are not warranted by the letter of what Scotus actually says. For example: "The entire universe is willed by God for the sake of Christ, and not the other way around"; "In Christ God willed to communicate himself in a manner so sublime as to introduce all creatures into the very bosom of the blessed Trinity"; and "Love is not a relationship between two 'things,' between two 'objects,' between two 'beings,' but between two persons." Scotus, quoted in Pancheri, *Universal Primacy of Christ*, 35–36. This chapter is an attempt to own up to the interpretative difficulties *and* possibilities that Scotus's argument offers.

of the acts of the human nature of Christ is the divine Word. Scotus may also be understood as saying that God so loved Christ's human nature that God assumed it and thereby gave it the ability to enjoy the highest bliss possible: to be united with Godself. However, Christ's human nature is called into being only in being elected to be the human nature of the divine Word. Creation follows election; election does not follow creation. Thus, there is nothing for God to love external to Godself before God decides to become incarnate. Moreover, both interpretations suffer from not being able to account for that which drives much contemporary Scotist theology: the idea that the circle of love is expanded beyond God and God's incarnation to draw in other creatures.

These challenges can, however, be met in a constructive rereading of Scotus's argument according to which the love expressed in the incarnation is directed at creation. In deciding to become incarnate, God decides to give Godself to that which is not God. The embodiment of this decision is Christ. The incarnation is not an expression of divine self-love but an expression of love for others. This interpretation squares with Chalcedonian Christology; it is consistent with other key elements of Scotus's theology; and it names the rest of creation as called into being as the recipients of the divine, self-giving love expressed by the incarnate One. And as such, Scotus's argument, as well as his wider Christological narrative, could be read as an early representative of the central argument that drives this book.

2

"To Know Nothing . . . Except Jesus Christ, and Him Crucified"

Supralapsarian Christology and a Theology of the Cross

Proponents of supralapsarian Christology do not deny that God deals with the sin problem through the incarnate Christ, but they hold that there are deeper and more important reasons for the incarnation than reconciliation and redemption. In this Christological model the goal of creation is a love relationship with human beings, and in this relationship God comes as close to God's creatures as God can—in becoming human. Supralapsarian Christology thus seems to decenter the cross. Although it acknowledges the cross as God's means of dealing with sin, the dynamic of sin, reconciliation, and redemption is not considered to be the sole or even deepest motivation for the incarnation. The cross is not the central moment in the story of God and humanity. How then does such a Christological approach sit with a theology of the cross (*theologia crucis*), which suggests the cross as the lens through which the relationship between God and human beings is to be seen? That is the question I address in this chapter.

Exploring this issue is complicated for at least two reasons. First, like *infralapsarianism*, *supralapsarianism* is a family name. It does not stand for a particular theory but for a family of ideas. Just as many theologians agree that the sin problem is the sole motivation for the incarnation while disagreeing on how the incarnate One deals with sin, so too supralapsarian theologians differ among one another in the argumentative strategies used to support their Christological position. Rather than exploring a variety of supralapsarian Christologies, I take for my starting point in this chapter a particular supralapsarian account, one that I developed several years ago in a book entitled *Incarnation Anyway*.[1] I will therefore begin with a section in which I summarize the supralapsarian argumentative strategy I propose in that book.

The second complication is that *theology of the cross* does not stand for one particular Christological theory either but for a number of different theological arguments. For this chapter I choose three prominent types of crucicentric arguments and explore whether or not these interfere with supralapsarian lines of thought.[2] The first crucicentric argument I will discuss is soteriological. The cross, so the argument goes, negates all anthropocentric methods for achieving salvation. It shows that there is no soteriological advancing from humans to the divine; salvation is not a divine perfecting of a promising human beginning but rather brings all human efforts to an end—salvation comes through the creature's death and resurrection. An example of such soteriological argument is the urtext of cross theology: Martin Luther's Heidelberg Disputation. I then engage an epistemological crucicentric argument, the soteriological argument's epistemic parallel: Just as the cross negates all anthropocentric methods for achieving salvation, it likewise puts an end to all suggestions that human beings can access God through their own devices.[3] As an example of such an argument I refer to the doctrine of

---

1. Edwin Chr. van Driel, *Incarnation Anyway: Arguments for Supralapsarian Christology* (Oxford University Press, 2008). In this book I analyze different versions of supralapsarian Christology, arguing that each of the three ways in which, according to the biblical narrative, God relates to that which is not God—in creation, in eschatological consummation, and in reconciliation—can be used as the basis for a supralapsarian argument. My own arguments, developed at the end of the book, are based on God's drawing creation into eschatological consummation. One reviewer, evaluating these arguments, commented that, for me, "supralapsarianism is opposed to a *theologia crucis*." David W. Congdon, review of *Incarnation Anyway*, by Edwin Chr. van Driel, Center for Barth Studies, Princeton Theological Seminary, October 6, 2010, https://barth.ptsem.edu/incarnation-anyway/. This seemed to me a rather premature, but also intriguing, comment. Premature, because in my discussion I had not mentioned a *theologia crucis* at all. Intriguing, because I do share Congdon's intuition that at least some arguments used in *theologiae crucis* seem inconsistent with some forms of supralapsarianism. This chapter is meant to bring some conceptual clarity regarding these relationships.

2. I follow Rosalene Bradbury's use of the adjective *crucicentric* as meaning "pertaining to the theology of the cross," whereas *cruciform* recalls the cross itself. Rosalene Bradbury, *Cross Theology: The Classical Theologia Crucis and Karl Barth's Modern Theology of the Cross* (Pickwick, 2011), 1n4.

3. In distinguishing between the soteriological and epistemological arguments, I was helped by the discussion in Rosalene Bradbury's *Cross Theology*.

revelation developed by Karl Barth in the first volume of his *Church Dogmatics*. Then I consider a hermeneutical argument according to which the very narrative about the relationship between God and human beings should be cruciform. Here I delve into the work of the New Testament scholar J. Louis Martyn. While I do not claim that these three arguments exhaust the range of *theologiae crucis*, I believe this exploration will at least begin to map the territory and lead to greater clarity regarding both supralapsarian Christology and theologies of the cross.

As to the relationship among these three crucicentric arguments themselves, the first two are formal: They want to shape the rules for what counts as a valid theological strategy. The last one is material, suggesting a particular shape to the actual narrative of the relationship between God and God's creatures. The three arguments could all be held simultaneously but do not necessarily need to be so, as will be illustrated by my contention that one could hold the first two in conjunction with my version of supralapsarian Christology, but not the last one. As a matter of fact, in a final section to this chapter I argue that the first two crucicentric arguments are driven by intuitions very similar to the ones that shape supralapsarian Christology and that holding these arguments while simultaneously embracing a supralapsarian position is not only possible but even fitting.

Before I embark on my discussion, it may be helpful to explicitly distinguish the topic of this chapter from a different topic: the relationship between supralapsarian Christology and doctrines of atonement. This, in itself, is a fascinating topic. As I mentioned above, while supralapsarian Christology posits that the incarnation is not contingent upon sin, it does not deny that, once sin has entered the picture, God takes care of the sin problem through the incarnate One. Supralapsarian Christology does not deny the atonement; it simply places it in the context of a larger story. As such, supralapsarian Christology could be combined with a multitude of atonement theories. However, particular kinds of supralapsarian arguments may limit the kinds of atonement theories one can consistently adhere to. I will return to this in a later chapter.[4] For now, however, the question is simply this: In what ways does a supralapsarian narration of the incarnation diverge from or align with intuitions about the centrality of the cross that have shaped major parts of especially Protestant theology?

---

4. See chap. 11, below. A different way to express this distinction is that whereas I concentrate in this chapter on the place of the cross in the wider narrative of the relationship between God and God's creatures, I forego a discussion of what exactly happened on the cross. For this reason, I will not engage Jürgen Moltmann's *The Crucified God*. Even though this book is often seen as a prime example of a twentieth-century *theologia crucis*, the heart of the book is a reinterpretation of what happened on the cross.

Incarnation Anyway

In *Incarnation Anyway*, I offer three arguments to support a supralapsarian Christology. The first of these is what I call an argument from eschatological superabundance. It starts from an observation that has been made by supralapsarians and infralapsarians alike: The eschaton, the final goal of creation, is better than the proton, the beginning of creation. The eschaton is not simply the restoration of the proton. There is in the eschaton an abundance, a richness in intimacy with God and in human transformation that the proton did not know. Traditionally, theology describes this intimacy with God as the *visio Dei*, the vision of God; in the eschaton we are so close to God that we will see God face-to-face. The gain of human transformation is usually described using the terms coined by the church father Augustine: While in the proton human beings were *posse non peccare* ("able not to sin"), in the eschaton they will be *non posse peccare* ("unable to sin").[5]

What is at stake for the supralapsarian in all of this is that in the Scriptures this eschatological extra is intimately bound up with the person of Christ. We will change for the better because we are modeled after Christ, both in body—in the resurrection, this "body of our humiliation" will be conformed to "the body of his glory," as Paul so poetically says (Phil. 3:21)—and in spirit, in that we will be like him in our minds and hearts (Rom. 8:29; Phil. 3:10; 2 Cor. 3:18). We will be modeled after Christ the closer we are to Christ. "We will be like him, for we will see him as he is" (1 John 3:2).

Well, says the supralapsarian, if the eschaton is thus a gain over the proton, and this gain is given to us in Christ, after whose incarnate presence we are modeled and in whose incarnate presence we are made to see the Father, then do we receive this eschatological extra, all this gain, because of sin? Because that is what one would have to say if Christ's coming is contingent upon sin. Without sin, no incarnation; without incarnation, no eschaton. And that cannot be true. Sin is powerful, but it is not that powerful. Sin does not bring us closer to God. We would therefore do better to understand all this in a supralapsarian way. The abundance of the eschatological life cannot be contingent upon sin. And since Christ is the embodiment of this abundance, neither is the incarnation contingent upon sin.

My second argument zooms in on one particular aspect of the eschatological consummation: the promised *visio Dei*, the vision of God. On the traditional understanding of this notion, the vision of God will fully wrap human beings in the enjoyment of God. For bodily, sensory beings this includes sensory contact. And eschatological humans will be bodily, sensory beings

---

5. See Augustine, *De civitate Dei* 20.30.

since the resurrected Christ is a bodily, sensory being, and he is the model for what we will be like in our eschatological resurrection. Therefore, if the eschatological goal of humanity is to enjoy God fully in the beatific vision, this vision should not be understood purely in terms of intellectual cognition but should also imply sensory perception. To fully enjoy God means that we should be able to hear, see, touch, and physically embrace God. However, this can take place only if God makes Godself present in bodily form.[6]

My third argument for supralapsarianism hinges on the notion of divine friendship. There is a small but discernible line in the biblical narrative that conceives of the relationship between God and God's people as a form of friendship. Abraham and Moses are called God's friends (Exod. 33:11; Isa. 41:8; see also 2 Chron. 20:7; James 2:23). Christ uses friendship language and says to his disciples, "I do not call you servants any longer, . . . but I have called you friends" (John 15:15).

The theologically important point about conceiving of God's relating to humanity as a form of friendship is friendship's motivational structure. Friendship is motivated by a delight in and a love for the other. It enjoys the other's goodness and the goodness the relationship with the other embodies. Of course, friendship can be disrupted, disregarded, betrayed. All of these can motivate friends to seek forgiveness, reconciliation, healing of their relationship. But the friendship itself is not based on the episodes of disruption and reconciliation but on a deeper sense of love and delight. Therefore, when God calls Abraham and Moses and when Jesus addresses his disciples as friends, not slaves, these relationships are defined not by human sin and a need for reconciliation but by a deeper, primordial sense of love. It is true that all of these relationships are also tainted by human failure and betrayal. The narratives of Abraham and Moses tell us about distrust, disobedience, and unbelief. Jesus calls his disciples friends in the context of a conversation about his imminent death: "No one has greater love than this, to lay down one's life for one's friends" (John 15:13). But while the death is motivated by the friendship, the friendship is not motivated by death. Jesus becomes his disciples' Savior because he is their friend, not the other way around.

If this is true, it would be an impoverishment to read all of Jesus's actions, all of his words, and finally, his very presence as motivated by human sin and the need for reconciliation. To do so would be to lose sight of other feelings and emotions, of a deeper layer of motivations that may be at play in

---

6. Of course, understanding the eschatological vision in this way, as the enjoyment of God both with the intellect and with our senses is to go against the standard understanding of the *visio Dei*, which is almost exclusively intellectual. For more on this, see "*Being With* and Seeing God" in chap. 12, below, 269–75.

the relationship between God and human beings. One of these motivations, I suggest, is laid bare in a fascinating story about Moses. God and Moses have just had a lover's quarrel. The issue being resolved, Moses wants to reconcile, and he, the friend of God, therefore asks to see God's face (Exod. 33:18). Moses wants to make sure things are right again between God and himself, and therefore he longs for the visible, tangible presence of the Lord. For embodied human beings, when it comes to crucial moments of our friendships, it is not enough to hear a voice calling to us from a pillar of clouds; it is physical presence that we want. And the Lord, understanding the longing of God's friend, makes Godself available to Moses, as much as God can (Exod. 33:21–23). I suggest we read the incarnation as God's final and permanent answer to humanity's longing, the ultimate availability of the Lord. God is no longer in a pillar of cloud, no longer seen in a momentary appearance of dazzling glory; God is now in a human form, with a human face—visible, tangible, audible.[7]

For the sake of a comparison with a theology of the cross, it is important, before we move on, to point out one central feature of these arguments. These three have a common starting point: the story as we have it, the incarnation event as it happened. And they press whether an infralapsarian account can fully make sense of this Scriptural narrative. In that sense these arguments thus follow a very different strategy than traditional supralapsarian arguments, which usually conceive of the supralapsarian case in terms of a counterfactual: Would God have become incarnate if we had not sinned? To which the supralapsarian then answers in the affirmative. The downside of this traditional strategy is that it leaves the supralapsarian open to the objection of *speculation*. As John Calvin, an infralapsarian, put it pointedly, in speculating about a counterfactual situation in which we had not sinned, supralapsarians can be accused of trying to get away from the fact that we actually have sinned, and their arguments can be dismissed as simply revealing that the supralapsarians are not "content with this very Christ who was given to us as the price of our redemption."[8] But my arguments are not open to such a critique. I do not ask what would have happened if we had not sinned. I ask about the incarnation as it happened, about the Christ as we have him. And my point is that the incarnation as it happened gives us

---

7. In other words, what the supralapsarian theologian is after is the intrinsic importance of the "play of the Word," which, as Andrew Louth explains, is missing in Maximos the Confessor. Andrew Louth, "Maximos the Confessor on the Foolishness of God and Play of the Word," in *The Wisdom and Foolishness of God: First Corinthians 1–2 in Theological Exploration*, ed. Christophe Chalamet and Hans-Christoph Askani (Fortress, 2015), 95–97.

8. John Calvin, *Institutes of the Christian Religion*, ed. John T. McNeill, trans. Ford Lewis Battles, 2 vols. (Westminster, 1960), 2.7.5.

so much, and is so rich in terms of divine friendship and intimacy, that it cannot be explained as only a divine countermeasure against sin. Granted, the biblical narrative does not carry supralapsarianism on its sleeves, and so the case has to be made in terms of inferences and arguments. But, in this regard, supralapsarian Christology is no different from the doctrine of the Trinity or the doctrine of the two natures of Christ. Thus, supralapsarian Christology is in good company.

Theologia Crucis: The Soteriological Argument

How does such an approach to supralapsarian Christology relate to a theology of the cross? An important first line of argument underlying *theologiae crucis* is soteriological in nature. The cross, so the argument goes, negates all anthropocentric methods for achieving salvation. It shows that there is no soteriological advancing from humans to the divine; salvation is not a divine perfecting of a promising human beginning but rather brings all human efforts to an end—salvation comes through the creature's death and resurrection.

An example of such a soteriological argument is the urtext of cross theology: Martin Luther's Heidelberg Disputation. It may be surprising to see Luther's text advanced as a soteriological argument. After all, the central theses in which Luther coins the terms *theologian of the cross* and *theologian of glory* are cast in epistemological terms:

> 19. That person does not deserve to be called a theologian who looks upon the invisible things of God as though they were clearly perceptible in those things which have actually happened (Rom. 1:20).

> 20. He deserves to be called a theologian, however, who comprehends the visible and manifest things of God seen through suffering and the cross.

> 21. A theologian of glory calls evil good and good evil. A theologian of the cross calls the thing what it actually is.[9]

However, a purely epistemological reading of these theses misses that they come at the conclusion of a soteriological train of thought.[10] In the preceding theses Luther has dealt with the desire of humans to offer building blocks for

---

9. Martin Luther, Heidelberg Disputation, in *Luther's Works*, vol. 31, *Career of the Reformer I*, ed. Harold J. Grimm (Fortress, 1957), 40.
10. See Gerhard O. Forde, *On Being a Theologian of the Cross: Reflections on Luther's Heidelberg Disputation, 1518* (Eerdmans, 1997), 69–70.

their salvation, "to advance on their way to righteousness" (thesis 1).[11] The first twelve theses deal with the notion of good works, the following six with the idea of good willing. Luther rejects both. Our good works actually make matters worse because they feed our religious aspirations and thereby seal us off from the gift of free grace. Our will is bound to evil, and therefore even imagining that doing our best will prepare us for grace "add[s] haughty arrogance" to our misery and thereby doubles our sin.[12] The theologian of glory now begins to cry out of despair. They find that there is nothing they can do, nothing to hold on to, nothing that can help to make progress toward salvation. This is exactly where one needs to be in order to receive grace, Luther believes: "It is certain that man must utterly despair of his own ability before he is prepared to receive the grace of Christ" (thesis 18).[13] The cross is not a moment in a larger train of advancing toward righteousness but the negation of any human salvific striving. Only in the face of the death of one's own abilities is one able to receive forensic grace: "He is not righteous who does much, but he who, without work, believes much in Christ" (thesis 25).[14] It is in this context that Luther formulates his theses about the theologian of glory and the theologian of the cross. These theses should thus be read as reflections on the soteriological argument Luther has just advanced. The theologian of glory believes they can make sense of the cross in a larger story of human advancing toward God, and they believe that cruciform grace is nothing more than the keystone of human works and willing. As such, they call "evil good and good evil." They do not realize that it is exactly our seemingly good acts and good desires that lead us away from grace. What they thought they knew about God only works against them; it blinds them to the grace of a God who is willing to die for them. In other words, their theological epistemology is wrong because it leads to soteriological disasters. By contrast, the theologian of the cross lets "suffering and the cross" expose them. This is what all our own striving leads to: death. Therefore, the theologian of the cross "calls the thing what it actually is."

How does this line of argument sit with a supralapsarian Christology? Three observations need to be made. First, the kind of soteriology implied by the Heidelberg Disputation and my supralapsarian arguments converge rather than clash; both emphasize the unconditional nature of God's gracious relating to humanity. My argument suggests neither a soteriological advancing from the human to the divine nor a human conditioning of the salvific will

11. Luther, Heidelberg Disputation, 39.
12. Luther, Heidelberg Disputation, 50.
13. Luther, Heidelberg Disputation, 40.
14. Luther, Heidelberg Disputation, 41.

of God. As in Luther's soteriology, there is rather the opposite move: depicting a God who freely condescends to become the friend of God's creatures.

This first observation helps us negotiate the next: Supralapsarian Christology and a theology of glory nonetheless seem to coincide in that both want to place the cross in the context of a larger story—something a *theologia crucis* is set against. The difference is, however, that a theology of glory sets the cross in a larger narrative of nature, whereas my supralapsarian approach places the cross in a larger narrative of grace. A theology of glory reduces the cross to the divine keystone in human progress on the path to righteousness. By contrast, the story told by supralapsarian Christology is one about a God who, from the beginning of creation, intends to condescend graciously in an incarnate form. It is a narrative that shapes humanity rather than one shaped by humanity.

This notion of a larger supralapsarian narrative of grace is, in turn, important for a third observation. Because of this larger narrative, there is one point of divergence between supralapsarianism and the soteriological argument for a *theologiae crucis*: the notion that the human "must utterly despair of his own ability before he is prepared to receive the grace of Christ" (thesis 18). This part of the argument reflects an infralapsarian logic. If the incarnation is solely contingent upon sin, then indeed one needs to be convinced of one's sin before one can welcome the incarnate One. After all, it is only because of sin that one is in need of Christ. However, on a supralapsarian logic Christ is welcome not only because of our sin but because he is the one for whom we were created.

In engaging this difference between supralapsarian Christology and a theology of the cross, the supralapsarian believes there are important theological and spiritual advantages to their position. First, on the logic of a *theologia crucis*, the preacher must preach sin before they can preach Christ. They have to lead hearers to despair before they can embrace the good news. It is for this reason that a Lutheran hermeneutic is shaped by the dynamic of law and gospel, sin and forgiveness. But a preaching that centers the narrative of Christ on the dynamic of sin and forgiveness leaves the preacher's message open to the misunderstanding that the most important thing the Christian faith has to say about human beings is that they are sinners. And of course, that is not the case. The most important thing the Christian faith has to say about human beings is that they are beloved children of God. The supralapsarian may preach exactly that. They do not have to preach sin in order to preach Christ; they can preach Christ as the offer of love and friendship with God, and it is after that, in the light of that offer of friendship and love, that human beings discover themselves as sinners.

Second, since on infralapsarian logic our relationship to Christ is triggered by a problem (sin), this relationship is, in its origin, therapeutic. Christ is the troubleshooter. The relationship can therefore be said to be functional. The believer needs Christ for something; they have a problem. But what happens when the problem is solved and the believer's need is met? What basis is there for a continuing relationship? There seems to be none. Believers may grow in their understanding of themselves and their relationship with God. They may come to see themselves as forgiven creatures, destined for an eschatological future in which the stains of sin are permanently removed and sin's guilt and shame are permanently cast behind God's back (Isa. 38:17). But there is no basis for an ongoing, future relationship with Christ. Since, by infralapsarian logic, believers' relationship to him is purely functional, it is a relationship permanently defined in terms of sinner and Savior, problem and solution, sickness and medicine. Once the problem of sin is removed, the basis for the relationship is removed as well. For a faith so centered on the person of Christ as Christianity, this is a serious theological, spiritual, and psychological problem. But on a supralapsarian understanding of Christ, we do not need sin in order to benefit from the incarnation. We do not need sin in order to relate to Christ. If the intimate presence of God in Christ is the goal of all things, then all aspects of our lives are related to him. It is here, I believe, that supralapsarianism has an important contribution to make.

Theologia Crucis: The Epistemological Argument

The epistemological argument for a *theologia crucis* parallels the soteriological argument laid out in the previous section. Just as the cross negates all anthropocentric methods for achieving salvation, it likewise puts an end to any suggestion that human beings can access God through their own devices. The cross, one could say, is an expression of the absolute otherness of God—of a God whose wisdom and strength are not located "on a scale extending *beyond* the human, as if the wisdom of God were continuous with, just considerably further along, the spectrum of human wisdom," but rather God's wisdom is "separated entirely from the human scale of norms."[15] In combination with some epistemological principles, this otherness of God leads to the conclusion that such a God can be known only by those to whom God gives Godself to be known in particular events of revelation.

---

15. John M. G. Barclay, "Crucifixion as Wisdom: Exploring the Ideology of a Disreputable Social Movement," in *The Wisdom and Foolishness of God*, ed. Christophe Chalamet and Hans-Christoph Askani (Fortress, 2015), 12.

An example of such an epistemological stance is the doctrine of revelation Karl Barth develops in his *Church Dogmatics*. Barth's doctrine of revelation is based on two correlated arguments concerning our inability to know God. Both arguments combine the notion of the otherness of God with an epistemological premise. In the first argument Barth draws on the epistemological premise that like is only known by like.[16] The conclusion is that divine revelation can happen only mediately. Humans cannot know God directly since God is completely unlike creatures. Only a medium that is alike to creatures can reveal God. The second argument combines the notion of God's otherness with the epistemological premise that knowledge of an object equals power over the object.[17] This combination leads to the conclusion that God can be known only if God gives Godself to be known. God, as the completely other, falls outside the scope of creaturely power. Only God is master over Godself.

Barth suggests that these two epistemological premises amount to the same content.[18] This is where Barth is mistaken, as is clear simply from the different results of these two arguments. The first argument amounts to the need for incarnation. If only a creature can reveal God, divine self-revelation calls for God to assume a creaturely form. Such a form would unveil God but also veil God. It would unveil, because God makes Godself an object of human knowledge; it would veil, because it would reveal God mediately, "under the sign and veil of other objects different from himself."[19] The second argument amounts to a need for the Holy Spirit. Only God has power over who will hear God's revelation: "The Lord of speech is also the Lord of our hearing."[20]

If that is what a theology of the cross wants to say, there is no conflict with the particular kind of supralapsarian Christology I put forward. As I have emphasized, my supralapsarian arguments are not rooted in speculation. Because they reflect solely on the story as we have it, the event of God's revelation, they do not try to access God on their own devices. Rather, they argue that the event as it happened cannot be understood other than as a supralapsarian story.

Therefore, the ontological and epistemological arguments that are at work in Barth's thought do not turn on what is a result of sin but on what is given with the nature of the Creator and creation. And this means that if divine

---

16. In Barth's terms, "We resemble what we can apprehend." Barth, *Church Dogmatics* II/1, trans. G. W. Bromiley (T&T Clark, 1957), 188.
17. In Barth's terms, "To apprehend certainly means to possess." Barth, *Church Dogmatics* II/1, 189.
18. Barth, *Church Dogmatics* II/1, 188–89.
19. Barth, *Church Dogmatics* II/1, 16.
20. Karl Barth, *Church Dogmatics* I/1, trans. G. W. Bromiley (T&T Clark, 1956), 182.

self-disclosure is part of the goal of creation, and this self-disclosure can take place only through incarnation, then the incarnation has to be supralapsarian in intent. Thus, if the epistemological argument for a *theologia crucis* looks anything like Barth's position, and Barth's position implies supralapsarian Christology, then the same has to be said about this form of crucicentric theology.[21]

Theologia Crucis: The Apocalyptic Argument

The previous two arguments for a *theologia crucis* want to help shape the rules for what counts as valid theological thinking: The cross negates all soteriological and epistemological advancing from humans to the divine. The crucicentric argument I discuss in this section is oriented differently. It is focused on material content. It does not seek to outline criteria for theologizing as much as to determine the shape of the narrative about the relationship between God and humanity. Such a narrative, the argument goes, needs to be cruciform. This argument is rooted in the apocalyptic reading of Paul advanced by the German New Testament scholar Ernst Käsemann and his American student J. Louis Martyn. Martyn's work in particular has received significant attention from theologians as of late, so I will focus on his work.[22]

According to Martyn, Paul believes he lives in a "twice-invaded world." Heaven and earth were created in such a way that the earth is permeable, subject to entry from outside.[23] The first such incursion happened when sin entered the world. For Paul, Martyn argues, sin is not so much an individual affair caused by volitional choices as a matter of suprahuman powers that have invaded and enslaved God's creation.[24]

---

21. For Barth's own development on this score, see Van Driel, *Incarnation Anyway*, 77n67.
22. See Douglas Harink, *Paul Among the Postliberals: Pauline Theology Beyond Christendom and Modernity* (Brazos, 2003); Nathan R. Kerr, *Christ, History, and Apocalyptic: The Politics of Christian Mission* (Cascade Books, 2009); David H. Kelsey, *Eccentric Existence: A Theological Anthropology* (Westminster John Knox, 2009), 478–500; Douglas Harink, ed., *Paul, Philosophy, and the Theopolitical Vision: Critical Engagements with Agamben, Badiou, Žižek, and Others* (Cascade Books, 2010); and Joshua B. Davis and Douglas Harink, eds., *Apocalyptic and the Future of Theology: With and Beyond J. Louis Martyn* (Cascade Books, 2012). The following analysis of Martyn goes back to Edwin Chr. van Driel, *Rethinking Paul: Protestant Theology and Pauline Exegesis* (Cambridge University Press, 2021), 262–69.
23. For a very clear sketch of Martyn's understanding of the relationship between creation (the world), fallen creation (*this* world), and new creation, see his essay "World Without End or Twice-Invaded World?," in *Shaking Heaven and Earth: Essays in Honor of Walter Brueggemann and Charles B. Cousar*, ed. Christine Roy Yoder et al. (Westminster John Knox, 2005), 117–32.
24. Martyn, "Twice-Invaded World?," 121; and J. Louis Martyn, *Galatians: A New Translation with Introduction and Commentary*, Anchor Bible 33A (Doubleday, 1997), 95–97.

This world was invaded again, however, when the earth was climactically and determinatively entered by God in the person of Christ. Paul calls this divine invasion apocalyptic (Gal. 1:12, 2:2) not in the sense of "God's unveiling something that was previously hidden, as though it had been eternally standing behind a curtain" and now finally, in the present age, is revealed but, rather, in the sense of a violent divine incursion that brings this world, the cosmos as we know it, to an end.[25] In this context Martyn points out that when Paul describes the result of Christ's coming, he speaks not of "a new age" but of "a new creation."[26] By speaking of "a new creation," Paul signals that God's invasion is not about "merely repairing this world"; rather, "in fundamental contrast to this world, God's new creation is *the* new."[27]

This new creation is established, Martyn holds—and this is key to the topic at hand—not in Christ's resurrection but in Christ's crucifixion. As such, the shape of the eschatological world goes against our expectations: "We should have preferred to hear that God has established the *new* creation by raising Jesus from the realm of those who have died. Or that God will establish the new creation at the parousia of Christ. Especially when speaking of God's new creation, can we not move *from* the odious cross *to* the glorious resurrection and the hoped-for parousia? Although Paul takes for granted the world-changing resurrection of Jesus, . . . he is far from allowing that event to avert his glance from the cross. He sees the new creation in the cross."[28] God's invasion and victory does not come in brutal power as, for instance, Caesar's army would; it rather comes and is fundamentally shaped by the weakness of the cross. Even the resurrection does not leave the cross behind; as Martyn says, quoting Käsemann, "'The theology of the resurrection is a chapter in the theology of the cross, not the excelling of it.' Seen through resurrection lenses, the cross itself remains the event of God's weak power, the event in which power is, in fact, transfigured and thus fundamentally redefined."[29] The new creation is, therefore, fundamentally cruciform. The bodily shape of the new creation is, says Martyn, the church, and this church is "cross-bearing"—it is "the community of those who . . . are conformed to the crucified one for the sake of others."[30]

Of the several crucicentric arguments, this one alone does not sit well with supralapsarian Christology. The reason is that on Martyn's reading of the

---

25. Martyn, *Galatians*, 99.
26. J. Louis Martyn, "The Apocalyptic Gospel in Galatians," *Interpretation* 54 (2000): 254.
27. Martyn, "Twice-Invaded World?," 126.
28. Martyn, "Apocalyptic Gospel," 259.
29. Martyn, "Twice-Invaded World?," 126.
30. Martyn, "Twice-Invaded World?," 128.

story, the incarnation is contingent upon God's invasion of the world, and this invasion in turn is contingent upon the invasion of sin. God's entering of the world is a response to a problem: sin invading and enslaving God's creation. It is motivated solely by a state of affairs that is an attack on God's original design of creation, not part of it. Thus, Jesus is plan B.

That, for Martyn, the incarnation is indeed solely contingent upon sin is underscored by his conceptualization of the eschaton. Martyn's account rightly suggests that Christ makes a twofold difference: He overcomes the power of sin, and he inaugurates an eschatological reality—the new creation. A theologically important question is how these two aspects of Christ's work relate. A supralapsarian account would argue that a Christocentric eschatological consummation is the essential goal of God's creation. On such an understanding, we are created "for [Christ]" (Col. 1:16). Because Christ is central to all of creation, he is also to be the one who, when creation is overcome by the powers of sin, draws creation back to God in reconciliation and redemption. This redemptive work of Christ is done for the sake of his eschatological work. We are redeemed so that we may be part of the new creation. The cross is thus a function of the eschatological difference that Christ makes. Whereas Christ's redemptive work is accidental to God's relating to creation (if sin had not invaded creation, redemption would not have been necessary), the eschatological work is essential; it is for this that we were created.

On Martyn's account, however, a Christocentric eschatological future is not the essential goal of creation. The cross is not a function of the eschaton, but the eschaton is a function of the cross. Only in the cross is the new creation established, and this eschaton is cross shaped. But the cross is, of course, contingent upon sin—and so is Christ's eschatological work.

At this point, the supralapsarian would want to press a variation of a concern I expressed earlier. It seems inevitable that, for infralapsarians, the eschaton is *cross shaped*. If the incarnation is contingent upon sin, then our relationship with Christ is, in a strong way, based on sin. No sin, no Christ. It is therefore, in a sense, a rather functional relationship. Jesus comes because we have a problem. He comes because there is a job to do. But what happens when the job is done? What if sin no longer is a problem? Then, it seems, we no longer have need of Christ. That suggestion goes against the central and enduring place Christ has both in Christian spirituality and in the biblical narrative of the eschaton. The only solution to that problem seems to be Martyn's: the eschaton is cross shaped. The less theologically sophisticated version of this is the idea that in the eschaton, for all eternity, we will be singing praises to Jesus for his sacrifice.

As a supralapsarian, I press this question: If the eschaton is cross shaped, then has sin not won? If for all eternity we are singing praises to Jesus for his sacrifice, then is our relationship with God, and subsequently our own identity, not permanently shaped by sin? Is sin then truly overcome? Supralapsarian Christology offers another option. Because, on the supralapsarian understanding, our relationship with Christ is not based on sin, we will not have to permanently remember either our sin or Christ's sacrifice. Because the cross is not central in our relationship with God, it can at some point be forgotten. That seems to be exactly what is promised to us. As Miroslav Volf argues in his book *The End of Memory*, the eschaton will entail exactly this, the gift of forgetting.[31] "The former things shall not be remembered or come to mind," as God promises (Isa. 65:17). On a hermeneutical theology of the cross, that is a problem. On a supralapsarian Christology, it is exactly right.[32]

A *Theologia Crucis* Argument for Supralapsarianism

In the previous sections I discussed three ways of construing a theology of the cross. The first two were formal arguments that seek to shape the rules for what counts as an acceptable theological argument. I argued that they can easily be squared with supralapsarian Christology. The problem lies with the third argument. For the apocalyptic theologian of the cross, the cross is the focal point of the relationship between God and humanity. The supralapsarian tells a different story. They believe the cruciform narration overestimates sin and underestimates divine love. The cross, therefore, will have to be decentered. While supralapsarian Christology and an apocalyptic *theologia crucis* thus

---

31. Miroslav Volf, *The End of Memory: Remembering Rightly in a Violent World* (Eerdmans, 2006), 131–213.

32. During an oral presentation of an earlier version of this chapter at a conference, it was pointed out to me that the notion of eschatological forgetting of sin and the cross sits uneasily with the idea that the resurrected Christ has the marks of his wounds, and that he will have them even in the eschaton. This is true. And so the supralapsarian will have to say that just as all memory of the cross will be erased, so will Christ's wounds be erased. This, in turn, means that while Christ was resurrected in a glorified body, his body is nonetheless not-yet perfected. While this may not be the way the tradition historically has conceived matters, I do not believe this is intrinsically problematic. Christ's resurrected and ascended *life* is not perfected—after all, he is sill "waiting 'until his enemies would be made a footstool for his feet'" (Heb. 10:13)—so why would we say that his *bodily existence* has been perfected? For more on this, see "*Being With*—Without Wounds" in chap. 12, below, 265–66.

Of course, embedded in the thought of eschatological forgetting is another supralapsarian argument: If it is true that Christ is the essential center of the eschaton, and if it is true that in the eschaton we will receive the gift of forgetting all evil and wrong, then the incarnation cannot be contingent upon sin, lest we forget why Christ is there in the first place.

part ways, in this final section I want to suggest, as a conclusion, that there is an interesting convergence of motives between the supralapsarian narrative and what drives the epistemological and soteriological crucicentric arguments.

For a *theologia crucis* as shaped by the first two formal arguments, what happens on the cross is completely contradictory to our usual religious thinking. It reveals that what we "naturally" take to be right and good about God and ourselves actually contradicts God's ways and truth. As the charter text of cross theology, 1 Corinthians 1:18–25, says, we expect God to act in wisdom, but God's saving act appears in foolishness; we think it would be fitting for the divine to act in power, but God acts in weakness. God's acts do not fit the mold we have designed for them. In order to see and understand God's acts for what they are, we need to be told about them. We do not recognize them by our own devices. We need revelation. In the light of this revelation, we discover that our criteria for the fittingness of divine acts are skewed, that the things we think are beneath God's dignity are actually expressions of God's very ways of dealing with us: condescension, humility, love.

This debate between a *theologia crucis* and a *theologia gloriae* about which acts are becoming of the divine has a parallel in discussions between infralapsarian and supralapsarian Christological thinkers. Much infralapsarian thought is premised on the idea that the incarnation is a humiliating act that God performs only because God's hand is forced, as it were. A prime example is Anselm's *Cur Deus Homo*, one of the key texts of infralapsarian Christological thought. The intention of Anselm's treatise was to contribute to an ongoing debate about the incarnation between Jewish and Christian medieval theologians in which the Jewish rabbis had argued that the incarnation was derogatory of the dignity of God.[33] As is clear from the discussion's progression, that argument had hit home. Thus, when Anselm enters the discussion, he does not challenge this fundamental premise but tries to show that, given the circumstances, God could not have done otherwise—there was no other way to solve the problem of sin.[34] Supralapsarian Christology challenges, however, the basic premise. What the infralapsarian regards as embarrassment, the supralapsarian regards as the heart of God's relating to

---

33. See R. W. Southern, *Saint Anselm: Portrait in a Landscape* (Cambridge University Press, 1992), 198–202. See also "Satisfaction: Anselm of Canterbury and John Duns Scotus" in chap. 11, below, 228.

34. As Anselm's conversation partner, Boso, frames the question, "I ask you, therefore, to reveal to me something which, as you know, many people besides me ask about, namely this: 'By what necessity or logic did God, almighty as he is, take upon himself the humble standing and weakness of human nature with a view to that nature's restoration?'" Anselm, *Cur Deus Homo*, in *Anselm of Canterbury: The Major Works*, ed. Brian Davies and G. R. Evans (Oxford University Press, 1998), 1.1.

creation. That the incarnation is a humiliating act that needs justification is true only if we try to fit God's actions into a preconceived mold. The actual events tell us that the incarnation is not an emergency measure brought about by the problem of sin but an expression of the very relationship of friendship and love for which God called us into being. Our understanding of what is fitting for divinity will need to be formulated in the light of God's actual acts, not the other way around.

The supralapsarian Christological stance is thus structurally parallel to the soteriological and epistemological arguments for a *theologia crucis*—parallel not only formally but also materially. Both positions emphasize that what is becoming of God should be determined not by a preconceived concept of divinity but by God's actual acts. And both positions underscore that in God's acts God reveals Godself as one who relates to creation in humility and love. If that is the case, could not these two positions be presented as causally ordered? That is, could theologians of the cross be persuaded that the fullest expression of God's condescending love—of God's own, incarnate presence—must include more than God's action in response to sin, that the cross should be placed in a larger, supralapsarian narrative? At the very least, given the intuitions undergirding the cruciform arguments, this seems to be fitting.

3

"Too Lowly . . . to Reach God Without a Mediator"

John Calvin's Supralapsarian Eschatological Narrative

Following a chronological order of historical explorations, having delved into an approach rooted in Lutheran theology (the *theologia crucis*), in this chapter I turn to John Calvin. Based on a surprising comment in Calvin's *Institutes*, some interpreters have recently suggested that Calvin might also be among the supralapsarian Christological theologians. In the midst of a discussion of how God became human so as to reach through the "cloud cast between us and him" by our iniquities, Calvin remarks that nonetheless, "even if man had remained free from all stain, his condition would have been too lowly for him to reach God without a Mediator."[1] The comment is almost made in passing, and Calvin elaborates no further. Calvin seems here to adhere to some form of supralapsarian Christology. But only a few pages later, discussing the work of Andreas Osiander, a well-known supralapsarian contemporary of his, Calvin firmly rejects any arguments for "incarnation anyway" (i.e., for supralapsarianism) as "vague speculations that captivate the frivolous and the seekers after novelty."[2] Our redemption was "the sole purpose of Christ's incarnation," Calvin propounds. "Since all

---

1. John Calvin, *Institutes of the Christian Religion*, ed. John T. McNeill, trans. Ford Lewis Battles, 2 vols. (Westminster, 1960), 2.12.1.
2. Calvin, *Institutes* 2.12.4.

Scripture proclaims that to become our Redeemer he was clothed with flesh, it is too presumptuous to imagine another reason or another end."[3] In fact, he says, whoever desires to say more "shows that he is not even content with the very Christ who was given to us."[4] Traditionally, commentators have therefore read Calvin's earlier remark not as hinting at a supralapsarian understanding of the incarnation, but rather as expressing the idea of a cosmic mediator, a conduit of God's creating and sustaining of that which is not God, a role fulfilled by the eternal Word independent of his incarnation in time.[5]

As of late, though, some readers of Calvin have suggested that Calvin's passing comment on the prelapsarian mediator suggests he has a much wider use for the incarnation than his polemics against Osiander would indicate. Oliver Crisp has argued that Calvin's comment is an expression of "a real tension in Calvin's doctrine of the motivation for the Incarnation" and that "on one plausible reading of the data, a case can be made for thinking that Calvin's thinking is broadly consistent with something like supralapsarianism, and even with an Incarnation anyway argument, though (admittedly) there are residual difficulties with this reconstruction."[6] Through careful consideration of Calvin's doctrine of mediation, Julie Canlis sees Calvin as weaving "Christ into the patterns of creation, not as one of its properties or potentials but as its orientation."[7]

---

3. Calvin, *Institutes* 2.12.4.

4. Calvin, *Institutes* 2.12.5.

5. "Calvin subjects . . . the idea of mediation to two different nuances: mediation as reconciliation and mediation as sustenance. . . . As sustainer, the Mediator always was the way creation was preserved and ordered." E. David Willis, *Calvin's Catholic Christology: The Function of the So-Called Extra Calvinisticum in Calvin's Theology* (Brill, 1969), 70. Likewise, Stephen Edmondson writes, "We find in the *Institutes* an elaboration of the mediatory involvement of the Son from the beginning of God's work, as the conduit whereby God pours God's grace out upon the world, in the assertion of the Son's involvement in the creation and providential care of the world." Stephen Edmondson, *Calvin's Christology* (Cambridge University Press, 2004), 144.

6. Oliver D. Crisp, *Revisioning Christology: Theology in the Reformed Tradition* (Ashgate, 2011), 38. As a side note, it may be helpful here to point out that the term *supralapsarian* is used in the context of two different theological loci: election and Christology. Crisp seems to think that supralapsarian Christology should be seen as a subset of a supralapsarian doctrine of election, and his formulation in the quotation above ("Calvin may be consistent with supralapsarianism, or *even* an Incarnation anyway argument") betrays this. I think it is more helpful to keep these conversations separate, as one can be a supralapsarian with regard to one doctrine while being an infralapsarian with regard to the other. For instance, most Reformed scholastics who were supralapsarian with regard to election were infralapsarian with regard to the incarnation, while the medieval theologian John Duns Scotus was a supralapsarian with regard to incarnation and election but an infralapsarian with regard to rejection.

7. Julie Canlis, *Calvin's Ladder: A Spiritual Theology of Ascent and Ascension* (Eerdmans, 2010), 71.

In this chapter, I will offer an alternative understanding of Calvin's idea that human beings are "too lowly . . . to reach God without a Mediator." First, I will discuss Crisp's arguments and show them wanting. Second, I will scrutinize Canlis's reading of Calvin. As it turns out, Canlis's interpretation hangs mostly on Calvin's two letters to Polish pastors concerning the teaching of traveling scholar Francesco Stancaro. I will show that these letters actually entail the opposite of a supralapsarian Christology. However, I will argue, third, that Crisp and Canlis are nonetheless right in discerning in Calvin's passing comments in the *Institutes* an important and hitherto not fully explored substructure of Calvin's thought. I will aim to show that what comes to the fore here is part of Calvin's eschatological expectations. The very formulation of his comment betrays that Calvin believes human beings are essentially created for an upward, eschatological journey that will carry them beyond the original baseline of creation. In their journey, they reach toward God, and for this they need a mediator. Calvin, I will show, does not conflate mediation and incarnation. While he is thoroughly infralapsarian in his understanding of incarnation, he is a supralapsarian in his understanding of mediation, which in turn is embedded in a supralapsarian eschatology. Fourth, I will argue that my interpretation is confirmed by and sheds new light on another puzzling claim in Calvin's Christology: that on the other side of the arch of salvation history, at the end of time, the triumphant Christ will "discharge the office of Mediator, will cease to be the ambassador of this Father, and will be satisfied with that glory which he enjoyed before the creation of the world."[8] Fifth and finally, I will show that detecting Calvin's supralapsarian eschatological narrative can help one negotiate the ongoing debate concerning Calvin's take on deification.

Oliver Crisp: Calvin Is Committed to Supralapsarianism

While acknowledging Calvin's explicit infralapsarian stance, Oliver Crisp argued in a recent essay that "when one pieces together different things Calvin says about the motivation for the Incarnation, it looks like Calvin is committed to—though he does not commit himself to—a species of supralapsarianism along with an Incarnation anyway argument."[9] Crisp has his eye on three lines of argument in Calvin's writing. The first is Calvin's comment that human beings are "too lowly . . . to reach God without a Mediator." Crisp believes the context of this remark shows that Calvin has in mind an *incarnate* mediator,

8. Calvin, *Institutes* 2.14.3.
9. Crisp, *Revisioning Christology*, 25.

not the preincarnate Word. After all, Crisp argues, right after this statement Calvin refers to 1 Timothy 2:5 and emphasizes that the mediator is not just God but also human. In this, he is "familiarly among us as one of ourselves. . . . He is near us, indeed touches us, since he is our flesh."[10] Calvin's statement should therefore be read as "an appeal to some species of Incarnation Anyway reasoning."[11] Second, in a section in the *Institutes* devoted to the "person" of the mediator, Calvin stipulates this interpretative maxim: "Those things which apply to the office of the Mediator are not spoken simply either of the divine nature or of the human."[12] This implies, Crisp argues, that every reference to a mediator needs to be to one who is incarnate. Therefore, if the need for a mediator is not contingent upon sin, as Calvin says, then the incarnation cannot be contingent upon sin. And third, Crisp points to the several places where Calvin argues that not only humans but also the angels need a mediator—not because they were alienated from God, like humans, but because without a mediator they run the risk of becoming alienated. For instance, commenting on Colossians's statement that through the Son "God was pleased to reconcile to himself all things, whether on earth or in heaven" (Col. 1:20), Calvin writes,

> It was . . . necessary that angels, also, should be made to be at peace with God, for, being creatures, they were not beyond the risk of falling, had they not been confirmed by the grace of Christ. . . . There is not on the part of angels so much of righteousness as would suffice for their being fully joined with God. They have, therefore, need of a peace-maker, through whose grace they may wholly cleave to God. Hence it is with propriety that Paul declares, that the grace of Christ does not reside among humankind alone, and on the other hand makes it common to angels. Nor is there any injustice done to angels, in sending them to a Mediator, that they may, through his kindness, have a well-grounded peace with God.[13]

10. Calvin, *Institutes* 2.12.1. See Crisp, *Revisioning Christology*, 27.
11. Crisp, *Revisioning Christology*, 27.
12. Calvin, *Institutes* 2.14.3.
13. John Calvin, *Commentaries on the Epistle of Paul the Apostle to the Philippians, Colossians, and Thessalonians*, trans. John Pringle (Baker, 2005), 156.

In his essay, Crisp also refers to a place in the *Institutes* where Calvin speaks of the relationship between the angels and Christ in the context of a discussion with Andreas Osiander. Osiander had argued that the notion of the *imago Dei*, which both humans and angels bear, implies a supralapsarian stance since, he believed, the image of God in whom humans are created is the incarnate Word. Calvin responds to this line of argument by denouncing supralapsarian Christology as a form of speculation and by reinterpreting the *imago Dei* as simply "a resemblance to the Father." But then, Crisp highlights, Calvin continues by stating that "the angels would have lacked [a] head [i.e., Christ] if God had not determined to clothe his Son with flesh, even apart from Adam's guilt" (Calvin, *Institutes* 2.12.7). With this, Crisp suggests,

Crisp believes that this line of thought implies a supralapsarian Christology. After all, he argues, in this passage Calvin assigns the role of cosmic mediator not just to the divine Word *simpliciter* but to the Christ, the Word incarnate.[14] And what else could Calvin have done? "Calvin's linking of the headship over the angels to the role of the God-man seems to include some confirmatory role, which it is difficult to square with Christ merely as Cosmic Mediator (How could a Cosmic Mediator be one through whom the elect angels are mystically united to God)?"[15]

Calvin's comments "appear to pull in several different directions at once." Calvin wants to say "that Christ is Head over the angels; that Christ would have been Head over the angels irrespective of Adam's sin; and that Christ is requisite in order that the angels have his headship over them"—while at the same time denouncing supralapsarian Christology (Crisp, *Revisioning Christology*, 31–32). This is an example of the tension Crisp sees in Calvin's Christology, causing him to suggest that while Calvin may not explicitly commit himself to supralapsarian Christology, he is nonetheless committed to it.

The problem with Crisp's argument, however, is that the line "the angels would have lacked this head if God had not determined to clothe his Son with flesh, even apart from Adam's guilt" is not Calvin's position but, rather, Calvin reporting on Osiander; Calvin characterizes this particular argument by Osiander as a "futile subtlety, which Osiander spreads abroad!" Thus what Crisp characterizes as an expression of tension within Calvin's position is in fact an expression of a consistent rejection of the idea of a supralapsarian decree of incarnation.

14. Crisp, *Revisioning Christology*, 30.

15. Crisp, *Revisioning Christology*, 34. That Calvin's notion that a mediator is needed to sustain the angels was not an occasional thought on his part but a considered position is clear from the fact that Calvin makes similar claims throughout his oeuvre. For instance, in one of his sermons on Ephesians, he writes, "Jesus Christ is the mediator to set the angels at full accord with God, insomuch that there would be no steadfastness or constancy in them if they were not upheld by him. And besides, their righteousness should not be perfect except they were blessed and elected in him." John Calvin, *Sermons on the Epistle to the Ephesians* (Banner of Truth, 1973), 45. In his commentary on Ephesians 1:10, he writes,

The angels also have been gathered together. Not that they were ever scattered, but their attachment to the service of God is now perfect, and their state is eternal. What comparison is there between a creature and the Creator, without the interposition of a mediator? So far as they are creatures, had it not been for the benefit which they derived from Christ, they would have been liable to change and sin, and consequently their happiness would not have been eternal. Who then will deny that both angels and men have been brought back to a fixed order by the grace of Christ? Men had been lost, and angels were not beyond the reach of danger. By gathering both into his own body, Christ hath united them to God the Father, and established actual harmony between heaven and earth. (John Calvin, *Commentaries on the Epistles of Paul to the Galatians and Ephesians*, trans. William Pringle [Baker, 2005], 205)

And, in his *Sermons on the Book of Job*, he writes,

Furthermore it behooveth us to mark well howe St. Paule sayth, that Jesus Christ is come too gather together the things that are in heaven and earth. And thereby he sheweth, that the Angells have their steadfastnesse in the grace of our Lorde Jesus Christ, forsomuch as he is the mediator between God & his creatures. True it is that Jesus Christ redeemed not the Angels, for they needed not to be ransomed from death whereunto they were not yet falne: but yet was he theyr mediator. And how so? To the intent to joyne them

I believe each of these lines of argument fails to make Crisp's case. With regard to Calvin's saying that human beings are "too lowly . . . to reach God without a Mediator," the wider context does indeed concern the incarnate One. The paragraph at stake begins with Calvin's assertion that "it was of the greatest importance for us that he who was to be our Mediator be both true God and true man." Calvin expounds this claim by pointing to humanity's sinful condition: "Since our iniquities, like a cloud cast between us and him, had completely estranged us from the Kingdom of heaven, no man, unless he belonged to God, could serve as the intermediatory to restore peace." Calvin then makes his claim that even if we had never sinned, we were in need of a mediator—but, significantly, continues *by contrasting* such a hypothetical situation with the actual one: "What, then, of man: plunged by his mortal ruin into death and hell, defiled with so many spots, befouled with his own corruption, and overwhelmed with every curse?" It is in response to this understanding of the current needs of humanity that Calvin returns to a discussion of the incarnation. The flow of Calvin's line of thought itself does therefore not commit Calvin to a supralapsarian take on the incarnation. Whether or not Calvin's idea that humanity finds itself in a position "too lowly . . . to reach God without a Mediator" implies in and of itself a form of supralapsarian Christology depends on what Calvin's argument is for this claim. As it stands, Calvin does not provide us with such an argument, nor does Crisp offer a suggestion about what this argument could be.

A similar observation could be made with regard to Crisp's second argument. Calvin makes the comment that "those things which apply to the office of the Mediator are not spoken simply either of the divine nature or of the human" in the context of a discussion of a mediatorship focused on the problem of sin—of a mediator who "received from the Father the power of remitting of sin, of raising to life whom he will, of bestowing righteousness, holiness, salvation," of one "appointed judge of the living and the dead," and so on.[16] Whether or not Calvin's maxim applies also to the mediatory role outside that context is exactly the issue at stake. It cannot be assumed; it has to be shown.

Finally, Calvin does indeed state at multiple places that not only humans but also angels have need of a mediator—and at some places he refers to this mediator explicitly as Christ, the incarnate One.[17] However, Calvin's reference

---

unto God in all perfection, and afterward to mainteyne them by his grace, that they may be preserved from falling." (Calvin, *Sermons on the Book of Job*, quoted in Crisp, *Revisioning Christology*, 33)

16. Calvin, *Institutes* 2.14.3.
17. See note 15, above.

to the mediator as Christ could simply be analogous to a man who points at a baby picture of his spouse and calls the child "my wife," even though at the time the picture was taken he obviously was not yet married to her. In addition, it does not go without saying, as Crisp surmises, that the angels need an *incarnate* mediator in order to be confirmed in their righteousness and brought into eternal bliss. That all depends on how Calvin conceives of the workings of this kind of mediation—but Crisp never offers an account of what he believes Calvin's conception of this to be. Therefore, here too, Crisp's argument assumes the very thing that has to be shown.

In sum, Crisp's case is that while Calvin commits himself to an infralapsarian form of Christology, some of his statements on a supralapsarian form of mediation commit him to the opposite. In order to make this case, Crisp has to show that these statements *imply* a supralapsarian take on the incarnation. But as Crisp never offers an analysis of what this supralapsarian form of mediation might be, or how it works, he never generates enough material on which to make his case.

Julie Canlis: A Christologically Ordered Creation

Another proposal to read Calvin as a Christological supralapsarian comes from Julie Canlis. Her book *Calvin's Ladder* traces the ways Calvin engages an idea deeply ingrained in Christian spirituality and theology—the idea of creation's ascent to God. According to Canlis, Calvin reworks this notion in two ways. First, he conceives of the ascent in Christological terms. Whereas much of the Christian tradition speaks of an ascent of the human soul, Calvin instead focuses on the ascent of Christ—who, through his mediatory work, brings believers with him on his journey to the Father. Second, Calvin places Christ's ascent in a supralapsarian context. According to Canlis, Calvin weaves "Christ into the pattern of creation, not as one of its properties or potentials but as its orientation."[18] Creation is, for Calvin, "christologically and pneumatologically ordered."[19] Key to this supralapsarian Christological interpretation is Canlis's observation that Calvin "refuses to collapse mediation into expiation."[20] Instead, Calvin "moves the notion of Christ as 'midpoint' between God and humanity from the cross, where we are accustomed to look for his mediation, all the way back into creation."[21] In other words,

---

18. Canlis, *Calvin's Ladder*, 71.
19. Canlis, *Calvin's Ladder*, 55.
20. Canlis, *Calvin's Ladder*, 56.
21. Canlis, *Calvin's Ladder*, 70–71. See also note 26, below.

"Calvin is positioning the forthcoming redemption (mediation-expiation) of Christ within a more comprehensive story, that of the God who intends us for communion (mediation-union)."[22] It is in this context that Canlis interprets Calvin's saying that human beings find themselves in a state "too lowly . . . to reach God without a Mediator."[23]

The problem with Canlis's interpretation is that it is not warranted by what Calvin actually says. Her case for a supralapsarian Christological reading of Calvin is based mainly on two collections of texts: Calvin's commentaries and sermons on Colossians and Ephesians, in which he expresses his notion of the angels' need for a mediator, and his letters against the traveling theologian Francesco Stancaro.[24] Canlis rightly calls attention to the fact that, in these texts, Calvin refuses to collapse mediation and expiation. But she misses that Calvin also refuses to collapse mediation and incarnation. This is not so clear in Calvin's comments on Colossians and Ephesians, but it is clear in the Stancaro letters. At stake in the latter documents is Stancaro's claim that Christ is mediator only according to his human nature.[25] Calvin levels a number of arguments against this position. The first is that Stancaro ignores the fact that Christ was already a mediator before his incarnation:

> But we maintain, first, that the name of mediator suits Christ, not only by the fact that he put on flesh, or that he took on the office of reconciling the human race to God, but from the beginning of creation he already truly was mediator, for he always was the head of the Church, had primacy over the angels, and was the firstborn of every creature (Eph. 1:22; Col. 1:15; 2:10). Therefore, we conclude that not only after Adam's fall did he begin to exercise his office of mediator, but since he is the eternal Word of God, both angels as well as men were united to God by his grace so that they would remain uncorrupted. . . . The only begotten Son of God was the same God and of the same essence with the Father, and nevertheless, he was the mid-point (*medium*) between God and creatures, so that the life that was otherwise hidden in God would flow from him. We add, then, that although he was predestined by God after man's alienation to restore the lost human race to life by expiating sin, nevertheless,

---

22. Canlis, *Calvin's Ladder*, 56–57.
23. Canlis, *Calvin's Ladder*, 65.
24. For references to Colossians and Ephesians, see Canlis, *Calvin's Ladder*, 57n17; 63n43; 64n48; 71nn74, 76; 82n116 (Colossians); 57n14; 62nn38, 42; 63n45; 64nn47, 50; 65n52 (Ephesians). For references to Calvin's letters against Stancaro, see 55nn5–6; 56nn8, 10–11; 57n12; 59n24; 61n37; 71n73. See also note 25, below.
25. For a wider discussion of the conflict with Stancaro, Stancaro's own position, and the dogmatic-historical context of Calvin's reply, see Edmondson, *Calvin's Christology*, 14–39. Quite importantly, Edmondson shows how Stancaro's identification of mediation and incarnation is rooted in a medieval tradition going back to Augustine. Calvin breaks with this tradition.

in the role of mediator he is no less head of the angels than of men. This can be seen from the first chapter of Colossians which is by no means appropriate to human nature alone.[26]

Canlis concludes from this that Calvin has a Christologically structured doctrine of creation, with Christ being the medium between God and creation. But Calvin's arguments in these texts hinge exactly on a disentangling of the Word's mediatory role from his incarnation. It is not Christ who is the medium between God and creatures; it is the non-incarnate divine Word. The Word exercised the role of mediator long before there was the need for him "to put on flesh" and to take on "the office of reconciling the human race to God." Stancaro cannot be right in thinking that only Christ's human nature mediates, Calvin argues, because the divine Word's mediatory role is not contingent upon incarnation. But likewise, Canlis cannot be right in thinking that creation is Christologically structured, because the Word does not become the midpoint of God and creation only upon taking on a human nature. To put it differently, Canlis collapses mediation and incarnation. While Calvin does indeed have a supralapsarian account of mediation, he has an infralapsarian account of incarnation.

An Alternative Reading: Calvin's Supralapsarian Eschatological Narrative

While the texts thus do not bear out the particular supralapsarian interpretation Crisp and Canlis offer, Canlis is nonetheless correct when she points out that Calvin's notion that humanity's state is "too lowly . . . to reach God without a Mediator" ought to be read in the context of a larger comprehensive

---

26. Calvin, quoted in Joseph Tylenda, "Christ the Mediator: Calvin versus Stancaro," *Calvin Theological Journal* 8, no. 1 (April 1973): 12–13. See a parallel comment in Calvin's second reply to Stancaro:
> In what pertains to the matter at hand we must first see what the word mediator means. Certainly, the eternal [*logos*] was already mediator from the beginning, before Adam's fall and the alienation and separation of the human race from God. In this sense, unless we are mistaken, he is also called by Paul the first-born of all creatures; and when John says that life was in him, he indicates the mode of communication from which otherwise hidden source, the grace of God flowed to men. Therefore, since Christ was head of angels and men in the still innocent state of things, he is rightly considered the mediator whom the elect angels even now see and acknowledge. It was man's rebellion that brought it about that expiation was necessary to reconcile us to God, and so Christ should be regarded as mediator together with his sacrifice, by which he appeased God's anger and restored us in the hope of the blessed life from which we were barred. We indeed teach that he is the mediator, not with regard to one nature alone, but inasmuch as he is God revealed in the flesh. (Calvin, quoted in Joseph Tylenda, "The Controversy on Christ the Mediator: Calvin's Second Reply to Stancaro," *Calvin Theological Journal* 8, no. 2 [November 1973]: 147)

story. The traditional interpretation of Calvin's notion, as if it were a simple reference to the divine Word's work of creation and preservation, falls short.[27] The actual wording of Calvin's phrase implies that the mediator's task does not have simply to do with the calling forth and sustaining of humanity. Rather, it suggests that human beings are set on a journey, an upward movement toward God, and that the mediator's role is to guide them onward toward their destiny. Calvin's comment is thus not concerned with creation or preservation; it is concerned with eschatology.

Calvin has sometimes been said to have a weak eschatology.[28] However, the opposite is true. Calvin has not only one but two eschatologies. One grouping of eschatological events is contingent upon the dynamic of fall, incarnation, and Christ's reconciliatory work—namely, Christ's resurrection, ascension, return, and last judgment. We can call this Calvin's infralapsarian eschatology. But Calvin also has a supralapsarian eschatology: his vision of the original, essential, eschatological goal for which God has destined human beings. In the *Institutes*, Calvin's infralapsarian eschatology is presented in book 2, the volume devoted to "the knowledge of God the redeemer in Christ."[29] Calvin's supralapsarian eschatology has no analogous clear location. Weary of speculation, Calvin does not like to probe into supralapsarian realties as if the fall had not happened. But careful reading allows us nonetheless, I believe, to gather together the contours of Calvin's understanding of an original eschatological destiny of humanity. This is mostly to be found in book 1 of the *Institutes*, the volume devoted to "the knowledge of God the creator." Calvin argues here that human beings were created with a *sensus divinitatis*, a sense occasioned by "the whole workmanship of the universe" that gives human beings an awareness of God.[30] However, the *sensus divinitatis* not only gives us knowledge of God; it also triggers in us an eschatological awareness and longing: "Knowledge of this sort, then, ought not only to arouse us to the

---

27. See note 5, above.
28. See John Bolt, "'A Pearl and a Leaven': John Calvin's Critical Two-Kingdoms Eschatology," in *John Calvin and Evangelical Theology: Legacy and Prospect*, ed. Sung Wook Chung (Westminster John Knox, 2009), 242–65; and W. Balke, "Some Characteristics of Calvin's Eschatology," in *Christian Hope in Context*, ed. A. van Egmond and D. van Keulen (Meinema, 2001), 30–64.
29. See his discussion of the creedal notions of Christ's resurrection, ascension, and return (Calvin, *Institutes* 2.17.13–16) as well as his chapter on the final resurrection (Calvin, *Institutes* 3.25).
30. "There is within the human mind, and indeed by natural instinct, an awareness of divinity." Calvin, *Institutes* 1.3.1. "The final goal of the blessed life, moreover, rests in the knowledge of God. Lest anyone then, be excluded from access to happiness, he not only sowed in men's minds that seed of religion of which we have spoken but revealed himself and daily discloses himself in the whole workmanship of the universe. As a consequence, men cannot open their eyes without being compelled to see him." Calvin, *Institutes* 1.5.1.

worship of God but also to awaken and encourage us to the hope of the future life."[31] The *sensus divinitatis* is given to make us see that we are eschatological creatures, made for a journey toward another, heavenly existence. Calvin describes this journey as characterized by the cultivation of righteousness,[32] the development of piety,[33] and a life of worship.[34] But each of these makes us live into the reality that we "were made for the meditation of heavenly life"—the very center of which is "to be united with God."[35]

It is in the context of this supralapsarian eschatological vision, I submit, that we are to understand Calvin's notion that humans find themselves "too lowly . . . to reach God without a Mediator." Human beings are made for an upward journey, to be united with God. They nonetheless do not have the internal resources to reach their destiny on their own. Therefore, as Calvin says in the first letter regarding Stancaro, the second person of the Trinity becomes the *medium*, the midpoint between God and creatures, "so that the life which was otherwise hidden in God would flow from him."[36] The mediator enables human beings to fulfil their upward eschatological journey.

When human beings sin, and thereby journey not upward but downward, "plunged into death and hell" (notice Calvin's use of the spatial metaphors), it is then also the divine Word who follows human beings on their downward journey, chasing after them as it were, and, having taken on a human nature, catches them in their fall, turns them around, and guides them on the ascent again. "It is Christ alone, therefore, who connects heaven and earth: he is the only mediator who reaches from heaven down to earth: he is the medium

---

31. Calvin, *Institutes* 1.5.10. See also the last quotation in the previous note. According to Calvin, a human being "should consider for what purpose he was created and endowed with no mean gifts. By this knowledge he should arouse himself to meditation upon divine worship and the future life." Calvin, *Institutes* 2.6.1.

32. Human beings "understand themselves to have been born to cultivate righteousness, in which the seed of religion is enclosed. But, without controversy, just as man was made for the meditation upon the heavenly life, so it is certain that the knowledge of it was engraved upon his soul. And if human happiness, whose perfection it is to be united with God, were hidden from man, he would in fact be bereft of the principal use of his understanding" (Calvin, *Institutes* 1.15.6). See also Calvin, *Institutes* 2.1.3: "Yet God would not have us forget our original immortality, which he had bestowed upon our father Adam, and which ought truly to arouse in us a zeal for righteousness and goodness. For we cannot think upon either our first condition or to what purpose we were formed without being prompted to meditate upon immortality, and to yearn after the Kingdom of God."

33. "The natural order was that the frame of the universe should be the school in which we were to learn piety, and from it to pass over to eternal life and perfect felicity" (Calvin, *Institutes* 2.6.1).

34. A human being "should consider for what purpose he was created and endowed with no mean gifts. By this knowledge he should arouse himself to meditation upon divine worship and the future life." Calvin, *Institutes* 2.1.3.

35. Calvin, *Institutes* 1.15.6.

36. Calvin, quoted in Tylenda, "Christ the Mediator," 13.

through which the fullness of all celestial blessings flow down to us, and through which we, in turn, ascend to God."[37]

Against the background of this eschatological narrative, we can also understand Calvin's remarks about the mediatory role of the divine Word vis-à-vis the angels. While they have a different status than human beings, they too are being prepared for an eschatological future in the presence of God; and they too need assistance. Not only were they "not beyond the risk of falling" and thereby needed to be confirmed in their state; they actually did not yet have "so much of righteousness as would suffice for their being fully joined with God" and thereby, like human beings, needed to be guided from their too lowly state on an upward journey.[38]

In either case—for angels or for human beings—the key requirement for the mediatory role is not that the mediator shares in the nature of those who benefit from his assistance. On Calvin's supralapsarian eschatological vision, the divine Word does not have to take on an angelic or human nature to accompany angels and humans on their eschatological journey. Rather, the key requirement is that he share in the nature of the one to whom creation is journeying: "He first had to be God to lead us back to the Father. What is the goal of our adoption which we attain through him, if it is not, as Peter declares, finally to be partakers of the divine nature?"[39] Here is then the proper response to Crisp's worry that one who is not incarnate could not mystically unite the angels to God.[40] The supralapsarian eschatological mediation Calvin has in mind is not one of a divine identification with creatures; it is one of creatures being graced with divine life flowing to them by way of the mediator. This then results in an eschatological narrative that is very different from the one offered by Canlis. Yes, a supralapsarian mediation is embedded in this narrative. But it is simply the mediation of the non-incarnate divine Word.

The End of Mediation

This way of reading Calvin's supralapsarian eschatological narrative both sheds new light on and is confirmed by another puzzling claim in Calvin's

---

37. John Calvin, *Commentaries on the First Book of Moses Called Genesis*, trans. John King, vol. 2 (Baker, 2005), 113. Note the verbal similarities with the statements in Calvin's reply to Stancaro. See also Calvin, *Institutes* 1.13.26: "And certainly for this reason Christ descended to us, to bear us up to the Father, and at the same time to bear us up to himself, inasmuch as he is one with the Father."

38. Calvin, *Philippians, Colossians, and Thessalonians*, 156. See also note 15, above.

39. Calvin, quoted in Tylenda, "Controversy," 148–49.

40. See note 15, above.

Christology. Commenting on Paul's remark that, at the end, Christ "hands over the kingdom to God the Father," at which point "the Son himself will also be subjected to the one who put all things in subjection under him, so that God may be all in all" (1 Cor. 15:24, 28), Calvin argues that Christ's mediatorship will come to an end at that point. Right now, Christ, subjecting all things to himself, "is the medium between us and the Father in such a way as to bring us at length to him."[41] But once that task is completed, "God, holding the government of the heaven and the earth by himself, and without any medium, will in that respect be all.... All things will be brought back to God, as their alone beginning and end, that they may be closely bound to him."[42] The means of the Word's current mediatory work is his human nature. "All power was delivered over to Christ, inasmuch as he was manifested in the flesh."[43] The goal is for Christ to "restore the kingdom which he has received, that we may cleave wholly to God."[44] At that point, he "will transfer [the kingdom] from his humanity to his glorious divinity, because a way of approach will then be opened up, from which our infirmity now keeps us back. Thus then Christ will be subjected to the Father, because the veil being then removed, we shall openly behold God reigning in his majesty, and Christ's humanity will then no longer be interposed to keep us back from a closer view of God."[45]

In the *Institutes*, Calvin makes similar statements:

> For what purpose were power and lordship given to Christ, unless that by his hand the Father might govern us? In this sense, also, Christ is said to be seated at the right hand of the Father. Yet this is but for a time, until we enjoy the direct vision of the Godhead.... Until he comes forth as judge of the world Christ will therefore reign, joining us to the Father as the measure of our weakness permits. But when as partakers in heavenly glory we shall see God as he is, Christ, having then discharged the Office of Mediator, will cease to be the ambassador of this Father, and will be satisfied with that glory which he enjoyed before the creation of the world.... That is, to him was lordship committed by the Father, until such time as we should see his divine majesty face to face.[46]

---

41. John Calvin, *Commentary on the Epistles of Paul the Apostle to the Corinthians*, trans. John Pringle (Baker, 2005), 31.
42. Calvin, *Corinthians*, 33.
43. Calvin, *Corinthians*, 31.
44. Calvin, *Corinthians*, 32.
45. Calvin, *Corinthians*, 33.
46. Calvin, *Institutes* 2.14.3. In this context, it is also noteworthy that Calvin references the same thought in his polemic against Stancaro: "As long as Christ sustains the role of mediator, he does not hesitate to submit himself to the Father.... Finally, on the last day the Son will hand over his kingdom to God the Father, because then, as I say, the splendor of the glory of

Commentators have debated whether Calvin means that the divine Word will actually lay down his human nature in the eschaton.[47] I do not believe the texts give us enough to come to a decision about that. But it is clear that, according to Calvin, in the eschaton the Word's human nature will no longer play any mediatory role. In the light of the previous sections of this chapter, it is now clear why. Calvin's take on the incarnation is purely infralapsarian. The divine Word takes on a human nature to chase after us when, instead of ascending upward to the Father, we descend into death and hell. Having reached us and turned our way upward again, the incarnate One continues his mediatory work by ruling his church and leading us to the seeing of God. But once that goal has been reached, once we safely have been ushered into the eschatological presence of God and are united with him, there no longer is any work for him to do in his human nature. The sin problem is taken care of.

I wonder whether, in the light of the previous arguments, we should read Calvin's notions that in the eschaton Christ will have "discharged the office of Mediator" and will "cease to be the ambassador of the Father" as concerning not only the Word's infralapsarian, incarnate mediatory work but also his larger supralapsarian mediatory work. In the latter function, the divine Word is, in terms of Calvin's first letter regarding Stancaro, the "mid-point (*medium*) between God and creatures," the one through whom divine grace was flowing so as to lead human beings from their lowly state to reach God. The divine Word guides human beings to their eschatological goal. But what if the goal has been reached? What if humans, having made their upward journey, now have been brought to "see the divine majesty face to face"? Does creation still need the Word to be a medium, or can the Word now completely give up being the ambassador of the Father, not just in his infralapsarian appearance but also in his supralapsarian mediation? As with the issue of whether, in the eschaton, the divine Word will lay down his human nature or simply not make use of it anymore, Calvin does not offer an answer to this question. But the logic of his eschatological narrative suggests the latter.[48]

God the Father will be instantly visible to us, the glory which now appears in Christ, his living image." Calvin, quoted in Tylenda, "Christ the Mediator," 16.

47. For example, that it is Calvin's view that in the eschaton Christ will lay down his human nature is argued by E. Emmen, *De Christologie van Calvijn* (H. J. Paris, 1935), 109; and Jürgen Moltmann, *The Crucified God* (Fortress, 1993), 257–59. That this may be Calvin's view is argued by Heinrich Quistorp, *Calvin's Doctrine of the Last Things* (John Knox, 1955), 170. That this is not Calvin's view is argued by Willis, *Calvin's Catholic Christology*, 99; Richard A. Muller, "Christ in the Eschaton: Calvin and Moltmann on the Duration of the *Munus Regium*," *Harvard Theological Review* 74, no. 1 (January 1981): 37; and J. F. Jansen, "1 Cor. 15:24–28 and the Future of Jesus Christ," *Scottish Journal of Theology* 40, no. 4 (October 1988): 559–61.

48. One might think that, on this interpretation, Calvin's position seems to imply subordination. This is true. If so, Calvin's retelling of the narrative would be inconsistent with his own

In either case, the limitations Calvin puts on the Word's incarnate presence underscore that Calvin does not have the supralapsarian Christological intuitions Crisp and Canlis assign to him. A supralapsarian who holds to a Christologically ordered creation, in which all that is not God is oriented toward the incarnation, will not simultaneously hold that in the eschaton the divine Word will lay his human existence dormant for the sake of returning to the glory he enjoyed before the creation of the world. After all, such a move on the part of the Word would leave the Christologically ordered creation without its very center.

Communicating Divine Life

Finally, tracing Calvin's supralapsarian eschatological narrative also allows us to negotiate another ongoing debate in Calvin interpretation: the debate concerning his take on deification. My reading of Calvin's narrative offers a measure by which to adjudicate this debate.[49]

At the heart of Calvin's description of the relationship between the incarnate mediator and creation we find language that speaks of believers participating in Christ, being grafted into his body, and being united with him. Scholars such as Carl Mosser, Julie Canlis, and J. Todd Billings have argued that fully mining these terms suggests an eschatological vision culminating in a form of deification. Other readers of Calvin, like Jonathan Slater and Bruce L. McCormack, have strongly opposed such a reading of Calvin. While it is not always clear what exactly is meant by the term

---

strong anti-subordination position, which came to the fore in the autothean controversies. On the autothean controversies, see Brannon Ellis, *Calvin, Classical Trinitarianism, and the Aseity of the Son* (Oxford University Press, 2012). This could therefore count as an argument against my line of interpretation—or it could be an illustration of how deeply entrenched Calvin's supralapsarian eschatological intuitions are.

49. For the debate, see Carl Mosser, "The Greatest Possible Blessing: Calvin and Deification," *Scottish Journal of Theology* 55, no. 1 (January 2002): 36–57; Julie Canlis, "Calvin, Osiander and Participation in God," *International Journal of Systematic Theology* 6, no. 2 (April 2004): 169–84; Jonathan Slater, "Salvation as Participation in the Humanity of the Mediator in Calvin's *Institutes of the Christian Religion*: A Reply to Carl Mosser," *Scottish Journal of Theology* 58, no. 1 (January 2005): 39–58; J. Todd Billings, "United to God Through Christ: Assessing Calvin on the Question of Deification," *Harvard Theological Review* 98, no. 3 (July 2005): 215–34; Yang-Ho Lee, "Calvin on Deification: A Reply to Carl Mosser and Jonathan Slater," *Scottish Journal of Theology* 63, no. 3 (August 2010): 272–84; Bruce L. McCormack, "Union with Christ in Calvin's Theology: Grounds for a Divinization Theory?," in *Tributes to John Calvin: A Celebration of His Quincentenary*, ed. David W. Hall (P&R, 2010), 504–29; and A. J. Ollerton, "*Quasi Deificari*: Deification in the Theology of John Calvin," *Westminster Theological Journal* 73, no. 2 (Fall 2011): 237–54.

deification,⁵⁰ a central question in this conversation is whether Calvin, when he speaks about participation in Christ, means a participation in Christ's human nature or a participation in Christ's divine nature. These two ways of reading imply two different eschatological narratives. If the believer is drawn into participation in Christ's divine nature, the eschatological goal of life is to be drawn beyond the baseline of human existence, however one wants to further unpack the nature of a participation in the divine. However, if Calvin only means to speak about a union with the human nature of Christ, there is no reason to expect such an eschatological movement. It is here that my own proposals regarding Calvin's eschatological narrative can help recognize the direction in which Calvin is thinking. If my reading of Calvin is correct, an upward movement beyond the baseline of creation is central to his eschatological expectations.

Jonathan Slater, denying that Calvin's notion of participation in Christ implies a participation in the divine, appeals to Calvin's concept of mediation: "Without in any way denying that it is the eternal Son who is our mediator, Calvin's emphasis is on the humanity of the mediator. . . . What we receive from him is what he has received *from* the Father according to his human nature, not what he has possessed *with* the Father from all eternity."⁵¹ But this argument falters on Calvin's refusal to conflate mediation and incarnation. According to the letters concerning Stancaro, the divine Word already mediated to humanity "the life which was otherwise hidden in God" without having taken on any human nature.⁵²

---

50. Thus, rightly, McCormack, states, "It is rarely if ever the case that the meaning of *divinization* is set forth in anything like a clear and consistent manner that would allow for meaningful discussion and debate." McCormack, "Union with Christ," 505. Case in point is Carl Mosser's essay, which is one of the papers that initiated this conversation. In the introduction to his paper, Mosser defines deification as "for believers to become by grace what the Son of God is by nature." Mosser, "Greatest Possible Blessing," 36. Later in the paper, Mosser elaborates in a footnote, "Believers, through union with the one true God, come to possess certain attributes that are natural only to the deity, not humanity. Primary among these are immortality and incorruptibility" (37n2). The problem with this definition is that immortality and incorruptibility do not have to be conceived of as divine rather than human attributes. One could think of the pairs mortality-immortality and corruptibility-incorruptibility as accidental properties, either of which could be gifted to human beings. We currently find ourselves to be mortal and corruptible; but rather than thinking about these as essential characteristics of humanity, which one day will be swapped for the loftier divine characteristics of immortality and incorruptibility, we could think of these as accidental characteristics—that is, as attributes we currently possess but that are not essential to our human nature and that, therefore, could one day be changed for other, better, characteristics that nonetheless do not carry us beyond the human baseline. If this is how to think of these pairs, then an eschatological future involving the gifts of immortality and incorruptibility need not involve deification.
51. Slater, "Humanity of the Mediator," 43.
52. On this, see also Lee, "Calvin on Deification," 276–77.

"Too Lowly . . . to Reach God Without a Mediator" 67

A more subtle position is developed by Bruce L. McCormack. He takes his starting point in Calvin's adherence to the Chalcedonian notion that Christ's two natures each retain their distinctive characteristics unimpaired. The two natures are united in one person, but without confusion or change. If there is thus no seepage from one nature to the other, "you simply cannot find the ontological ground needed for a divinization theory in Calvin's Christology."[53] Union with the human nature of Christ does not entail union with his divine side, since the two natures are not mixed. At the same time, McCormack acknowledges that there are texts in which Calvin seems to contradict this picture. For instance, writing about Christ's presence in the Lord's Supper, Calvin says,

> We are taught from the Scriptures that Christ was from the beginning that life-giving Word of the Father, the spring and source of life, from which all things have always received their capacity to live. . . . Therefore, John sometimes calls him "the Word of life." . . . The same John afterward adds that life was manifested only when, having taken our flesh, the Son of God gave himself for our eyes to see and our hands to touch. For even though he previously poured out his power upon the creatures, still, because man (estranged from God through sin and having lost participation in life) saw death threatening from every side, he had to be received into communion of the Word in order to receive hope of immortality. . . . But when the Source of life begins to abide in our flesh, he no longer lies hidden far from us, but shows us that we are to partake of him. . . . He is life since he is the eternal Word of God, who came down from heaven to us but also . . . by coming down he poured that power upon the flesh he took in order that from it participation in life might flow unto us.[54]

In the next section, Calvin adds, "Water is sometimes drunk from a spring, sometimes drawn, sometimes led by channels to water the fields, yet it does not flow forth from itself for so many uses, but from the very source, which by unceasing flow supplies and serves it. In like manner, the flesh of Christ is like a rich and inexhaustible fountain that pours into us the life springing forth from the Godhead into itself. Now who does not see that communion with Christ's flesh and blood is necessary for all who aspire to heavenly life?"[55] Clearly, Calvin here goes beyond the notion that in the Lord's Supper we are united with Christ's human nature; rather, in being united to Christ's humanity, it is life springing forth from the Godhead itself that is being communicated

---

53. McCormack, "Union with Christ," 516.
54. Calvin, *Institutes* 4.17.8.
55. Calvin, *Institutes* 4.17.9.

to us. McCormack rules these passages out of bounds, as he judges them inconsistent with Calvin's own Christology.[56]

One indeed may question whether the Chalcedonian formula allows for this kind of conceptualization; however, Calvin's remarks here are exactly what one should expect given his supralapsarian eschatological narrative.[57] As I noted above, Calvin states in his letters concerning Stancaro that the non-incarnate divine Word was to be the midpoint between God and creatures "so that the life which was otherwise hidden in God would flow from him." This gift is not contingent upon an incarnation on the part of the divine Word; it is a gift coming forth directly from the Word's divine riches. Of course, when human beings sin and fall, and the Word therefore has to take on a human nature so as to chase after falling humanity and reverse its downward course, the Word's human nature then becomes the conduit through which the Word communicates his gifts. But the nature of the gift does not differ from the gift God intended prior to the need for incarnation: It is "life springing forth from the Godhead into [Christ's flesh] itself . . . for all who aspire to heavenly life." In this respect, Calvin's use of the image of a fountain or channel is quite illuminating. In an infralapsarian context, believers are united to Christ's human nature, but this nature serves only as a channel through which the real gift, coming from elsewhere, is being communicated. Calvin uses the same image in his commentary on John 6:51:

> As this secret power to bestow life, of which [Christ] has spoken, might be referred to his divine essence, he now comes down to the second step, and shows that this life is placed in his flesh. . . . But an objection is brought, that the flesh of Christ cannot give life, because it was liable to death, and because even now it is not immortal in itself. . . . I reply, though this power comes from another source than the flesh, still there is no reason why the designation may not accurately apply to it; for as the eternal Word of God is the fountain of life, so his flesh, as a channel, conveys to us that which dwells intrinsically, as we say, in his divinity. And in this sense it is called life-giving, because it conveys to us that life which it borrows for us from another quarter.[58]

In fact, this is a pattern discernable throughout Calvin's description of the benefits offered by the incarnate One: Believers are participating in Christ's

---

56. McCormack, "Union with Christ," 511, 516.

57. This would then be the second moment in which Calvin's eschatological narrative pushes beyond the boundaries of the ontology codified in the ecumenical creeds (see also note 48, above). Again, this could count as an argument against my line of interpretation—or it might invite us to rethink the ontological shape of Calvin's Christology.

58. John Calvin, *Commentary on the Gospel According to John*, trans. William Pringle, 2 vols. (Baker, 2005), 1:262.

human nature, but by way of this human nature gifts are bestowed upon them that have their source in his divinity. We see the same in other comments on John 6,[59] in Calvin's teaching about Christ's work in atonement and resurrection,[60] in his formulation of the glorious exchange,[61] and even in his polemics against Osiander's doctrine of justification.[62]

A question that remains open is the exact nature of the gifts given to the believer. Calvin speaks of life springing forth from the Godhead itself. But is this life created or uncreated? For the debate on divinization, the answer to this question is quite important. Sometimes it sounds like Calvin means the former. In the only place with direct comment on the notion of divinization, in his commentary on 2 Peter 1:4 ("so that . . . [we] . . . may become participants of the divine nature"), Calvin says, "The word nature is not here essence but quality. . . . The holy Apostles only intended to say that when divested of all

---

59. Commenting on John 6:57, Calvin writes,
Hitherto Christ has explained the manner in which we must become partakers of life. He now comes to speak of the principle cause, for the first source of life is in the Father. . . . For though the Father is the beginning of life, yet the eternal Word himself is strictly life. . . . He points out here three degrees of life. In the first rank is the living Father, who is the source, but remote and hidden. Next follows the Son, who is exhibited to us as an open fountain, and by whom life flows to us. The third is, the life which we draw from him. We now perceive what is stated to amount to this, that God the Father, in whom life dwells, is at a great distance from us, and that Christ, placed between us, is the second cause of life, in order that what would otherwise be concealed in God may proceed from him to us." (Calvin, *John*, 1:269)

60. Calvin, *Institutes* 2.12.2:
It was imperative that he who was to become our Redeemer be true God and true man. It was his task to swallow up death. Who but the Life could do this? It was his task to conquer sin. Who but very Righteousness could do this? It was his task to rout the powers of world and air. Who but a power higher than world and air could do this? Now where does life or righteousness, or lordship and authority of heaven lie but with God alone? Therefore our most merciful God, when he willed that we be redeemed, made himself our Redeemer in the person of his only-begotten Son.

61. Calvin, *Institutes* 4.17.3:
This is the wonderful exchange . . . ; that, becoming Son of man with us, he has made us sons of God with him; that, by his descent to earth, he has prepared an ascent to heaven for us; that, by taking on our mortality, he has conferred his immortality upon us; that, accepting our weaknesses, he has strengthened us by his power; that, receiving our poverty unto himself, he has transferred his wealth to us; that, taking the weight of our iniquity upon himself . . . , he has clothed us with his righteousness.

62. Having strongly polemicized against Osiander's notion that Christ is made our righteousness with respect to his divine rather than his human nature, Calvin nonetheless adds, "I usually say that Christ is, as it were, a fountain, open to us, from which we may draw what otherwise would lie unprofitably hidden in that deep and secret spring, which comes forth to us in the person of the Mediator. In this way and sense, I do not deny . . . that [the] righteousness of which Christ makes us partakers with himself is the eternal righteousness of the eternal God." Calvin, *Institutes* 3.11.9.

the vices of the flesh, we shall be partakers of divine and blessed immortality and glory, so as to be as it were one with God as far as our capacities will allow." Calvin describes this as only a form of deification.[63] Here it sounds as if God will change our makeup such that we can commune more naturally with the divine. Instead of our lives being mortal and temporal, they will become immortal and eternal. But this change does not have to lift us beyond the essential capacities of created existence. Being mortal or immortal, temporal or eternal can be described in philosophical terms as accidental properties of created human nature. God can give a human being one or the other characteristic. The eschatological life gifted by the divine Word can thus be understood as still created, not uncreated, life. However, at other places Calvin seems to go beyond this. He speaks of the eschatological goal of humanity not just as receiving life but as "union with God," "participation in the Father," and "union with God the Father."[64] To be united with God, and to *participate in* God, is more than to receive the capacity to simply *be with* God. The former requires that humanity be beefed up beyond the essential baseline of its creaturely existence, while the latter does not.

In the end, Calvin may not give us language exact enough to further unpack his understanding of the eschatological life mediated by the divine Word.

---

63. God "should make himself ours, so that all things should in a manner become our things. . . . Let us then mark, that the end of the gospel is, to render us eventually comfortable to God, and, if we may so speak, to deify us." John Calvin, *Commentaries on the Catholic Epistles*, trans. and ed. John Owen (Baker, 2005), 371.

64. "Just as man was made for meditation upon the heavenly life, so it is certain that the knowledge of it was engraved upon the soul. And if human happiness, whose perfection it is to be united with God, were hidden from man, he would in fact be bereft of the principal use of his understanding." Calvin, *Institutes* 1.15.6. Christ "took upon himself the person and the office of the Mediator, that he might join us to God." Calvin, *Institutes* 1.13.24. "Endowed with heavenly glory he gathers believers into participation in the Father." Calvin, *Institutes* 1.13.26. "Thus, while for the short time we wander away from God, Christ stands in our midst, to lead us little by little to a firm union with God." Calvin, *Institutes* 2.15.5.

And compare Calvin's comments on John 14:28, in which all the themes of the last two sections of this chapter come together:

> As it has not been granted to us to reach the height of God, Christ descended to us, that he might raise us to it. "You ought to have rejoiced," he says, "because I return to the Father"; for this is the ultimate object at which you ought to aim. By these words he does not show in what respect he differs in himself from the Father, but why he descended to us; and that was, that he might unite us to God; for until we have reached that point, we are, as it were, in the middle of the course. . . . There is a similar passage in the writings of Paul, where he says that Christ "will deliver up the kingdom to God his Father, that God may be all in all." . . . It is, because the divinity which is now behold in Christ's face alone, will then be openly visible in him. . . . Let us therefore learn to behold Christ humbled in the flesh, so that he may conduct us to the fountain of a blessed immortality; for he was not appointed to be our guide, merely to raise us to the sphere of the moon or of the sun, but to make us one with God the Father. (Calvin, *John*, 2:102–3)

What can be shown, though, is that the passages that the debate on deification has drawn attention to are not aberrations in Calvin's overall theological framework. They cohere with a larger eschatological narrative according to which human beings were always destined for an upward journey, a journey made possible by the life communicated to us by the divine Word.

Conclusion

Calvin is usually mined for his take on singular theological questions—such as those having to do with the church, or union with Christ, or predestination. But underneath his arguments regarding this or that theological topic lies a coherent account of the overall narrative of the relationship between God and humanity. In this chapter, I have argued that a central and governing part of that narrative is its supralapsarian eschatological intent. Human beings were created for an eschatological future in the presence of and in union with God. Their creation was only a first step toward that eschatological goal. They were to lead a life in meditation upon their heavenly future, a life shaped as an upward journey toward God. Since they would not be able to reach their destination by their own devices, the divine Word would be their mediator, accompanying them on their journey. But rather than reaching upward, human beings fell downward. Therefore, the divine Word was to chase after them, take on a human nature, catch humans in their fall, and set them back on the road toward their eschatological goal.

On theological analysis, this story can be divided into two parts. There is the infralapsarian narrative of the incarnate mediator, a narrative that consumes the bulk of the biblical materials and also of Calvin's own theological work. But this infralapsarian narrative can be read as embedded in a supralapsarian story, one that began before the need of incarnate mediation and that will continue even when the need for incarnate mediation has long subsided. This supralapsarian story receives significantly less airtime in the biblical material and in Calvin's writings. But if my argument is correct, it is consistently present in the background of Calvin's thinking.

Having unearthed this narrative substructure, one might wonder how Calvin's telling of the story sits within the wider theological tradition. We could raise questions about the genealogy of Calvin's understanding of the supralapsarian mediation of the divine Word, but maybe even more interesting is the issue of whether, and if so how, Calvin's understanding of the biblical narrative has influenced subsequent developments in Reformed theology. For example, Calvin's late contemporary Jerome Zanchi (1516–90) still taught that the Word was a mediator in God's relating to us not only in reconciliation but also in creation and preservation. But lost in Zanchi is Calvin's understanding of the eschatological dimension of the Word's mediation.[65] In the work of the great surveyor of Reformed scholasticism Francis Turretin (1623–87), any notion of a supralapsarian mediatory role of the divine Word disappears. For Turretin, the need for mediation is purely infralapsarian.[66] However, is it nonetheless possible to recognize in the narrative structures of Reformed federal theology—of which Turretin is a representative—Calvin's notion of a supralapsarian eschatology. Federal theology develops the notion of a twofold covenant: an original, pre-fall, covenant of works, in which human beings were promised a glorious eschatological future in exchange for their obedience, and a later covenant of grace, which offers a way out of humanity's post-fall misery. If this could be read as residue of Calvin's twofold eschatological narrative, it would offer an account of humanity's supralapsarian eschatological journey without a mediator. We were thought to be empowered to reach our destiny on our own.

Constructively speaking, this historical exploration introduces the idea that, in addition to supralapsarian Christology, one might entertain supralapsarian accounts of other key parts of the Christian story; and it raises the question of how these various supralapsarian accounts hang together with a supralapsarian Christology. In the second part of this book, I will engage this question, exploring several examples of such supralapsarian accounts.

---

65. See Stefan Lindholm, "Would Christ Have Become Incarnate Had Adam Not Fallen? Jerome Zanchi on Christ the Mediator," *Journal of Reformed Theology* 9, no. 1 (2015): 19–36. Lindholm is incorrect, though, in equating Zanchi's understanding with Calvin's (33). He misses the eschatological dimension of Calvin's account.

66. Francis Turretin, *Institutes of Elenctic Theology*, trans. George Musgrave Giger, ed. James T. Dennison, vol. 2 (P&R, 1992), 14.1.4.

4

"His Death Manifested Its Power and Efficacy in Us"

The Role of Christ's Resurrection in John Calvin's Theology

In the previous chapter, I offered a novel interpretation of Calvin's eschatological imagination and the ways it shapes his overall theological narrative. In addition to his explicit infralapsarian eschatology, which circles around the reconciling work of the incarnate Christ, Calvin also has an implicit supralapsarian eschatology, according to which human beings were created for an upward journey toward God, mediated by the non-incarnate divine Word. In this chapter, I will further explore this interpretation by zooming in on one aspect of Calvin's explicit infralapsarian eschatology: Christ's resurrection. What kind of work does Christ's resurrection do in John Calvin's theology? How does it shape the ways in which Calvin tells the story of God and creation? And, in particular, how does Christ's resurrection shape Calvin's eschatological imagination?[1]

---

1. As far as I am aware, no studies have been devoted to these questions. Some attention is given to Christ's resurrection in books devoted to wider Christological issues in Calvin, but these studies do not probe in any depth the work Christ's resurrection does in his larger theological narrative. See E. Emmen, *De Christologie van Calvijn* (H. J. Paris, 1935), 105–7; Paul van Buren, *Christ in Our Place: The Substitutionary Character of Calvin's Doctrine of Reconciliation* (Oliver and Boyd, 1957), 81–89; and Stephen Edmondson, *Calvin's Christology* (Cambridge University Press, 2004), 133–36.

Focusing in on these questions will strengthen the value of my hermeneutic of this part of Calvin's thought. But it will also help focus attention on an intrinsic aspect of the particular supralapsarian Christological proposal advanced in this book. In chapter 2, I outlined three arguments for a supralapsarian Christology. Each of these takes its starting point in a particular aspect of the biblical narrative and traces the hermeneutical pressure exerted by the narrative on our systematic accounts of the incarnation. In each case, the launching point for the argument is an eschatological part of the Scripture's narrative: the eschaton's superabundance, the eschatological seeing of God, and divine friendship—a continued thread of the story and the anticipation of eschatological life. In each case, embodiment is central to the story. For the first argument, it is particularly the embodiment of Christ's own resurrection and ascension life that gives rise to a supralapsarian read of the incarnation. In short, Christ's embodied resurrected existence both shapes the nature of the eschaton and gives us a richness in divine intimacy and friendship that cannot be explained as a countermeasure against human sin.

Calvin, as I have argued in the previous chapter, has a rich eschatological imagination. The way he tells the story of God and humanity is driven by eschatological intentions and goals. Nonetheless, Calvin shows no sign of being susceptive to the pressures of the narrative that give rise to my supralapsarian Christological argument. His is a supralapsarian eschatology but an infralapsarian Christology. In this chapter, I further explore why this is the case. Calvin's Christology—not his account of the work of the divine Word but his understanding of the Word's enfleshment—has little space for the theological importance of the resurrection in the first place. In fact, Calvin pays scant attention to Christ's resurrection. In his *Institutes*, the only place where Calvin pauses to consider explicitly the meaning of Christ's resurrection is in his commentary on the Apostles' Creed. In the final version of the *Institutes*, this discussion takes barely three pages, which is telling in itself.[2] As I will argue in this chapter, even while Calvin affirms the reality of the resurrection of the flesh—both Christ's and ours—on analysis, Christ's resurrection does only very limited work in Calvin's theological imagination. Christ's resurrection is only revelatory and applicatory of a transformative event that previously occurred. As Calvin says in his discussion in the *Institutes*, the full measure of salvation is obtained in Christ's death, not in his resurrection. Christ's resurrection makes us aware of this salvific reality and allows us to be drawn into it, but it does not inaugurate a salvific transformation itself. Moreover,

---

2. John Calvin, *Institutes of the Christian Religion*, ed. John T. McNeill, trans. Ford Lewis Battles, 2 vols. (Westminster, 1960), 2.16.13.

while Calvin holds that Christ's resurrection is a guarantee and model for our resurrection, embodiment plays no role in his eschatological vision. We are finally drawn into union with God, but Calvin gives us no reason to believe we need resurrection in order to participate in this reality. A simple continued spiritual existence would do.

By offering what amounts to the opposite of my theological reading of Christ's resurrection, Calvin's example illustrates the underlying issue: the strong ties between a focus on the eschatological difference Christ makes and a supralapsarian understanding of the incarnation's intentions. Embracing the former puts pressure on the theologian to embrace the latter. And vice versa: The only way to escape the latter is to deny the former.

To demonstrate my interpretation of Calvin's position, I take four steps. First, I analyze Calvin's commentary on the creedal confession: "On the third day he rose again from the dead." I compare what I find in the *Institutes* with what Calvin says in his Romans commentary concerning two key passages from Paul's letter, discussions Calvin explicitly references in the *Institutes*. Second, I explore Calvin's notion of an eschatological resurrection guaranteed by and modeled on Christ's rising from the dead. I focus on a worry expressed in the secondary literature: While Calvin affirms the physical nature of the resurrection, his vision of the eschatological life tends to be spiritual and disembodied. I believe this concern is demonstrably warranted. Third, I place my findings from the first two steps in the context of Calvin's larger eschatological vision, as developed in chapter 3. I believe that, however we may want to evaluate constructively the results of the analysis in the first two steps, they actually fit quite consistently within the larger eschatological narrative about God and humanity that is operative in Calvin's theology. Any evaluative concerns that may arise about Calvin's engagement of the theological meaning of Christ's resurrection will therefore have to result in questions about his wider vision. Fourth and finally, I raise some of these concerns and return to the debate between supralapsarian and infralapsarian interpretations of the incarnation.

The Difference Christ's Resurrection Makes

Reading through John Calvin's discussion of the Apostles' Creed in his *Institutes*, one may be struck by the lackluster beginning of what amounts to fewer than three pages of discussion: "Next comes the resurrection from the dead."[3] Calvin's prose does not get more enthused when he continues:

3. Calvin, *Institutes* 2.16.13.

"Without this what we have said so far would be incomplete. For since only weakness appears in the cross, death, and burial of Christ, faith must leap over all these things to attain its full strength." Calvin's formulation seems to suggest resurrection is needed only to counter the *appearance* of weakness in the events that preceded it, not for any intrinsic reason. That this is not just a matter of rhetoric becomes clear as Calvin continues: "We have in his death the complete fulfillment of salvation, for through it we are reconciled to God, his righteous judgment is satisfied, the curse is removed, and the penalty paid full."[4] If salvation was already completely obtained in Jesus's death, why then did he still need to rise? Why could the Son, having completed the salvific work he had come to undertake, not take this moment to leave a human nature that was subject to suffering and death and return to his celestial glory? Because, says Calvin, "we are said to 'have been born anew to a living hope' not through his death but 'through his resurrection' (1 Pet. 1:3). For as he, in rising again, came forth victor over death, so the victory of our faith over death lies in his resurrection alone." To further unpack what he means, Calvin reaches for Paul's words: "[Jesus] was handed over to death for our trespasses and was raised for our justification" (Rom. 4:25). Based on this saying, Calvin says, "we divide the substance of our salvation between Christ's death and resurrection as follows: through his death, sin was wiped out and death extinguished; through his resurrection, righteousness was restored and life raised up, so that—thanks to his resurrection—his death manifested its power and efficacy in us."[5] These last words are key for Calvin's understanding of the difference Christ's resurrection makes. For him, the resurrection is not, as is the case with some theologians today, "the proleptic disclosure of the end of history," "a beginning of the fulfillment of the promised life," or "the symbol and starting point of the new world."[6] Rather, Christ's resurrection is "the closing scene" of what went before—the story of the cross.[7] Christ's resurrection does not make a difference in and of itself. That difference, the radical break, the transformative moment, is

---

4. Calvin, *Institutes* 2.16.13.
5. Calvin, *Institutes* 2.16.13.
6. Respectively: Wolfhart Pannenberg, *Jesus—God and Man* (Westminster, 1968), 53–66; Jürgen Moltmann, *Theology of Hope* (Fortress, 1993), 211; and N. T. Wright, *Surprised by Hope: Rethinking Heaven, the Resurrection, and the Mission of the Church* (HarperCollins, 2008), 67.
7. As Calvin says in the opening lines to his commentary on the synoptics' narration of Christ's resurrection, "We now come to the closing scene of our redemption. For the lively assurance of our reconciliation with God arises from Christ having come from hell as the conqueror of death, in order to show that he had the power of a new life at his disposal." John Calvin, *Commentary on a Harmony of the Evangelists*, ed. William Pringle, 3 vols. (Baker, 2005), 3:338.

found in Christ's death.[8] Christ's resurrection offers us the *revelation* and *application* of what is obtained in Christ's death.[9] Without Christ's resurrection, salvation would still have been complete. Sin would still have been wiped out, and death, which Calvin interprets as punishment for sin, would thereby have been extinguished. But if the grave had not broken open on Easter morning, we would not have *known* that sin and its consequence had been overcome. We would only have known the appearance of weakness in which Christ's victory was clothed. And so our faith would not be able to jump over it and be victorious in the face of death itself. Christ's resurrection allows us to have this kind of faith.

Calvin continues by listing briefly two more benefits of Christ's resurrection. Referring to Paul's words that, just as we were grafted into the likeness of Christ's death, we may walk in newness of life as participants in Christ's resurrection (Rom. 6:4) and his injunction that, as people who have been raised with Christ, we ought to set our minds on things that are above (Col. 3:1–2), Calvin holds that Christ's resurrection means "we are reborn into righteousness through his power."[10] Christ's resurrection and ascension lay bare a way of sanctification. And finally, a third benefit is "that we are assured of our own resurrection by receiving a sort of guarantee substantiated by his."[11] This last point demands some further reflection. After all, if Christ's resurrection were only revelatory and applicatory, as Calvin suggests, then it would not be needed for the eschatological unfolding of his own life. It would be needed only for the salvation of our lives. But where does this leave us with regard to the role of our own resurrection? I will return to this question below.

The main takeaway of Calvin's discussion—that Christ's resurrection obtains no benefits not already acquired in Christ's death but, instead, reveals and applies benefits previously obtained—is confirmed by the exegesis,

---

8. Commenting on Acts 3:21, Calvin writes, "Christ has already restored all things by his death; but the effect does not yet fully appear . . . [For] the kingdom of Christ is only begun." John Calvin, *Commentary upon the Acts of the Apostles*, ed. Henry Beveridge, 2 vols. (Baker, 2005), 1:153.

9. Here I have to correct what I said in "Gospeling: Paul, Protestant Theologians, and Pittsburgh Theological Seminary." In that address, I posited that, for Calvin, Christ's resurrection is only declarative. That is too narrow an interpretation. Not only does Christ's resurrection reveal the salvation previously obtained, but it also applies this salvation to believers, setting them on a road of sanctification. Edwin Chr. van Driel, "Gospeling: Paul, Protestant Theologians, and Pittsburgh Theological Seminary," address at the installation of the Directors' Bicentennial Chair in Theology (Pittsburg Theological Seminary, May 12, 2014), 12.

10. Calvin, *Institutes* 2.16.13.

11. Calvin, *Institutes* 2.16.13.

referenced in the *Institutes*,[12] that Calvin offers of two passages from Paul's Letter to the Romans.

In the opening verses of his letter, Paul summarizes what he considers to be "the gospel," and in this summary Christ's resurrection has a prominent place: It is "the gospel concerning his Son, who was descended from David according to the flesh and was declared to be Son of God with power according to the spirit of holiness by resurrection from the dead, Jesus Christ our Lord" (Rom. 1:3–4). In his comments on this verse, Calvin zooms in on the word *declared* and reads Paul as saying that the role the resurrection played was to give witness to Christ's divinity: "The power, by which he was raised from the dead, was something like a decree, by which he was proclaimed the Son of God. . . . Christ was declared the Son of God by openly exercising a real celestial power. . . . Power, peculiar to God, shone forth in him, and uncontestably proved him to be God."[13] In other words, the meaning of Christ's resurrection is, again, epistemic; it reveals something—namely, that the one resurrecting is truly divine.[14]

Finally, the same interpretive strategy that we found in the *Institutes* emerges in Calvin's reading of Romans 4:25 ("[Jesus our Lord] was handed over for our trespasses and was raised for our justification"). Here too, Calvin invests the accomplishment of our salvation in Christ's death on the cross, while the revelation and application of salvation to us are included as functions of Christ's resurrection. That Paul seems to attribute salvation to both cross and resurrection is only an accommodation to our ignorance, says Calvin. "For it is also true that righteousness has been obtained for us by that obedience of Christ, which he exhibited in his death. . . . But as Christ, *by rising from the dead, made known how much he had effected by his death*, this distinction is calculated to teach us that our salvation was begun by the sacrifice . . . and was at length completed by his resurrection: for the beginning of righteousness is to be reconciled to God, and its completion is to attain life by having death abolished."[15] That's the revelation. Continuing, Calvin says, "As it would not have been enough for Christ to undergo the wrath and judgment of God, and to endure the curse due to our sins, without his coming forth a conqueror, and without being received into celestial glory, that by

12. See Calvin, *Institutes* 2.16.13.
13. John Calvin, *Commentaries on the Epistle of Paul the Apostle to the Romans*, trans. and ed. John Owen (Baker, 2005), 45–46.
14. In "Gospeling," I contrasted Calvin's approach to this verse with the far different reading by N. T. Wright, drawing out the theological implications of both readings. For Wright, Paul's summary of the gospel is not about revealing Christ's divinity but about the vindication of Christ and his proclamation of the inbreaking of God's reign (Van Driel, "Gospeling," 9–13).
15. Calvin, *Romans*, 185 (emphasis added).

his intercession he might reconcile God to us, the efficacy of justification is ascribed to his resurrection."[16] That's the application.

Christ's Resurrection and Ours

As previously noted, Calvin holds that Christ's resurrection guarantees our own. In the twenty-fifth chapter of the third book of the *Institutes*, "The Final Resurrection," Calvin underscores this point. He starts out by acknowledging that "it may be difficult to believe that bodies, when consumed with rottenness, will at length be raised up in their season."[17] Thus the notion of bodily resurrection is significantly less popular than that of the immortality of the soul. But Christ's resurrection is the pledge that "the resurrection hoped for is that of the body."[18] It is like a mirror in which we see our own rising, Calvin argues.[19] In fact, "Christ rose again that he might have us as companions in the life to come."[20] His resurrection was not just for his own sake, but "rather there was begun in the Head what must be completed in all the members, according to the rank and station of each."[21]

Calvin's emphasis on the reality and impact of a bodily resurrection notwithstanding, scholars have raised questions about the function of this notion in Calvin's eschatological imagination. For instance, Beth Felker Jones argues that Calvin's descriptions of the eschaton remain ultimately ambiguous on its embodied nature. She ascribes this to a tension between the Christian tradition Calvin inherited—which understands the body as a created good— and a deep personal antipathy toward the body that consistently rises to the surface of his thought.[22] In her analysis, Jones harkens back to the older study of Heinrich Quistorp, who also raises questions about the consistency of Calvin's thought regarding resurrection and eschatology. In Quistorp's analysis, there is in Calvin

> a tension between his loyalty to the Biblical message of the return of Christ and of the kingdom of God as a visible all-embracing reality, and on the other hand his humanistic tendency to confine and spiritualize. . . . He thinks of the future life preeminently as a heavenly and spiritual life which definitely begins

---

16. Calvin, *Romans*, 185.
17. Calvin, *Institutes* 3.25.3.
18. Calvin, *Institutes* 3.25.3.
19. Calvin, *Institutes* 3.25.3.
20. Calvin, *Institutes* 3.25.3.
21. Calvin, *Institutes* 3.25.3.
22. Beth Felker Jones, *Marks of His Wounds: Gender Politics and Bodily Resurrection* (Oxford University Press, 2007), 49–68.

at death with the liberation of the immortal soul, and which is completed in the immediate vision of God without the mediation of the humanity of Christ. For this reason the new creation, in so far as it is a new earth and the new Jerusalem, the fulfilled communion of saints in the new world, is only occasionally referred to by Calvin.[23]

It strikes me that Quistorp and Jones rightly point out the ambiguous nature of Calvin's thinking about the embodied nature of the eschaton. In fact, I would like to draw out a further consequence of their critique. If Christ's resurrection is the guarantee of our resurrection, and Calvin's thinking about the embodied nature of our eschatological resurrection life is ambiguous, then we should wonder about the importance Calvin attaches not only to the embodied nature of our resurrection but to that of Christ himself.

I would like to lift up four moments from Calvin's larger theological narrative that support Quistorp's and Jones's concerns. First, throughout book 1 and the first chapters of book 2 of the *Institutes* Calvin describes human beings as essentially eschatologically oriented. They are created with a *sensus divinitatis*, a sense that, occasioned by "the whole workmanship of the universe," gives them an awareness of God.[24] This sense also triggers in us an eschatological awareness and longing: "Knowledge of this sort, then, ought not only to arouse us to the worship of God but also to awaken and encourage us to the hope of the future life."[25] The *sensus divinitatis* makes us see that we are eschatological creatures, made for a journey toward another existence. This journey is characterized by the cultivation of righteousness,[26] the

---

23. Heinrich Quistorp, *Calvin's Doctrine of the Last Things* (John Knox, 1955), 192–93.

24. "There is within the human mind, and indeed by natural instinct, an awareness of divinity." Calvin, *Institutes* 1.3.1. "The final goal of the blessed life, moreover, rests in the knowledge of God. Lest anyone then, be excluded from access to happiness, he not only sowed in men's minds that seed of religion of which we have spoken but revealed himself and daily discloses himself in the whole workmanship of the universe. As a consequence, men cannot open their eyes without being compelled to see him." Calvin, *Institutes* 1.5.1.

25. Calvin, *Institutes* 1.5.10. See also the last quotation in the previous note. Calvin also writes that a human being "should consider for what purpose he was created and endowed with no mean gifts. By this knowledge he should arouse himself to meditation upon divine worship and the future life." Calvin, *Institutes* 2.6.1.

26. Human beings "understand themselves to have been born to cultivate righteousness, in which the seed of religion is enclosed. But, without controversy, just as man was made for the meditation upon the heavenly life, so it is certain that the knowledge of it was engraved upon his soul. And if human happiness, whose perfection it is to be united with God, were hidden from man, he would in fact be bereft of the principal use of his understanding." Calvin, *Institutes* 1.15.6. See also Calvin, *Institutes* 2.1.3: "Yet God would not have us forget our original immortality, which he had bestowed upon our father Adam, and which ought truly to arouse in us a zeal for righteousness and goodness. For we cannot think upon either our first condition

development of piety,[27] and a life of worship.[28] Each of these has us "meditate upon immortality, and to yearn after the Kingdom of God."[29] However, in these chapters of the *Institutes* Calvin's description of this eschatological reign is ambiguous as to whether it is an earthly, embodied existence or, rather, a heavenly, spiritual life. What Calvin in some places calls the "meditation upon . . . the future life"[30] in other places he refers to as the "meditation upon the heavenly life."[31]

Second, the same ambiguity is present in the chapter famously devoted to the *meditatio vitae futurae* (meditation on the future life), a chapter Calvin situates within the context of a description of the Christian life.[32] Right in the chapter's opening sentences, Calvin interchanges "future" life and "heavenly" life: "Whatever kind of tribulation presses upon us, we must ever look to this: to accustom ourselves to contempt for the present life and to be aroused thereby to meditate upon the future life. . . . There is not one of us, indeed, who does not wish throughout his life to aspire and strive after heavenly immortality."[33] Calvin then unpacks the opposition between present and future in terms of an opposition between earthly, embodied existence and heavenly, eternal life. Close to the end of his chapter, Calvin writes in a way that could not have painted a clearer picture of the scope of his eschatological imagination:

> Let the aim of believers in judging mortal life, then, be that while they understand it to be of itself nothing but misery, they may with greater eagerness and dispatch betake themselves wholly to meditate upon that eternal life to come. . . . For, if heaven is our homeland, what else is the earth but our place of exile? If departure from the world is entry into life, what else is the world but a sepulcher? And what else is it for us to remain in life but to be immersed in death? If to be freed from the body is to be released into perfect freedom, what is the body but a prison? If to enjoy the presence of God is the summit of happiness, is not to be without this, misery?[34]

---

or to what purpose we were formed without being prompted to meditate upon immortality, and to yearn after the Kingdom of God."

27. "The natural order was that the frame of the universe should be the school in which we were to learn piety, and from it to pass over to eternal life and perfect felicity." Calvin, *Institutes* 2.6.1.

28. A human being "should consider for what purpose he was created and endowed with no mean gifts. By this knowledge he should arouse himself to meditation upon divine worship and the future life." Calvin, *Institutes* 2.1.3.

29. Calvin, *Institutes* 2.1.3.
30. Calvin, *Institutes* 2.1.3.
31. Calvin, *Institutes* 1.15.6.
32. Calvin, *Institutes* 3.9.
33. Calvin, *Institutes* 3.9.1.
34. Calvin, *Institutes* 3.9.4.

Interestingly, in the same chapter Calvin denotes the future life that he encourages his readers to meditate upon as "the final day of resurrection."[35] No one "has made progress in the school of Christ who does not joyfully await the day of death and final resurrection."[36] But while he says this, the embodied, earthly nature of a resurrection that is modeled after Christ's resurrection does not seem to determine in any way the shape of this future life.

Third, in between Calvin's thoughts on the *meditatio vitae futurae* in creation and recreation stands his treatment of the biblical narrative of salvation. One might wonder how Calvin's thoughts about the heavenly nature of our eschatological existence square in particular with the promises to the patriarchs, reiterated by the prophets, who seem to imagine much more earthly blessings for God's people. Calvin's treatment of this material is, however, quite in line with the way he has framed his eschatological expectations elsewhere. He acknowledges at the outset that the promises of the Old Testament may seem draped in "carnal prosperity and happiness,"[37] but he believes that to take them as such would be a misreading of the actual intent of these promises. After all, according to Paul, the promises of the Old Testament were promises of the gospel, and "surely the gospel does not confine men's hearts to delight in the present life, but lifts them up to the hope of immortality. It does not fasten them to earthly pleasures, but by announcing a hope that rests in heaven it, so to speak, transports them thither."[38] Therefore the Old Testament should be read as "particularly concerned with the future life."[39] To make his case, Calvin then gives a cursory reading of the Old Testament narrative, touching on Adam, Abraham and the patriarchs, David, Job, and the prophets, aiming to show that in all these stories "the believers were so taught by the Lord as to perceive that they had a better life elsewhere; and, disregarding the earthly life, to meditate upon the heavenly."[40]

These three moments from Calvin's larger theological narrative all concern his imaginary regarding the eschatological future of all humanity. All three cast doubt on the embodied, earthly nature of that future. The last moment I want to lift up concerns Christ's own eschatological life. In the current age, Christ's resurrection reveals and applies to us the completion of salvation. His human nature functions, therefore, as a means of mediation. But this mediatory role of Christ's humanity will come to an end, argues Calvin. Right

---

35. Calvin, *Institutes* 3.9.5.
36. Calvin, *Institutes* 3.9.5.
37. Calvin, *Institutes* 2.10.2.
38. Calvin, *Institutes* 2.10.3.
39. Calvin, *Institutes* 2.10.3.
40. Calvin, *Institutes* 2.10.10.

now God is ruling creation through Christ "inasmuch he was manifested in the flesh."[41] Yet, once creation's history has run its course, Calvin says, commenting on 1 Corinthians 15:28, "Christ will transfer [the kingdom] in a manner from his humanity to his glorious divinity."[42] At that point "Christ's humanity will . . . no longer be interposed to keep us back from a closer view of God." Rather, "God, holding the government of the heaven and the earth by himself, and without any medium, will in that respect be all. . . . All things will be brought back to God, as their alone beginning and end, that they may be closely bound to him."[43]

In the *Institutes*, Calvin makes similar statements:

> For what purpose were power and lordship given to Christ, unless that by his hand the Father might govern us? In this sense, also, Christ is said to be seated at the right hand of the Father. Yet this is but for a time, until we enjoy the direct vision of the Godhead. . . . Until he comes forth as judge of the world Christ will therefore reign, joining us to the Father as the measure of our weakness permits. But when as partakers in heavenly glory we shall see God as he is, Christ, having then discharged the Office of Mediator, will cease to be the ambassador of this Father, and will be satisfied with that glory which he enjoyed before the creation of the world. . . . That is, to him was lordship committed by the Father, until such time as we should see his divine majesty face to face.[44]

As I recorded in the previous chapter, commentators have debated whether Calvin means that the divine Word will actually lay down his human nature in the eschaton.[45] I do not believe the texts offer enough evidence to decide. It is however clear that, for Calvin, the Word's human nature will not play a role in the eschaton. This has important implications for how we analyze the place of Christ's resurrection in Calvin's theology. First, it aligns with my findings in the previous section. If Christ's humanity has no eschatological role to play, the impact of his resurrection is limited to this side of the eschaton. This is also the upshot of the notion that Christ's resurrection is revelatory and applicatory but not transformative. Second, Calvin's argument raises a question, as Quistorp rightly points out, about the nature of the union between Christ and believers.[46] If this union continues in the eschaton but Christ's

---

41. John Calvin, *Commentary on the Epistles of Paul the Apostle to the Corinthians*, trans. John Pringle, 2 vols. (Baker, 2005), 2:31.
42. Calvin, *Corinthians*, 2:32.
43. Calvin, *Corinthians*, 2:33.
44. Calvin, *Institutes* 2.14.3.
45. See "The End of Mediation" in chap. 3, above (esp. chap. 3, note 47).
46. Quistorp, *Calvin's Doctrine of the Last Things*, 170–71.

humanity plays no mediatory role in the eschaton, then the union cannot be based on Christ's humanity—neither his originally incarnated humanity nor his resurrected humanity.[47]

Christ's Resurrection in Calvin's Eschatological Narrative

Jones and Quistorp believe that the limited theological work that Christ's resurrection does in John Calvin's theology is due to internal tensions between Calvin's theological convictions and heritage, on the one hand, and personal or cultural antipathies toward the body, on the other hand. Such personal and cultural attitudes are hard to prove. I therefore want to offer another line of interpretation, one that shows Calvin's ambiguous interpretation of resurrection and its embodied nature nonetheless consistently fits within his larger Christological and eschatological narrative.

Calvin's telling of the story of God and humans has from the beginning an eschatological bent. As I noted in the previous section, Calvin believes that we are essentially created for an upward journey. Our *sensus divinitatis* makes us aware of our eschatological orientation and triggers in us a longing for heavenly life, the very center of which is communion with God. However, Calvin also makes clear that while human beings are created for this upward journey, they do not have the internal resources to reach their destiny on their own. The ontological gap between God and creation is too large to be bridged by humans on their own accord. They need help. Their state is, as Calvin puts it, "too lowly . . . to reach God without a Mediator."[48] This mediator is the divine Word. He becomes, Calvin says, the *medium*, the midpoint between God and creatures, and he will enable human beings to complete their eschatological journey by letting "life which was otherwise hidden in God flow from him."[49] It is through the work of the divine Word that creatures are enabled to journey beyond their natural status.

---

47. This would be another argument for the reading of Calvin as holding that believers participate not just in the human but also in the divine nature of Christ. See "Communicating Divine Life" in chap. 3, above, 65–71.

T. F. Torrance convincingly argues that, for Calvin, eschatology is an unfolding of union with Christ. See T. F. Torrance, *Kingdom and Church: A Study in the Theology of the Reformation* (Oliver and Boyd, 1956), 90–137. Torrance repeatedly describes this union as "union with Christ in his death and resurrection" (Torrance, *Kingdom and Church*, 94, 100, 112–13). But he nowhere pauses to consider what the end of the mediation of Christ's humanity means for the union or, subsequently, for the shape of the eschaton.

48. Calvin, *Institutes* 2.12.1.

49. This is how Calvin puts it in a letter opposing Francesco Stancaro, quoted in Joseph Tylenda, "Christ the Mediator: Calvin versus Stancaro," *Calvin Theological Journal* 8 (1973): 13. In

However, humans do not follow their intended upward trajectory. Instead, they sin and thereby journey downward, "plunged into death and hell."[50] In order to fulfil his mediatory mission, the divine Word therefore needs to follow them in their downward journey—to chase after them, catch them in their fall, turn them around, and guide them on the ascent again. This is what necessitates the Word's incarnate existence. The Word was always to be a mediator, enabling humans' eschatological journey toward God. Subsequent to the fall, this mediation must take the form of incarnation, so as to reach humans as they move in the direction opposite to the one they were intended to move in.

Human beings' status already was too lowly for them to reach God on their own accord. Because of their downward fall, they have created an extra barrier: "God's righteous curse bars our access to him." The core of Christ's mediatory work in his incarnate existence is therefore to take away this hindrance, for "an expiation must intervene for us and appease [God's] wrath."[51] While Calvin underscores that Christ's whole life stands in the service of "banishing the separation between us and God," he stipulates that "to define the way of salvation more exactly, Scripture ascribes this as peculiar and proper to Christ death."[52] For this reason, Calvin can say that in Christ's death our salvation is completed.[53]

Christ's salvific work needs, however, to be applied to us. Thus, the mediatory role of the incarnate One continues after the completion of salvation on the cross. The ascended Christ advocates for the church to the Father and transfuses us with his power.[54] "Thus, while for the short time we wander away from God, Christ stands in our midst, to lead us little by little to a firm unity with God. And surely, to say that he sits at the right hand of the Father is equivalent to calling him the Father's deputy, who has in his possession the whole power of God's dominion. For God mediately, so to speak, wills to rule and protect the church in Christ's person."[55]

Once this work has come to an end—that is, once Christ's role in protecting the church has been accomplished—and the last resistance of sin has been overcome in Christ's return and the final judgment, then there will be no need for a continued mediatory role of the incarnate One in the eschaton. Here

---

addition to the statement quoted above, from *Institutes* 2.12.1, Calvin is most explicit about this in his dispute with Francseo Stancaro about Christ's mediatorship. See "Communicating Divine Life" in chap. 3, above, 65–71.
    50. Calvin, *Institutes* 2.12.4.
    51. Calvin, *Institutes* 2.15.6.
    52. Calvin, *Institutes* 2.16.5.
    53. Calvin, *Institutes* 2.16.13.
    54. Calvin, *Institutes* 2.16.16.
    55. Calvin, *Institutes* 2.15.5.

Calvin's notion of the end of Christ's mediation, as discussed in the previous section, enters the picture. As Christ's humanity will no longer interpose, "the veil being removed, we shall openly behold God reigning in majesty. . . . All things will be brought back to God, as their alone beginning and end, that they may be closely bound to him."[56] In that day, human beings will have come to their own. They receive, as Calvin calls it, union with God, "participation in the Father," or "union with God the Father."[57] They have finally reached the destiny for which they were created, albeit in a roundabout way.

Calvin summarizes the narrative in a remark in his commentary on John:

> As it has not been granted to us to reach the height of God, Christ descended to us, that he might raise us to it. "You ought to have rejoiced," he says, "because I return to the Father"; for this is the ultimate object at which you ought to aim. By these words he does not show in what respect he differs in himself from the Father, but why he descended to us; and that was, that he might unite us to God; for until we have reached that point, we are, as it were, in the middle of the course. . . . There is a similar passage in the writings of Paul, where he says that Christ "will deliver up the kingdom to God his Father, that God may be all in all." . . . It is, because the divinity which is now beheld in Christ's face alone, will then be openly visible in him. . . . Let us therefore learn to behold Christ humbled in the flesh, so that he may conduct us to the fountain of a blessed immortality; for he was not appointed to be our guide, merely to raise us to the sphere of the moon or of the sun, but to make us one with God the Father.[58]

The upshot of this narrative is, as I argued in the previous chapter, that we best analyze Calvin as having two complementary eschatologies. Calvin himself does not describe it thus, but framing it in this way clarifies conceptually how he tells the story. The first eschatology is the narrative of God's original intent for human beings: They were created "to meditate upon heavenly life." Through the mediation of the divine Word, they were set on an upward journey toward the ultimate destination for which they were created—to be "united with God." The second eschatology can be found in the final chapters of the story of the

---

56. Calvin, *Corinthians*, 2:32–33.

57. "Just as man was made for meditation upon the heavenly life, so it is certain that the knowledge of it was engraved upon the soul. And if human happiness, whose perfection it is to be united with God, were hidden from man, he would in fact be bereft of the principal use of his understanding." Calvin, *Institutes* 1.15.6. Christ "took upon himself the person and the office of the Mediator, that he might join us to God." Calvin, *Institutes* 1.13.24. "Endowed with heavenly glory he gathers believers into participation in the Father." Calvin, *Institutes* 1.13.26. "Thus, while for the short time we wander away from God, Christ stands in our midst, to lead us little by little to a firm union with God." Calvin, *Institutes* 2.15.5.

58. John Calvin, *Commentary on the Gospel According to John*, trans. William Pringle, 2 vols. (Baker, 2005), 2:102–3.

divine Word who "descends so that he may raise us," becoming incarnate so as to chase humans in their downward fall, catch them through the salvation obtained on the cross, and guide them on their way back until the day of his return and the final judgment. The first eschatology is supralapsarian: Its motivation precedes logically and ontologically the need for incarnate mediation, and its realization will continue long after the need for incarnate mediation has disappeared. The second eschatology is infralapsarian: It is contingent upon human sin. And while it is true that the second eschatology entails a series of events that feature most prominently in our imagination—Christ's return, the resurrection of the dead, and the last judgment—none of these events are part of the original intent of God for creation, and therefore they do not contain the key to our eschatological future. In fact, it is only *after* these events have been completed that our *true* eschatological destiny—the immediate vision of God—unfolds.

Distinguishing between these two kinds of eschatologies, each with its own particular shape, meaning, and place within the larger narrative, allows us to hold together what Quistorp and Jones consider to be ambiguous or in tension. For Calvin, Christ's death and resurrection, as well as our resurrection, are part of the infralapsarian eschatological story. But this story does not determine the shape of our ultimate eschatological future. Resurrection tells us that sin and the punishment for sin, death, have been overcome. It does not yet entail the fulfillment of our eschatological goal, the upward journey toward God.

Conclusion: Christ's Resurrection, Reconciliation, and Eschatological Consummation

With this analysis of Calvin in mind, let us take a step back. According to the biblical narrative, God relates to that which is not God in three distinct but interrelated ways. God is the one who calls all things into being and the one on whom all things depend for their continued existence—that is, God relates to that which is not God as the Creator. Further, God does not just give creatures existence and a history; God also draws creation to a final eschatological goal—that is, God relates to what is not God as the Consummator. Finally, when creation wanders away, God draws it back to Godself—that is, God relates to that which is not God in reconciliation. In the biblical narrative, these three ways of divine relating are deeply intertwined. Yet, each way of divine relating has its own particular logic and storyline.[59]

---

59. For further reflections on these three ways of divine relating and their connections, see David H. Kelsey, *Eccentric Existence: A Theological Anthropology* (Westminster John Knox, 2009), 120–31.

Exactly which events and stories are assigned to which of these three ways of divine relating is part of the theological debate. Crucial to the way Calvin tells the biblical narrative are his decisions to conceptualize Christ's resurrection as the closing scene of God's relating to creation in reconciliation, his interpretation of resurrection as only the revelation and application of a previously obtained salvation, and his tying together of incarnation and reconciliation. Each of these decisions has important theological implications.

If Christ's resurrection is the closing scene of God's relating to creation in reconciliation, this frames the relationship between Christ's resurrection and eschatological consummation in one of two ways. Either eschatological consummation must have its own shape and logic independent of the notion of resurrection or, if Christ's resurrection rather inaugurates eschatological consummation, one's eschatological imagination will be absorbed by the notion of reconciliation. Calvin's read of the narrative is an instance of the first way of framing things. Christ's bodily resurrection, and our resurrection as modeled on his, have no discernable influence on the ways in which Calvin imagines eschatological life. Our eschatological future is consistently described as spiritual and heavenly. Embodiment plays no meaningful role. The role of Christ's humanity as a means to draw us closer to the Godhead has ended. The eschaton is imagined independently of his resurrected existence. One may believe that because of these things Calvin does not do right by the biblical narrative. One may think that the eschaton will in fact be embodied and that the resurrected Christ as such will be the center of eschatological life, as we will be "heirs of God and joint heirs with Christ" (Rom. 8:17)—joint heirs not with a disembodied divine Word but with "Jesus raised from the dead" (Rom. 8:11). In that case, if one also agrees with Calvin that Christ's resurrection is nothing but the closing scene of the act of reconciliation, one will have to conceive of eschatological life as nothing more than the extended application and celebration of reconciliation. The eschaton is then the eternal wedding feast of the Lamb, the continued celebration of the Lamb's gift of forgiveness and reconciliation. The problem with this concept is that God's relating to creation in eschatological consummation loses its own logic. The logic of the eschaton is de facto determined by the dynamic of sin and grace. But this cannot be the dynamic for which God created that which is not God in the first place. One may wonder whether, in this conception, sin does not succeed in permanently altering the course of history—and if so, whether sin does not, ultimately, win.

In addition to interpreting Christ's resurrection as the closing scene of God's relating to creation in reconciliation, Calvin conceives of the resurrection as only the revelation and application of a salvation that is already completed on the cross. These two moves are conceptually distinct. One could imagine an understanding of reconciliation that includes the act of resurrection but in which Christ's resurrection is as transformative as his death. Such is not Calvin's position. His notion of penal substitution locates the full force of atonement in Christ's death. Combined with the decision to understand resurrection within God's relating to that which is not God in reconciliation, rather than in eschatological consummation, this view of atonement cannot yield anything other than the picture that Calvin offers us.

Finally, decisive for Calvin's larger narrative, including the role of Christ's resurrection, is his infralapsarian understanding of the incarnation. If the incarnation is needed only for the sake of the sin problem, this raises the question of the meaning of a continued embodied presence of the divine Word in the eschaton. If the sin problem has been dealt with, why would the Word continue to be incarnate? This is the question I press in the supralapsarian Christological arguments summarized in chapter 2, which gave rise to the exploration of Calvin's account of the resurrection in the present chapter.[60] Most infralapsarian Christologies ignore this problem, but not so Calvin's. Even while he does not clearly state that Christ will give up incarnate existence, he bites the bullet: Eschatologically, Christ will no longer relate to creation through his human nature. This betrays the import of Christ's resurrection—it does not extend any further than the role Christ's humanity plays. At the same time, this raises a question that, in some shape or form, applies to all infralapsarian Christologies: Does a functional understanding of the incarnation fit with the larger biblical narrative, which speaks about the relationship to the incarnate One not only in functional terms but also in relational terms? Believers are "conformed to the image" of the resurrected Christ "in order that he might be the firstborn within a large family" (Rom. 8:29). This goes beyond the notion that Christ is incarnate only to take care of the problem. It extends the role of his resurrection far beyond that of a Christological intermezzo. It makes the resurrected Christ the model and center of the eschatological people of God.

---

60. See "*Theologia Crucis*: The Apocalyptic Argument" in chap. 2, above, 46–47.

5

Sharing in Nature or Encountering a Person

A Tale of Two Different Supralapsarian Strategies

Supralapsarian Christology holds that God's relating to what is not God by becoming incarnate is embedded in a reality deeper than the dynamic of sin and forgiveness. The gift of the incarnation does more than counteract the result of the fall. On this, supralapsarian theologians agree. But they do not all agree on what then should be said about the difference the incarnation makes. In this respect, the name *supralapsarian Christology* stands for a family of theological accounts.

In this chapter, I conceptualize and examine a hitherto unexplored difference among two kinds of supralapsarian Christologies. The difference concerns our understanding of the nature of the gift given to us in God's becoming incarnate. To analyze this difference, I draw on a Chalcedonian account of persons and natures. According to Chalcedon, the second person of the Trinity, the divine Word, who from all eternity shares in the divine nature of the triune God, in a moment in time assumes a second, human nature in the incarnation. On this ontological framework, person and natures relate to each other as *who* relates to *what*. The incarnation is the event in which the *who* of the divine Word assumes a *whatness*—humanity—that he shares from that moment onward with human beings.[1] Both kinds of supralapsarian

---

1. For a recent account of Chalcedonian Christology, see Ian A. McFarland, *The Word Made Flesh: A Theology of the Incarnation* (Westminster John Knox, 2019).

Christologies I discuss in this chapter consider this divine act to have a transformational effect on creation, but they differ on how this transformation comes about. One kind thinks of it as a gift coming to us through the *natures* of the incarnate One. In the incarnation the Word takes on a human nature, which, transformed as it is in the act of assumption, becomes the conduit of grace for those who share in the same humanity. The other kind thinks of the transformation as taking place through the presence of the incarnate *person*. In taking on human form, the person of the divine Word comes as close to us as God can—the invisible God now can be seen, touched, heard—and draws us into a community of friendship and love.

These two different supralapsarian approaches are exemplified in the work of two contemporary theologians, Kathryn Tanner and Samuel Wells. In this chapter, I engage Tanner and Wells as my main conversation partners. First I explore the internal logic of each of their accounts. For each, I identify the main supralapsarian Christological intuition that drives their theological proposal and then analyze how that intuition shapes a resulting account of creation, atonement, and the eschaton. Then I switch from an analytic to a constructive mode. I argue that while Tanner's approach is better represented in both ancient and modern theological traditions, Wells's approach is constructively more fruitful. While the logic of thinking about the incarnation as a gift channeled by Christ's natures may be internally consistent, it is challenging to weave this position together with other theological commitments concerning Christology and eschatology.

A Tale of Two Different Supralapsarian Strategies

Kathryn Tanner: Grace Communicated Through Christ's Human Nature

Kathryn Tanner's supralapsarian Christological design can be found in her books *Jesus, Humanity and the Trinity* and *Christ the Key*.[2] At the core of her theological vision is the image of a God who is the ultimate gift giver who engages the world in an ongoing communication of goodness cumulating in the giving of Godself.[3] The incarnation is the climax of this divine self-giving:

---

2. Kathryn Tanner, *Jesus, Humanity and the Trinity: A Brief Systematic Theology* (Fortress, 2001); and Kathryn Tanner, *Christ the Key* (Cambridge University Press, 2010).

3. See Tanner, *Jesus, Humanity and the Trinity*, 1–2: "In short, God, who is already abundant fulness, freely wishes to replicate to every degree possible this fulness of life, light, and love outward in what is not God; this is possible in its fullness only to the extent the world is united by God to Godself over the course of the world's time." See also Tanner, *Christ the Key*, vii–viii: "The central theological vision of [this book is]: God wants to give us the fulness of

"Jesus is the one in whom God's relationship with us attains perfection. In Jesus, unity with God takes a perfect form; here humanity has become God's own.... The effect of this perfect relationship with God is perfect humanity, humanity to which God's gifts are communicated in their highest form."[4] This perfected humanity of Christ in turn becomes the conduit of God's transformative self-giving to the rest of humanity: "The point of incarnation is . . . the perfection of humanity. By way of this perfected humanity in union with God, God's gifts are distributed to us—we are saved—just to the extent we are one with Christ in faith and love; unity with Christ the gift-giver is the means of our perfection as human beings, just as the union of humanity and divinity in Christ was the means of his perfect humanity."[5]

In *Jesus, Humanity and the Trinity* this distributing of divine gifts is made possible by what is best described as a qualified transitivity of God's assumption of human nature. Just as Christ the Word assumes a human nature and perfects it, so other human beings are "assumed into Christ's life," which allows for the transformative "workings of Christ in us through the powers of the Spirit."[6] In this way, "Christ's incarnation is matched by our assumption into Christ. Assumed by Christ, Christ becomes the subject of our actions in much the way the second Person of the Trinity is the subject of Jesus' acts."[7] The qualification is that "there are two subjects here, where a human being is assumed by Christ, and not one, as when the Son of God assumed humanity rather than a man.... Our relation to Christ has more the flavor, then, of Christ's own relation to the Father, a relationship of fellowship and correspondence of wills."[8] In *Christ the*

God's own life through the closest possible relationship with us that comes to completion in Christ.... In order to give us the entire fulness of what God enjoys, God must give us God's very own life and not simply some created version of it. God cannot give us everything that God has to give by merely transforming human life itself into some created approximation of divinity. God must attach us, in all our frailty and finitude, to God."

4. Tanner, *Jesus, Humanity and the Trinity*, 9.

5. Tanner, *Jesus, Humanity and the Trinity*, 9. See also Tanner, *Jesus, Humanity and the Trinity*, 53:

Once perfected by the inpouring of gifts from the Father, Jesus' humanity becomes the means by which those gifts are poured out to us through the working of the Holy Spirit. . . . The Spirit radiates the humanity of Jesus with the Father's own gifts of light, life, and love; and shines through him, not simply back to the Father, but through his humanity to us, thereby communicating to us the gifts received by Jesus from the Father. . . . The condition for this inclusion of us in the dynamic of the Trinity's own life is our humanity with Christ, which is also worked by the Holy Spirit as the Spirit of Christ, the Son, sent by him for the completion of the Father's work *ad extra*.

6. Tanner, *Jesus, Humanity and the Trinity*, 58.

7. Tanner, *Jesus, Humanity and the Trinity*, 56.

8. Tanner, *Jesus, Humanity and the Trinity*, 57. See also Tanner, *Jesus, Humanity and the Trinity*, 55–56: "Our humanity is not assumed by Christ's, as Christ's was by the Word; our already formed persons are.... This union with Christ requires tending in a way that humanity's

Key, Tanner wields the notion of assumption as well, but she embeds it in the concept of participation. The divine Word mirrors the Trinity's first person, says Tanner, echoing the church fathers. A perfect image must reproduce its original from top to bottom. This can happen only when the image "shares or participates wholly in what its archetype is. . . . Perfect imaging requires a community of nature."[9] By contrast, creation mirrors the Word by participating in what it is not: God. Tanner distinguishes two kinds of creaturely participation in the divine. In a weak sense, all creatures participate in God by deriving their existence from God and being shaped according to their paradigms as held within the divine Word.[10] In a strong sense, human creatures participate in God not simply "by imitating God, but in virtue of the gift to them of what remains alien to them, the very perfection of the divine image that they are not, now having become their own."[11] Of this form of participation the incarnate Christ is the paradigm and source.[12] The assumed human nature in Christ becomes in turn, as we are attached to Christ, "the very means" of our strong participation in God.[13]

Tanner stresses that humans enjoy their strong participation in God from the moment of their creation. From the beginning the Spirit modeled human nature into imaging the divine Word.[14] Human beings were, however, too immature to receive this gift.[15] Here the incarnate One makes the difference. "Jesus Christ, the perfect human image of God because the perfect divine image, brings human life in himself back to its perfect beginning—the perfect beginning that in a sense never was."[16] In Christ is realized the gift of self that, from the beginning, God offered to humanity. This human nature participates in the Word not as something that is foreign to it but by being identical to it.[17] This in turn has a transformative effect on us, as

> in virtue of the humanity we share with him because the Word has made our humanity its own in him . . . we can have the Spirit that forms Christ's humanity

---

assumption by the Son of God in Christ did not. Our union with Christ must be nurtured through the workings of the Spirit."

9. Tanner, *Christ the Key*, 6.
10. Tanner, *Christ the Key*, 9–10.
11. Tanner, *Christ the Key*, 12.
12. Tanner, *Christ the Key*, 13.
13. Tanner, *Christ the Key*, 14: "Jesus Christ is more than a paradigm for what is involved here; he has become for us the very means. The humanity of Jesus has the perfect attachment or orientation to the Word in virtue of his being one with the Word, nothing apart from it; and we gain the capacity of something like that through our connection to him."
14. Tanner, *Christ the Key*, 24, 26.
15. Tanner, *Christ the Key*, 34.
16. Tanner, *Christ the Key*, 35.
17. Tanner, *Christ the Key*, 35.

according to the divine image as our own too, with the same sort of consequences. Before Christ came, the divine image of the Word was simply foreign to us. . . . Now that the Word has taken our humanity to be its own, the Word has become in a sense proper to us. . . . We can be knit into the Word as never before in virtue of the fact that the Word has made our humanity its own in the incarnation.[18]

In fact, "by being in a hypostatic union with it, by being one with the second person of the trinity, humanity gains a sort of natural connection to the divine comparable to the natural connection that the Word enjoys with other members of the Trinity."[19]

It is possible to read this part of Tanner's argument as an infralapsarian understanding of the incarnation: God intends to give humans the gift of participating in Godself; as this fails, due to human immaturity, God finds another way by binding humanity to Godself through incarnation. However, this reading runs into trouble when Tanner places her Christological argument within the dynamic of nature and grace. The incarnation should be understood as "the highest possible form in which the good of God's own life can be given to us," and, as receiving the grace of God's own life is that for which nature is created, the incarnation is the culmination of the original design of creation.[20]

This account of the role of incarnation shapes how Tanner reads the subsequent stages of the relationship between God and humanity. For example, when it comes to the work of countering sin, Tanner does not locate the atonement in a particular moment of Jesus's life (such as the cross) but asserts that incarnation itself is "the primary mechanism of atonement."[21] In the incarnation, the Word brings "the life-giving powers of the divine nature" to bear upon Christ's human nature and, through him, upon all of humanity.[22] The cross only "exemplifies in paradigmatic fashion" the very character of the pain and sin of human life that the incarnate One redeems.[23]

Tanner's understanding of the incarnation as transforming our existence through our share in Christ's humanity also shapes her account of humanity's eschatological future. Confronted with the scientific expectation of creational entropy, Tanner refuses to contest the finality of the world's end by appealing to God's creative and recreative powers. Instead, she explores what it looks like

18. Tanner, *Christ the Key*, 36.
19. Tanner, *Christ the Key*, 73.
20. Tanner, *Christ the Key*, 60.
21. Tanner, *Christ the Key*, 252.
22. Tanner, *Christ the Key*, 254.
23. Tanner, *Christ the Key*, 260.

to embrace the scientists' expectation that the world does not have a future and to design an eschatology in which preoccupations "would not center on the world of the future but on the world as a whole and on an ongoing redemptive (rather than creative) relation to God that holds for the world of the past, present, and future."[24] The key to such an eschatology lies in the unity we have with God as we are assumed into the humanity of Christ.[25] We can now imagine eternal life as a spatialized existence—that is, "a living *in* God, a kind of placement within the life of God" even "when the world no longer exists."[26] Were eternal life understood in this way, Tanner holds, "death itself, . . . in the sense of temporal cessation, in the sense that each of us, the species, and the planet have a limited duration, would remain a simple fact of existence, a concomitant of the finite constitution of things as we know them."[27] Instead, "we are taken up into the life of God as the very mortal creatures we are. It is only in God that we gain immortality; considered independently of this relation to God we remain mortal. . . . Immortality is not, then, granted to the world in the form of some new natural principles that prevent loss or transience; instead, God's own animating eternity shines through or suffuses the very mortal being of those who hold their existence in God."[28]

Samuel Wells: Grace Communicated Through Christ's Person

In turning to the work of Samuel Wells, we are encountering a supralapsarian approach in which the gift of the incarnation is not located in our transformation through Christ's human nature but rather through the presence of his person. Wells situates his Christological account within a network of four models of social engagement: working for, working with, being for, and being

---

24. Tanner, *Jesus, Humanity and the Trinity*, 102.
25. Tanner, *Jesus, Humanity and the Trinity*, 108. See also Tanner, *Jesus, Humanity and the Trinity*, 110:
> Jesus is the one who lives in God, the one who is all that he is as a human being without existing independently of God, the human being whose very existence is God's own existence—that is the meaning of the hypostatic union. Otherwise expressed, in Jesus God becomes the bearer of our very human acts and attributes. By grace—by virtue, that is, of a life-giving relationship with Jesus that is ours in the power of the Spirit—we enjoy something like the sort of life in God that Jesus lives. We (and the whole world) are to live in God as Jesus does, through him. In short, there is an approximation to the hypostatic union that the world enjoys through grace, most particularly after the world's death, when it transpires that, like Christ, the only life or existence we have is in and through God. . . . When the fire of our own lives grows cold, we come to burn with God's own flame.

26. Tanner, *Jesus, Humanity and the Trinity*, 111.
27. Tanner, *Jesus, Humanity and the Trinity*, 114.
28. Tanner, *Jesus, Humanity and the Trinity*, 116.

with. *Working for* focuses on doing things to make the lives of others better. Like *working for*, *working with* is aimed at problem solving, but *working with* is interested in building coalitions with those who are to benefit from one's work. *Being for* orients one's life toward the well-being of others—although there is no reason why, on this model, one would actually have to engage these others personally. *Being with*, finally, is not so much focused on problems that need solving or a well-being that needs to be enhanced but on personal encounter and enjoyment of presence.[29] When it comes to God's relating to what is not God, Wells holds that the driving force and purpose is a divine desire to *be with*.[30] And the very heart of this is the incarnation:

> The crucial point is that the humanity of the Son is prior to the existence of the world: that the incarnation is prior to the fall; that God's desire to be in relationship is the trigger for the universe's coming into being. But a theology of with assumes more than this. It does not define the Son through the lens of the term "Savior": the Son is the principal, determinative way in which God is with us—but God is with us not primarily to do things for us, even to secure our salvation; God is with us because that is the purpose of creation. Immanuel is prior to Savior. God's working for is subordinate to and designed to restore God's being with. The fall does not determine the shape or character or purpose of God; such things are defined by the original decision of God—the decision to be with.[31]

"The most important word in theology," Wells therefore claims, is "the word with."[32]

Exegetically, Wells roots his prioritizing of *being with* in a surprising place: the "hidden 90 percent" of Jesus's life in which the incarnate One was not working for, or with, his disciples and all of humanity—that is, in the "30-odd years Jesus spent in Nazareth" simply being with those he loved. "Nazareth is important," Wells submits, "not because it is a stage on the way to something more significant, but precisely because it is an extended window into heaven: God and humanity in peaceable interaction, perhaps with good work,

---

29. See Samuel Wells, *A Nazareth Manifesto: Being with God* (Wiley Blackwell, 2015), 20–21; Samuel Wells, *Incarnational Ministry: Being with the Church* (Eerdmans, 2017), 7–10; and, earlier, Samuel Wells and Marcia A. Owen, *Living Without Enemies: Being Present in the Midst of Violence* (InterVarsity, 2011), esp. 19–47.

30. "All the other actions of God—in being for us, working with us, and working for us—are all ways of preparing and redeeming the ground for the fundamental purpose of creation, salvation, and final redemption: God being with us. That is what was ever in God's heart, and what ever shall be." Wells, *Nazareth Manifesto*, 24.

31. Wells, *Nazareth Manifesto*, 232–33.

32. Wells, *Nazareth Manifesto*, 11.

perhaps with good food, perhaps with learning and growing and nurturing and celebrating, but fundamentally just being, because there is no better place to be and no better company to keep and no better thing to be doing. This is Sabbath—the crown of creation; simply being with God."[33]

Being with is the lens through which Wells reads the narrative of creation, reconciliation, and eschatological consummation. He takes creation itself to be embedded in a divine design to *be with*. He therefore rejects theological models that describe God's creative activity as flowing forth out of divine goodness—either as an unselfish sharing of being with that which is not God or as a demonstration of divine glory and power. Both of these accounts, Wells charges, are governed not by the logic of *being with* but by the logic of *being for*. God is thought to create either for the sake as of as-yet-nonexistent creatures, with whom God shares that which they did not have by themselves, or for the sake of Godself, as God shows forth divine perfection. Instead, Wells suggests, "creation is not principally *for* anybody—God or us. Creation is to bring about with. With means creation is God's decision never to be except to be with us. . . . God's desire to be in relationship is the trigger for the universe's coming into being."[34]

---

33. Wells, *Nazareth Manifesto*, 27. Wells admits that his is an argument from silence; the gospel writers seem to devote very little attention to what, according to Wells, is the crux of the matter. But Wells argues that the gospel writers' silence goes back to Jesus's own attitude:
> I suggest that Jesus took the centrality of with for granted. Part of my evidence for this comes in the frequent controversies in which Jesus reacts with exasperation when disciples and others don't grasp what seems to Jesus to be something that goes without saying. . . . Over and again Jesus is in debate about the company he keeps—about whom he is with. . . . Examples abound, but perhaps the most familiar arises in the controversies over whom Jesus eats with. . . . All these stories demonstrate the same principle: that Jesus takes for granted that being with the Father means being with this whole range of people; and that it is so intrinsic to his ministry that he only articulates it when he is criticized by those who find that ministry of being with problematic. (Wells, *Nazareth Manifesto*, 146–48)

In this chapter, I am less interested in the arguments for the respective supralapsarian positions of Tanner and Wells than I am in their theological shapes. However, in chap. 7, below, I offer an exegetical case for a position much akin to Wells's that is, I believe, on sounder footing than his argument from Nazareth.

34. Wells, *Nazareth Manifesto*, 232. Wells continues on this same page by drawing out an explicit supralapsarian Christological position:
> The incarnation is the epitome of with; together with the resurrection, it is the epistemological center of a theology conceived around the notion of with. The question that discloses the dividing line between a theology grounded in with and a theology rooted in for is, . . . "If there had been no Fall, would Christ still have come?" A theology rooted in for invariably replies, "No—since what would there be for the Messiah to do?" Such a perspective presupposes sin, in that it makes Christ's humanity dependent on a deficit—on a problem to be solved. By contrast a theology oriented to and shaped by with takes for granted that Christ would have become incarnate had there been no

As that which motivates creation, *being with* is an eschatological notion.[35] The eschaton is the place where *being with* comes to full fruition.[36] The Christian hope for eternal salvation is, Wells argues, really a reaching for the fullness of communion—"a state of being with God and being with one another and being with the renewed creation."[37] The eschaton is shaped by "a rejoining of such relationship, a restoration of community, a discovery of partnership, a sense of being in the presence of another in which there is neither a folding of identities that loses their difference nor a sharpening of difference that leads to hostility, but an enjoyment of the other that evokes cherishing and relishing."[38]

Atonement in turn relates to eschatological consummation as a means relates to a goal. It is a divine *being for* in the service of God's desire to *be with*.[39] As such, this act *for us* takes once again the shape of *being with*. Wells rejects traditional atonement models, such as *Christus victor*, Anselmian satisfaction theory, or Abelard's subjective account, as expressions of a *working for* or *working with* understanding of God's relationship with humanity. Instead, he proposes that we understand the cross as God's ultimate enactment of *being with*. If sin is our desperate effort not to be with God, on the cross Christ embodies God's absolute commitment to be with us whatever happens. If being with people is what brought Jesus to the cross, then Jesus's "Father, forgive them" is Jesus's finding a way to be with them even when they have abandoned him. Jesus "outlasted humanity's hatred, cruelty, and enmity. After everything the crowds and authorities could throw at him, he was still there. His endurance demonstrated the love that holds on, whatever happens—the love that will never let go. His perseverance showed that nothing can separate us from the love of God. Our isolation has been overcome—from his side."[40]

Sharing in Nature vs. Encountering a Person: A Constructive Analysis

The common nature of Christ and humanity appeals to theologians' ontological imaginations. From Gregory of Nyssa to T. F. Torrance, theologians have used Christ's human nature as the springboard to account for the ways the

---

fall—since Christ being incarnate was the *raison d'etre* of the universe. The incarnation is the heart of a mystery, not the solution to a problem.
35. Wells, *Nazareth Manifesto*, 244.
36. Wells, *Nazareth Manifesto*, 58.
37. Wells, *Nazareth Manifesto*, 43.
38. Wells, *Nazareth Manifesto*, 44.
39. Wells, *Nazareth Manifesto*, 25.
40. Wells, *Nazareth Manifesto*, 243.

incarnation transforms human existence. Tanner's Christology thus exemplifies a longstanding tradition. Wells's approach represents a road less traveled. Nonetheless, I will argue that the latter account is the constructively more fruitful one. When we try to weave each of these two approaches into a larger theological tapestry, an account based on a common humanity causes things to unravel. I will argue this is the case with regard to Christological ontology, eschatology, and a supralapsarian read on the goal of the incarnation.

Natures and Persons

On Tanner's account, the human nature of Christ is the central link in the giving of Godself to creation. In assuming a human nature, the divine Word perfects this nature by making it God's own; by virtue of the humanity we share with him, this nature becomes the means through which God's gifts are distributed to other human beings.

What does this assume about the nature of *nature*? On the philosophical framework from which the distinction between persons and natures stems, a distinction is made between primary and secondary substances. A secondary substance is a generic nature—for example, humanity. A primary substance is an individual substance nature—for example, Paul. When Tanner says that the Word's assumption of a human nature has a transformative effect on all of humanity due to our sharing in nature with the incarnate One, does she take the divine Word to have assumed a primary or a secondary substance?[41]

At numerous places of her argument, Tanner seems to hold to the assumption of a secondary substance. For example, she argues that "in virtue of our community of nature with the humanity of Christ—in virtue of the humanity we share with him because the Word has made our humanity its own in him—we can have the Spirit that forms Christ's humanity according to the divine image as ours too."[42] Likewise, she argues that we are "one with Christ in and through the humanity we share with him," and that "by being in a hypostatic union with it, by being one with the person of the trinity, humanity gains a sort of natural connection to the divine comparable to the natural connection that the Word enjoys with other members of the Trinity."[43] All these statements assert that the very act of incarnation in and of itself had immediate implications not just for the humanity of Christ but for the humanity of all. It is hard to make sense of this without the notion

---

41. Oliver D. Crisp also wrestles with this interpretative question concerning Tanner's Christology. See Oliver D. Crisp, *Revisioning Christology: Theology in the Reformed Tradition* (Ashgate, 2011), 124–28.
42. Tanner, *Christ the Key*, 36.
43. Tanner, *Christ the Key*, 72, 73.

that humanity as a secondary substance exists and was assumed in the act of incarnation. Such a reading would be confirmed by Tanner's seeming admission (this time in the context of a discussion on incarnation and atonement) that her preferred account of the incarnation "trades on a Platonic reification of universal terms such as 'humanity.'"[44]

To premise one's Christological account on the idea of an assumption of a secondary substance is, however, highly problematic theologically. If a secondary substance like humanity indeed exists in such a way that what happens to it in the particular events of Christ's life has a direct effect on all human beings, the very same thing should be said about what happens in the particular events of other people's lives. That is, if there exists an ontological web of connections between all human beings that allows for the Word's assumption of a particular life in first-century Palestine to result in me being assumed by the divine, that very same web would allow for ontological connections to go in other directions. It would allow for the events of my life to also count as the events of Christ's life—but, more than that, it would allow for the events of every single human being to be counted as the events of all other human beings, and vice versa. However, central to the Christian life are events that are particular to some but not to all: sin, love, repentance, forgiveness, conversion, faith, and so on. If every human being shares in the same, singular human nature, no particular events would count as a particular human being's events, and only theirs. This is theologically undesirable.

At other places Tanner explicitly asserts that in the incarnation Christ assumes an individual and not a universal human nature: "We are not included in Christ's life simply because the humanity assumed by the Son in Christ is common, shared by Christ and every other human being. It is this particular person—and not the humanity of Christ *per se*—that has universal efficacy, in so far as everyone else is drawn to it, united with Christ's own life."[45] This in turn raises the question of *how* we are united with Christ's life. If the transformative effect of the incarnation comes to us by way of Christ's human nature but the nature assumed is an individual human nature (primary substance), not a universal nature in which we all share (secondary substance), how does what happened to Christ's human nature affect us?

As I observed above, Tanner employs here a move that amounts to the idea of a qualified transitivity of assumption. Because they are in Christ, other human beings also share in his assumption and thereby participate in the divine life—although in their case it is not only their natures but also their

---

44. Tanner, *Christ the Key*, 258.
45. Tanner, *Jesus, Humanity and the Trinity*, 54.

persons that are assumed.[46] The problem with this move is that it is inconsistent with the Chalcedonian logic of assumption. Chalcedonian Christology employs the notion of assumption to differentiate the unique relationship between the divine Word and his human nature from other ways in which God takes hold of human beings. In the act of assumption, the human nature—its properties, powers, and acts—become the Word's very own. The Word is therefore said to be this nature's term, or supposit—its ontological owner. The Word *personifies* this nature.

To unpack this further, we may turn to Tanner's own explanation of the Chalcedonian logic. The church fathers hold that Christ's human nature is anhypostatic, which means that "apart from his existing in the Word, Jesus has no existence of his own." Moreover, Jesus's existence is also enhypostatic: "Jesus has a human existence but only in virtue of having his existence in God. Jesus does not just get his existence *from* God, as we do; he exists in God; his very existence is God's existence."[47] To put it still differently, because Jesus's human nature is assumed by the divine Word, there is no interpersonal over-againstness between the divine Word and Jesus's humanity. According to this understanding, when we encounter Jesus's human nature, we encounter the person of the Word.

This is different from the case of encountering another human being. The human natures of human beings other than Jesus are personified not by a divine person but by human persons; thus, even when God draws such humans into the closest intimacy, there continues to exist an interpersonal over-againstness between God and the human persons who personify these particular natures. For example, God may inspire a prophet through the Spirit; the prophet may start speaking and acting in the name of God; but, on Chalcedonian Christology, we would not say that in encountering this prophet we encounter God in the same way that in encountering Jesus we encounter God. In the prophet's case there continues to be an interpersonal over-againstness between God and the human that does not exist in the case of Jesus. This difference goes back to the logic of assumption.

It is also for this reason that later medieval theologians, reflecting on Chalcedonian Christology, would argue that while God could assume any human nature, God cannot assume another person. God can inspire, transform, sanctify, and recreate another person. But it belongs to the definition of a person that a person cannot be assumed, and thereby personified, by another person.[48]

---

46. Tanner, *Jesus, Humanity and the Trinity*, 55.
47. Tanner, *Jesus, Humanity and the Trinity*, 25.
48. Thomas Aquinas, *Summa Theologiae* III.4.2; John Duns Scotus, *Quodlibet* 19.61. To approach the same point from a different angle again, this is where the logic of creation, on

And so, if a human person's human nature were to be assumed by another person—say, the second person of the Trinity—it would thereby cease to be that human person's nature. In fact, since a human person by definition needs to have a human nature in order to exist as a person, if their nature were to be assumed by another person, they (the original ontological owner of that nature) would thereby cease to exist.

To summarize, Tanner's account of divine self-giving through the means of the human nature of Christ either presupposes the existence of numerically one universal human nature, which is a notion that runs into steep theological difficulties, or it relies on the idea of a transitivity of assumption, which runs afoul of the logic of Chalcedonian Christology.[49]

However, these problems disappear if we unpack divine self-giving not in terms of the communication of natures but in terms of the presence of a person. While Wells does not clarify this explicitly, his account of the incarnation also relies on the Chalcedonian logic of assumption. In the incarnation, the divine Word takes a human nature as his own, and when we meet and engage this nature—that is, when we are *with* Jesus of Nazareth—we truly are with the one who personifies this nature, the divine Word. The *who* we meet is the Word; in the incarnation, this *who* acquires the *what*, the nature, that makes this meeting possible. At the same time, to *be with* demands that the ones who are meeting are truly distinct. To *be with* implies difference, not sameness. It implies an interpersonal over-againstness, not the assumption of one by another. Therefore, what on Tanner's account is a problem—the enduring interpersonal over-againstness between the person of the divine Word and the persons of those human beings that encounter Jesus—is the very core and strength of the proposal. In the incarnation, the Word acquires the embodied, human properties and powers that allow us to see, to hear, and to touch the otherwise invisible Creator of heaven and earth. It is because of

---

the one hand, and of incarnation and assumption, on the other hand, are diametrically different. In creation, as Tanner rightly argues, the relationship between God and what is not God is noncompetitive (see *Jesus, Humanity and the Trinity*, 2ff.). Given God's transcendence, God and humanity do not operate within the same plane of causality, and therefore the creature does not have to decrease as God increases. But acts like assuming a human nature and thereby becoming incarnate mean God entering the created nexus of causality in which rules of ontological competitiveness do apply.

49. An additional question for the account represented by Tanner is how God perfects the human nature of Christ so that it may become an instrument of transformation for Christ's fellow human beings. Tanner locates this in a deifying communication between Christ's divine and human natures (see, e.g., Tanner, *Jesus, Humanity and Trinity*, 26–27, 30–32). This is a neo-Chalcedonian understanding of the metaphysics of the incarnation that is not universally accepted as legitimate. For this chapter, though, I set this issue aside and concentrate on the transformative interaction between the incarnate One and other human beings.

the incarnation that we can sit down with him, that he can look us in the eye, and that we can engage this person and become friends. Without incarnation, God would continue to be at a distance. God could have been *for* us, but not *with* us. God could have interacted with us, but only as one whose appearance would have resulted in our death (Exod. 33:20). But in the incarnation, the God who could not be seen has been made known (John 1:18).

Eschatology

If Christ's nature is the channel through which God's gift giving reaches our nature, it is unclear how God's grace also engages our personhood. Tanner's assertions notwithstanding, on a Chalcedonian logic, natures can be assumed, but persons cannot be. God can assume and thereby cleanse, elevate, and perfect my nature, but not my person. The implications of this become clear in Tanner's eschatology.

Responding to the scientists' claim that the cosmos is on its way to an inevitable end, Tanner refuses to appeal to God's creative and recreative powers to imagine an eschatological future for creation beyond its dooming collapse. Instead, Tanner embraces the scientist's claim and enfolds it in an eschatological imagination according to which one day the world will, indeed, no longer exist, but all of creation, mortal as it ever was, will nonetheless have an eschatological future. Finite and finished creatures will, as such, receive a place within the life of God. Not only does this eschatological construction align with the scientists' expectation, but it also flows forth from Tanner's understanding of the gift of grace.[50] On Tanner's proposal, the world has eschatological life—but as a world that has been. Our histories will be preserved as histories that definitively have come to an end. We will receive a place in God—but as beings whose lives have come to end, not as agents who continue to make history and whose lives continue to unfold in new chapters. This fits with Tanner's belief that divine grace is ultimately expressed by the assumption of our natures. As I argued above, on a Chalcedonian logic, the assumption of our natures comes at the price of casting aside that which makes us persons. If the logic of assumption rules the relationship between us and the incarnate Word, our natures can be assumed, but not our persons, not the *whos* who are the ontological agents of our natures. And if our

---

50. Tanner first formulated her eschatology in "Eschatology Without a Future?," in *The End of the World and the Ends of God: Science and Theology on Eschatology*, ed. John Polkinghorne and Michael Welker (Trinity Press International, 2000), 222–37. There she still presented it as a "thought experiment" (224). In the last chapter of *Jesus, Humanity and the Trinity*, a slightly expanded version of "Eschatology Without a Future?," Tanner makes clear that her position on eschatology flows forth from her wider systematic theological commitments (97).

eschatological future as creatures depends on our assumption by God, then we as persons fall outside the reach of eschatological life. Human beings can only be preserved as creatures whose histories have come to an end.[51]

Tanner's eschatological account fits her Christology. One might wonder, however, whether it coheres with the promise not just of a creation that once existed but of a creation that is created anew (Rev. 21)—a world in which creatures continue as active agents as every tongue confesses Christ as Lord (Phil. 2), a world in which humans thus continue to exist in interpersonal over-againstness vis-à-vis the incarnate One. These biblical themes cannot easily be woven into Tanner's eschatological design.

Wells's account does not suffer from these challenges. The very goal of *being with* is for God and creation to enjoy each other in an ongoing personal encounter and enjoyment of presence. This demands a twofold agency. Since *being with* is, for Wells, an eschatological notion, on his model such interpersonal engagement describes the shape of the eschaton. This eschatological expectation does not deny that, within the current framework, creation's energy necessarily will run out, the cosmos will collapse, and the world will come to an inevitable end. It also does not suggest that simply by creating people, God thereby is obliged to them eschatologically. But if this *being with* is the very goal of creation, then God thereby commits Godself to do to creation what God already did to Jesus—that is, to recreate it into a life of transformed-but-continued existence of agency and interaction. This seems to be what Paul lifts up as the eschatological ordering of and promise to creation: Human beings will be conformed to the image of the resurrected Son "in order that he might be the firstborn within a large family" (Rom. 8:29).

The Incarnation as Instrumental Good or Intrinsic Goal

When we think about the overall intentions of God for that which is not God, where does the incarnation fit? Supralapsarians agree that incarnation is not contingent upon sin, but this still leaves multiple ways open for how one conceives of the incarnation among God's eschatological intentions.

Some supralapsarians think of the incarnation as a means by which God accomplishes a larger goal. The incarnation may not be contingent upon sin, but it is still an instrumental good contingent upon something else. For

---

51. Even while she does not mention him in this context, Tanner develops an eschatology that is virtually identical to Karl Barth's, according to which the eschatological future of creation is the preservation of the life lived. I analyze Barth's eschatology in Edwin Chr. van Driel, *Incarnation Anyway: Arguments for Supralapsarian Christology* (Oxford University Press, 2008), 111–18. For a wider analysis and critique, see Nathan Hitchcock, *Karl Barth and the Resurrection of the Flesh: The Loss of the Body in Participatory Eschatology* (Pickwick, 2013).

example, Friedrich Schleiermacher took the incarnation to be the supralapsarian means by which God imparts Godself to all humanity.[52] On this line of thought, God's desire to be imparted to humanity is logically prior to the intention to become incarnate. Other supralapsarian theologians think of the incarnation as that which has absolute priority within God's relating to that which is not God. For example, Karl Barth argued that Christ is not just the object of election but also its subject—the very first divine self-determination in relation to that which is not God is to be a God for others.[53] This line of supralapsarian thought amounts to the assertion that the incarnation is an intrinsic good.

Tanner's model is another expression of a model in which the incarnation is a supralapsarian instrumental good. In some ways, the structure of her model is in this respect remarkably similar to Schleiermacher's.[54] The incarnation is the means by which God distributes the gift of Godself to humanity. Incarnation is not the ultimate gift itself; the assumed human nature of Christ is the conduit through which the ultimate divine intention is accomplished, the participation of the creature in the divine. This is particularly visible in Tanner's eschatological expectations, in which no further personal interaction between the incarnate One and humanity is imagined. Like all of creation, humanity is preserved as that which has been, and having lost creaturehood and particular identity, it continues to exist "in God."[55]

Wells's model on the other hand is an expression of a supralapsarian model according to which the incarnation is an intrinsic good. The very goal of creation is for God to be with others, and incarnation is not the means to this goal but its very expression. The eschaton is the celebration of incarnation: "God and humanity in peaceable interaction . . . fundamentally just being, because there is no better place to be and no better company to keep."[56]

The theological issue at stake in the difference between these approaches is the priority of Christ. Significant supralapsarian traditions take their cue

---

52. See Van Driel, *Incarnation Anyway*, 22–25.
53. Van Driel, *Incarnation Anyway*, 63–82.
54. Tanner hardly ever refers to Schleiermacher, and, as far as I know, the relationship between their theological models has never been explored. The structural parallels are, however, remarkable. Schleiermacher's notion of absolute dependence could be read as a version of Tanner's principle of non-competitiveness. In both theological designs, the relationship between God and what is not God is conceived of as a salvation ontology rather than a salvation history. For neither design does God's covenant with Israel, Jesus's resurrection, his ascension, or his return play a substantial role.
55. Tanner, *Jesus, Humanity and Trinity*, 119. Presumably, the same holds for Christ. If creation will continue to exist eschatologically only as "having been," this would apply also to the created human nature of the incarnate One.
56. Wells, *Nazareth Manifesto*, 27.

from the imagery in Colossians and Ephesians, in which all things are said to be created for Christ (Col. 1:16) and to be gathered in him (Eph. 1:10). If all things were created for Christ, the incarnation cannot be in the service of a larger goal; rather, Christ is the goal of whatever is created. A Christological model that implies the functional good of the incarnation can be supralapsarian, but it will have to downplay the priority of Christ implied by these Pauline notions.[57] On such a functional understanding, Christ can be the *key* to creation, as the title of one of Tanner's studies reads; but a key is neither the goal nor the center of that which it unlocks.

Conclusion

To locate the transformative effect of the incarnation on other human beings in the assumption of our common nature leads to theological complications. To assume a nature is to personify it. What this nature is and does count as the being and actions of the divine Word. In this, the Word's relationship to his nature is different from his relationship to other human beings; in the latter case, there is a personal over-againstness that is lacking in the former case. Assumption is therefore not a category that can be applied to Christ's relationship to other human beings; for Christ to assume us would be for Christ to cancel out *us*, the supposits who presently personify our natures. And thus, *we* would not receive the transformative grace of Christ; only our natures would. This in turn has important implications for eschatology. The much better way forward is to locate the incarnation's transformative effect in the *being with* of the person of the divine Word who, in taking on a human nature, comes to us as close as he can and engages us in a relationship of friendship and love. On such an account, the incarnation is not a means to a larger goal; it embodies the very goal itself: God's *being with* God's people. I will explore such an account in the constructive part of this book.

---

57. Such is indeed the position of Schleiermacher. See Friedrich Schleiermacher, *Christian Faith*, trans. Terrence N. Tice, Catherine L. Kelsey, and Edwina Lawler, 2 vols. (Westminster John Knox, 2016), §99, addendum.

6

All Things Summed Up in Christ

Reading Lesslie Newbigin's Missional-Ecumenical Project in a Supralapsarian Key

In the previous chapters, I have introduced various concepts, distinctions, and ways of considering the difference the incarnation makes that, in part 2, will help formulate a set of supralapsarian Christological explorations. Before we turn to that, however, I want to add one more consideration—that telling the Christian story from the perspective of the priority of Christ might be particularly fruitful in a new missional era. In a later chapter, I will address this idea directly; in this chapter, I will address it indirectly, by delving into the work of the missiologist and ecumenist Lesslie Newbigin. As many have looked to his work for inspiration in how to address the crisis of Christianity in the West, I will argue that Newbigin's responses are best read as shaped by what can only be called supralapsarian Christological intuitions.

Lesslie Newbigin was instrumental in shaping the missional and ecumenical imagination of the church in the last century. Following the formation of the Church of South India in the 1940s, he articulated that church's ecclesiology in his early work *The Household of God* (1953). His thinking shaped both Protestant and Roman Catholic thought on the church for another generation and a half. Newbigin's fingerprints are all over key ecumenical theological statements, including "The Calling of the Church to Mission and to Unity," issued by the World Council of Churches in its 1951 meeting in Rolle (and also by the International Missionary Council meeting in Willingen in the same year); the 1961 New Delhi WCC statement, "The Church's Unity"; and the 1984 report of the Anglican-Reformed International Commission, *God's Reign and Our Identity*. Even *Lumen Gentium*, Vatican II's dogmatic constitution on the church, bears Newbigin's imprint. As bishop of the Church of South India, general secretary of the IMC, and associate general secretary of the WCC, he spoke to countless audiences all over the globe. After retiring to his native Great Britain, he wrote several books on being church in the secular West, which, at the end of the twentieth century, gave rise to the Gospel and our Culture Network, first in England and later in North America. This network still shapes conversations about the missional church in the present day.[1] For all these reasons, G. Wainwright has called Newbigin a church father of the twentieth century.[2]

But what theological vision drives Lesslie Newbigin's missiological and ecumenical project? It is well documented that Newbigin roots his ecclesiology in his missiology and his experience in the mission field. Increasingly throughout his life, his conviction that a Christian community that is in conflict with itself cannot be a believable witness for a gospel of reconciliation drove his understanding of the imperative for Christian unity.[3] However, less attention has been given to the Christological impetus and shape of Newbigin's theological vision. In this chapter, I surface a particular and critical component of Newbigin's Christology—his use of the Ephesians metaphor of all things

---

1. See the discussion in Craig Van Gelder and Dwight H. Zscheile, *The Missional Church in Perspectives: Mapping Trends and Shaping the Conversation* (Baker Academic, 2011), 36–40, 46–52; and Michael W. Goheen and Timothy M. Sheridan, *Becoming a Missionary Church: Lesslie Newbigin and Contemporary Church Movements* (Baker Academic, 2022), 78–84.

2. Geoffrey Wainwright, *Lesslie Newbigin: A Life* (Oxford University Press, 2000), v, 390–93; on the influence of Newbigin's work on Vatican II, see 98; on his role as the drafter of the Rolle/Willingen statement, see 164–68; on the New Delhi statement, see 113–14; and on the report of the Anglican/Reformed International Commission, see 123–28.

3. Helpful studies of Newbigin's missional-ecumenical project include George R. Hunsberger, *Bearing the Witness of the Spirit: Lesslie Newbigin's Theology of Cultural Plurality* (Eerdmans, 1998); Jürgen Schuster, *Christian Mission in Eschatological Perspective: Lesslie Newbigin's Contribution* (VTR Publications, 2009); M. Scot Sherman, "*Ut Omnes Unum Sint*: The Case for Visible Church Reunion in the Ecclesiology of Bishop J. E. Lesslie Newbigin" (PhD diss., University of Wales, 2010); Mark T. B. Laing, *From Crisis to Creation: Lesslie Newbigin and the Reinvention of Christian Mission* (Pickwick, 2012); Jeppe Bach Nikolajsen, *The Distinctive Identity of the Church: A Constructive Study of the Post-Christendom Theologies of Lesslie Newbigin and John Howard Yoder* (Pickwick, 2015); Michael W. Goheen, *The Church and Its Vocation: Lesslie Newbigin's Missionary Ecclesiology* (Baker Academic, 2018); Paul Weston, *Humble Confidence: Lesslie Newbigin and the Logic of Mission* (Cascade Books, 2023); the essays in Mark T. B. Laing and Paul Weston, eds., *Theology in Missionary Perspective: Lesslie Newbigin's Legacy* (Pickwick, 2013); and the essays in Scott W. Sunquist and Amos Yong, eds., *The Gospel and Pluralism Today: Reassessing Lesslie Newbigin in the 21st Century* (IVP Academic, 2015).

being summed up in Christ—and the ways in which this metaphor is reflected in his account of salvation, election, and the church's mission.

All Things Summed Up in Christ

Ephesians 1:10 speaks of "a plan for the fullness of time, to sum up all things in [Christ], things in heaven and things on earth" (NRSV alt.). Among the multitude of images that the New Testament uses to speak about the difference Christ makes, this Ephesians metaphor of all things being summed up in Christ stands out for several reasons. First, it is linguistically uncommon: the Greek term translated here as "sum up," *anakephalaioō*, is used only twice in the New Testament, and only once in reference to Christ. Therefore, it is easily recognizable when later thinkers, such as Newbigin, employ it, even when they do not explicitly reference the Ephesians text. Second, it stands out theologically, since the image evokes a rich theological narrative that is different from other Christological stories. Three features characterize this narrative: First, while the Ephesians letter does not ignore those aspects of Christ's work that have been completed in the past, such as forgiveness and redemption (1:7), this image focuses on Christ's work that is ongoing in the present and the future. Christ's work takes the shape of an ongoing history as things are gathered into him. The Ephesian church has found itself drawn into this history, and thus it receives a destiny (1:11), an inheritance (1:14), and hope (1:18). Second, this history is eschatological in nature. It is not a phase within a much wider, unfolding process; it is, rather, the consummation of all of history. It is the enactment of a plan for the fullness of time (1:10) that was set from before the foundation of the world (1:4). In being gathered into Christ, creation is drawn into that for which it was called into existence. And third, this image therefore invites us to see the forging of a community as the core and goal of history. The center of this community is Christ; its reach is universal. Its formation begins small, in the covenant with the people Israel, but it widens as gentiles are folded into the covenant (2:12–13) and form with Israel a new people (2:22), a new household of God (2:23). Finally, it will encompass "all things . . . , things in heaven and things on earth" (1:10).

The Christology that arises out of this metaphor can in turn be mapped onto a larger theological canvas. In terms gleaned from the previous chapter, there are Christologies that unpack the ways Christ relates to us primarily in terms of *being for* and those that unpack these primarily in terms of *being with*. Relationships that are grounded in *being for* focus on a perceived need. They assume deficits that are to be remedied, problems that are to be solved.

They are relationships in the service of a larger goal. In contrast, relationships grounded in *being with* are themselves the goal. These are relationships in which the partners enjoy each other's company for its own sake. Christologically speaking, *being with* and *being for* are not mutually exclusive. Most Christologies hold that Christ does things for us and is with us. The question is how best to theologically order these relationships. Does Christ come to be with us (incarnation) in order to do something for us (usually, take care of the sin problem)? Or is Christ's work for us a means to achieving a larger goal—his being with us and our being with him? The Christology of the Ephesians letter is shaped by the latter logic. Forgiveness and redemption, wrought by Christ, serve the primordial and eschatological goal of forging a community in which all things are gathered to be with him.

In this chapter, I argue that the Ephesians metaphor is a critical component of Newbigin's Christology. My thesis unfolds in four directions. First, I show that references to the image of all things being summed up in Christ form an as-yet-undetected line of thought in Newbigin's work. While this line of thought is present most prominently in his early ecclesiological work, he does not abandon it in later phases. Second, I argue that the logic of Newbigin's theological imaginary follows the logic embedded in the Ephesians metaphor, and thus it is not farfetched to assume an ongoing impact of the image from Ephesians on Newbigin's thinking. Third, I show that detecting the particular shape of Newbigin's Christology allows us to map his project onto wider Christological conversations, and I suggest we most fruitfully read him in the context of a supralapsarian Christological approach. Fourth and finally, if we read Newbigin's work in this way, it can once again make a fresh contribution to the conversation as practitioners today seek a new narrative to support their work in this missional era.

Newbigin's Use of Ephesian Christological Imagery

In his study of Newbigin's account of election, George R. Hunsberger distinguishes three periods in Newbigin's life and writings: an early period, including the late 1940s and most of the 1950s, when Newbigin served the Church of South India as bishop; the end of the 1950s through the earlier part of the 1970s, during part of which Newbigin had returned to the West and became deeply involved with ecumenical organizations and debates; and the period after his return to England in the mid-1970s, when he faced up to the new missional age in the Western world.[4] Without committing to any

---

4. Hunsberger, *Witness of the Spirit*, 47.

further implications of this for the reading of Newbigin's work, I will adopt this periodization as an heuristic device to show how throughout each of these periods Newbigin drew on the imagery of Ephesians 1:10 to explain the difference Christ makes. In later sections, I will trace what theological work the Ephesians metaphor does for Newbigin. For now, I wish simply to establish the centrality of the metaphor in the various phases of his work.

The Household of God is the central text that grew out of Newbigin's early work as bishop in the Church of South India. Over against ecclesiologies that locate the *esse* of the church in something it has and is—such as Word, sacraments, or order—Newbigin argues that the *esse* of the church lies in the eschatological gathering and transformation work of God.[5] In unpacking this argument, Newbigin repeatedly turns to the metaphor of Ephesians 1:10 to make his point. The "salvation of which the Gospel speaks," and which we experience in the community of the church, is "the summing up of all things in Christ."[6] Salvation comes to us through an act of election, "the end of which is to sum up all things in Christ."[7] The unity of the community thus established "is the sign and the instrument of the salvation which Christ has wrought and whose final fruition is the summing-up of all things in Christ."[8]

By the end of the 1950s, Newbigin's work focused more and more on questions fueled by the ecumenical and missiological dialogues and organizations he was involved in, circling particularly around questions concerning the relationship between world, history, and the gospel. In all this, his description of the difference Christ makes continued to return to the Ephesians metaphor.

---

5. Lesslie Newbigin, *The Household of God: Lectures on the Nature of Church* (1953; repr., Wipf & Stock, 2008), 132.

6. Newbigin, *Household of God*, 140. In his very early essay "The Church and the Gospel," for the benefit of the newly forming Church of South India, Newbigin already sketches the ecclesiological lines that will come to full development in *The Household of God*. Newbigin draws on John 12:32, one of the few places in the New Testament where a metaphor similar to the one in Eph. 1:10 is used, and he weaves it together with notions from Ephesians:

> The work of Christ is to draw all men unto Himself. Where the Gospel is truly proclaimed and believed, . . . men . . . will be knit together in a common dependence upon the grace of God alone. The fruit of the Gospel is the fellowship of the Holy Spirit—a visible fellowship expressing itself in the common life of the organized church. . . . The church is the means by which the gospel reaches every individual. . . . This is the constant refrain of the Epistle to the Ephesians—that in the miracle of a visible unity of Jew and Gentile in the Church, God has revealed the hidden depths of his will "to the end that now unto the principalities and the powers in the heavenly places might be made known through the church the manifold wisdom of God" (Eph. 3:10). Thus the church is not only the fruit of the gospel: it is also the indispensable means by which the Gospel reaches us" (Lesslie Newbigin, "The Church and the Gospel," in *The Church and Union*, papers by members of the South India United Church [CLSI, 1944]), 58.

7. Newbigin, *Household of God*, 103.
8. Newbigin, *Household of God*, 149.

In *Trinitarian Doctrine for Today's Mission* (1963), he characterizes history as directed toward being "summed up in Christ, and creation as called into being to that end."[9] In *Honest Religion for Secular Man* (1966), Newbigin explores the relationship between the then-sought-after "secular, this worldly unification" of humankind to "the biblical promise of the summing up of all things in Christ."[10] Elsewhere, he describes conversion as "being so turned round that one's face is towards that 'summing up of all things in Christ' which is promised, and of which the resurrection of Jesus is the sign and first-fruit. It means being caught up into the activity of God which is directed to that end."[11] The church is said to be the sign, foretaste, and instrument of God's intention to sum up all things in Christ.[12] This idea in turn becomes Newbigin's guide as he negotiates the diversity of and therefore sometimes needed differentiation among different Christian communities while at the same time holding fast to the idea that "separation cannot be the last word. The gospel is about God's purpose to unite all things in Jesus Christ."[13]

At various places, Newbigin combines or replaces the verbiage of Ephesians 1:10 with other biblical notions that have the same visual connotations. Quoting Colossians 1, he tells us that "All things created . . . have been created through Christ and for Christ. They are to be summed up in Christ. This is therefore the norm by which they are to be interpreted."[14] Evoking John 12:32, he calls the congregation "the visible sign and first fruit of Christ's promise, 'I, if I am lifted up from the earth, will draw all men to myself.'"[15] In a passage in which he gives an account of Christ's multiple ways of relating to creation, he combines Ephesians 1:10 and John 12:32 to describe the ongoing, salvific work of Christ:

> The Church is the provisional incorporation of mankind into Jesus Christ. . . . The essential words are "into Jesus Christ." By this name we are referring to a three-fold reality.

---

9. "All things have been created that they may be summed up in Christ the Son. All history is directed towards that end. All creation has this as its goal." Lesslie Newbigin, *Trinitarian Doctrine for Today's Mission* (1963; repr., Wipf & Stock, 2006), 83.

10. Lesslie Newbigin, *Honest Religion for Secular Man* (SCM, 1966), 19.

11. Lesslie Newbigin, "From the Editor," *International Review of Missions* 54 (1965): 149, quoted in Hunsberger, *Witness of the Spirit*, 161.

12. Lesslie Newbigin, "What is a 'Local Church Truly United'?," in *In Each Place: Toward a Fellowship of Local Churches Truly United* (WCC Publications, 1977), 22–23.

13. Newbigin, "What is a 'Local Church Truly United'?," 24.

14. Newbigin, *Trinitarian Doctrine for Today's Mission*, 63.

15. Newbigin, *Honest Religion*, 108. Again, the use of the image from John 12 can be traced as far back as an early sketch for the argument that would eventually shape the 1952 Kerr Lectures and evolve into *The Household of God*. See Newbigin, "The Church and the Gospel," 58.

(a) We are referring to the One who lived and taught and died and rose again under Pontius Pilate. . . .
(b) We are referring to the One who is, who lives now in his risen power and who is present in the midst of his church. . . .
(c) We are referring to the One who is to come as the consummation of all human and cosmic history in order to gather up all things into himself. We are referring not to one of the strands of history, but to that which is the true meaning and end of all history.[16]

Finally, when in the last period of his work Newbigin turns to ask what the gospel might mean for the post-Christian West in his two major missiology books, he continues to draw on the Ephesians metaphor. Salvation is once again defined as "the summing up of all things with Christ as head (Eph. 1:10)."[17] And using all of Ephesians 1 to describe the "universality of God's purpose and the particularity of his calling," Newbigin takes "the uniting of the whole cosmos . . . with Christ as head (Eph. 1:10)" to be the purpose of salvation.[18] And the secret of this divine action, the goal of which is "the final unity of the whole creation in Christ," is now entrusted to the church.[19]

How the Ephesians Christological Imagery Shapes Newbigin's Account

It is not just that Newbigin returns to the Ephesians Christological metaphor; it is also—and this is central to this chapter's argument—that the particular logic of this imagery is recognizable in the shape of some of the most characteristic elements of Newbigin's theological vision. In this section I tease this out in a cumulative argument touching on Newbigin's account of salvation, election, and the church and its mission. To illustrate the fruitfulness of this analysis, I conclude by showing how it sheds new light on the tensions between Newbigin's theological intuitions and the approach of missiologist J. C. Hoekendijk.

Salvation

When the image of all things being summed up in Christ is taken as a central metaphor through which to understand the difference Christ makes, then one

---

16. Lesslie Newbigin, "The Form and Structure of the Visible Unity of the Church," in *So Sende Ich Euch: Festschrift für D. Dr. Martin Pörksen zum 70. Geburtstag*, ed. Otto Waack, Justus Freytag, and Gerhard Hoffmann (Evangelische Missionsverlag, 1973), 127–28.
17. Lesslie Newbigin, *The Gospel in a Pluralist Society* (Eerdmans, 1989), 178.
18. Lesslie Newbigin, *The Open Secret: An Introduction to the Theology of Mission*, rev. ed. (Eerdmans, 1995), 71.
19. Newbigin, *Open Secret*, 71–72.

will understand the salvation he brings as intrinsically communal. Salvation means that one is knitted into a new set of relationships, both with other humans and, finally, with the cosmos as a whole—a set of relationships of which Christ is the center. The beginning, the foretaste of this salvific, gathered community, is the church. This is indeed how Newbigin presents it. Throughout his oeuvre, he polemicizes against soteriologies—be they traditional Protestant or more liberal—that are concerned primarily with the fates of individuals as displaying too narrow an understanding of the difference Christ makes.[20] Instead,

> the salvation of which the Gospel speaks and which is determinative of the nature and function of the Church is—as the very world itself should teach us—a making whole, a healing. It is the summing-up of all things in Christ. It embraces within its scope the restoration of the harmony between man and God, between man and man and between man and nature for which all things were at the first created. It is the restoration to the whole creation of the perfect unity whose creative source and pattern is the unity of perfect love within the being of the triune God. It is in its very essence, universal and cosmic.[21]

As such, it is also not spiritual or otherworldly but embodied and earthly. It is the gathering of people and creation in all their concreteness: "We are not speaking of an abstract noun, or of an invisible platonic idea. . . . We are called upon to recognize and join ourselves to God's visible congregation here on earth. . . . The whole core of biblical history is the story of the calling of a visible community to be God's own people, his royal priesthood on earth, the bearer of his light to the nations."[22]

---

20. Newbigin makes these claims already in *The Household of God*: "There can therefore be no private 'salvation,' no perfection of joy and rest until the passion of that love is quenched, until he has seen of the travail of his soul and is satisfied. It belongs to the very heart of salvation that we cannot have it in fulness until all for whom it is intended have it together" (140). And, "When the eschatological and missionary perspective has been lost from the thinking of the church, its task comes to be conceived in terms of the rescue of individuals one by one out of this present evil age and their preservation unharmed for the world to come. . . . The root of the error lies in the failure to keep in view throughout the *whole* salvation of which the church is the sign and first-fruit and instrument" (146). Newbigin expresses similar thoughts still at the end of his career. See Newbigin, *Gospel in a Pluralist Society*, 82–84, 179.

21. Newbigin, *Household of God*, 140. Maybe the most succinct argument for Newbigin's position is his observation that Christ left behind not a book but a community (Newbigin, *Household of God*, 27; see also Newbigin, *Gospel in a Pluralist Society*, 133). Had Christ left behind a book, the difference he made could have been accessed on an individual basis, as people could immerse themselves in such writings on their own and thereby build up an individual relationship with the Savior. But, Newbigin points out, this is not the case. Christ left behind a community; therefore, finding access to the presence and ongoing work of the Savior comes only by being drawn into this circle.

22. Newbigin, *Household of God*, 26–27.

Understood in this way, salvation is not only communal but also progressive. It is not obtained once for all; it is realized more, and experienced more deeply, as Christ draws more and more people into the salvific community:

> It is because this is the nature of salvation, that our experience of it now must have the character of a foretaste, an earnest; that we who have the first fruits must yet groan waiting for our adoption. . . . We cannot enjoy the fullness of salvation until we have it together in the fullness of body the church. The new man into which we would fain grow up is a corporate humanity, wherein all the redeemed from every tribe and tongue are made one harmonious whole. . . . We cannot "grow up in all things into him, which is the head" (Eph. 4:15), except by going out into the world to make all men one with us in the fullness of his body.[23]

Election

If salvation is thus intrinsically communal, and if thereby salvation is concrete, embodied, and within time, then salvation presupposes the existence of a concrete, embodied, historic community to which one can be gathered. On this account, salvation cannot be offered or grasped in an individual, spiritual, or after-worldly manner; it can be offered and received only through the presence of a group of people whose common life embodies the salvation that the gospel speaks about. It is here, Newbigin holds, that the notion of election comes in. That is, salvation presupposes the existence of that which it promises. And election is the way in which God establishes that which is being promised: the people of God.[24] Election is that "one race is chosen in order that through it God's salvation may be mediated to others, and it may thus become the nucleus of a new redeemed humanity."[25] As such, "the source of election is in the depths of God's gracious will 'before the foundation of the world'; its context is 'in Christ'; its instrument is the apostolic mission to the ends of the earth"—and, once again, underscoring this chapter's thesis, "its end is to sum up all things in Christ."[26]

Newbigin's account of election stands out from the ways his own Reformed tradition has conceived of election. On more traditional Reformed accounts,

---

23. Newbigin, *Household of God*, 140–41. Again, for similar themes expressed in the last phase of Newbigin's career, with reference to Eph. 1:10, see Newbigin, *Gospel in a Pluralist Society*, 110, 178–79.

24. On how, in distinction from an individualistic understanding of salvation, a corporate and cosmic salvation will necessarily lead to a doctrine of election, see Newbigin, *Household of God*, 141; Newbigin, *Open Secret*, 70–71; and Newbigin, *Gospel in a Pluralist Society*, 82–83.

25. Newbigin, *Household of God*, 100. See also Newbigin, *Open Secret*, 68–90; and Newbigin, *Gospel in a Pluralist Society*, 80–88.

26. Newbigin, *Household of God*, 103.

election leads to the formation of a community but does not presuppose the community's existence. Election means, as the Westminster Confession of Faith says, "the predestination unto everlasting life" (3.3). It is the determination of an individual's eternal fate. As such, one is joined to others who are similarly predestined, but community with others is not essential to being elected. For Newbigin, however, to be elected is to be made part of a people—a people whose peoplehood is determined by their being gathered by and around Christ: "We are not elect as isolated individuals, but as members in [Christ's] body."[27]

Church and Mission

Finally, this salvific, electing, gathering work of Jesus Christ becomes visible in the church: "The life of the visible church on earth is thus the reality within which alone the doctrine of election is to be understood. The church . . . is both the first-fruits and the instrument of God's gracious election, for his purpose is precisely the re-creation of the human race in Christ."[28] The church is, as Newbigin is wont to say, the foretaste, instrument, and sign of salvation. It is salvation's foretaste because already in the church what it means for God to be with God's people and for the people to be drawn into community with each other becomes visible and tangible. It is a salvific instrument because through this community others have a chance to be knitted into the gathering work of Christ. And the church is a sign of salvation because here God's eschatological reality becomes already visible.[29]

---

27. Newbigin, *Household of God*, 102. In George R. Hunsberger's otherwise very helpful study *Bearing the Witness of the Spirit*—in which he offers the most penetrating study of Newbigin's doctrine of election to date (45–112)—he contrasts Newbigin's account of election with that of Karl Barth. Barth speaks of election as "the sum of the gospel," because for him "election" refers to God's primal decision to be a God with humanity in Jesus Christ (Karl Barth, *Church Dogmatics* II/2, trans. G. W. Bromiley [T&T Clark, 1957], 13–14). According to Hunsberger, Newbigin, on the other hand, "would never see in election the content of the gospel, always its method"—that is, "God's acting personally and particularly in history, selecting a people to be uniquely his own" (85–86). However, on the reading of Newbigin I have offered here, this *is* exactly the content of the gospel: all things summed up in Christ, an act of gathering that finds visible expression in the formation of a people through the act of election. Because the gospel is about *being with*, there is no distinction between means and goal: the act of gathering *is* the act of salvation the gospel proclaims. In that sense, Barth and Newbigin are much closer to each other on the doctrine of election than Hunsberger suggests.

28. Newbigin, *Household of God*, 103.

29. On the relationship between foretaste, instrument, and sign as characteristics of the church, among many places, see Lesslie Newbigin, *A Word in Season: Perspectives on Christian World Missions* (Eerdmans, 1994), 59–64.

Newbigin's argument amounts to an authentic reclaiming of the early church's adage that "outside the church is no salvation."[30] Medieval ecclesiology had interpreted this patristic saying to mean that the church mediates salvation through the actions of the priesthood. On this interpretation, church and salvation are two different things, and one is obtained by way of the other. The Reformation's ecclesiology continued to understand church and salvation as distinct elements of the economy of salvation. However, in resisting the idea that salvation has to be acquired through the works of the church—and holding instead that salvation can be obtained directly by the believer as she trusts in the promises of the gospel through faith—the church became accidental to salvation. While the Reformers may not have intended this relegation of the church, in many subsequent Protestant ecclesiologies the church was conceived of as the result of believers' faith rather than as effecting such faith. On this understanding, faith can be kindled in many ways, not least by personal engagement with the Scriptures. The church, meanwhile, is the place where believers who recognize one another's faith come together to express and deepen it. The result of this is denominationalism: the fragmentation of the Christian community by theological, liturgical, and spiritual preferences. Theologians reconciled this dimension of the church to the New Testament's call for unity by employing a distinction between the visible and the invisible church. While the institutional, visible church may be broken, the invisible, true church was still united.[31] Over against this trajectory, Newbigin reclaims the essential relationship between church and salvation and denies the Protestant separation between the two. Newbigin does not conceive of the church as the mediator of salvation, as medieval theology had done, but rather *identifies* church with salvation: To be saved is to be knitted into the community of the church. With the Reformation, Newbigin emphasizes that salvation comes to us by grace and not by works. But salvation comes to us by incorporating us into the visible, embodied, concrete community of the church by the gathering work of Jesus Christ. Newbigin therefore rejects the visible-invisible distinction because it ignores how God establishes actual, concrete, embodied communities.[32] These

---

30. See Newbigin, *Household of God*, 142, 145: "This truth about the nature of salvation in Christ must obviously be determinative of the doctrine of the church. . . . St. Paul is working with a doctrine of the Church which is dominated by the hope of the coming consummation, a consummation which will be wholly the victory of God, but of which the witness of the Church is the sign and instrument, and of which its life is the foretaste."

31. For an analysis of this trajectory in Reformed theology, see Edwin Chr. van Driel, "Outside the (United) Church Is No Salvation," in *Liturgical-Missional: Perspectives on a Reformed Ecclesiology*, ed. Neal D. Presa (Pickwick, 2016), 244–78.

32. Newbigin, *Household of God*, 28–29, 56–57.

communities, in turn, are constituted not by doctrinal agreement but by Christ's salvific intervention.[33]

In *The Household of God*, Newbigin uses the same Christologically shaped vision of the church to criticize what he calls the Catholic and Pentecostal approach to ecclesiology. These two, together with the Protestant tradition, locate the *esse* of the church in something it *has* and *is now*—be it doctrinal unity (Protestantism), sacramental community (Roman Catholicism), or life in the Spirit (Pentecostalism). But if the church is constituted by Christ's gathering work, it cannot be rooted in past or present. Rather, it is rooted in the future because it is constituted by something that comes from beyond itself. The *esse* of the church is eschatological, and therefore the church ought to let its visible life be shaped by the eschatological uniting work of Christ rather than by current agreements or disagreements. For Newbigin, ecumenism should not be focused on finding doctrinal or liturgical or orderly consensus but on letting oneself be drawn into Christ together with believers of other doctrinal convictions and liturgical practice. As Newbigin says, invoking once more his favorite image from Ephesians, "The Church's unity is the sign and the instrument of the salvation which Christ has wrought and whose final fruition is the summing-up of all things in Christ. . . . In so far as we, who share that faith and that baptism, prove ourselves unwilling or unable to agree together in one fellowship, we publicly proclaim our disbelief in the sufficiency of that salvation."[34] Only by living in a visible unity, even when, and maybe especially when, that unity is one characterized by real diversity and disagreements, can the church fulfill its missional call to be a foretaste, instrument, and sign of salvation.[35]

---

33. Newbigin, *Household of God*, 59. In the moves Newbigin makes here, he can be said to offer an authentic *post-Protestant* ecclesiology: While incorporating the Reformers' rediscovery of grace, Newbigin overcomes their subsequent tendency to justify church schism and to make human confessional, liturgical, or spiritual agreement rather than divine grace constitutive of the church's existence.

34. Newbigin, *Household of God*, 149–50.

35. Newbigin, *Household of God*, 150–51. As Newbigin makes explicit, the ecclesiological vision developed in *The Household of God* wants to give voice to the lived ecclesiology of the Church of South India. In its 1947 unification of Anglicans, Methodists, Presbyterians, and Congregationalists, it found visible unity not by solving all doctrinal and liturgical differences but by constituting their common life on the recognition of Christ's gathering work among them all. With his book, Newbigin intended to interject this experience from the Global South into the ecumenical movement, which he thought to be in danger of getting stuck in Western denominationalism (Newbigin, *Household of God*, 18–20, 22, 24–25). As such, Newbigin's ecclesiology, which can be characterized as post-Protestant, is also one of the earliest *postcolonial* ecclesiologies. For the ways in which Newbigin's own theological and ecclesial development was bound up with the formation of the Church of South India, see Mark T. B. Laing, "The International Impact of the Formation of the Church of South India: Bishop Newbigin Versus the

J. C. Hoekendijk and Lesslie Newbigin

Newbigin's career paralleled that of the Dutch missiologist J. C. Hoekendijk. They met at the 1951 mission conference in Willingen, where Hoekendijk and the American Paul Lehmann attempted to "swing missionary thinking away from the 'church-centered' model which had dominated it since Tambaram and to speak more of God's work in the secular world, in the political, cultural and scientific movements of the time."[36] Over the next few decades, Hoekendijk's vision began to exert significant influence in missional and ecumenical conversations.[37] In his *The Church Inside Out*, Hoekendijk argues that the goal of mission is the establishment of God's messianic shalom: the redemption of the whole of creation, the destruction of all solitude, and the obliteration of all injustice.[38] Within this radical messianic work of transformation, the church is an instrument—and nothing more: "I believe in the church, which is a function of the apostolate, that is, an instrument of God's redemptive action in this world. . . . The church is (nothing more, but also nothing less!) a means in God's hands to establish shalom in this world."[39] The church proclaims this messianic shalom (kerygma), it lives it (koinonia), and it demonstrates it (diakonia); but within the ordering of these things, the church's life stands completely in the service of the church's kerygmatic and diaconal work.[40] This is, Hoekendijk holds, because the focus of God's messianic reign is the world and not the church. He writes, "The nature of the church can be sufficiently defined by its function, i.e., its participation in Christ's apostolic ministry. . . . The church lives for the world. . . . The church cannot be more than a sign. She points away from herself to the Kingdom; she lets herself be used for and through the Kingdom in the oikoumene.

Anglican Fathers," *International Bulletin of Missionary Research* 33 (2009): 18–34; Mark T. B. Laing, "The Indian Church and the Formation of Lesslie Newbigin's Ecclesiology," in *Theology in Missionary Perspective*, ed. Mark T. B. Laing and Paul Weston (Pickwick, 2012), 49–69; and the unpublished dissertation by Sherman, "*Ut Omnes Unum Sint*." See also Newbigin, *That All May Be One: A South India Diary* (Association, 1952); and Newbigin, *The Reunion of the Church*, rev. ed. (SCM, 1960).

36. Lesslie Newbigin, *Unfinished Agenda: An Updated Autobiography* (Wipf & Stock, 2009), 130.

37. Some even hold that the decade after Willingen inaugurated a "Hoekendijkian interlude" in which ecumenical and missional conversations moved away from a Christological, congregational focused paradigm to focus on societal and social issues, with a recovery of some of the old paradigm in the emergence of missional church conversations inspired by David Bosch, Wilbert Shenk, and Newbigin's later work. Thus the narrative in Michael W. Goheen and Timothy M. Sheridan, *Becoming a Missionary Church: Lesslie Newbigin and Contemporary Church Movements* (Baker Academic, 2022).

38. J. C. Hoekendijk, *The Church Inside Out* (Westminster, 1964), 21–22.

39. Hoekendijk, *Church Inside Out*, 24.

40. Hoekendijk, *Church Inside Out*, 30.

There is nothing that the church can demand for herself and can possess for herself.... The church exists only ... in the proclamation of the gospel of the Kingdom to the world."[41]

While Newbigin was sympathetic to Hoekendijk's understanding of mission as essential to the being of the church, Newbigin resisted the functional nature of the church in Hoekendijk's design.[42] From *The Household of God* onward, Newbigin emphasizes that the church can be a means and an end only *insofar as* it is a foretaste.

> The Church can only witness to ... the community of the Holy Spirit ... because her life is a *real* foretaste of it, a real participation in the life of God himself.... It is precisely because she is not *merely* instrumental that she can be instrumental.... The means by which the good news of salvation is propagated must be congruous with the nature of the salvation itself.... The Church's task is to reconcile men to God in Christ. She can only do that in so far as she is herself living in Christ, a reconciled fellowship in him, bound together in the love of the Father. This life in Christ is not merely the instrument of the apostolic mission, it is also its end and purpose.[43]

When we place this disagreement between Hoekendijk and Newbigin in the context of this chapter's argument, we can see that their disagreement is not primarily ecclesiological but primarily *Christological*. Like Newbigin, Hoekendijk holds that the church can fulfill its mission only insofar as she has her existence in *actu Christi* (i.e., in the act of Christ).[44] But they differ sharply in their understanding of what Christ actually does. Hoekendijk's book contains remarkably little Christology. In what he says it is nonetheless clear that, for Hoekendijk, the existence of Christ is no less functional than that of the church. The church exists for the sake of diakonia because

---

41. Hoekendijk, *Church Inside Out*, 42–43.

42. It may not be too much to say that one can detect in Newbigin's work a life-long wrestling with Hoekendijk's claims, with a particular fascination for Hoekendijk's "secular theology" in the 1960s. See Wainwright, *Lesslie Newbigin*, chaps. 7 and 10, esp. 341–54. At the same time, Newbigin never wavered from the criticism of Hoekendijk he formulated early on in the *Household of God*. See Newbigin, *Unfinished Agenda*, 130, 144, 165.

43. Newbigin, *Household of God*, 147–48. See also Newbigin, "Form and Structure of the Visible Unity of the Church," 128–29:

> Those who gather ... are the *pars pro toto*, the "first fruits" of the harvest which is intended to include all men.... Membership in the church involves communion with God the Father through Jesus Christ in the Holy Spirit. This is not a means to an end, but the true end of life itself. And yet, in another sense, it is not yet the end—for God's purpose is that all men should be brought in to this communion. The church is thus neither an end in itself, nor merely an instrument. It is the *arrabon*, the first-fruit, of God's purpose in Christ. Only as such is it also sign and instrument.

44. Hoekendijk, *Church Inside Out*, 41.

the Messiah exists for the sake of diakonia: "The whole story of the New Testament, with its variety of close-ups, revolves around this one theme. . . . Someone has come, not to be served . . . but to serve. Everything that was done by the Son of Man who came, Jesus Christ, including humiliation, self-emptying, cross, and death, is summarized in eight letters: diakonia."[45] The church lives "for the world" because it imitates a Messiah whose identity is determined by "self-emptying, service, solidarity with the people."[46] In other words, Hoekendijk has a *being for* Christology. Read through the lens of Newbigin's Christological account, Hoekendijk's argument misses a sense of Christ's *being with*. The Messiah is there to usher in the messianic age but is not that age's center. Christ works for the people but does not draw them to himself. He offers them his service but not his presence. This is exactly what drives Newbigin's critique. For him, Christ cannot be just a means to some end but is the end of all things, because the center of the gospel is that all things are being summed up into Christ.

Newbigin's Christological Narrative

If we place this analysis of the ways in which the Ephesians metaphor shapes Newbigin's thinking against a wider canvas of Christological conversations, what picture emerges? Throughout his writings, Newbigin maintains that the Christian faith first of all be understood as a claim about the course and goal of history. In contrast to other sacred books, the Bible is not so much interested in the individual's self, or in religious truth, but in narrating "human history as a whole, beginning with a saga of creation and ending with a vision of the gathering together of all the nations and the consummation of God's purpose for mankind. The Bible is an outline of world history."[47] What are the implications of Newbigin's emphasis on all things being summed up in Christ for the way one ought to understand the overall shape and rhythm of this history?

One way to think about the difference between infralapsarian and supralapsarian Christologies is as different ways to think about the relationship

---

45. Hoekendijk, *Church Inside Out*, 146.
46. Hoekendijk, *Church Inside Out*, 71.
47. Newbigin, *Honest Religion*, 20. In *The Gospel in a Pluralist Society*, Newbigin assigns this insight to a Hindu friend, who had pointed out to him it is a missional mistake to present the Bible as another book of religion, of which there are already plenty. What makes the Christian Scriptures different is that they assign meaning to history and claim that this meaning is embodied in a person (89, 97). For this aspect of Newbigin's thought, see Weston, *Humble Confidence*, 43–62.

between Christ and history. The infralapsarian view holds that God becomes human in order to take care of the sin problem. The incarnation is a divine intervention to put history back on track and to return creation to the originally intended relationship with God. On such a view, the incarnation, like sin itself, interrupts history; it is not part of its original design. It embodies a reconciling, atoning, and restorative act of God. It is within this context that the difference that Christ makes is understood. Salvation, election, and church are all countermeasures to sin. Mission is literally a rescue mission. It aims to draw people, and all of creation, away from its downward spiral and return it to its original intent. Hoekendijk's account is an example of infralapsarian Christology: Christ's coming is a function of the need for a diaconal intervention. By contrast, the Christological approach explored in this book believes that the infralapsarian Christological account is too narrow and that God has deeper motives for the incarnation than a desire to remedy the sin problem. On this account, the incarnation is not an otherwise-unintended intervention, contingent upon sin, but is the very reason God created in the first place. In calling forth that which is not God, God first decides to be a God-with-others, an intention that is embodied in the person of Jesus Christ. God then decides to call forth humanity, and all of creation, to be this Jesus's companions and friends. This does not exclude the idea that it is also through the incarnate One that God counters sin and draws creation back to Godself when this creation refuses to be with God and wanders away from God. In that sense, this view is not meant as an alternative to infralapsarian Christology. Rather, it includes redemption in a larger theological imagination—according to which God intends, from the beginning, that all of creation be gathered into Christ. Christ is thus the goal of history. The difference he makes is first of all eschatological, in that his appearance inaugurates the realization of God's ultimate intentions for creation. Salvation, election, and church are the outworking of these intentions—they are the ways in which Christ's gathering work becomes visible and begins to be realized. Mission, in turn, is the way in which Christ enacts this gathering work and draws creation into the telos for which it was created: to be Jesus's companions and friends.

    I suggest that, given the conceptual structures of his missional-ecumenical project that I have surfaced in this chapter, Newbigin's account of the gathering Christ—and of salvation, election, and church—can be best understood as an expression of supralapsarian Christology. This is not to argue that Newbigin himself claims to be of the supralapsarian Christological tribe; as far as I am aware, the debate between infralapsarian and supralapsarian Christologies never makes it into his writings. This is also not to argue that, if the question were to be put to him, Newbigin would readily embrace a supralapsarian point of view. There simply is not enough in Newbigin's work to supply such an argument. As a matter of fact, there are some passages in which Newbigin seems to espouse an infralapsarian narrative—in particular, where he characterizes the difference Christ makes as a "restoration."[48] This suggests that Christ is simply an instrument to return creation to how it once was. But then, by contrast, there is also a passage like this: "There is a way in which the doctrine of election has been distorted by separating it from the doctrine of Christ. . . . It is in Jesus Christ that, as Paul says, we are elect from the foundation of the world. Jesus is not a latecomer into the world. He is the one in whom and through whom and for whom we and all things exist."[49] Such a statement simply cannot be made within an infralapsarian Christological design, in which Christ precisely *is* a latecomer into the world. On such a view, all things do not exist for Christ, but Christ exists for all things. Newbigin's statement makes sense only within a supralapsarian Christological account.

The center of my argument for a supralapsarian reading of Newbigin's Christology is simply the image from Ephesians of all things summed up in Christ. This image speaks of an eschatological future in which all of humanity, in all its diversity and difference, is joined together in a common life in which harmony and peace permeate the whole cosmos and in which the center of all this is the glorious, embodied divine presence of the incarnate One. In all of this, God does much more for creation than overcome sin, more than repair what is broken, and more than restore creation's original design. This is an eschatological future shaped by a divine presence, which, in its intimacy and embodiment, goes far beyond creation's original baseline. The harmony of this eschatological life goes far beyond anything creation has ever experienced.

---

48. See Newbigin, *Household of God*, 140, 141. As I observed above, the Christological impetus of Newbigin's ecumenical-missional project has received remarkably little attention in the secondary literature. Those who do reflect on Newbigin's Christology either ignore the issues I raise here (as Jürgen Schuster does in his *Christian Mission in Eschatological Perspective*, where he explores Newbigin's understanding of the kingdom of God and attempts to offer a systematic description of Newbigin's account of the story of God with creation [155–70] but never analyzes the nature and rhythm of Newbigin's Christological narrative) or read him as expounding a Christology focused on recovery and restoration (as Goheen does in *The Church and Its Vocation*, 26–39). None of these authors observes the centrality of the Christological point about all things being summed up in Christ for Newbigin's theological imagination, and thus they also miss its constructive theological implications.

49. Newbigin, *Gospel in a Pluralist Society*, 86. It is highly likely that Newbigin makes this remark influenced by his retirement reading of Karl Barth's *Church Dogmatics*, which is a thoroughgoing supralapsarian Christological design. As he tells in his autobiography, in the early 1950s Newbigin had encountered Barth in several committees of the WCC they both served on; but it was only in retirement in the 1970s that he read through the *Church Dogmatics* and found it "an immensely rewarding experience." Newbigin, *Unfinished Agenda*, 228; see also 109–111, 123–24, 131, 164.

An infralapsarian account has difficulty making sense of this theologically. If incarnation is only a countermeasure to sin, there is no need for this eschatological superabundance.[50] This makes the idea of all things being summed up in Christ an unstable element in an infralapsarian theological design.

The opposite is true for the supralapsarian Christological approach. For the supralapsarian, Ephesians's vision expresses the purpose of creation's existence. On such a reading, to *be with* is at the very heart of the cosmos. God decided to be Jesus Christ—that is, God decided to be with what is not God and called all of creation into existence to be Jesus's friends and companions. Creation's history is nothing but the unfolding of this divine intention. Salvation is the enactment of God's eschatological purposes. Election is the name for the formation of the firstborn's large family (Rom. 8:29). The church is the place where God's dwelling among God's creatures is already experienced (Eph. 2:19–21). Christ's gathering of all things is what the gospel is all about.

Newbigin and the Need for a New Soteriological Narrative

In several recent articles, Dutch missiologist Stefan Paas observes that new missional communities in the West are in need of a fresh, coherent soteriological narrative. Old narratives, especially of an evangelical orientation, have lost cultural relevance and plausibility. Many of these narratives are predicated on the idea that the gospel is God's response to the sin problem. This means that, in order to invite people into the gospel, they first need to be told that they are sinners. This is no longer acceptable or intelligible to many people, which makes the communication of the gospel both difficult and embarrassing. Other parts of these narratives are shaped by highly individualistic notions of the believer and his or her agency. This sits uncomfortably with current missional practices, which focus on forging relationships and building community. Because of this, traditional soteriological narratives function for many practitioners as a negative benchmark. A convincing alternative is lacking, however. As a result, many practitioners focus on the *what* and *how* of mission as opposed to the *why*. In the long run, this lack of reflective accounting may lead to uncertainty about the whole missional enterprise.[51]

---

50. The infralapsarian way out is to say that, since it is given to us nonetheless, sin, in the end, was a felicitous occurrence: O *felix culpa!* This approach brings, however, its own significant theological problems. See Van Driel, *Incarnation Anyway*, 127–32, 151–53, 165–66.

51. Stefan Paas and Hans Schaeffer, "Reconciled Community: On Finding a Soteriology for Fresh Expressions," *Ecclesiology* 17 (2021): 325–47; Stefan Paas, Sake Stoppels, and Karen Zwijze-Koning, "Ministers on Salvation: Soteriological Views of Pioneers and Pastors in the Protestant Church in the Netherlands," *Journal of Empirical Theology* 35, no. 2 (2022): 1–20;

I believe the reading of Newbigin's Christological narrative offered in this chapter contains the contours of such a convincing alternative soteriological story. It is a story shaped by five characteristics. First, relationships and community are at the very core of what the story is about. It is a story about *being with*, about Christ gathering all things into himself. People are saved by being knit into the community Christ draws around himself. Community formation is not distinct from salvation; salvation is given, received, and experienced precisely in being gathered into Christ's community. Second, as such, this community formation overcomes old and tired oppositions between *vertical* and *horizontal* relationships and missional orientations. A new humanity is being formed out of people with many different convictions and from many different walks of life—a vision that translated into Newbigin's missional and ecumenical work—the center of which is God incarnate. Third, this is a narrative about a community of reconciliation. Knitting together people from a variety of backgrounds includes overcoming difference, learning to live with conflict, and finding healing for past hurts. But reconciliation is a means in the service of a larger goal; it is embedded in a larger vision. The story of sin and forgiveness is, therefore, not the required entryway into this community; rather, the story of a gathering God is. Fourth, this gathering work is progressive, and therefore, while it has a clear center—the incarnate One—its boundaries are fuzzy and change all the time. Christ draws all things into himself, but this drawing is an ongoing process in which people find themselves relating in a great variety of ways, levels of intensity, and degrees of closeness to one another and to the one who is drawing them. This fits the reality of our new missional era and gives the theological justification for letting this process play out with patience and forbearance. And finally, fifth, as such this is a story that describes an intrinsically missional process. This is the *missio Dei*! But at the same time, it is an intrinsically ecclesial process: The gathering work of Christ becomes visible as people are knitted into concrete, embodied communities in which they already taste and see the future that God has in store for them.

Stefan Paas, "Soteriology in Evangelical Practice: A View from the Street," *Exchange* 51 (2022): 323–42.

PART 2

Constructive Explorations

In part 1, I engaged several voices and ideas from the history of theology that can function as building blocks for a narration of the story of God and what is not God set in a supralapsarian Christological key. Before I explore some of the constructive contours of such a narrative in the next seven chapters, it may be helpful to first gather some of the insights generated in the previous chapters. I can count at least five:

First, the fundamental intuition that undergirds this book is that the very first divine intention vis-à-vis that which is not God is to become incarnate. That is, God's first decision is to be Jesus Christ, and everything that is not God is created in the context of, and for the sake of, this decision. In this decision, God decides to be a God-*with*-others. As John Duns Scotus argues, God becomes incarnate for the sake of love, and since incarnation is first in the divine intentions, love is the center of the universe. This love thus has a particular face—that of Jesus—and, as I suggested we interpret Scotus's argument, this love has an addressee: humanity and creation, called into existence to receive this love.

Second, embedded in this understanding of the motivation for the incarnation is thus an understanding of an ontological over-againstness. God identifies with a human being so as to *be with* other human beings who are not God but are created to be the incarnate One's family and friends. Chalcedon gives us the language to further unpack these claims. In the incarnation, God takes on and personifies a human nature. When we meet the incarnate One, *what* we meet is a human nature, but *who* we meet is the Creator God. Everything this human nature is, does, and undergoes is, is done, and is undergone by God. Through this incarnate One, the invisible, awesome God can now engage little critters like us, human beings: God can walk with us, sit with us, engage with us, have a meal with us. God can engage us in interpersonal relationships—God is *with us*.

Third, what fuels this understanding of the divine motives for the incarnation are, among other parts of the Scriptural narrative, the events of Christ's resurrection and ascension. Christ's mission is not complete upon his death on the cross. He does not lay down his humanity once the work of atonement and reconciliation has been accomplished. Resurrection and ascension, and the ongoing nature of the incarnation, open up vistas of an eschatological life decisively shaped by intimacy with the divine presence gifted to us in the incarnation. In this is an eschatological superabundance that cannot be sufficiently explained on an infralapsarian Christological framework.

Fourth, the insight that the incarnation is essentially bound up with the eschaton and is, therefore, first in the order of divine decisions (as a well-ordered decider, God decides on ends before means) in turn raises the question, Which other divine intentions and commitments should be understood as supralapsarianly located? That is, the idea that everything that exists is embedded in, and called into being for the sake of, the incarnate One invites us to rethink the whole ordering of the narrative about God relating to what is not God. Central to the reordering of this narrative is a supralapsarian commitment to community formation: God creates us to *be with* God and, thereby, to *be with* one another, as Christ gathers all things into himself.

Fifth and finally, such a fresh telling of the "story of everything" has the potential to create new ways in which the Christian community might relate missionally to a culture that is setting aside its Christian heritage as worn, tired, and irrelevant.

With these insights in hand, I turn next to a set of constructive explorations of the theological potential of this way of understanding the story of God and all that is not God.

7

"All Things Have Been Created . . . for Him"

On Christ, Election, and Creation

What happens when we read the doctrine of election as a doctrine centered on the incarnation? That is, what happens when we take seriously Paul's statement that election is for the sake of being "conformed to the image of [the] Son, in order that he might be the firstborn within a large family" (Rom. 8:29)? Or the notion in Ephesians that God chose the elect "in Christ before the foundation of the world[,] . . . destined us for adoption as [God's] children through Jesus Christ, according to the good pleasure of his will" (Eph. 1:4–5)? And what if we were to take seriously the further claim that this incarnationally focused act of divine election, this "good pleasure that [God] set forth in Christ," results in the unfolding of "a plan for the fullness of time, to gather up all things in him, things in heaven and things on earth" (Eph. 1:9–10), because "all things have been created through him and for him" (Col. 1:16)? This chapter offers an answer to these questions, setting the stage for a theological program for rethinking the relationship between Christ and election and, embedded in this, the divine intention for creation as it moves from the proton to the eschaton. The aim is to take the themes developed in the previous chapters and apply them now in constructive directions.

Of course, I am not the first to observe that the doctrine of election and the doctrine of the incarnation ought to go hand in hand. Augustine pointed out that the incarnation itself is a form of election. On a Chalcedonian framework, in the incarnation the second person of the Trinity takes a human nature as his own. This human nature is a particular nature among many. Any human nature is assumable; that the divine Word takes on this particular nature is a form of election. Moreover, there is no intrinsic reason why the Word would assume this nature rather than another; its election is therefore an expression of grace.[1]

Working with this Augustinian insight, medieval theologian John Duns Scotus argues that Christ's election is best understood as a supralapsarian decision of God. Scotus premises this idea on the notion that every purposefully acting person sets a goal before deciding on the means to achieve the goal. Election destines someone for eschatological bliss—the enjoyment of God. For a human, the means to reach eschatological bliss are faith and love, the opposite of which are unbelief and sin. As a well-ordered decider God determines people's eschatological bliss before taking into account whether or not they have the means of faith and love. God also elects people therefore before sin enters into consideration. Election is thus supralapsarian.[2] Turning to Christology, Scotus observes that incarnation is not only a form of election but is also the predestination of a particular human nature to bliss in the hypostatic union with the divine Word. Since predestination is supralapsarian, so is the predestination of the human nature of Christ. Moreover, to be assumed as the very human nature of Godself is the highest form of enjoyment of God that a nature could experience. A most-ordered decider will not only determine a purpose before determining the means of achieving it but will also decide on the most-central object of the purpose before deciding on those that are included in the purpose at a greater distance. Christ's human nature, therefore, must be predestined first. Not only is the incarnation supralapsarian; it also has priority over everything else.[3]

Finally, Reformed theologian Karl Barth held that election is not simply a predestination of Christ's human nature or a prioritizing of incarnation but is, rather,

---

1. Augustine writes, "There is also the most brilliant beacon of predestination and of grace, the savior himself, the very mediator between God and human beings, the man Jesus Christ. By what preceding merits of his, either of works or of faith, did the human nature which is him obtain such a dignity?" Augustine, *The Predestination of the Saints*, in *Answer to the Pelagians*, trans. Roland J. Teske, ed. John E. Rotelle, The Works of Saint Augustine I/4 (New City Press, 1999), 15.30–31. See also Augustine, *The Gift of Perseverance*, in *Answer to the Pelagians*, trans. Roland J. Teske, ed. John E. Rotelle, The Works of Saint Augustine I/4 (New City Press, 1999), 24.67.

2. See, e.g., Scotus, *Lectura*, in *Duns Scotus on Divine Love: Texts and Commentary on Goodness and Freedom, God and Humans*, ed. A. Vos, H. Veldhuis, E. Dekker, N. W. den Bok, A. J. Beck (Ashgate, 2003), 1.41.

3. See Scotus' *Ordinatio*, in *Franciscan Christology: Selected Texts, Translations and Introductory Essays*, ed. Damian McElrath (St. Bonaventure University, 1980), 3.7.3. For an analysis of Scotus's supralapsarian Christology, see chap. 1, above.

first and foremost a form of divine self-determination. God's first decision has a twofold determination. It is a choice of the other, an election that chooses "the other to fellowship with himself." But it is also, and preeminently, "a self-election [by God] in favor of this other."[4] God "determines the human for himself, having first determined himself for the human."[5] God determines "that he should not be entirely self-sufficient as he might be." God determines to reach out to what is not God, and the character of this divine reaching out is one of self-giving: "God constitutes himself as benefit or favor."[6] God determines to unite Godself with the other, and the embodiment of this determination is the incarnation.

In this programmatic chapter, I offer an argument in the tradition of Augustine, John Duns Scotus, and Karl Barth. With Augustine, I believe that incarnation is itself a form of election; with John Duns Scotus, I hold that this election ought to be understood as supralapsarian; with Karl Barth, I argue that this supralapsarian election is, first of all, a form of divine self-determination. Further, I offer material content to these rather formal observations about the nature of election and Christology. In particular, I argue that in the incarnation God moves to be *with* creation. In becoming Jesus Christ, God intends to create a family, a circle of friends to whom God comes as close as God can—by coming among them as a human creature. I argue that this reading makes the most sense of the supralapsarian Christological motives we find particularly in Paul's letters and the Gospel of John. Election, I argue, is the name of this family formation. And as election is primordially God's relating to what is not God, this in turn becomes a hermeneutical lens through which to view creation, Israel, the church, and creation's eschatological future.[7]

The Firstborn of All Creation

I would like to introduce my argument as a theological reflection on the Colossians hymn, which praises Christ:

> Who is the image of the invisible God,
>   the firstborn of all creation,
>   because in him were created

---

4. Karl Barth, *Church Dogmatics* II/2, trans. G. W. Bromiley (T&T Clark, 1957), 10.
5. Barth, *Church Dogmatics* II/2, 91.
6. Barth, *Church Dogmatics* II/2, 10.
7. I call this a programmatic chapter, first, because it sets the framework for further discussions on these doctrinal topics, particularly in chaps. 8 (Israel), 12 (the eschaton), and 13 (the church) and, second, because it sketches some of the contours of the multivolume supralapsarian Christology for which this book is an interim report.

> all things in heaven and on earth;
> the visible and the invisible things,
> whether thrones or lordships,
> whether rulers or authorities—
> all things have been created through and for him.
> And he is before all things,
> and all things have been held together in him.
>
> And he is the head of the body, the church,
> who is the beginning,
> the firstborn from the dead,
> in order that he may be holding the first place in all things,
> because in him was pleased to dwell the fullness,
> and through him to reconcile all things to himself,
> having made peace through the blood of his cross,
> whether the things on earth or in heaven. (Col. 1:15–19, my trans.)

Four exegetical observations can be made about this text. First, the hymn concerns the incarnate Christ, who as such is said to relate to God and creation as God's image (*eikōn*) and creation's firstborn (*prōtotokos*). That is, the subject of the hymn is not the *logos asarkos*, the non-incarnate Word, or wisdom as it existed before the creation of the world, or the second person of the Trinity.[8] The hymn sings of Christ in the flesh. This is clear from the outset as the Colossians writer comes to the hymn having just spoken of the economy of salvation, in which the Father is said to have rescued the gentile readers of the letter from the power of darkness and given them a share in the heritage of the saints, the chosen ones, by ushering them into the kingdom of the beloved Son (Col. 1:12–14). This one, the Son in whom all this has come about, is the *he* to whom the opening lines of the hymn refers. This one is said to be God's *eikōn*, the one who makes the invisible God visible.[9] This cannot be said of the *logos asarkos*, the second person of the Trinity. The divine Word in and of itself is just as invisible as the Father and the Spirit. But the triune Godhead becomes visible as the Son takes on flesh. As he takes on flesh, he does not do so as one among many but as the *prōtotokos*, a word that stands both for first in birth order and preeminence in rank.[10]

---

8. Pace many of the church fathers. See the essays in Peter Gorday, ed., *Colossians, 1–2 Thessalonians, 1–2 Timothy, Titus, Philemon*, Ancient Christian Commentary on Scripture 9 (IVP Academic, 2000), 12–21.

9. *Eikōn* connotes a physical representation. See Markus Barth and Helmut Blanke, *Colossians: A New Translation with Introduction and Commentary*, Anchor Bible 34B (Doubleday, 1994), 195; and Scot McKnight, *The Letter to the Colossians* (Eerdmans, 2018), 147.

10. *Eikōn* and *prōtotokos* are thus notions that refer to the selfsame action of the Son, be it under different aspects: the incarnate Son in his relationship to God (*eikōn*) and in his

Second, the hymn's extraordinarily artful composition reveals that it is meant as a concentrated Christological gloss on the creation story. The evidence for this is gathered in a recent essay by New Testament scholar Richard Bauckham.[11] Each of the hymn's two sections (vv. 15–17 and 18–20) consists of fifty-five words. Fifty-five is a triangular number, which ancient people regarded as significant. This tells us from the get-go that we should not read the text as a composite of different sources but as a carefully orchestrated poem.[12] This impression is underscored by another numerical aspect of the text. A central notion of this poem is the Greek word *pas* and its plural *panta* (all). With reference to creation, it is used seven times—echoing the special role of this number in the Hebrew Scriptures, not least in Genesis 1. The word *pas* is used an eighth time in reference to God: In Christ the whole fullness (*pan to plērōma*) of God dwells (v. 19). Thus, in the text, the whole of creation in all its diversity is indicated by the seven occurrences of *all*, and the uniqueness of God is expressed by the single reference to all God's fullness.[13] Another recurring word is *autos*, which occurs eleven times, all referencing the one whose name is not mentioned in the hymn at all: Jesus. Bauckham points out that in all its declined forms *autos* has five letters, and therefore the total number of letters used in the hymn to reference Jesus is fifty-five.[14] In other words, the numerical structure of the hymn in and of itself focuses the attention on God and creation, and in a way that weaves Christ into every aspect of this relationship. To this Bauckham adds the observation that two of the text's key Christological notions, *archē* (beginning) and *eikōn* (image), are drawn from Genesis's creation story.[15] The ways these notions function in the hymn invite the reader to see Christ as central both to the story of creation and to the story of recreation.

Third, the text anchors creation's Christological determination by way of three prepositions: All things are created *in*, *by*, and *for* the incarnate One. That is, Christ is the context within which all other creatures live and move

---

relationship to creation (*prōtotokos*). See Barth and Blanke, *Colossians*, 194: "Both titles, 'image' and 'firstborn Son' are closely associated with each other; they are grounded and explained by the causative clause in v. 16: the 'image and son of God' are in a direct relationship to all of creation." That *prōtotokos* should not be read as referring to an inner-trinitarian relationship is also underscored by its use in v. 18: he is also the "*prōtotokos* from the dead," clearly referencing the Son in his incarnate relationship to creation. As Barth and Blanke point out, "It is unlikely that the same title is used within the hymn in a different way" (207).

11. Richard Bauckham, "Confessing the Cosmic Christ (I Corinthians 8:6 and Colossians 1:15–20)," in *Monotheism and Christology in Greco-Roman Antiquity*, ed. Matthew V. Novenson, Supplements to Novum Testamentum 180 (Brill, 2020), 138–71.
12. Bauckham, "Confessing the Cosmic Christ," 148.
13. Bauckham, "Confessing the Cosmic Christ," 150.
14. Bauckham, "Confessing the Cosmic Christ," 150.
15. Bauckham, "Confessing the Cosmic Christ," 156–57.

and have their being; he is the instrument through whom they have been called into existence; and he is the intended goal for whom they were created in the first place. The text does not further explicate what these extraordinary claims mean. This task is left to the theologian. But it is clear from the start that the logic of the text cuts off significant avenues of theological reflection. Jesus does not exist for the sake of creation. His appearance is not a chapter added to creation's original narrative, brought in to troubleshoot when history goes off track. Rather, all of creation exists for him.

Fourth, while the text does not limit Christ's presence and work to the need for reconciliation and divine redemption, it does not deny his centrality to these aspects of God's relating to what is not God. Rather the opposite is true: The hymn's second verse is completely devoted to cross and resurrection. But the text does set forth an explicit logic for the relationship between these various aspects of Christ's role and work. Christ is the firstborn from the dead *so that* he may be first in everything (v. 18). In other words, the hymn calls for an account of cross and resurrection that is contingent upon the incarnate One's primacy in creation.[16]

Taking these observations together, the Colossians hymn demands a supralapsarian Christology. An infralapsarian account, in which the incarnation is contingent upon sin, simply cannot make sense of the logic of the text. On an infralapsarian Christology, Christ exists for the sake of the world—the incarnation happens to take care of the sin problem. But on the hymn's logic, it is the other way around: The world exists for the sake of Christ.

Thus, not only does the hymn demand a supralapsarian Christology; it implies the primacy of Christ. Supralapsarian Christologies come in different kinds. Their commonality rests in the way they embed God's incarnational relating to what is not God in a reality deeper than the dynamic of sin and forgiveness. These Christologies differ in their understanding of why the incarnation happened. Some supralapsarian accounts think of the incarnation as the way in which God completes creation. Without it, creation would be missing its center.[17] Others conceive of it as the means by which God draws

---

16. Obviously, while the logic of the Colossians hymn takes its starting point in Christ's primacy in creation, historically the Christian kerygma begins with Christ's crucifixion and resurrection. Elsewhere I have given an account of how the Colossians writer—whom, following such exegetes as Markus Barth and Helmut Blanke, as well as N. T. Wright and Douglas A. Campbell, I take to be the apostle Paul—may have inferred Christ's primacy in creation from Christ's centrality in God's act of reconciliation and eschatological consummation. For this, see Edwin Chr. van Driel, *Rethinking Paul: Protestant Theology and Pauline Exegesis* (Cambridge University Press, 2021), 281–82.

17. Such an approach is reflected in many medieval supralapsarian arguments. See Robert Grosseteste, *On the Cessation of the Laws*, trans. Stephen M. Hildebrand (Catholic University of America Press, 2012), 3.1.3.

creation to Godself. As both human and divine, the incarnate One bridges an otherwise unending qualitative difference.[18] On either account, the incarnation is still serving a larger goal. Christ still exists for the sake of creation. But according to the Colossians hymn, all things have been created for Christ. Christ does not come to complete or elevate a preconceived reality; rather, he precedes all things.

Finally, the hymn says not only that all things have been created for Christ but that they have been created in him and by him. The incarnate Christ himself stands at the beginning of all things. This calls for an account in which it makes sense to talk about the incarnate One's existence before he has come into being. Christ is at work before he was born, not just in his divinity, but already in his humanity. It is a humanity that at that point exists only in God's intentionality but that, as such, already determines the identity of the one who at some point will embody it. He is both the second person of the Trinity and the firstborn of creation. While exploring this would go far beyond the confines of this chapter, a theological anthropology and a doctrine of creation may be implied here, since the hymn evokes not only an image of a God whose identity is determined by the decision to be creation's firstborn but also an image of a God in whose intentionality all of creation is already called into being before it exists, as it is held together in him.

Being With

If all things were created for Christ, then by implication the very first decision God made in relation to that which is not God did not concern "all things"; it concerned Christ. God's first decision must have been to *be* Jesus Christ. If God had not decided beforehand to be Jesus Christ, it would not have been possible to create all things for him. No other decision can be prior to this, because if God had any intentions regarding that which is not God prior to God's intention to be Jesus Christ, it could not then be said that "all things" are for the sake of him.[19]

---

18. This strategy is employed by Schleiermacher, for example. See Friedrich Schleiermacher, *Christian Faith*, trans. Terrence N. Tice, Catherine L. Kelsey, and Edwina Lawler, 2 vols. (Westminster John Knox, 2016), §164. See also Edwin Chr. van Driel, *Incarnation Anyway: Arguments for Supralapsarian Christology* (Oxford University Press, 2008), 22–25.

19. *First*, *prior*, and *beforehand* are all theologically loaded terms. Classical theology has wanted to think about God as beyond time and would therefore suggest we understand these terms as expressing a logical ordering rather than a time sequence. I sympathize with this suggestion. Similarly, theologians have argued that God should not be thought of as engaging in several decisions; God's will is one, and there is one eternal act of divine willing. John Duns Scotus therefore suggests we distinguish between "moments" or "instances" within the divine

If God's first decision was to be Jesus Christ, then God's first decision with regard to what is not God was a form of self-determination. It involved creation, but first of all it involved Godself. In fact, it was a form of election. God determined for Godself a future. And the content of this self-determination was an act of self-giving. In deciding to be Jesus Christ—that is, in deciding to become incarnate—God determined to give Godself to that which is not God. It is an act in which God establishes that which is not God as the recipient of Godself. But Barth is right: It is first of all an act in which God decides to be a particular kind of God. God determines to be God-with-others. In deciding to become incarnate, God determines to be a God who is *with* creatures.

As I discussed in chapter 5, in several publications Samuel Wells reflects on the difference between *being with* and *being for*. *Being for*, along with its more active partner *working for*, describes attitudes and relationships built on a perceived need. It assumes a deficit that can be remedied, a problem that needs to be solved. It describes relationships that do not demand that the relating parties engage one another for the relationship's own sake. The relationships are functional, constituted by and focused on the work that must be done. *Being with* is fundamentally different. It describes a relationship in which the partners enjoy one another for the sake of enjoying one another. *Being with* is not based on a deficiency that needs to be remedied, a problem that needs to be solved. It is not a relationship contingent upon a larger goal; *the relationship is the goal*. Infralapsarian Christologies unpack the difference Christ makes in terms of *being for* and *working for*. Supralapsarian Christologies understand the primary reason for the incarnation in terms of *being with*.[20]

The Colossians hymn itself does not explicate *why* God decides to be a God-with-others and to become Jesus Christ. The hymn's logic implies that God's determination to become incarnate logically and ontologically precedes all things, but it does not go further in addressing the divine intentions. In other texts this divine intention comes closer to the surface. In Romans 8 Paul writes that "those whom he foreknew he also predestined to

---

will, rather than different acts of willing (see Scotus, *Reportatio Parisiensis* 3.7.4). Finally, some theologians object to the notion of divine *decisions*, as if God were to make choices among alternative courses of action. I am not very concerned about these objections. I would, however, be happy to translate the notion of decision I employ in this section into the notion of intentionality. It strikes me that, whatever particular concept of divine willing we favor, Christian theologians ought to agree that God's will has a particular intention. Thus, at a minimum, the question at stake is, What intention shapes the incarnation?

20. Samuel Wells, *A Nazareth Manifesto: Being With God* (Wiley Blackwell, 2015). See also Samuel Wells, *Incarnational Ministry: Being With the Church* (Eerdmans, 2017), 7–10; and Samuel Wells and Marcia A. Owen, *Living Without Enemies: Being Present in the Midst of Violence* (InterVarsity Press, 2011), esp. 19–47. I analyze Wells's exploration of Jesus's ministry as an embodiment of *being with* as a form of supralapsarian Christology in chap. 5, above.

be conformed to the image of his Son, in order that he might be the firstborn [*prōtotokos*] within a large family" (Rom. 8:29). The goal of election is for the Son not to be alone but to be, rather, the center of a community. Again, notice the ordering here. The Son does not come for the sake of the elect, but the elect are gathered for the sake of the Son. And the divine intentionality behind this election is family formation. To be elected is to be determined to be the Son's eschatological company and friend. The goal of election is *being with*. If this is the case, then in addition to saying something about the election of God's creatures, Paul is also says something here about the election of Godself—and, thereby, about the motive for the incarnation. *Being with* is not an instrumental relationship. It has no larger goal in mind; it is its own goal. *Being with* is the simple act of mutual enjoyment. This means that if creatures are elected to *be with* the elected God, God becomes incarnate for the sake of the enjoyment of *being with* God's creatures.

Once we take hold of the notion of incarnation as primarily motivated by God's intention to *be with*, we can observe it right under the surface of many other texts. For example, the Ephesians letter speaks of the plan that God has for the fullness of time, "to gather up all things in [Christ], things in heaven and things on earth" (Eph. 1:10). It is a plan that has been set in motion in the death, resurrection, and ascension of Christ, as he is now knitting Jews and gentiles together into a new humanity, a new household of God, with Christ as the cornerstone (Eph. 2:15, 20). No reason for this plan, which preceded "the foundation of the world" (1:4), is given other than its grand finale: God living among God's people, who are "a holy temple in the Lord[,] ... built together spiritually into a dwelling place for God" (2:21–22). The goal is to be with Jesus. Likewise, John's prologue offers a retelling of the Genesis creation story through the lens of the incarnation. Its opening scene takes us to a beginning before Genesis's beginning, narrating the speaking of the Word, a speaking that is life; and this life is the light—the light that is the very presence of the Word and that seems to come closer and closer until it becomes visible to all as the Word steps onto the world scene on Christmas night. "The true light, which enlightens everyone, was coming into the world" (John 1:9). This in turn expresses something about the nature of the world: "He was in the world, and the world came into being through him. . . . He came to what was his own" (vv. 10–11). This world is not strange to the Word. It is the place he calls his own. It is a place created to host the Word, to be the Word's home. The world is created with an eye to the Word's incarnation and his taking up residence in creation. The world is meant to be the stage, the theater, of God's *being with* God's creatures. It is the place where the Word tabernacles and lives among us (v. 14), making visible the one who otherwise cannot be seen (v. 18).[21]

Creation

That all things have been created for Christ has implications not only for our understanding of God and of Christ but also for our understanding of creation. *Creation is intended to be the recipient of God's presence.* This is the deepest word that can be said about creation. Humanity is created to be Jesus's family. The earth is created to be Jesus's home. All of creation is to be gathered up in him. Creation is meant to be with God.

Ultimately, *being with* is an eschatological category. The plan to gather up all things in Christ is for "the fullness of time." *Being with* God describes the ultimate future God has in mind for that which is not God. In and of itself, the act of creation has no eschatological direction. God is under no obligation to give creatures, who essentially have a limited existence, a future beyond their natural lifespan. But on the logic of the argument I am exploring, the divine act of creation is embedded in the divine intention to *be with* creation.[22]

The theological name for God's determination of creation as the recipient of the divine *being with* is election. Election is the determination of the creature for eternal bliss, says John Duns Scotus.[23] That is as good a definition as any. The creature's eternal bliss is to be with God. The plan to gather up all things in Christ at the fullness of time is expressed in God's choosing us "in Christ before the foundation of the world to be holy and blameless before

---

21. I develop three further arguments for supralapsarian Christology in Van Driel, *Incarnation Anyway*, 150–62.

22. Some theologians are concerned about telling the biblical story in a way that would subject the diverse ways of divine relating to a monolithic theological logic. The most articulate objections of this kind come from David H. Kelsey, who argues that the biblical narrative is best understood as telling the story of a threefold divine way of relating to that which is not God—in creation, eschatological consummation, and reconciliation. These three ways are complexly interrelated, but each has its own logic and integrity. See David H. Kelsey, *Eccentric Existence: A Theological Anthropology* (Westminster John Knox, 2009), esp. 120–31. It strikes me that Kelsey is completely correct in pointing out the different logic of God's threefold relating to what is not God. Kelsey is also correct when, in the course of his argument, he emphasizes that the theological logic of creation does not entail "that God must necessarily also draw what is created to eschatological consummation or that God must reconcile them if they are alienated from God" (121–22). The question, however, is how we tease out the relationships among the threefold divine relating. On the logic of *being with*, God's act of creation has an eschatological intention and direction. In this respect, Barth is correct: The covenant is the internal basis for creation (Barth, *Church Dogmatics* III/1, 231).

23. John Duns Scotus, *Ordinatio* 3.7.3, in *Franciscan Christology: Selected Texts, Translations and Introductory Essays*, ed. Damian McElrath (Franciscan Institute, 1980), 147.

[God] in love" (Eph. 1:4). In this choosing, we are "destined . . . for adoption as [God's] children" (Eph. 1:5). Creation is thus embedded in election because creation is embedded in God's self-determination to be Jesus Christ, a God-with-others.

To say that creation is called into being as the recipient of God's *being with* is not yet to give an account of why God creates in the first place. Why is there something and not nothing? Or, to put the question more sharply in line with my argument so far, Why does God decide to be a God-with-others? In Anselm's words, *Cur Deus homo?*

Answers to these questions tend to focus either on God's goodness or on God's glory.[24] As a first option, a significant part of Christian theologizing about creation is shaped by the Dionysian intuition that creation is the result of God's overflowing essential goodness. Even Barth makes use of this notion.[25] A variation on this idea is that perfect goodness does not begrudge anyone anything and therefore wants others to exist—a notion voiced by Plato that also made its way into the writings of the church fathers.[26] Another variation is the notion that since God is essentially love, and therefore essentially

---

24. See the discussion in Herman Bavinck, *Reformed Dogmatics*, vol. 2, *God and Creation* (Baker Academic, 2004), 430–35.

25. When God turns to us, this is "an overflow of his essence." Karl Barth, *Church Dogmatics* II/1, trans. G. W. Bromiley (T&T Clark, 1957), 273. God's "inner glory overflows and becomes outward." Barth, *Church Dogmatics* II/2, 121. In a longer passage, Barth writes,

> The fact that God makes this movement, the institution of the covenant, the primal decision "in Jesus Christ," which is the basis and goal of all his works—that is grace. Speaking generally, it is the demonstration, the overflowing of the love which is the being of God, that he who is entirely self-sufficient, who even within himself cannot know isolation, willed even in all his divine glory to share his life with another, and to have that other as the witness of his grace. This love of God is his grace. It is love in the form of the deepest condescension. It occurs even where there is no question of claim or merit on the part of the other. It is love which is overflowing, unconstrained, unconditioned.

(Barth, *Church Dogmatics* II/2, 9–10)

26. Plato writes, "Let us now give the reason why the maker made becoming, and the universe. He was good, and in him that is good no envy ever arises regarding anything. Being devoid of envy, he wanted everything to be like himself, as far as possible. . . . God desires that everything should be good and nothing evil, as far as possible. . . . For him who is most good it neither was nor is permissible to do anything other than what is most beautiful." Plato, *Timaeus* 29E–30B, quoted in Norman Kretzmann, "A General Problem of Creation: Why Would God Create Anything at All?," in *Being and Goodness: The Concept of the Good in Metaphysics and Philosophical Theology*, ed. Scott MacDonald (Cornell University Press, 1991), 214–15.

Athanasius writes, "For one that is good can grudge nothing: for which reason he does not grudge even existence, but desires all to exist, as objects for his loving-kindness." Athanasius, *Contra Gentiles*, in *A Select Library of Nicene and Post-Nicene Fathers of the Christian Church*, 2nd series, vol. 4, *Athanasius: Select Works and Letters*, ed. Philip Schaff and Henry Wace (Hendrickson, 2004), §41.

ecstatic, it is a matter of course for the three trinitarian persons to expand God's love by creating that which is not God.[27]

As to the second option, another line of thought holds that the end of all God's works *ad extra* is the advancement of God's glory. Tertullian says that God created the world "for the glory of his majesty."[28] As Herman Bavinck puts the argument, "God can rest in nothing other than himself and cannot be satisfied in anything less than himself. He has no alternative but to seek his own honor."[29]

The problem with the arguments from divine goodness is that they make creation natural to God. They imply that creation flows forth out of the perfection of God's nature. If creation is natural to God, and, as these arguments presume, it is also essential to God's nature that God lives out God's full potential, God will create necessarily. If God did not create, God would not fully express God's goodness, which would not fit the perfection of God's being. On the argument from divine love, God naturally seeks to expand the objects of God's love. This implies that God's being would remain unfulfilled if God did not create. This would make God dependent on our existence, and it would mean that God's love is an expression of God's self-interest. On this understanding, God would create us as objects of God's love not so much for love's sake but because God *needs* to love us for God's sake.

Something similar can be said about the arguments from divine glory. First, these arguments fail to notice that nothing could glorify God more fully than the perfection of God's own essential glory; it is hard to see how creation could add anything to this. Second, they also make God's acts of incarnation, election, and creation the means to a larger goal. If God incarnates, elects, and creates for the sake of God's glory, God does not create to *be with* us. As I argue above, *being with* is a form of relationality that does not seek anything higher than the very intimacy it creates.[30]

I proposed we read the Colossians hymn as saying that creation exists to *be with* God because God becomes Jesus Christ to *be with* creation. This invites a radically different reading of the relationship between God's perfections and God's act of creation. God's perfections are not the basis from which to understand why God creates; rather, they tell us why God does not have to create. God in Godself is enough. God's goodness excludes any divine

---

27. Jürgen Moltmann, *The Trinity and the Kingdom* (Fortress, 1993), 116–17.
28. Tertullian, *Apology*, in *The Ante-Nicene Fathers: Translations of the Writings of the Fathers down to A.D. 325*, vol. 3, *Tertullian*, ed. Alexander Roberts and James Donaldson (Hendrickson, 2004), §17.
29. Bavinck, *Reformed Dogmatics*, 2:434.
30. See Wells, *Nazareth Manifesto*, 231–32.

need; the intrinsic glory of the divine goodness cannot be embellished. This implies an absolute divine freedom with regard to anything that is not God. In this freedom God determines to live a life of *being with*. In fact, it is the freedom of God's perfections that allows God to live into the *being with* to the fullest. As imperfect, finite, vulnerable creatures, humans will engage in *being with* either with guardedness or with neediness, but this is not so with God. If God decides to *be with* the other, God can give Godself completely in this relationship, because God has nothing that God could lose, nor does God have needs to be fulfilled. Therefore, God's creative *being with* can take the self-giving form of incarnation.

If there is any metaphor that could best express the divine intentionality here, it is the metaphor of play. Creation does not flow forth out of divine goodness, nor does it serve to display divine glory. Rather, it is an expression of divine playfulness. God created the Leviathan for the sport of it, say the Scriptures (Ps. 104:26). Why not think of all of creation as an expression of God's playfulness? Sport is not done for the sake of anything else. It does not need to accomplish anything beyond itself; its goods are internal to itself.[31] It is incumbent upon no one's nature to engage in it. It is purely an expression of joyous freedom. But, as such, it is not random. There is intentionality to it. One can fully give oneself to it, express oneself fully in it. As such, it is analogous to *being with*. There is for God no imperative to engage in it; but once God does so, it is shaped by intentionality and commitment.[32]

Israel

If creation is embedded in election, this gives God's act of election a universal reach. On the logic of the Colossians hymn, I do not see how it can be otherwise. If *all* things have been created for Christ and he holds *all* things together, there is no way around this universal claim. The text does not lie.

At the same time, Scripture's narrative is not of a universal election but of a particular one. In this story, God choses one particular people, not all of them. It is a story in which God commits Godself not to all the nations but to one nation, one family, and does so irrevocably: "I will establish my covenant between me and you, and your offspring after you throughout their

---

31. See Alasdair MacIntyre's reflections on games as practice in *After Virtue*, 2nd ed. (University of Notre Dame Press, 1984), 187–88.
32. For the notion of creation as an act of divine play, see A. A. van Ruler, *Verzameld Werk*, vol. 3, *God, Schepping, Mens, Zonde* (Boekencentrum, 2009), 15 (with further references).

generations, for an everlasting covenant, to be God to you and to your offspring after you" (Gen. 17:7).

The universal reach of election as understood by supralapsarian Christology does not contradict the particular focus of the biblical narrative of election. On the contrary, particularity is implied by Christological supralapsarianism. In the incarnation, God becomes a human being. This does not mean that God assumes generic humanity, for such a thing does not exist. To be a human being is to be in a context; it is to be located somewhere. To be a human being is to have a particular family, to be part of a particular tribe, to have a particular ethnicity. To be a human being is to find one's roots in a place and to partake in a specific history. All this flows from the fact that a human being is a creature; creatures are by definition limited, and therefore situated somewhere. If God is to become human, God is therefore to become a particular human: God is to become part of a family, a tribe, an ethnicity, located in a place and rooted in a history. Incarnation therefore is not just the election of a human nature; it is also the election of a community, a place, and a time in history. According to the biblical narrative, Israel is this elect community; Israel's place and history are set aside to be the recipients of God's presence. In making a covenant with Abraham, God designates Israel to be God's family, to be the ones God will *be with*.[33]

Abraham's family is thus the recipient of God's decision to *be with* that which is not God. Israel is determined to be the Son's eschatological company and friend. As such, the covenant that God makes with Israel is not functional. It is not instituted for the sake of a larger goal; it is a relationship God engages for its own sake.

This understanding goes against a long-standing Christian tradition of regarding Israel as elected for the sake of the nations. On this traditional reading, the covenant with Abraham is God's answer to a world gone awry. The point of Israel's election is to set the world aright and to bless the nations. Israel serves this wider salvific goal.[34]

However, understanding Israel as elected for its own sake, and not for the nations, is much more in line with the ways the biblical narrative describes the nature of God's covenantal relating to this people. For example, a functional understanding of Israel's election cannot make sense of the repeated use of the imagery of Israel as God's bride:

---

33. For a more extensive version of this argument, see chap. 8, below.
34. In *Rethinking Paul*, I discuss as contemporary examples of this line of thinking Gerhard von Rad's Genesis commentary, the work of the New Testament scholar N. T. Wright, and the missional hermeneutics as developed by Christopher J. H. Wright and Michael Goheen (see Van Driel, *Rethinking Paul*, 288–91).

> For your Maker is your husband,
> > the LORD of hosts is his name;
> > the Holy One of Israel is your Redeemer,
> > the God of the whole earth he is called. (Isa. 54:5)[35]

Marital relationships are good for their own sake. One doesn't choose a bride for the sake of a larger good, as that would devalue the relationship. Marital love is not functional but personal.

A similar observation could be made regarding Scriptural portrayals of Israel as God's child:

> Listen to me, O house of Jacob,
> > all the remnants of the house of Israel,
> who have been borne by me from your birth,
> > carried from the womb;
> even to your old age I am he,
> > even when you turn gray I will carry you.
> I have made, and I will bear;
> > I will carry and will save. (Isa. 46:3–4)[36]

Moreover, a functional understanding of election cannot make sense of the repeatedly emphasized everlasting nature of God's love for Israel as God's bride or child, as expressed in the preceding verses or in strophes like these:

> For a brief moment I abandoned you,
> > but with great compassion I will gather you.
> In overflowing wrath for a moment
> > I hid my face from you,
> but with everlasting love I will have compassion on you,
> > says the LORD, your Redeemer. (Isa. 54:7–8)

If God engages Israel in covenant only for the sake of a larger goal, the ground for this relationship disappears as soon as the goal is reached. This is not, however, what God promises Israel. God's love for Israel is not contingent upon a larger goal; it is everlasting, as promised through the words of the prophet. All these images suggest, therefore, that God relates to Israel simply for the sake of being in relationship with Israel.

---

35. For a discussion of the bridal imagery for Israel as the object of God's election, see Seock-Tae Sohn, *The Divine Election of Israel* (Eerdmans, 1991), 10–44; see also 184–89, 241–44.

36. See Sohn, *Divine Election*, 61–73.

Although only a few Scripture passages offer a reason why God chose Israel, an important one suggests that God was motivated by love. The Deuteronomist tries to make sense of God's choice of Israel, saying,

> For you are a people holy to the Lord your God; the Lord your God has chosen you out of all the peoples on earth to be his people, his treasured possession.
> It was not because you were more numerous than any other people that the Lord set his heart on you and chose you—for you were the fewest of all peoples. It was because the Lord loved you and kept the oath that he swore to your ancestors, that the Lord has brought you out with a mighty hand, and redeemed you from the house of slavery, from the hand of Pharaoh king of Egypt. (Deut. 7:6–8)

If there were ever a place where it would be theologically useful to introduce a functional account of Israel's election, it would be here: to provide a reason for what seems unreasonable. Instead, the writer doubles down. God's choice for Israel cannot be defended by pointing to a reason. God's choice for Israel is motivated by love.

That said, in the election of Israel there is blessing for the nations. The story of Abraham's call explicitly confirms this: "I will make of you a great nation, and I will bless you, and make your name great, so that you will be a blessing. I will bless those who bless you, and the one who curses you I will curse; and in you all the families of the earth shall be blessed" (Gen. 12:2–3). But the logic of this promise is that the nations are blessed for the sake of Abraham's election.[37] As Abraham is elected for his own sake, God's grace will nevertheless spill over Israel's boundaries. So it is in Ephesians: God's covenant with Israel is the very core of God's gathering work to which now also the gentiles are being joined.[38]

The Church

There is thus not blessing just for Israel; in Israel's election, and the promise to Abraham that he will be a father of many descendants and inherit the world, there is also blessing for the nations. The Genesis texts do not further unpack how these promises relate. Later Jewish traditions have interpreted them in a

---

37. See also Joel S. Kaminsky, *Yet I Loved Jacob: Reclaiming the Biblical Concept of Election* (2007; repr., Wipf & Stock, 2016), 85.
38. For similar critiques of the idea that Israel's election is instrumental, see Kaminsky, *Yet I Loved Jacob*, 153–57; and R. W. L. Moberly, *Old Testament Theology: Reading the Hebrew Bible as Christian Scripture* (Baker Academic, 2013), 43–48.

variety of ways. The apostle Paul gives a particular twist that is fundamental to both his ministry and his writings: Abraham will bless the nations as they become his heirs. He will inherit the world by becoming the ancestor of both the circumcised and the uncircumcised.

In Romans 4, in a remarkable piece of exegesis, Paul describes how, through the faithfulness of Christ Jesus, God is making good on the promises God once made to aging, childless Abraham. As Abraham had trusted in God's commitment and power to give life to the dead and to bring into existence the things that do not exist, in the present time this trust has been justified as both the circumcised and the uncircumcised trace their lineage back to Abraham and are brought into one family, thus making him the father of many nations.[39]

We find the same thoughts in the parallel text in Galatians 3. The goal of Paul's argument is to convince the Galatians that the basis for God's justifying work is not the works of the law but the faithfulness of Christ. The narrative Paul works with is the same as in Romans: Through the faithfulness of Christ the promises God made to Abraham now come to the Gentiles as well, as in Christ they are counted among Abraham's offspring. By being baptized into Christ they have been knitted into Abraham's lineage, and thus is fulfilled the Scriptures' declaration that "all the Gentiles shall be blessed in you" (Gal. 3:8).[40]

Without mentioning Abraham, this same narrative is folded into the supralapsarian Christological vision of Colossians and Ephesians. In Colossians, immediately before the hymn, Paul writes to his gentiles readers that he rejoices in the Father, having "enabled you to share in the inheritance of the saints in the light" (1:12). In the lines after the hymn, Paul picks up this theme again as he asserts that these very same readers, who "were once estranged" have now been reconciled (1:21–22). This is "the mystery that has been hidden throughout the ages and generations but has now been revealed" (1:26)—namely, Christ himself (2:2), the God who decides to be with and for others, for whom all things have been created, not just the Jews but also the gentiles.

In Ephesians, this narrative is even more explicit. The narrative that governs the letter mirrors the supralapsarian Christological reach of Colossians. It is a narrative rooted in God's act of election before the foundation of the world—an election that is "in Christ" (Eph. 1:4). This election spans till the "fullness of time," at which point God has planned "to gather up all things in [Christ]"—that is, "things in heaven and things on earth" (Eph. 1:10). And this gathering follows a distinct pattern. This becomes clear when the writer addresses his

---

39. See Van Driel, *Rethinking Paul*, 46–59.
40. Van Driel, *Rethinking Paul*, 77–81.

readers as people who were "Gentiles by birth," and were therefore formerly "without Christ, being aliens from the commonwealth of Israel, and strangers to the covenants of promise" (2:11, 12). But now they "who once were far off have been brought near by the blood of Christ" (2:13). These words imply that the gathering of all things had started much earlier, with the gathering of Israel. However, as the writer states, the wall that once divided Jews and gentiles has been broken down. "In himself" Christ is creating a "new humanity" (2:15). The writer reassures his gentile readers: "You are no longer strangers and aliens, but you are citizens with the saints and also members of the household of God" (2:19). The gathering that began with Israel now extends to the gentiles, and it will encompass all of creation. That all things were meant to be gathered into Christ is a "mystery" that was not known "in former generations" (3:5), but it has now been revealed. What was hidden in the past is now visible for everyone to see (3:9). Where? "Through the church" (3:10). It is, in particular, through the gentiles becoming "fellow heirs, members of the same body" (3:6) that "the rulers and authorities in the heavenly places" are being put on notice about God's intentions for creation (3:10). That is, in the forming of this new community, this new household of God, from groups that were previously hostile to one another, the resurrected and ascended Christ makes clear to the powers-that-be that their time is up. Powers that have established their grip on people by pitting one group against another—political powers, socioeconomic powers, powers of ethnicity, nationality, race, class, or gender—are now being conquered by Christ, not by a direct confrontation but because their subjects are being drawn out from under their authority.

If the church is the community of those who have been knit into the community of Israel as the result of Christ's gathering all things to himself, this has significant consequences for both the doctrine of election and the doctrine of the church.[41] First, it means that God's act of election is not individually focused but, rather, ecclesially shaped. Election is the determination of the creature for eternal bliss, but eternal bliss is not an individual affair. It is inclusion in the family of Jesus—the community with whom he lives in intimacy and friendship in the eschaton. This family is already proleptically formed in Israel, and now, in the circle around Israel, in the community of the church. To be elect means to be brought by Christ's gathering work into the community of the church. This cuts against long-standing traditions that define election as distinct from the community of the church. On the logic of Colossians and Ephesians, there is no election apart from the *ekklēsia*. Second, if the church is the community of those who have now been knitted into the community of

---

41. See my analysis of Lesslie Newbigin's account of church and election in chap. 6, above.

Israel, this makes the church essentially a visible community—because Israel is a visible community. The very core of Israel's existence is a public life—a public set of habits, practices, and ordinances that show the world what it looks like to live in intimate fellowship with the God of Israel. If to be church means that one is now included in Israel's covenantal life, church life should be shaped similarly. This cuts against long-standing traditions of distinguishing the visible and the invisible church, with only the latter thought to embody the ecclesial existence of the elect. To be elect is to live into the visible reality of Christ's eschatological family formation. Third, the visible and communal nature of election shapes the relationship between church and mission. As the visible expression of Christ's mission to draw all things to himself, the church is essentially missional. But this mission is essentially ecclesial, since the expression and result of Christ's mission is the formation of a visible community, Christ's family and friends. This cuts against recent conversations that subordinate God's concern for the church to God's concern for God's reign or for the world. The church is not a means for a greater good, such as the inauguration of God's kingdom—because the church is the embodiment of God's *being with* God's creatures, and *being with* is itself the goal. In fact, all of creation is called into being in order to *be with* Christ—which leads to the fourth and last consequence: Not only is the church not a means in the service of the world but the world is created so as to become the church.

Eschatology

On the line of thought explored in this chapter, election is eschatological in intention, Christological in shape, and communal in nature.[42] Election is God's self-determination to be Jesus Christ; that is, election is God's self-determination to be a God with others. As such, election is the determination of others to be with God; that is, election is a determination to bliss. And since it is the very first thing that God decides with regard to God's relationship to that which is not God, it is eschatological: It is the determination of creation's ultimate goal, since a well-organized decider determines goals before means.

If all this is true, the eschaton is also Christological in shape. Christ is the center of creation's ultimate future. Moreover, just as election is communal and interpersonal in nature, so is the eschaton. Creation is called into being to be with God; humanity is created to be Jesus's family.[43] All this in turn implies

---

42. For more on the arguments in this section, see also chap. 12, below.

43. See Wells, *Nazareth Manifesto*, 58: "Heaven is not a freeze-frame of ecstatic or euphoric stillness: it is a dynamic interaction of God, redeemed creatures, and the renewed creation,

that the eschaton is embodied because the resurrected and ascended Christ is embodied. It is a transformed embodiment, but embodiment nonetheless—the kind of embodiment consisting of flesh and bones, breakfasts and suppers, even a messianic meal with the tables laden with the finest foods and aged wine.[44]

In this eschatological future of God *being with* creation and creation *being with* God, history continues unendingly. Because embodiment moves in space and time, time and history do not come to an end. If resurrection is new life in a recreated embodied existence, then space and time may likewise be renewed, but they may not be discarded. The eternal now is not conducive to the joy and embrace of resurrection life. But even more importantly, time and history will not have come to an end because the eschaton is the full enjoyment of *being with*. In the eschaton we will enjoy what it means to be with God to the fullest. As Gregory of Nyssa points out, this can only mean that we move unendingly toward God, since God is always bigger than we can conceive.[45] Gregory understood this process mostly in mental and spiritual terms. Scripture's Christ-centered eschatological universe invites us also, and maybe primarily, to understand this in embodied terms: Our physical eyes will see Jesus, crowned with glory and honor (Heb. 2:9).[46] And thus time and history become the unending unfolding of election—as we will be that which we were created to be, a large family for the firstborn of creation, a family *with him*.

Conclusion: All Things Have Been Created for Him

In this chapter, I have offered an account of the relationship between Christology and election in the tradition of Augustine, John Duns Scotus, and Karl

---

in which there is partnership without pain and expression without envy. . . . In heaven, God, humanity, and the renewed creation continue to interact with one another, but this interaction issues in continuous iterations of ceaselessly new fruits. There is change, but no death; growth, but no loss; creativity, but no suffering."

44. Here I part from Karl Barth, whose eschatology does not seem to have the conceptual space to make these claims. See Van Driel, *Incarnation Anyway*, 114–18; and, more extensively, Nathan Hitchcock, *Karl Barth and the Resurrection of the Flesh: The Loss of the Body in Participatory Eschatology* (Pickwick, 2013).

45. See the helpful collection of essays in Giulio Maspero, Miguel Brugarolas, and Ilaria Vigorelli, eds., *Gregory of Nyssa's Mystical Eschatology* (Peeters, 2021).

46. In *Incarnation Anyway*, I argue from the physical seeing of Christ in the eschaton as part of the *visio Dei* to a supralapsarian Christology (155–59). Here I make the opposite programmatic move: A supralapsarian Christology invites us to rethink the *visio Dei* in relation to the seeing of Jesus. This touches on a significant contemporary conversation. For a report on the conversation, see, e.g., Marc Cortez, "The Body and the Beatific Vision," in *Being Saved: Explorations in Human Salvation*, ed. Marc Cortez, Joshua R. Farris, and S. Mark Hamilton (SCM, 2018), 326–43.

Barth, read through the lens of a primordial divine intention to *be with* that which is not God. Taking a step back from the argument developed here, How does this theological commitment to incarnation as motivated by a divine desire to *be with* bend the shape of the doctrine of election? I suggest the resulting account is supralapsarian but not instrumental, particular and universal, communal and personal, and participatory but not divinizing.

The resulting account is *supralapsarian but not instrumental*. The traditional Reformed supralapsarian understanding of predestination holds that in the first step of God's decrees God establishes as the purpose for creation the manifestation of the divine virtues: God's mercy in the eternal blessedness of the elect, and God's justice in the eternal damnation of the reject. All of creation is the unfolding of these divine intentions. On this account, God's supralapsarian act of election thus serves a primordial goal: the revelation of God's glory. The account of election offered in this chapter is likewise supralapsarian, but it is decisively non-instrumental. Any sense of election serving a larger goal is cut off by the notion that election is God's self-determination to *be with* creation and for creation to *be with* God. The relationship established in election is not contingent upon a deeper intention; it *is* the intention for the sake of which all of creation unfolds. And the name of this relationship is Jesus.

This account of election is both *particular and universal*. In the act of election, God commits Godself to becoming a particular human being. God's *being with* that which is not God comes to pass in a particular place, has roots in a specific history, and shapes a particular family. The incarnation of God means the election of Israel as the recipient of God's *being with* that which is not God. But in electing Israel God also blesses the nations—as, in the fullness of time, those who were far off are brought near, as gentiles are knit into this particular community and allowed to partake in this new household of God. God's particular presence to the family of Abraham turns out to have a universal reach. *All* things have been created for him.

Election is both *communal and personal*. Contrary to large swaths of the tradition, on this account election is not an individual affair. As it is the first determination of Godself in relationship to anything that is not God, election is the determination of the identity and goal of all of creation. It is a determination that works itself out in the formation of the communities of Israel and of the church—of the "large family" (Rom. 8:29) of the Son. But this does not make it any less personal. The relationship into which any member of these communities, into which any creature, has been called is that of *being with* God, of finding joy and grace in the presence of the One in whom we look God in the eyes, in whom we can be embraced by God, sit down with God, have a meal with God.

Finally, this account of election calls for a narrative that is deeply *participatory but not divinizing*. As theologians are rediscovering the notion of participation as a central, governing metaphor for the relationship between God and that which is not God, I want to be clear that this account does offer participation—but the participation it offers is not the creature's participation in God; it is, rather, God's participation in the life of the creature. The life of all of creation is established exactly in God's primordially decision to be God with others—that is, to be Jesus Christ. Election tells us not that our destiny is to be lifted up beyond our creaturely baseline and to be given a participation in divine realities but, rather, that our existence and eschatological destiny is embedded in and upheld by God, who comes as close to us as God can as God becomes one of us.

These four characteristics, however, hold for more than just a revised doctrine of election. As I continue, in the following chapters, with further constructive explorations in the light of a commitment to the absolute priority of Christ, it will become clear that this kind of supralapsarian Christological approach bends all doctrinal reflection in this direction. Such is the essential effect of God's primordial commitment to be a God-*with*-others.

8

"So That He Might Be the Firstborn Within a Large Family"

On Supralapsarian Christology and Israel's Election

Why is there election rather than not? Why does God's relating to that which is not God take the shape of a narrow concentration on a particular people rather than an equal divine engagement of all nations? Is not God's preferential love for Israel inconsistent with the very attributes the Scriptures assign to God? As the good and just Creator of all things, shouldn't God love all things equally? As Michael Wyschogrod puts it, "Why does God proceed by means of election, the choosing of one people among the nations as his people? Why is he not the father of all nations, calling them to his obedience and offering his love to man, whom he created in his image? More fundamentally, why must the concept of nation intrude itself into the relationship between God and man? Does not God address each individual human being as he stands alone before God?"[1]

---

1. Michael Wyschogrod, *The Body of Faith: God in the People Israel* (Rowman & Littlefield, 1983), 58. In a similar vein, Will Herberg writes, "A truly rational and universal God, it is maintained, could not do anything so arbitrary as to 'choose' one particular group out of mankind as a whole. . . . God is the God of all alike, and, therefore, cannot make distinctions between nations and peoples. To this is added the moral argument that the doctrine of 'chosenness' is little better than crude ethnocentrism, in which a particular group regards itself as the center of the universe and develops doctrines that will flatter its pride and minister to its glory." Will Herberg, "The 'Chosenness' of Israel and the Jew of Today," in *Arguments and Doctrines: A Reader of Jewish Thinking in the Aftermath of the Holocaust*, ed. Arthur

The goal of this chapter is to offer a fresh answer to these questions. In doing so I will build on the overall thesis of this book and further unpack the argument of the previous chapter. I proceed in three steps: First, I lay out three contemporary ways in which Christian theologians speak about Israel's election and engage its challenges for a Christian understanding of God's relating to what is not God. Second, I offer an alternative account of Israel's election, premised on a supralapsarian understanding of the incarnation. Third, I turn to the problem of supersessionism. Supralapsarian Christology has been accused of aggravating the deeply rooted tendency to write Israel's election out of the rhythm of the canonical narrative. I argue that my account actually does the opposite by anchoring the ongoing priority of Israel more deeply in God's relating to what is not God.

The Problem of Israel's Election

Contextualized Election

One strategy for dealing with the theological challenge of Israel's election is to contextualize it. For example, Naim Stifan Ateek proposes we distinguish between three streams of tradition stemming from the Hebrew Scriptures: a nationalist, a Torah-oriented, and a prophetic. Between these traditions Ateek sees tensions regarding the themes of particularism and universalism. The nationalist tradition found its first-century expression in the Zealot movement, drawing its inspiration from the historical books and early prophetic traditions within the Old Testament. Ateek holds that this stream of tradition represents the belief "that the Jews had a special, privileged relationship with God."[2] He contrasts this tradition with the prophetic one and "its deep, profound, and mature understanding of God." Even while they may still wrestle with a view that is "narrow, nationalist, and exclusive," Israel's later prophets were "able to produce profound truths about the universal and inclusive nature of God."[3] Ateek identifies Jesus as a first-century representative of this tradition.[4] On this kind of reading, the notion of God's particular commitment to Israel as expressed in election is acknowledged, but its theological challenges are dealt with by placing the notion within a theological tradition that is superseded by others.

Cohen (Harper & Row, 1970), 280, quoted in Joel S. Kaminsky, *Yet I Loved Jacob: Reclaiming the Biblical Concept of Election* (2007; repr., Wipf & Stock, 2016), 1.

2. Naim Stifan Ateek, *Justice and Only Justice: A Palestinian Theology of Liberation* (Orbis Books, 1989), 94.

3. Ateek, *Justice*, 96.

4. Ateek, *Justice*, 97.

Ateek's approach is heir to a longstanding Christian tradition. For example, Friedrich Schleiermacher describes a hierarchy of religious states of mind, the highest stage of which is occupied by the monotheistic religions. Here the idol worship that clouds the feeling of absolute dependence has been overcome. Schleiermacher includes Judaism among the monotheistic communities, although "by its restriction of Jehovah's love to the Abrahamic tribe, Judaism still displays its affinity with the stage of fetishism.... Only after their Babylonian exile had [monotheistic] faith emerged in an unalloyed and complete form."[5]

The theological problem with this strategy is that it uses election's context to neutralize its content. The Old Testament's witness to God's election of Israel aims to lift God's commitments beyond their particular contexts: "I will establish my covenant between me and you, and your offspring after you throughout their generations, for an everlasting covenant, to be God to you and to your offspring after you" (Gen. 17:7).[6] Within a contextualized understanding of election, this notion of an everlasting covenant, transcending time and place, is void of meaning. Rather than understanding the divine promises as promises to carry Israel beyond its immediate horizon, these promises are read as only the expressions of a particular form of Israel's self-understanding—expressions that, as such, are limited by their immediate horizon and superseded by later, supposedly different theological accounts.

Instrumentalized Election

A second Christian strategy for dealing with the challenge of Israel's election acknowledges it as a genuine moment within the divine economy, not just as an expression of Israel's religious self-consciousness, but deals with the theological challenges therein by interpreting Israel's election as serving a larger goal.

One example of this approach is the way the influential New Testament scholar N. T. Wright retells the biblical narrative. In response to a world gone awry, a world described in Genesis 1–11, God "called Abraham so that through his family he, God, could rescue the world from its plight."[7] Call it, says Wright, "the reason God called Abraham" or "the Creator's purpose, through Israel,

---

5. Friedrich Schleiermacher, *Christian Faith*, trans. Terrence N. Tice, Catherine L. Kelsey, and Edwina Lawler, 2 vols. (Westminster John Knox, 2016), §8.4.

6. It is telling that Schleiermacher can observe that the Jewish community "is almost in a process of extinction" (Schleiermacher, *Christian Faith*, §8.4) without pausing to note not only that this would be a historical tragedy but also that it would call for a theodicy (though on Schleiermacher's account, it wouldn't).

7. N. T. Wright, *Justification: God's Plan and Paul's Vision* (IVP Academic, 2009), 94.

for the world."[8] Whereas "the whole world had been cursed through Adam and Eve, through the human pride which led to Babel, the Creator God would now bring blessing to that same whole world. That was the point of the covenant."[9] Therefore, "The point of 'election' was not to choose or call a people who would somehow mysteriously escape either the grim entail of Adam's sin or the results it brought in its train. It was not—as in some low-grade proposals!—about God simply choosing a people to be his close friends. The point was to choose and call a people through whom the sin of humankind, and its results for the whole creation, might be brought to the point where that sin, and those results, could at last be defeated, condemned, overcome."[10]

Other prominent representatives of this instrumental understanding of Israel's election can be found in contemporary missional hermeneutics, a movement that arose out of reflection on the *missio Dei* in the second half of the twentieth century. Missiologists and theologians reinterpreted *mission*, understanding it not primarily as a human response to the gift of the gospel but, rather, as God's work as expressed in the gospel. Missional hermeneutics anchors the *missio Dei* deep within the biblical narrative, tracing it all the way to God's election of Israel. This election is, however, interpreted as serving God's wider mission to the nations. For example, missiologist Christopher J. H. Wright holds that "it is God's mission in relation to the nations, arguably more than any other single theme, that provides the key that unlocks the biblical grand narrative."[11] The Abrahamic call and Israel's election stand in the service of this missional movement.[12] Wright refers here in particular to Abraham's blessing in Genesis 12:3, reading the second part as the goal of the first part—that is, he believes Abraham is blessed *so that* in him the nations will be blessed. "The election of Israel is," therefore, says Wright, "instrumental, not an end in itself. God did not choose Israel that they alone should be saved, as if the purpose of election terminated with them. They were chosen rather as the means by which salvation could be extended to others throughout the earth."[13] For this reason, Wright can say that "the nations are the matrix of Israel's life, the raison d'être of her very existence."[14] Likewise, Michael W. Goheen describes Abraham's and Israel's election as "means to a

---

8. Wright, *Justification*, 94.
9. Wright, *Justification*, 99.
10. N. T. Wright, *Paul and the Righteousness of God* (SPCK, 2013), 1208.
11. Christopher J. H. Wright, *The Mission of God: Unlocking the Bible's Grand Narrative* (IVP Academic, 2006), 455.
12. Wright, *Mission of God*, 194. Wright appeals for his reading explicitly to the work of N. T. Wright (Wright, *Mission of God*, 212, 329).
13. Wright, *Mission of God*, 263.
14. Wright, *Mission of God*, 454.

greater end."[15] After God's initial plan failed in the events described in Genesis 3–11, chapter 12 describes how Abraham is called "to sort out the mess that Adam has created."[16] Therefore, says Goheen, "God's particular attention to Abraham and Israel in the Old Testament was for the sake of *all* nations; for *all* creation."[17] Thus, "God's chosen people do not exist for themselves. Rather, they exist for the sake of God's glory and his mission, and for the sake of others toward whom God's mission is directed. They are indeed 'chosen by God' to play a prescribed role in God's mission to restore the creation and to glorify himself. But this choosing is 'for the sake of the world.'"[18]

Here is then another response to the objection that the Creator God ought to love all peoples and not just Israel: This is exactly what motivates Israel's election. This people is elected not for its own sake but for the sake of the well-being of the nations. The problem with this account of Israel's election is that it does not honor the logic of the biblical narrative. God's relationship to Israel is described as that of a husband to a wife (Isa. 54:5), or a parent to a child (Isa. 46:3–4). These are not simply instrumental relationships; they express a relationship in which the other is loved for their own sake. It is for this reason that God also emphasizes the everlasting nature of Israel's election (Isa. 54:7–8). If Israel were elected only for the sake of a larger goal, the grounds for this relationship disappear as soon as the goal is reached. Similarly, while the covenantal promises that God makes to Abraham involve the nations, the logic of the promise does not suggest that Abraham is elected for the nations' sake; rather, the nations will be blessed for Abraham's sake. The nations are blessed based on how they relate to this chosen people: "I will make of you a great nation, and I will bless you, and make your name great, so that you will be a blessing. I will bless those who bless you, and the one who curses you I will curse; and in you all the families of the earth shall be blessed" (Gen. 12:2–3). The blessing of the nations is thus a consequence that flows from God's special election of Abraham and his descendants, not a larger purpose that explains that special election.[19]

---

15. Michael W. Goheen, *A Light to the Nations: The Missional Church and the Biblical Story* (Baker Academic, 2011), 38.

16. Goheen, *Light to the Nations*, 28.

17. Goheen, *Light to the Nations*, 29.

18. Goheen, *Light to the Nations*, 26. Goheen, too, appeals for his proposals to N. T. Wright (Goheen, *Light to the Nations*, 205–6). I have analyzed the instrumental understanding of Israel's election as expressed in the work of N. T. Wright and missional hermeneutics more deeply in Edwin Chr. van Driel, *Rethinking Paul: Protestant Theology and Pauline Exegesis* (Cambridge University Press, 2021), 257–62, 274–75, 288–91.

19. For a more extensive critique of a functional understanding of Israel's election, see Van Driel, *Rethinking Paul*, 291–97.

Irrational Election

A third strategy for dealing with the theological complications implied by Israel's election is to characterize election as a "falling in love." A love that really loves the other for her own sake, Michael Wyschogrod argues, in his own response to the challenges, has to differentiate. "Undifferentiated love, love that is dispensed equally to all must be love that does not meet the individual in his individuality but sees him as a member of a species."[20] But such is not God's love for Israel. "There are those whom God loves especially, with whom he has fallen in love, as with Abraham. There is no other way of expressing this mystery except in these terms. God's relationship to Abraham is truly a falling in love. The biblical text tells us this when it fails to explain the reason for the election of Abraham."[21]

However, because love embraces the other in all aspects of existence, God's love encompasses not only Abraham but also Abraham's carnal offspring. They belong to Abraham and therefore fall within the realm of God's love. "To believe that the individual can be lifted out of his nation and brought into relation with God is as illusory as to believe that man's soul can be saved and his body discarded. Just as man is body and soul, so man is individual and member of a nation."[22] To love Abraham is to love all who are his, and thereby to create a people that is in God's service in the totality of its human existence.[23] Nonetheless, as God continues to love Israel "it is because he sees the face of his beloved Abraham in each and every one of his children as a man sees the face of his beloved in the children of his union with his beloved."[24]

Wyschogrod received support for his approach from Jon D. Levenson and R. W. L. Moberly.[25] They both point to Deuteronomy 7:

> For you are a people holy to the LORD your God; the LORD your God has chosen you out of all the peoples on earth to be his people, his treasured possession. It was not because you were more numerous than any other people that the LORD set his heart on you and chose you—for you were the fewest of all peoples. It was

---

20. Wyschogrod, *Body of Faith*, 61.
21. Wyschogrod, *Body of Faith*, 63–64.
22. Wyschogrod, *Body of Faith*, 68.
23. Wyschogrod, *Body of Faith*, 67.
24. Wyschogrod, *Body of Faith*, 64.
25. Jon D. Levenson, "The Universal Horizon of Biblical Particularism," in *The Bible and Ethnicity*, ed. Mark G. Brett (Brill, 1996), 143–69; Jon D. Levenson, "Miscategorizing Chosenness," in *Partners with God; Theological and Critical Readings of the Bible, in Honor of Martin A. Sweeney*, ed. Shelley L. Birdsong and Serge Frolov (Claremont School of Theology Press, 2017), 327–43; R. W. L. Moberly, *Old Testament Theology: Reading the Hebrew Bible as Christian Scripture* (Baker Academic, 2013), 43–52.

because the LORD loved you and kept the oath that he swore to your ancestors, that the LORD has brought you out with a mighty hand, and redeemed you from the house of slavery, from the hand of Pharaoh king of Egypt. (Deut. 7:6–8)

According to this text, "the choice of Israel is grounded in passion," observes Levenson. The verb used "suggests an affair of the heart, with all the irrationality and unpredictability of such things. Who can specify the reasons why he loves someone above all others of the same class, and even if he can, do those reasons ever account in full for that love?"[26] An appropriate response to such love is "an astonished 'Why me?'" adds Moberly. "This is a question that always looks for more than actual reasons and explanations. . . . The question expresses sheer marvel at the gratuitous wonder of being loved. . . . The reality of love surpasses the realm of reason. In this sense love is a mystery."[27]

Levenson and Moberly thus embrace the argument that God's election of some, rather than all, is not rational. This is simply in the nature of love, they argue, and election is an expression of love. This move also reveals the theological problems embedded in this third strategy. On a classical understanding of God, such that as explored by medieval and post-Reformation scholastics, it is part of divine perfection that even God's love never conflicts with God's reason. In fact, for this tradition, God is, in the words of Marilyn McCord Adams, "a maximally well-organized lover," loving that which is to be loved most (i.e., Godself) first and loving others in a manner appropriate to their loveliness in an ever-enlarging circle.[28] For those who, for theological reasons, embrace such an understanding of divine perfection, the picture of a God whose acts of election are the expressions of a lover's foolishness may be a bridge too far.

Supralapsarian Christology and Israel's Election

I wish to put forward a different theological understanding of Israel's election. My argument acknowledges the centrality of Israel's chosenness in God's relationship to what is not God, but it also takes seriously the theological questions this raises, while addressing the objections often raised to the three strategies I laid out in the previous section. I will proceed in three steps. All theological arguments are embedded in underlying theological assumptions, so it is with my proposal. Thus, first, I articulate the three major theological

---

26. Levenson, "Universal Horizon of Biblical Particularism," 156.
27. Moberly, *Old Testament Theology*, 44.
28. Marilyn McCord Adams, *Christ and Horrors: The Coherence of Christology* (Cambridge University Press, 2006), 181.

notions I take for granted. Second, I lay out my argument and its internal logic. Third, I further unpack my understanding of Israel's election by juxtaposing it with what motivates the alternative accounts and with the challenges they face.

Supralapsarian Christology[29]

For my argument, I assume three major ideas. First, I assume that supralapsarian Christology is correct. Second, I assume the absolute priority of Christ. The incarnation is not contingent upon anything else; the very first thing God decides is to become incarnate. Third, I assume that to be a human being is to be a *particular* human being. That is, when God becomes incarnate, God does not assume generic humanity, for such a thing does not exist. This flows forth from the fact that a human being is a creature, and creatures are by definition limited and therefore situated somewhere. To be a human being is to have a particular family, to be part of a particular tribe, to have a particular ethnicity. Incarnation means God finds God's roots in a place and partakes in a specific history.

Israel Elected for the Sake of the Incarnate One

On the assumptions I just laid out, the very first thing in the order of divine intentions is to become incarnate. That is, the very first thing God decides is to be Jesus Christ. All that follows is embedded within this decision.

To become Jesus Christ is, however, for God to become that which is not God. To become incarnate is therefore a form of divine self-giving. In the incarnation, God reaches outside of Godself to participate in that which is not God—specifically, to assume a human nature, to identify with this nature as God's very own, as an extension of God's own life and an expression of God's own being. To become incarnate is for God to give Godself to what is not God. It is a decision to be a God-with-others. This is, of course, what the whole biblical narrative drives at: God is not just the Creator, the one who calls that which is not God into being; God is also the one who commits to this creation, who sees it through, who is creation's eschatological Consummator. The insight of supralapsarian Christology is that this commitment is embedded in the ultimate act of divine self-giving: the decision to be Jesus Christ. Everything else is subsequently called into being for him.

---

29. Readers of the original essay version of this chapter will realize I have here significantly abbreviated my discussion of the first two assumptions, since they are sufficiently covered in earlier parts of this book. Cf. Edwin Chr. van Driel, "Incarnation and Israel: A Supralapsarian Account of Israel's Chosenness," *Modern Theology* 39 (2023): 9–10.

To become Jesus Christ—that is, to assume a human nature and become incarnate—means, however, to become a particular human being. As noted above, to be a particular human being means to have a family, to be part of a tribe, an ethnicity, a nation; it means being rooted in a history and located in a place. For the incarnating God, this family is Abraham's family. This tribe, this ethnicity, this nation is the people of Israel. The history in which the incarnate One is rooted and the place where he is located are the history and land of this people. But this implies election. This family, this people, is elected for the sake of the incarnation.

To put it differently, incarnation itself is a form of election.[30] God can take any human nature as God's own, but because taking on a human nature means taking on not an imaginary, generic humanity but a particular human nature, the decision to become incarnate is also a decision to predestine a particular human nature as God's own. This election does not limit itself to this particular human nature. For this nature to be truly human, it must be a contextual human nature, woven into a particular location of space and time, of family and relationships. To elect this human nature is therefore to elect a people.[31]

Particularity and Universality

God's incarnation thus has a particular location and focus. But one cannot deny that it also has a universal scope. After all, Colossians declares that *all things* have been created for the incarnate One, not just Israel (Col. 1:16). Similarly, Ephesians holds that in Christ is revealed "a plan for the fullness of time, to gather up all things in him" (Eph. 1:10). The theological logic of these letters entails that, rather than holding particularity and universality in tension, the reach of the particular history of Jesus and his people is universal.

This aligns with the way the biblical narrative unfolds. God promises to be God to Abraham and his people in an everlasting covenant. But God also promises that, in this particular choice for Abraham, all the nations will be blessed. The Genesis text does not unpack how this will be. But for the apostle Paul (or for Paul and the Pauline school) it is clear: In Christ the gates

---

30. See the discussion in chap. 7, above.
31. Some of the same logic I employ here made the medieval supralapsarian theologian John Duns Scotus reflect deeply on the predestination of Jesus's mother, Mary. If God elected Jesus's particular nature to be his own, what about the one from whom this nature came? In addition to becoming one of the intellectual fathers of supralapsarian Christology, Scotus therefore also became known as the "Marian theologian." See John Duns Scotus, *Four Questions on Mary*, trans. Allan B. Walter (Franciscan Institute, 2000). In some ways, my argument simply extends Scotus's reflections.

of the covenant with Israel have been opened, and those who once were "far off"—that is, "aliens from the commonwealth of Israel, and strangers to the covenants of promise"—have been brought near and made to be "members of the household of God" (Eph. 2:12–14, 19). The nations are blessed by Abraham by being incorporated into his family and being made honorary Jews.[32]

The contextualizing interpretation of Israel's election is premised on the notion that particularity and universality are opposites. It reads the history of Israel's religion as a superseding of particularity by universality. This approach creates space for the nations by erasing the everlasting nature of God's relationship with Israel. I suggest that the logic of the Pauline statements and the larger biblical narrative points in a different direction: God's relationship with Israel is expanded to include those who once were far off. The covenant becomes universal, but it continues to be shaped by the particularity of Abraham's family. Admittedly, Paul does not spell out exactly what this means for the life of the gentiles. How do their identities change as they are incorporated into a new community, Israel? What does it mean to be a member of the nations and then to come near to the covenant and be incorporated into the household of Israel's God?

The church has often wanted to avoid these questions, preferring, with the contextualizing interpretation, to think about the church superseding the covenant with Israel rather than becoming guests in a household not its own. Nonetheless, no gentile Christian can escape the thorough Jewishness of Christian existence. From pagan polytheists, gentiles became monotheists. From believers in violent or dualistic cosmogonies, they embraced the Jewish idea of a good creation through a simple divine word. Christian liturgies are shaped decisively by Jewish sources. Christians look for the glorious rule of a Jewish Messiah who will seat them with Abraham at a Jewish meal that they anticipate weekly in their worship services. All this expresses the universal reach of Jewish particularity. And according to Ephesians, not only does this entail gentiles accepting new practices and beliefs; it also expresses a change in their identity. Gentiles are now woven into the commonwealth of Israel (Eph. 2:11–13).

Means and Goal

On the instrumental understanding of Israel's election, Israel is called to repair what humanity has broken. Israel's election is in the service of a larger goal. God's relationship with Israel is thus simply a means. As N. T. Wright

---

32. For a further exposition of how Paul interprets gentiles as being blessed by incorporation into Abraham's family, see Van Driel, *Rethinking Paul*, 38–67, 189–224.

says, Israel is not chosen to be God's friends but because there is a job to do. Israel's election is infralapsarian, contingent upon sin. Such a reading of the biblical narrative often goes hand in hand with an infralapsarian Christology: Incarnation takes place because of the sin problem.

The supralapsarian account of incarnation and Israel's election that I advance does not deny that God deals with sin through Israel and through Israel's Messiah. In that sense, my account is not an alternative to infralapsarianism. Rather, I argue that on the logic of the biblical narrative, the need to take care of sin is not the only, and not even the deepest, word that can be said about incarnation and election. The Colossians hymn that frames my argument also recounts the story of Jesus's death and resurrection (Col. 1:18) and emphasizes that in Christ "God was pleased to reconcile to himself all things, whether on earth or in heaven, by making peace through the blood of his cross" (Col. 1:20). However, the hymn places Christ's atoning work in a supralapsarian context. All things have been created for the one who would make the invisible God visible. Once creation wanders away from God, God decides that the one for whom all things were called into being, the one who is the eschatological goal of everything that exists, will also be the one through whom God draws creation back, "so that he might come to have first place in everything" (Col. 1:18). Atonement, reconciliation, Christ's mediatorship—these are means in the service of the previously set goal that in Christ all things may hold together (Col. 1:17).

A similar logic may be applied to Israel's existence. As the people from whom and to whom the incarnate One comes, Israel lives with him through the agony of sin and redemption. But these are not the reasons for Israel's existence. Rather, the Israelites exist to be God's friends (which is exactly the opposite of what N. T. Wright asserts). As Paul puts it elsewhere, "Those whom [God] foreknew he also predestined to be conformed to the image of his Son, in order that he might be the firstborn within a large family" (Rom. 8:29). The intention of God's work of election is to provide the One who was to come with a family. Paul here sums up my thesis in a single sentence.

Election and Love

Family relationships are shaped by ties of love. On the account I am proposing, one can happily agree with the third strategy: God's election is an expression of divine love. If God's first decision is to be a God-with-others by becoming incarnate, and if subsequently other creatures are called into being so as to provide the incarnate One with a large family named Israel, then love can indeed be said to be the driving force of Israel's election.

But it makes no sense to describe election as the result of a "falling in love," nor is there reason to describe God's love as irrational. The logic of "falling in love" implies that the object of one's affection exists before it is loved. It suggests an encounter with another the result of which is love. But on my account of divine election, there is love before the other even exists. God does not first create Israel and then fall in love with it; God creates Israel in order to love it. I believe this reflects the biblical narrative. The Scriptures emphasize that through Abraham God creates for Godself a people. Israel's existence is, as Paul puts it, a life out of death, a *creatio ex nihilo* (Rom. 4:17). When the promise comes to Abraham, Abraham, looking at himself, sees one who is "as good as dead," and his wife is barren (Rom. 4:19). But out of nothing God calls forth a people to love. This movement repeats itself when the gates of Israel's covenant open and the gentiles are ushered in. They who "were dead" have now been made alive and have been knit into Christ and his covenantal family (Eph. 2:4–5). Election precedes creation. Love precedes the existence of a people.

This love is not determined by reason. God is free to elect or not; God is free to exist solely in the eternal bliss that is God's internal life or to step outside of Godself and to call forth that which is not God. There is nothing, no logic or reason, that requires God to make a people for Godself. But once God decides to be a God-with-others by God's self-giving act of incarnation, the election of Israel is entirely reasonable. To become human is to become part of a human family, and that is exactly what God does. Becoming incarnate implies, not just calling into existence a human nature with which God unites, but creating a community. Nothing makes God do it; but once God decides to do it, God follows through with all the implications of God's choice, the way a maximally committed and organized lover does.

Supralapsarian Christology and Supersessionism

It may be surprising to see supralapsarian Christology lifted up as the basis for an argument on the centrality of Israel's election. Supralapsarian Christology has been accused of being a bedfellow of supersessionism, the belief "that since Christ's coming the church has taken the place of the Jewish people as God's chosen community, and that God's covenant with the Jews is now over and done."[33] Christian theology in general has a regrettable history of writing Israel out of the narrative concerning God and that which is not

---

33. R. Kendall Soulen, "Supersessionism," in *A Dictionary of Jewish-Christian Relations*, ed. Edward Kessler and Neil Wenborn (Cambridge University Press, 2008), 413.

God. Supralapsarian Christology is thought to strengthen this tendency by overwriting the history of God and Israel by prioritizing the story of Jesus. In this part of the chapter, I argue that the opposite is true. I will first summarize this argument, as expressed by R. Kendall Soulen, as well as Soulen's own alternative approach. I will then analyze Soulen's line of thought by mapping the various ways in which Christian theology can logically conceive of the relationship between God, incarnation, Israel, and sin. Finally, I will use this map to advance my own arguments. My main claim is that Soulen is incorrect in saying that supralapsarianism is supersessionist by definition. Secondarily, I will argue that my particular supralapsarian approach actually has an advantage over Soulen's Christology in that my approach offers a more consistent non-supersessionist account of the biblical narrative regarding election and incarnation.

Structural Supersessionism

According to Soulen, the canonical narrative that originated in the patristic era and that until quite recently was familiar to virtually every Christian "recounts God's history with human creation in four crucial episodes: God's intention to consummate the human pair whom God has created, the first parents' disobedience and fall, the redemption of lost humanity in Christ, and final consummation."[34] This standard model is deeply implicated in the problem of supersessionism, Soulen charges. It "is structurally supersessionist because it unifies the Christian canon in a manner that renders the Hebrew Scriptures largely indecisive for shaping conclusions about how God's purposes engage creation in universal and enduring ways."[35] In other words, the standard Christian way of telling the biblical narrative is to tell it coherently without God's covenant with Israel playing any essential role. The only part of the Hebrew Scriptures the standard model includes is the first three chapters of Genesis. The story of Israel is structurally irrelevant for the ways in which God relates to what is not God, and thus "God's identity as the God of Israel and God's history with the Jewish people become largely indecisive for the Christian conception of God."[36]

The structural supersessionism of the Christian canonical narrative is only heightened in modern times, Soulen continues. Classical Christian theologians subordinate God's relationship with Israel to a more basic drama concerning the Creator and creation. On such a reading, God's relationship with Israel

---

34. R. Kendall Soulen, *The God of Israel and Christian Theology* (Fortress Press, 1996), 25.
35. Soulen, *God of Israel*, 31.
36. Soulen, *God of Israel*, 33.

"was indecisive in fact but not yet inessential in principle."[37] In the modern period, theologians create, however, an opposition between the particularity of the Old Testament narrative and the universality of its Christian pendant. Theologians like Schleiermacher, Barth, and Rahner narrate the Christian story in terms of the relationship between the particular person Christ and certain universal features of the human condition. For Soulen, this move is connected to the supralapsarian Christology these theologians share. He seems to think the relationship cuts two ways. On the one hand, supralapsarian Christocentrism maintains "the doctrinal integrity of Christian theology after its internal reference to the God of Israel has been wholly cut away."[38] That is, Christian supersessionism needs Christological supralapsarianism to hold together a story that spans both the Old and New Testaments. On the other hand, by referencing Christ as the original goal of God's consummating work, supralapsarian Christology brings traditional structural supersessionism to its full conclusion.[39] Any need for Israel is now excluded.[40]

Over against these two ways of telling the canonical narrative, Soulen proposes an alternative according to which God's covenant with Israel is essential to God's eschatological intentions and goals and, as such, is part of an "overarching plot [that] revolves chiefly not around 'an economy of redemption' contingent on sin but rather around an antecedent economy of consummation based on the Lord's blessing."[41] That is, with the Christological supralapsarians Soulen distinguishes between two kinds of economies, one concerning "God's power to deliver the creature from sin, evil, and oppression," the other focused on "the ultimate good that God intends for human creation antecedent and subsequent to the calamity of sin."[42] But for Soulen it is not so much Christ but Israel who is at the core of God's economy of eschatological consummation.[43] Israel's election, Soulen proposes, should be understood in the context of this "divine purpose antecedent to the crisis of sin and evil."[44] Subordinate to this eschatological plot,

---

37. Soulen, *God of Israel*, 58.
38. Soulen, *God of Israel*, 77.
39. Soulen, *God of Israel*, 76.
40. Soulen, *God of Israel*, 86–90.
41. Soulen, *God of Israel*, 115.
42. Soulen, *God of Israel*, 115.
43. Soulen, *God of Israel*, 110, 115, 131.
44. Soulen, *God of Israel*, 110. As Soulen points out in support of his proposal, and in an argument that echoes the position of Michael Wyschogrod and, later, Jon D. Levenson and R. W. L. Moberly, nothing in the actual call story of Abraham in Genesis 12 "suggests that God's primary motive in calling Abraham is any special concern with the problem of sin, evil, or wickedness. To the contrary, God's motive seems chiefly to be the sheer fecundity and capaciousness of the divine good pleasure." Soulen, *God of Israel*, 120.

and occasioned by sin, is then the work of God as Redeemer and Deliverer.[45] It is the story of a God who "acts in fidelity to God's work as Consummator by refusing to let curse have the last word."[46] This is the story of the gospel, and, as such, the story of incarnation.[47] The story of Jesus is thus subordinated to the story of consummation.[48] He is the one who proclaims God's fidelity to God's coming reign and whose life, death, and resurrection embody the trust and hope that God will do what God promises.[49] As such, "God's victory in Jesus is the center but not the totality of Christian faith."[50] To put it differently, "The unity of the Christian canon is not best unlocked by insisting that everything in the Bible points toward Jesus. . . . More helpful for discerning the unity of the canon is the recognition that the Scriptures and the Apostolic Witness are both centrally concerned with the God of Israel and the God of Israel's coming reign of *shalom*. Without a doubt everything turns on Christ, but not everything concerns Christ. Redemption is for the sake of consummation, not consummation for the sake of redemption."[51]

Mapping the Options

To evaluate Soulen's critique of supralapsarian Christology as well as his alternative proposal, it is helpful to place them both on a larger conceptual map. When it comes to telling the biblical narrative regarding Israel's election and the incarnation, four options are logically possible: One can be an infralapsarian regarding both. One can be an infralapsarian regarding Israel's election but a supralapsarian regarding the incarnation. One can be a supralapsarian regarding Israel's election but an infralapsarian regarding the incarnation. Or one can be a supralapsarian regarding both.

In the West, according to Soulen, the dominant narration of the biblical story moves along the plotline of creation, fall, redemption in Christ, and consummation, without an essential role for God's election of Israel. God elects Israel in response to human history going awry, but only as a preparation for God's work in Christ. This version of the story is therefore infralapsarian regarding Israel's election. It should be observed though that the plotline is also infralapsarian regarding incarnation. For most of the Western theological

---

45. Soulen, *God of Israel*, 141.
46. Soulen, *God of Israel*, 148.
47. Soulen, *God of Israel*, 156.
48. Soulen, *God of Israel*, 159
49. Soulen, *God of Israel*, 161.
50. Soulen, *God of Israel*, 156.
51. Soulen, *God of Israel*, 175.

tradition, neither Israel nor the incarnate One belong to the original divine intentions for creation; they are both contingent upon sin.

Friedrich Schleiermacher is an example of one who is supralapsarian regarding Christology but infralapsarian regarding Israel's election. On his account, Christ's presence is not contingent upon sin but is the supralapsarian means by which God imparts Godself to all humanity.[52] The notion of a particular election of Israel is, however, the result of a sinful, clouded God-consciousness.

Soulen's own proposal, on the other hand, entails a supralapsarian account of Israel's election combined with an infralapsarian Christology. Israel is central to God's eschatological purposes. God's covenant with Israel is not contingent upon sin. Christ and his ministry, however, are an expression of redemption, of God's faithfulness to the covenant and God's eschatological purposes even when sin threatens to undermine God's intentions. On Soulen's reading, the incarnation is infralapsarian.

My own proposal, finally, is supralapsarian regarding both the incarnation and Israel's election. The incarnate One is the embodiment of God's very first intention with regard to that which is not God; it is God's decision to be a God-with-others. Abraham and his family are these others, the recipients of the divine self-giving.

Both Soulen's proposal and my own are thus supralapsarian regarding Israel's election. The question is, then, which proposal better helps us move away from the damaging history of supersessionism.

Infralapsarianism, Supralapsarianism, and Supersessionism

One of the challenges faced by infralapsarian Christology is how to account for the continued presence and role of Christ in the eschaton. If the incarnation is motivated solely by the divine desire to take care of the sin problem, what happens if the problem has been solved? Eschatologically, sin will be no more. So why would Christ still be there? And if Christ is still there, does this not suggest that the eschaton is better than the proton? In the incarnation, God is more intimately present than before. But if the incarnation is solely contingent upon sin, and the incarnation continues in the eschaton, then sin leads to an eschatological abundance we would not have received if sin had not existed. This has led infralapsarians to embrace a form of the *felix culpa* argument: "Oh happy guilt, that merited us to possess such a great Redeemer," as the Latin liturgy of Holy Saturday sings. On this line of thought, we should

---

52. For an analysis, see Edwin Chr. van Driel, *Incarnation Anyway: Arguments for Supralapsarian Christology* (Oxford University Press, 2006), 9–32.

be grateful for sin. This seems theologically incongruent.[53] Would it therefore be better to say that eschatologically, the incarnation does end? But does this not run afoul of the widespread New Testament expectation that Christ is the very center of the new creation? An infralapsarian account of incarnation thus leads to an eschatological conundrum.

Similar questions can be raised about an infralapsarian understanding of Israel's election. If Israel were chosen only in the context of God's dealings with sin, the covenant with Israel would then not be part of the original design or goals of creation. Therefore, it can also be conceived of as coming to an end or being overcome. Supersessionism draws this conclusion. But it is unclear how this reading of the biblical narrative is consistent with the content of the covenantal promises that God establishes an eternal relationship with this people.

Soulen instead offers a supralapsarian reading of Israel's election. God's relationship with Israel is not contingent upon sin but embedded in creation's goals. But his proposal combines this supralapsarian take on Israel with an infralapsarian understanding of the incarnation. Israel is part of God's original intention, but Christ is not. Thus, while Israel's eschatological future is guaranteed, the incarnate One's is not. It is telling that Soulen's proposal is inspired by the work of the Dutch theologian A. A. van Ruler.[54] Van Ruler was one of the few theologians who was willing to think consistently through the consequences of infralapsarian Christology and to bite the bullet. On his account, Christ embodies only a "Messianic intermezzo." His presence is contingent upon sin, and therefore, eschatologically, once sin has been overcome, he will hand the reins back to the Father and fade into the background. The incarnation, on an infralapsarian reading, is only functional.[55]

However, a combination of an everlasting divine covenant with Israel and a functional messianic intermezzo opens the door for the inversion of Christian supersessionism. On this picture, God's relationship with Israel outlasts God's relationship to creation through Christ. This in turn raises the question of how such an account makes sense of the insistence of the Ephesians letter that by being "in Christ" (Eph. 2:13, 2:21) the gentiles have entered into the covenant with Israel. If Christ's reign stretches only as far as needed to counter sin, and if the gentiles' inclusion into the covenant is contingent upon the rule of Christ, what happens when sin is no longer there and Christ's rule

---

53. For the theologically problematic nature of the *felix culpa* argument, see Van Driel, *Incarnation Anyway*, 130–32, 152–53.
54. Soulen, *God of Israel and Christian Theology*, 190n30.
55. See A. A. van Ruler, *Verzameld Werk*, vol. IV.A., *Christus, de Geest en het heil* (Boekencentrum, 2011), 17–40ff.

has ended? God's covenant with Israel will continue, but the basis for the inclusion of the gentiles will have fallen away.[56]

Things look very different on my proposal, where neither incarnation nor Israel's election are contingent upon sin. Both are embedded in creation's eschatological goal, with Christ being the embodiment of divine self-giving and Israel its recipient. One cannot be understood without the other. The arrival of the incarnate One is not the covenant's undoing but its confirmation. The covenant does not outlast Christ's reign but is upheld by it. The gentiles do not replace Israel, nor are they excluded from the gift Israel receives; they are blessed in receiving the gift by being included in Israel.[57]

Conclusion

Supralapsarian Christology provides a basis for a fresh account of Israel's election. The incarnation is the embodiment of God's decision to be a God-with-others, a decision in which God gives Godself to that which is not God. Israel is the recipient of this decision. To become incarnate is to become a concrete human being, and that means becoming part of a family, a tribe, a nation. It means being located in a particular place and history. Israel is called into being to be the incarnate One's family.

---

56. It should be noted that, as of late, Soulen has distanced himself from his original proposal. See R. Kendall Soulen, "The Standard Canonical Narrative and the Problem of Supersessionism," in *Introduction to Messianic Judaism: Its Ecclesial Context and Biblical Foundations*, ed. David Rudolph and Joel Willitts (Zondervan, 2013), 285; and R. Kendall Soulen, *Irrevocable: The Name of God and the Unity of the Christian Bible* (Fortress, 2022), 14–20.

57. Based on other grounds, some may still consider this a supersessionist position. For example, Bruce D. Marshall holds that the irrevocable nature of God's covenant with Israel implies Israel's continued existence as a people separate from the nations, and any account that does not allow for this leads to supersessionism. See Bruce D. Marshall, "Christ and Theology: An Unsolved Problem in Catholic Theology," in *The Call of Abraham: Essays on the Election of Israel in Honor of Jon D. Levenson*, ed. Gary A. Anderson and Joel S. Kaminsky (University of Notre Dame Press, 2013), 330–50.

Since this argument does not pertain to the particular supralapsarian aspect of my position, I will not further engage it here other than to say two things: First, I do not think the covenantal promises imply this. They say that Abraham will be a blessing to the nations and will inherit the world. They do not say how this will be or what the ensuing relationship between Israel and the nations will look like. I take Paul's account to be an original-but-legitimate exegesis of these promises: They are fulfilled in the nations becoming Abraham's children (see Van Driel, *Rethinking Paul*, 201–2, 294–97). And second, if supersessionism is the claim that since Christ's coming the church has taken the place of Israel as God's chosen people, this reading of Paul is not supersessionist. It entails that, in Christ, gentiles give up on their gentile identity and become honorary Jews. These gentiles do not take the place of Israel; rather, they join Israel. In fact, what is lost in this is not the ongoing, distinct existence of Israel but the ongoing, distinct existence of the gentiles.

The objection that rather than choosing one people, God ought to be the Father of all nations, or that God ought to love individuals rather than nations, fundamentally misunderstands what happens in the incarnation. God could have dealt with all people equally—from afar. But for God to give Godself as it happens in the incarnation, taking on a human nature as God's own, is for God to enter the particularity of human existence. Incarnation entails election. This does not mean that those of other tribes and histories are excluded from this gift of divine self-giving. They are included, but not on their own terms. They are blessed by being folded into the particularity of Jesus's family.

This reading offers a sure defense against long-standing traditions of Christian supersessionism. The covenant with Israel cannot be superseded because it is rooted in the very being of the incarnate One himself. To narrate the story of God's history with creation is to begin with Jesus, but to begin with Jesus is to begin with Israel.

9

"In Him All the Fullness of God Was Pleased to Dwell"

On Trinitarian Theology and Supralapsarian Christology

Most of the explorations in this second part of the book concern issues "downstream" from the incarnation. If we think about God's decision to be Jesus Christ as the bedrock of all things that exist, what does this mean for our understanding of creation, or election, or Israel? Another question to ask is whether a commitment to supralapsarian Christology has any consequences "upstream": What does supralapsarian Christology mean for our understanding of God in Godself, the triune nature of God, and how we conceive of the relationship of the triune God to what is not God? In this chapter, I explore one such kind of consequence. Supralapsarian Christology invites us to read differently some of the New Testament passages that concern the second trinitarian person's involvement with the origins of creation. Since, on an infralapsarian Christology, the incarnate One comes only late to God's relating to what is not God, in this tradition these texts are usually read as concerning the non-incarnate divine Word. They are taken as telling us something about the personal properties of the second person and his particular role within the taxis of the Trinity. But once one embraces a supralapsarian Christology, another reading becomes possible: These texts can then be taken as speaking about the *logos incarnandus*, about the God who is committed to be Jesus Christ. And therefore, texts that previously were thought to take us all the way into the immanent Trinity, revealing to us something about the difference between the trinitarian persons, might actually not reveal much beyond the economic Trinity at all.

I wish to explore what this means for trinitarian theology by juxtaposing this hermeneutic with two dominant, but different, lines of thought that together have shaped much of Western trinitarian theology. The first line of thought emphasizes the *similarity* of the trinitarian persons. It thinks about the fact that *one* of these persons becomes incarnate, and that *this* person becomes incarnate as embedded in an absolutely free, contingent decision of God. The other line of thought emphasizes the *difference* between the trinitarian persons. It thinks about the Trinity in terms of self-differentiation and sees the incarnation, and the fact that this particular person becomes incarnate, as embedded in the divine unfolding of Father, Son, and Spirit—a form of self-differentiation that can be conceived as either necessary or free, depending on one's wider theological commitments. My exploration in this chapter is driven by a twofold intuition—that a supralapsarian Christological hermeneutic draws us toward the first, rather than the second, trinitarian model and that, theologically speaking, this is a good thing because the first model fits better the thought that in Jesus Christ God gives Godself fully to that which is not God, that "in him all the fullness of God was pleased to dwell" (Col. 1:19).

Two Ways of Conceiving of the Trinity

Within Western trinitarian thought, two competing intuitions shape theologians' approaches to thinking about the Trinity and its relationship to what is not God. One line of thought conceives of the Trinity's relation to incarnation and creation in the context of divine freedom and contingency. The most pointed expression of this is the thesis, commonplace since Peter Lombard, that not just the Trinity's second person but any of the three trinitarian persons could have become incarnate.[1] Neither the being of God nor the being of creation limits the possibility of incarnation to only the second person. The ties that hold together God, incarnation, and creation are completely contingent, embedded only in the free will of God. Salvation history could have been radically different. The contingent nature of reality is further illustrated by the fact that, on this line of thinking, the incarnability of all three persons goes together with the assumability of all of creation. All of

---

1. Peter Lombard, *The Sentences*, bk. 3, *On the Incarnation of the Word* 1.2, trans. Giulio Silano (Pontifical Institute of Mediaeval Studies, 2010), 5.

creation is *capax Dei* (open to God). As any of the divine persons could have become incarnate—as, indeed, could the triune being itself[2]—any one of them could have assumed a human nature other than the one that was assumed; in fact, any one of them could have assumed any individual substance in nature, whether human or not. In other words, creation lies completely open to God's free ways of engagement.[3] Everything in creation hinges on the free will of God.

The other line of thought binds Trinity, incarnation, and the structures of creation much more tightly together. The central argument here is the fittingness of the second person's incarnation—a fittingness anchored not in the freedom and contingency of God's will but in the essential self-differentiation of God's being. As the first trinitarian person generates the second and the first and second generate the third, they thereby establish difference; and this difference within God is thought to create the space for, and the impetus toward, God's calling into being what is different from God. Moreover, the eternal and essential self-differentiation within God comes in the form of a certain taxis, or ordering, among the trinitarian persons; and this ordering continues to express itself in the ways in which the triune God calls forth and engages all that is not God. The divine *processiones*, and the distinctions they establish among the trinitarian persons, find a continuation in the divine *missiones*—the distinct ways in which the persons make themselves present in creation. And in all of this, only the second person has the distinct personal characteristics that make him capable of incarnation.

In the course of Western theology, this notion of divine self-differentiation takes various forms and shapes. Medieval theologians such as Bonaventure and Thomas Aquinas combine a sense of the congruity of the second person's incarnation with that of the divine freedom to incarnate otherwise. For the eighteenth-century theologian Jonathan Edwards, the divine self-differentiation takes the form of a necessary unfolding of the triune nature of God: Incarnation and creation are the expressions of God's essential creative disposition, which itself is rooted in God's necessary trinitarian self-differentiation. For the nineteenth-century philosopher G. W. F. Hegel, and a whole generation of Hegelian theologians, the necessary divine self-differentiation unfolds over time as the Absolute realizes itself in producing the world of the finite. For twentieth-century social trinitarians, the unfolding happens along the lines of

---

2. Thomas Aquinas, *Summa Theologiae* III.3.3; Bonaventure, *Commentaria in Librum Tertium Sententiarum* 1.1.4.

3. I briefly discuss the theological logic and ontology that undergirds this view in Edwin Chr. van Driel, "The Logic of Assumption," in *Exploring Kenotic Christology*, ed. C. Stephen Evans (Oxford University Press, 2006), 265–90.

interpersonal interaction among the self-differentiating trinitarian persons, each with their own consciousness and center of action.

Within the limited confines of this chapter, I will focus on the theological arguments for the incarnability of all trinitarian persons and the fittingness of the second person's taking on flesh. I will bracket the different ontological contexts in which the latter line of thought has been located. I will, however, consider the position of contemporary theologians who, in opposition to their medieval predecessors, do not believe that both lines of thought can be held together and argue that the incarnation should be grounded solely in divine self-differentiation.

I believe that grounding incarnation and creation in divine self-differentiation comes with significant drawbacks. Some of these have to do primarily with trinitarian concerns, such as the need to conceptualize the essential unity of the one Godhead. The more we differentiate among the characteristics of the trinitarian persons, the more challenging it becomes to uphold their unity and equal divinity. But as I will argue below, there are also specifically Christological questions at stake in this debate. The more we differentiate among the individual participation of the trinitarian persons in the being of God *ad intra* and the work of God *ad extra*, the more it raises the question whether we can say, in any meaningful way, that in Jesus Christ "all the fullness of God was pleased to dwell" (Col. 1:19). In the incarnation, are we dealing with the self-giving of *God*, or only *part* of God?

I want to affirm the incarnability of all three trinitarian persons. At the same time, I believe the medieval scholastics did not effectively deal with those aspects of salvation history that speak to the fittingness of the incarnation of the Trinity's second person. They left themselves open to the objections and construals that would be offered by their modern critics. Therefore, I will explore an alternative. I will read the fit between the second person's incarnation and the nature of creation and salvation history in the light of God's first intention—the intention to be Jesus Christ.

My exploration will develop in four steps: First, I will focus on the trinitarian account of Thomas Aquinas. Here we already see developed, side by side, both ways of conceiving of the Trinity. Given the essential unity of God, the three persons of the Trinity are identical in power and capacity; it is the free decision of God that the second person becomes incarnate. At the same time, given this person's personal properties, it is most fitting that it is he, and not the other two, who takes on a created nature. Second, I will report on the critique recent Roman Catholic theologians have advanced against Aquinas's position in their positing of an essential continuation of the *processiones* in the *missiones*. Third, analyzing the exegetical and theological arguments for this position, it will become clear that it is undergirded by a particular reading of the ways in which the New Testament characterizes the incarnate One as the primordial, eternal image and word of God, after whom human beings are fashioned and through whom they are adopted as God's children. These notions are read as expressing an inner-trinitarian relationship. On an infralapsarian Christology, this is indeed the only reading possible. If the incarnation is not part of God's original intentions for creation, Christ's human nature is not primordial in creation and cannot be the model for or eschatological goal of humanity. On this, supralapsarian Christology paints a very different picture. Fourth and finally, I will explore the exegetical space created by a supralapsarian Christological reading of the biblical narrative and argue that, in fact, a different reading of the relevant texts is not only possible but exegetically preferable.

Thomas Aquinas on the Incarnation's Contingency and Fittingness

The best way to understand Aquinas's account of the clustered relationship between Trinity, incarnation, and creation is to juxtapose two questions from the *Summa Theologiae*: on whether each trinitarian person can assume a human nature and on whether it is fitting for the second person to be the one to do it. In this section, I will trace Aquinas's arguments as he responds to both of these questions positively and situate these arguments in the wider framework of Aquinas's theological narrative.[4]

The Contingency of the Second Person's Incarnation

Aquinas engages the question whether each trinitarian person has the power to assume a human nature with a four-fold response. First, he lays out three arguments that hold that it is impossible for the Father or the Spirit to become incarnate due to their particular personal characteristics. One, through incarnation God becomes the Son of Man. For the Father or the Spirit to become a Son would obscure that which distinguishes each of them from the second person. Two, through the incarnation human beings can receive adoption as children of God (Rom. 8:15). By such an adoption, human beings

---

4. Due to his centrality in contemporary trinitarian discussions, in this chapter I concentrate on Aquinas. However, we should not understand his trinitarian account as unique to him. For example, his contemporary Bonaventure offers an account that is structurally very similar. See Zachary Hayes, "Incarnation and Creation in the Theology of St. Bonaventure," in *Studies Honoring Ignatius Charles Brady Friar Minor*, ed. Romano Stephen Almagno and Conrad L. Harkins (Franciscan Institute, 1976), 309–30.

participate in the likeness of the one who is Son by nature (Rom. 8:29). But neither the Father nor the Spirit is a Son by nature, and therefore neither would be able to give to humanity what the incarnation aims to accomplish. And three, as the one who takes on flesh, the incarnate One is said to be "sent." But the Father cannot be sent because he is unbegotten.[5]

Second, Aquinas argues that each person nonetheless must have the power to assume, given the unity of God, which is grounded on the sameness of the persons' powers: "What the Son can do, the Father can do, for otherwise the three persons would not be equal in power."[6] Aquinas appeals here to a line of thought that is crucial to the development of patristic trinitarian theology. Because in the biblical narrative Father, Son, and Spirit are all said to do the same thing, the church fathers held that the persons' power must be identical.[7]

Third, Aquinas appeals to a sophisticated set of distinctions that allows him to deal with what drives the arguments against the incarnability of each. With regard to an act, Aquinas says, we can distinguish between that by which the act is effected and that in which the act terminates. For example, in an act of assumption, that which makes the act happen is divine power. This power is part of the divine being; all three persons have the same being—and thereby, as established, the same power. The term of an act is that in which the act terminates. In the case of an act of assumption, the term is a person. Regarding a person, we can again make a distinction—this time between different kinds of characteristics. There are those characteristics that make one a person, and

---

5. Aquinas, *Summa Theologiae* III.3.5 arg. 1–3.

6. Aquinas, *Summa Theologiae* III.3.5 s.c., ed. and trans. Thomas Gilby et al., 61 vols. (Blackfriars, 1964–80).

7. For the relationship between trinitarian unity and power, see the discussion in Stephen R. Holmes, *The Quest for the Trinity: The Doctrine of God in Scripture, History and Modernity* (IVP Academic, 2012), 107–10. Historians such as Michel Barnes and Lewis Ayers have highlighted the importance of the argument from divine power for the patristic development of the doctrine of the Trinity. See Michel Barnes, "'One Nature, One Power': Consensus Doctrine in Pro-Nicene Polemic," in *Historica, Theologica et Philosophica, Critica et Philologica*, ed. Elizabeth A. Livingstone, Studia Patristica 29 (Peeters, 1997), 205–23; and Lewis Ayers, "On Not Three People: The Fundamental Themes of Gregory of Nyssa's Trinitarian Theology as Seen in *To Ablabius: On Not Three Gods*," in *Re-thinking Gregory of Nyssa*, ed. Sarah Coakley (Blackwell, 2003), 15–44. See also Adonis Vidu, *The Same God Who Works All Things: Inseparable Operations in Trinitarian Theology* (Eerdmans, 2021), esp. chaps. 2 and 3. As Vidu points out in a discussion pertinent to our overall exploration of the relationship between Trinity, incarnation, and creation, a key illustration for this argument is the act of creation. If creation is *ex nihilo*, it cannot be the result of cooperating powers; it has to be the result of one and the same power. There are no preparatory works for this kind of act that one of the persons could engage in first. It is not an act that can be distributed over multiple agents, since God's calling things into being is not belabored. Therefore, if all three persons are said to be the Creator, the power through which they are acting is not similar, nor jointed, but identical and one (Vidu, *Same God*, 55–56).

there are those that make one this particular person. The first kind of characteristics one has in common with all those who are also persons. These are the characteristics that allow a person to be the term of an act. The three trinitarian persons have this set of characteristics in common, and therefore they not only all have the same power to assume, they also all have the ability to be the term of the act of assumption. However, they differ from one another in the characteristics that make them particular persons—in other words, in personal characteristics such as unbegotten, begotten, and proceeding. While each person can become incarnate due to their shared power and similar personhood, their distinguishing personal characteristics allow Aquinas to make his last move.[8]

Even while each person has the power to become incarnate, how that incarnation would be enacted and what the ensuing salvation history would look like are different based on the personal characteristic of the person who is the term of the act of assumption. Based on this insight, in his fourth response, Aquinas returns to the objections to the whole argument. One, if the Father or the Spirit were to become incarnate—that is, to become "Son of Man" in time—this would not obscure what distinguishes each from the second person of the Trinity since the act of assumption in time would not erase their distinguishing personal characteristics in eternity. Two, if the Father or the Spirit were to become incarnate, we could still receive adoption as a participation of the Son in nature. The way in which we would receive this gift would, however, be different: Rather than receiving it through a history shaped by the Son's presence, we would receive it through a history shaped by the presence of the Father, who would now be the source both of natural and of adopted sonship, or we would receive it through a history shaped by the presence of the Spirit, who forms the bond of love between the Father and the Son. Three, the Father's personal characteristic—that he is unbegotten in eternity—does not exclude him from being begotten in time. But he would definitely not be sent; and, likewise, the Son's eternally being sent would not, then, continue in time. In these alternative histories, *processiones* and *missiones* would not line up with each other.[9] As such, on this picture the relationship between *processiones* and *missiones* is radically contingent—that is, it is subject to the free will of the triune God.

The Fittingness of the Second Person's Incarnation

Or not quite. While any of the three trinitarian persons has the power to become incarnate, and it was a free, contingent divine act for the second

---

8. For Aquinas's introduction to these distinctions, see Aquinas, *Summa Theologiae* III.3.5 co.
9. Aquinas, *Summa Theologiae* III.3.5 ad. 1–3.

person to assume a human nature, Aquinas holds that it was nonetheless fitting for this person, and not either of the other persons, to become incarnate. With "fittingness" Aquinas refers to "those things that truly suit a thing by reason of its distinctive nature."[10] Such is the case with the second person and incarnation.

Aquinas's argument is woven into his understanding of the economy of salvation, which itself is tightly knit into the unfolding of God's trinitarian existence. Aquinas adopts the conception of *exitus* and *reditus*: Creation goes forth from God and returns to God. At the heart of this is God's own going forth and returning; through incarnation and inspiration God gives Godself to creation and draws creation back to Godself. And this movement *ad extra* is in turn rooted in God's trinitarian self-differentiation *ad intra*, as the Father, the source of all things, issues forth Son and Spirit. Thus,

> in the coming out of creatures from the first principle, one observes a certain circulation or "re-gyration," in the fact that all things take as their end point of return that which produced them as their principle. And therefore it is necessary that the return to the end come about through the same realities through which the "exit" from the principle was achieved. Thus, in the same way that the procession of the persons is the rationale for the production of creatures by the first principle, so likewise the procession of the persons is the rationale of this return to the end; since, in the same way that we have been created through the Son and the Holy Spirit, so likewise it is through them that we are united to the ultimate end, as Augustine makes clearly apparent when he writes, "the principle to which we return," that is, the Father, "and the form which we imitate," that is, the Son, "and the grace through which we are reconciled [that is, the Holy Spirit]." And Saint Hilary says: to one alone without-principle and the principle of all things we refer all things by way of the Son.[11]

---

10. Aquinas, *Summa Theologiae* III.1.1 co. For Aquinas's notion of fittingness, see Corey L. Barnes, "Necessary, Fitting, or Possible: The Shape of Scholastic Christology," *Nova et Vetera*, English Edition, 10, no. 3 (2012) 669–78; and Frederick Christian Bauerschmidt, *Thomas Aquinas: Faith, Reason, and Following Christ* (Oxford University Press, 2013), 160–75. For how arguments of fittingness, rather than necessity, shaped already earlier medieval discussions (such as Anselm's) of the incarnability of the three trinitarian persons, see David Brown, "Necessary and Fitting Reasons in Theology," in *The Rationality of Religious Belief: Essays in Honour of Basil Mitchell*, ed. William J. Abraham and Steven W. Holtzer (Oxford University Press, 1987), 211–30. For, again, very similar notions in Bonaventure, see Zachary Hayes, OFM, "The Meaning of *Convenientia* in the Metaphysics of St. Bonaventure," *Franciscan Studies* 34 (1974): 74–100.

11. Thomas Aquinas, I *Scriptum super libros sententiarum* 14.2.2, quoted in Gilles Emery, *The Trinitarian Theology of Saint Thomas Aquinas* (Oxford University Press, 2007), 173–74. See also Dominic Legge, *The Trinitarian Christology of St. Thomas Aquinas* (Oxford University Press, 2017). Emery's and Legge's books are both critical of the recent unearthing of the ways

At the heart of this "circulation," as Aquinas calls it, is a form of mirroring that happens in the issuing forth of the second person by the first person and in the calling forth of creation by the second person's agency. The Son goes forth from the Father as the Father's Word—a Word in which the Father knows himself and knows everything else. As such, this Word is the exact reflection of the one whose knowledge it is. As the Father then calls forth creation, this Word, in which the Father knows all possibilities embedded in himself, is the blueprint of all that is created. Creation is thus the image of the Word, who himself is the image of the Father:

> Since, of course, God understands both himself and other things, . . . his act of understanding is the principle of things understood by him, since they are caused by his intellect and will; but his act of understanding is referred to the intelligible which he himself is as to a beginning, for this intelligible is identified with the intellect understanding, whose emanation, so to say, referred to the other things understood by God as exemplar, and must be referred to God himself whose word he is as image. Hence, one reads in the Word of God in Colossians (1:15) that he is "the image of the invisible God."[12]

In this context Aquinas observes the fittingness of the Word's incarnation. His discussion of this topic in the *Summa Theologiae* begins, according to the practice of medieval scholastic exposition, with the statement of several objections to his thesis. It is clear, however, that this is not where Aquinas's energy is, and these objections never rise to the level of serious issues. The incarnation is meant to give humans true knowledge of God, holds the first objection; thus, the incarnate presence of the Father would have been more convincing. The incarnation inaugurates a new creation, asserts another; thus, it would have, again, been more appropriate for the Father, to whom the power of creation is appropriated, to become incarnate. The purpose of the incarnation is forgiveness of sins, states a third; since forgiveness is appropriate to the Spirit, there was more reason for the third person to take on human flesh.[13] Aquinas rejects these objections almost offhand. Everything can be misused by human sin, so the first person would not have been trusted more than the second. The first person creates through the second, and thus the first person ought also to recreate through the second. And finally, the Spirit is a gift of the second person, and therefore it is actually more fitting

---

in which Aquinas's understanding of the economy of salvation is embedded in his account of trinitarian self-differentiation.

12. Thomas Aquinas, *Summa Contra Gentiles* IV.11.14, trans. Charles J. O'Neil (University of Notre Dame Press, 1975).

13. Aquinas, *Summa Theologiae* III.3.8 arg.

that the second person become incarnate so as to give this gift.[14] Notably, in these responses Aquinas actually goes beyond the positive thesis he wishes to defend. He does not say just that it is appropriate and fitting for the second person to become incarnate; he says it is "more appropriate," and it "ought to happen."[15]

Aquinas reserves most of his creative energy for the body of his positive statement. It is structured along the threefold way in which God, in the actual salvation history, relates to what is not God: in creation, in eschatological consummation, and in redemption. Aquinas juxtaposes each of these with the personal characteristics of the second person and argues from this that it was fitting for exactly this person to become incarnate.

As to creation, Aquinas holds that there is a "sort of general affinity between the Son, the Word of God, and all creatures: the craftsman's mental word, i.e., his idea, is a pattern for whatever he fashions; so too the Word, God's eternal conception, is the exemplar for all creation."[16] Here Aquinas harkens back to the ways in which, in his account of the Trinity, he had exegeted the second person's personal characteristic of being "the Word." Aquinas's position is based on a philosophical theory reflecting on the working of an intellect. In the act of understanding, Aquinas argues, something proceeds from the intellect: a conception of the object understood. This concept can be called the word of the heart, as distinct from the word of the voice.[17] Applying this theory to God, Aquinas states that this is how one is to understand the procession of the Word.[18] In knowing Godself, the Word proceeds from the Father, and in knowing Godself through the Word, God also knows all possibilities that are within God's power. These possibilities function as the exemplar for what God creates. This leads Aquinas to conclude that while the three trinitarian persons always act together—after all, they act in and through the very same power—there is an ordering in their actions based on the personal characteristics of the persons. In the act of creation, God creates through the Word. In fact, given his understanding of

---

14. Aquinas, *Summa Theologiae* III.3.8 ad. 1–3.
15. "Unde et recreation per Verbum fieri debuit Dei Patris"; "Et ideo convenietius fuit." Aquinas, *Summa Theologiae* III.3.8 ad. 2.
16. Aquinas, *Summa Theologiae* III.3.8 co.
17. Aquinas, *Summa Theologiae* I.27.1 co.
18. Aquinas, *Summa Theologiae* I.27.1 co.; I.27.2 ad. 2. For further accounts of this understanding of the generation of the Word—in particular in an exegesis of John 1:1–2—see Aquinas's lecture on John 1:1–2. Thomas Aquinas, *Commentary on the Gospel of John: Chapters 1–8*, trans. Fabian Larcher (Aquinas Institute for the Study of Sacred Doctrine, 2013), 11–28. See also Aquinas, *Summa Contra Gentiles* IV.11. For a virtually identical argument in Bonaventure, see Bonaventure, *Commentaria in librum primum sententiarum* 27.2.1.3 (on which, see Hayes, "Incarnation and Creation," 316–17).

the immanent working of the Trinity, Aquinas holds that "it is impossible that [God] would make anything except through the Son."[19] But then it is also appropriate for the Word to be the one to become incarnate when creation needs to be restored. After all, when a craftsman has made that which he had imagined, and at some point his handiwork is damaged and needs repair, the craftsman will proceed based on the same mental model he used to make the thing in the first place.[20]

It should be noted that in his responses to the objections against the fittingness of the Word's incarnation, Aquinas makes a related point that nonetheless follows a different line of argument. Here too Aquinas appeals to the ordering of the three persons in the divine act of creation. This argument, however, is based not on the personal characteristics but on the way in which the divine nature is distributed among them. According to Aquinas, the first person is the font of divinity. The divine nature is common to all three trinitarian persons, but the Son receives it from the Father, and the Spirit receives it from both the Father and the Son. Therefore, the work that God does is shaped by the same *taxis*: "To be the Creator is attributed to the Father as to the one not having the power from another. Of the Son we process that through him all things were made, for while yet not having this power yet from himself, for the preposition 'through' in ordinary usage customarily denotes an intermediate cause, or a principle from a principle."[21] Based on this ordering in the act of creation, Aquinas now concludes to the appropriateness of the Word's incarnation in the act of recreation: "The first creation of things is by the power of God the Father through the Word. Hence also the second creation ought to be by the power of God the Father through the Word, so that re-creation corresponds to creation."[22]

As to consummation, Aquinas works with the notion that the eschatological goal of the predestined is to be adopted as children of God, joint heirs with Christ (Rom. 8:16–17). Based on Romans 8:29 ("For those whom he foreknew he also predestined to be conformed to the image of his Son"), Aquinas holds that this adoption takes the shape of a transformation in the likeness of the Son. Aquinas reads "Son" as a reference to the incarnate One's divine personhood, not his human nature.[23] Based on this, Aquinas concludes that it is appropriate for the second person to become incarnate.

---

19. Commenting on John 1:3. See Aquinas, *Commentary on the Gospel of John*, 32.
20. Aquinas, *Summa Theologiae* III.3.8. co.
21. Aquinas, *Summa Theologiae* I.45.6 ad. 2.
22. Aquinas, *Summa Theologiae* III.3.8 ad. 2.
23. For Aquinas, his being "the Word" is the hermeneutical key to understand the second person's "sonship." See Aquinas, *John: Chapters 1–8*, 15.

Finally, as to redemption, Aquinas draws a parallel between the structure of the fall and of salvation. Referencing Genesis 3:5, he observes that humans sinned because they desired knowledge. Salvation therefore fittingly comes from the incarnate presence of the one who is "the Word of true wisdom."[24]

Processiones and *Missiones*

Aquinas thus aims to hold together the freedom and fittingness of God's trinitarian relating to what is not God. Given the divine nature, God's actions toward creation are absolutely contingent. God could have acted differently; and, since all three trinitarian persons share in the very same divine power, the trinitarian persons could have been involved in the divine activity *ad extra* in different ways. Nevertheless, the divine actions as enacted are congruent with the nature of divine self-differentiation. The trinitarian *missiones* are understood as a continuation of the trinitarian *processiones*. The divine work *ad extra* mirrors the divine work *ad intra* and fittingly mirrors the mirroring within the inner-trinitarian self-differentiation.

At the same time, the notion of divine self-differentiation exerts a pressure on Aquinas that pushes him beyond the idea of the simple fittingness of the divine actions *ad extra*. Given the inner-trinitarian relationships, it is "more than fitting" that the second person becomes incarnate. In fact, God the Father cannot create any differently than through the Word. Therefore, God also "ought" to recreate through the Word. Aquinas never seems to fully weigh the implication of these statements. The stipulation about the act of creation seems to imply a difference in power between the trinitarian persons, which then in turn limits the capacity for incarnation. It is difficult to square this with the sameness in power that upholds the unity of the Trinity.

Nonetheless, as trinitarian thinking developed, the balance between divine freedom and self-differentiation decidedly moved in the direction of divine self-differentiation. For modern and contemporary trinitarian thought, this is now the governing paradigm. The self-differentiating divine processions are thought to find their essential continuation in the divine missions.

To support these moves, at least two lines of thoughts are lifted up. First, the (exegetical) arguments from fittingness are essentialized. For example, in a recent essay Thomas Weinandy takes Aquinas to task for his thesis of the incarnability of all three trinitarian persons.[25] Weinandy's main strategy is to

---

24. Aquinas, *Summa Theologiae* III.3.8 s.c.
25. Thomas G. Weinandy, "Trinitarian Christology: The Eternal Son," in *The Oxford Handbook of the Trinity*, ed. Gilles Emery and Matthew Levering (Oxford University Press, 2011), 387–99.

press in on the three arguments Aquinas himself formulated for the fittingness of the second person's incarnation and to argue that these imply more than fittingness; rather, they describe the only possible avenue for an incarnational divine relating to what is not God. Agreeing with Aquinas's philosophical exegesis of the second trinitarian person as "the Word," Weinandy holds that through the Word the Father knows himself and all that is and could be, and therefore the Word must be the one through whom God created the world and in whom it finds its order. Weinandy suggests that for another person to become incarnate in order to carry out the work of restoration of creation would be to "undermine the very identity of the Son as Word . . . of the Father."[26] Likewise, Weinandy points out that as the Word, the second person is the "divine person whose very identity, who he is as a divine person, is defined as the Word of wisdom and truth."[27] Since it is central to the work of redemption to engender the Father's wisdom and truth in the believers, only the Word can appropriately become incarnate to engage in this work. However, "the heart of the issue," for Weinandy, is humanity's eschatological end to become the adopted children of the Father.[28] As the Word, the second person contains all that the Father is and is therefore "the perfect image of the Father."[29] When God, through the Word, calls creation into being, God fashions human beings in God's image and likeness. This means that the Father creates them in the likeness of the Son, who, after all, is the Father's image and likeness.[30] To be created in God's likeness therefore contains an eschatological destination: to know, live, and reflect the Father's truth the way the Son does.[31] But this means, Weinandy holds, that "it would not only be inappropriate but also ontologically impossible" to obtain such sonship through the incarnation of the Father or the Spirit, "given that only the divine Son is ontologically the Son of the Father and thus only he could obtain humankind's adopted sonship."[32]

A second line of argument is rooted in the notion of divine revelation. Karl Rahner is probably the most prominent representative of this widely endorsed argument. For Rahner, the core of God's dealing with creation is God's self-communication: God gives Godself to that which is not God, and God gives Godself completely as God is.[33] Self-communication implies

26. Weinandy, *Handbook of the Trinity*, 393.
27. Weinandy, *Handbook of the Trinity*, 394.
28. Weinandy, *Handbook of the Trinity*, 394.
29. Weinandy, *Handbook of the Trinity*, 391.
30. Weinandy, *Handbook of the Trinity*, 392.
31. Weinandy, *Handbook of the Trinity*, 392.
32. Weinandy, *Handbook of the Trinity*, 394.
33. See Karl Rahner, *The Trinity* (Crossroad, 1999), 34–38.

self-involvement. This means, Rahner believes, that the economy of salvation cannot just be an expression of what God can and will do but must touch on the very being of who God is. The act of divine self-giving must be rooted in the very identity of God. Without this rooting, it would amount to nothing but a role God plays, and thereby fall short of self-communication. Reflecting on the doctrine of the Trinity, this conviction leads Rahner to a two-way argument—one that moves from the economy to the immanent Trinity and from the immanent Trinity to the economy.

In the economy of salvation we experience a form of divine self-differentiation. We encounter God as Father, Son, and Spirit—persons who, in the way they relate to creation, express particular characteristics; and we experience between them a certain kind of ordering, expressed in a particular set of relationships. If God's relating to that which is not God is a form of self-communication, and if self-communication is an expression of divine identity, then what is being expressed and lived out by God in the economy must reveal the essence of who God is. Thus, the divine self-differentiation experienced in the economy is not a contingent feature, accidental to the divine being; it expresses God's very essence. For instance, in the economy we experience two distinct-but-related ways in which the unoriginated Father communicates himself to creation: one through the Son's incarnation and one through the Spirit's drawing creation to acceptance. Given Rahner's understanding of self-communication, this must mean that when God freely steps outside of Godself, this twofold way of relating is itself not contingent but reflects the essential features of who God is within Godself and thereby is the only way in which God could communicate Godself.[34]

In this way, we can travel from the economic to the immanent Trinity. But we can also travel in the opposite direction. If in the economic Trinity God gives creation that which is essential to the identity and life of the triune God, then the economic *missiones* are to be described as continuations of the immanent *processiones*. The divine self-differentiation within God expresses itself in, and finds a continuation in, the divine self-communication to what is not God—and this self-differentiation could not communicate itself in another way.[35] Thus, in the act of divine revelation, there is a straight line from the shape of the immanent Trinity to the economic Trinity.

---

34. Rahner, *Trinity*, 83, 86.

35. In these last two paragraphs, I have tried to describe what Rahner himself summarizes as follows: "The 'economic' Trinity is the 'immanent' Trinity and the 'immanent' Trinity is the 'economic' Trinity" (Rahner, *Trinity*, 22). This summary is generally known as "Rahner's rule." It strikes me that calling it a rule is not helpful; it suggests that this quote is the axiomatic starting point from which Rahner's trinitarian account unfolds. Rahner does indeed call it an

Given all of this, Rahner rejects the idea that each of the trinitarian persons has the power to become incarnate. In fact, he thinks this notion has had a devastating effect on our understanding of the Trinity and its relationship to what is not God, for it implies that the divine revelation given to us in the incarnation is not a form of self-revelation, since it does not teach us anything about the inner-trinitarian life. "If we admit that *every* person might assume a hypostatic union with a created reality, then the fact of the incarnation of the logos 'reveals' properly nothing about the Logos *himself*, that is, about his own relative specific features within the divinity."[36]

Against Trinitarian Self-Differentiation

As I noted in the introduction, a trinitarian model in which divine self-differentiation overrules divine freedom comes at a significant theological cost. The more we read the self-differentiated reality of the economic Trinity into the immanent Trinity, the more difficult it becomes to avoid saying that each of the three persons has substantial attributes that the other two do not have.[37] And the greater the distance between the trinitarian persons, both in their ontological makeup and in their economic engagement with what is not God, the harder it is to speak of one God. As I noted above, the commitment to oneness in divine power and act was central to the development of the doctrine of the Trinity.

Given the topic of this book, it might be worthwhile to point out one Christological consequence of the modern emphasis on trinitarian self-differentiation. The more we differentiate among the persons of the Trinity, the more difficult

---

axiom, but in his argument it functions more as a conclusion. As Rahner himself points out, its correctness can only be established based on his trinitarian account (Rahner, *Trinity*, 22), and thus not the other way around. Given the well-known interpretative difficulties with Rahner's rule, it might be better to avoid using it altogether. In particular, Rahner's formulation makes it hard to avoid the conclusion that the economic Trinity—and, thereby, all of God's actions—are necessary. For a discussion of the various interpretive options, see Randal Rauser, "Rahner's Rule: An Emperor Without Clothes," *International Journal of Systematic Theology* 7, no. 1 (2005): 81–94; Vincent Battaglia, "An Examination of Karl Rahner's Trinitarian Theology," *Australian eJournal of Theology* 9 (2007): 1–18; and Dennis Jowers, "An Exposition and Critique of Karl Rahner's Axiom: 'The Economic Trinity is the Immanent Trinity and Vice Versa,'" *Mid-American Journal of Theology* 15 (2004): 165–200.

36. Rahner, *Trinity*, 37.

37. It is for this reason that, for instance, Augustine wished to avoid saying that the Father, while bringing forth wisdom, would become wise through the Son, because otherwise he would be lacking an essential attribute of divinity. See Vidu, *Same God*, 68. This argument seems to undermine the kind of self-differentiation Aquinas pursues in his understanding of the Word's generation by the Father.

it is to maintain that in Jesus Christ *God* becomes incarnate. If the *missiones* are extensions of the *processiones*, does the *missio* of the second person truly amount to the incarnation of the Godhead? Because surely the *processio* that generates the second person is not the *processio* of *God*.

However, how convincing are the arguments for the idea that the self-differentiating divine processions find their essential continuations in the divine missions? I believe Rahner's argument is the least impressive, notwithstanding its significant influence. The difficulties in interpretating the notion that "the 'economic' Trinity is the 'immanent' Trinity and the 'immanent' Trinity is the 'economic' Trinity" are well documented.[38] A strict reading would imply the complete identification of God's immanent life and economic life, which would make creation and history, as the space in which the economic Trinity moves and has its being, constitutive of the divine existence. Most Christian theologians are not willing to pay this price. But even if we interpret Rahner in a way that does not demand the strict identification of God's being and God's incarnate history, Rahner's epistemological concerns are based on a deeply problematic premise. When Rahner argues that God's economic self-giving needs to be grounded in God's essential being—otherwise, in God's economic life, God would be only playing a role, not truly self-involved, and not truly self-revealing—he is working with the premise that only those things are real to someone that are essential to their existence. This is a premise deeply ingrained in the structures of Greek philosophy, but it is also one that Christian metaphysics emancipated itself from. After all, the Christian story is concerned with many things that are real but nonetheless not essential: election, covenant, creation, sin, forgiveness, love. On a Christian understanding, God and human beings must be able to truly give themselves without their essences requiring them to act in this way.

These concerns about the implications of Rahner's epistemological argument can be further unpacked when applied to the incarnation. For example, if one holds that the economic Trinity is the immanent Trinity and one recognizes any form of subordination in the economic Trinity, one then has to affirm essential subordination in the immanent Trinity—which would threaten the equality of the divine persons, and therefore their unity as one God. However, if, because of this, we were to understand the subordination in the economic Trinity not as an essential feature of God's triunity but, rather, as a voluntary act on the part of the second person, Rahner's argument would make us say that the incarnation cannot qualify as divine self-revelation.[39]

---

38. Rahner, *Trinity*, 22. See note 35, above.
39. A version of this argument can be found in Vidu, *Same God*, 48–49.

Weinandy's arguments are much more forceful. Weinandy presses on the very places where Aquinas's own language goes beyond his official position. Given Aquinas's account of the second person's personal properties and his place within the trinitarian *taxis*, it is "more appropriate" for the second person to become incarnate, and it "ought to happen," Aquinas says. Weinandy's essentialist reading of the biblical speech about the Son draws out the consequences of these statements.

It is exactly here that a supralapsarian Christological hermeneutic can offer a new path. Aquinas's account of the trinitarian personal properties is based on a particular interpretation of three New Testament designations for the incarnate One: image, Son, and Word. Aquinas, and Weinandy with him, read these as expressing essential attributes of the incarnate One's divine nature: He is the perfect, eternal, and essential *image*, or *likeness*, of the Father, in whose likeness creation is called forth. He is the Father's *Son*, expressing an essential inner-trinitarian filial relationship that serves as a model for the economic relationship God establishes with human beings when they are adopted as the Father's children. And he is the *Word* of the Father, established in the Father's act of knowing himself and the possibilities embedded in his power, and as such the exemplar of all that is not God. In the following sections, I will explore how the central intuition of this book, that the first divine intention *ad extra* is to be Jesus Christ, allows us to read these biblical notions differently—as characteristics not of the inner-trinitarian *processiones* but of the Christologically determined *missiones*.

The Incarnate One as Image

The idea of *imaging* is central to the arguments that draw on trinitarian divine self-differentiation. The Son is thought to be the inner-trinitarian, perfect reflection of the Father, the font of divinity; when creation is called into being, it in turn is made to reflect the Son.

Jonathan Edwards sees in this very train of thought the basis for another supralapsarian Christological argument. The Father's producing One who is exactly like him is usually taken to be the expression of the Father's essential desire for self-communication. However, if the Son is the exact image of the Father, then the Son will have the very same essential desire. As the Father produces the Son, the Father also delights in the Son's reflection of the Father's own perfection—including the Father's inclination to communicate himself. For Edwards, this delight results in an inner-trinitarian election: The Father wills the Son's eternal happiness. The Son's happiness, however, calls for an act of self-communication. Since there is no inner-trinitarian object to which the Son can communicate himself—the Father already has everything the Son might wish to give—the object of the Son's self-communication must be external. And thus, the Son is united with a creaturely nature in the incarnation for the purpose of communicating the Son's perfections.[40]

Edwards's argument brings out an unexpected consequence of the idea of divine self-differentiation. However, his argument also illustrates the theological problem of this form of trinitarian modeling. On this kind of account, the Father, as the font of divinity, has all divine properties independently of the other trinitarian persons and can operate these independently of the other trinitarian persons. This finds expression in the Father's delight in and election of the Son. Moreover, if the Son is the exact image of the Father, then in producing the Son, the Father gives the Son the ability to likewise will and act in distinction from other trinitarian persons such as the Father.[41] But this undermines the unity of the Godhead in such a way that it is hard to see how this model does not lead to the conclusion that there are three gods.

The theological argument about *imaging* is rooted in the New Testament's notion that Jesus Christ is the image of God (2 Cor. 4:4; Col. 1:15; "imprint," Heb. 1:3) and that humanity in turn is to be transformed into the image of

---

40. Here is one of several passages in which Edwards addresses this: "God the Son, having the infinite goodness of the divine nature in him, desired to have a proper object to whom he might communicate his goodness: to have this object in the nearest, strictest union with himself, and therefore desires (to speak of him after the manner of men) a spouse to be brought and presented to himself in such a near relation and strict union as might give him the greatest advantage to communicate his goodness to her." Jonathan Edwards, "Approaching the End of God's Grand Design," in *The Works of Jonathan Edwards*, vol. 25, *Sermons and Discourses, 1743–1758*, ed. Wilson H. Kimnach (Yale University Press, 2006), 117. For a thorough discussion of Edward's supralapsarian Christology, see Phillip A. Hussey, *Supralapsarianism Reconsidered: Jonathan Edwards and the Reformed Tradition* (T&T Clark, 2024), esp. 91–120.

41. That this interpretation is not far-fetched is clear from the way in which Edwards elsewhere analyzes the Trinity *ad extra* and the new covenant. See Jonathan Edwards, "Economy of the Trinity and the Covenant of Redemption," in *The Works of Jonathan Edwards*, vol. 20, *The Miscellanies, 833–1152*, ed. Amy Plantinga Pauw (Yale University Press, 2002), 431–43. Edwards argues that while "the persons of the Trinity are not inferior to one another in glory and excellence of nature," there exists subordination among them "by mutual free agreement, whereby the persons of the Trinity of their own will have as it were formed themselves into a society for carrying on the great design of glorifying the Deity and communicating its fullness." Edwards, "Economy of the Trinity," 430–31. Within this, the Father "acts as the head of the society of the Trinity" and as such appoints the Son as the mediator of redemption and promises the Son "honor and award"—something that, Edwards points out, witnesses to the Father's capacity to act on his own, as these promises were not made "by all persons of the Trinity, acting conjunctly." Edwards continues, describing the "covenant of redemption" as "a free covenant entered by [the Father] and his Son," in which the Son "acts altogether freely, and as in his own right," and the Son "becomes obliged to the Father with respect to it by voluntary covenant engagement." Edwards, "Economy of the Trinity," 433–36. All this presupposes a trinitarian ontology in which the three trinitarian persons do not essentially act through one will and one mind, but in which each has their own will and mind.

Christ (Rom. 8:29; 1 Cor. 15:29; Col. 3:16). The notion of image is, of course, taken from the Old Testament notion that human beings were created *in* God's image (Gen. 1:26).

As we embark on an exegetical exploration of this notion, three things should be observed from the outset. First, the phrase *image of God* is relatively rare in the Old Testament, and exegetes differ greatly about its meaning.[42] This is important background to the fact that in the New Testament the phrase is used exclusively for Jesus. It is as if the canon only then knows what to make of it. Second, a similar contrast can be drawn concerning the way both parts of the canon apply the phrase. One of the reasons exegetes and theologians offer a wide range of interpretations of the phrase is that the Old Testament is not clear about the phrase's terms of comparison between the Creator and creation. Exactly which aspect of human existence mirrors divinity, and how? Influential theological traditions have located the *imago Dei* particularly in human spiritual or mental capacities. But in the New Testament, the notion clearly refers to Jesus in his embodied form. In particular, it expresses the idea that Jesus makes God present and visible in the very thing that itself is not God.[43] This goes far beyond what the Old Testament seems to be saying. In this respect it is also noteworthy that the New Testament does not speak about Jesus being *in* the image of God; rather, it says he *is* God's image. Third, human beings are said to be transformed into this image. That is, their imaging is mediated by the way Christ's embodied existence makes visible the invisible God. This is actually in line with the Jewish exegetical tradition: When humans are said to be created *in* God's image, this assumes God already has an image after which humanity is patterned.[44] The New Testament writers seem to claim that they know who this original image is: Jesus.

Colossians 1

In chapter 7 I paid extensive attention to Colossians 1 as a place where the supralapsarian Christological logic of the biblical narrative comes to the

---

42. It is therefore all the more remarkable that the notion has taken such a central position in Christian theological anthropology. One might wonder whether the biblical notions can carry the theological weight that the Christian tradition has put on them. On this, see David H. Kelsey, *Eccentric Existence: A Theological Anthropology* (Westminster John Knox, 2009) 895–1051; and Marc Cortez, *Resourcing Theological Anthropology: A Constructive Account of Humanity in the Light of Christ* (Zondervan, 2017), 99–129.

43. The New Testament repeatedly emphasizes that through Jesus God can finally be seen. See John 1:14, 18; 14:9; Col. 2:9.

44. See Chris Kugler, *Paul and the Image of God* (Lexington Books / Fortress Academic, 2020), 61–88.

surface.⁴⁵ For the sake of this chapter's argument, I would like to summarize my earlier conclusions.

The hymn concerns the incarnate Christ, who as such is said to relate to God and creation as God's image (*eikōn*) and creation's firstborn (*prōtotokos*). That is, the subject of the hymn is not the *logos asarkos*, the non-incarnate Word, or wisdom as it existed before the creation of the world, or the second person of the Trinity. The hymn sings of Christ in the flesh. This is clear from the outset: the Colossians writer comes to the hymn having just spoken of the economy of salvation, in which the Father is said to have rescued the letter's gentile readers from the power of darkness and given them a share in the heritage of the saints, the chosen ones, by ushering them into the kingdom of the beloved Son (Col. 1:12–14). This One, the Son in whom all this has come about, is the *he* to whom the opening lines of the hymn refer. This One is said to be God's *eikōn*, the one who makes the invisible God visible.⁴⁶ This cannot be said of the *logos asarkos*, the second person of the Trinity. The divine Word in and of itself is just as invisible as the Father and the Spirit. But the triune Godhead becomes visible as the Son takes on flesh. In other words, that this one is called God's image does not in and of itself express consubstantiality; rather, it implies the opposite.

As this one takes on flesh, he does so not as one among many but as the *prōtotokos* (a word that stands both for first in birth order and for preeminence in rank). *Eikōn* and *prōtotokos* are thus notions that refer to the selfsame action of the Son, albeit under different aspects: the incarnate Son in his relationship to God (*eikōn*) and in his relationship to creation (*prōtotokos*). Therefore, claims the hymn, all of creation has the incarnation as the context in which it lives. The incarnate Son is the instrument through which creatures have their existence and the goal for which they were created.

Within the Colossians hymn, then, *eikōn* does not refer to an innertrinitarian reality. Rather, its use indicates that in Jesus we have a form of divine self-expression in what is not God. But it is a supralapsarian form of divine self-expression: It precedes everything else, and everything else exists for its sake.⁴⁷ And thus, this text does not have to support divine self-differentiation;

---

45. See "The Firstborn of All Creation" in chap. 7, above, 133–37.

46. *Eikōn* connotes a physical representation. See Markus Barth and Helmut Blanke, *Colossians: A New Translation with Introduction and Commentary*, Anchor Bible 34B (Doubleday, 1994), 195; and Scot McKnight, *The Letter to the Colossians* (Eerdmans, 2018), 147.

47. Characterizing the ways in which we may interpret the Christological use of the *imago Dei* concept in the New Testament, Marc Cortez suggests the primarily options are to take it either as advancing an anthropological claim identifying Jesus as the perfect expression of what it means to be human or as advancing a trinitarian claim about the relationship between the Father and the Son in eternity. Cortez argues for the former (Cortez, *Resourcing Theological*

it speaks only of the economy in which God becomes visible by becoming incarnate.

2 Corinthians 3:1–4:6

This interpretation of the iconic character of the incarnate Christ is supported by the way in which Paul uses the notion of the *imago Dei* elsewhere. In 2 Corinthians 3 and 4 Paul speaks of Christ as a mirror in whom we see the glory of God:

> All of us, with unveiled faces, seeing the glory of the Lord as though reflected in a mirror, are being transformed into the same image [*eikōn*] from one degree of glory to another. . . . [But] the god of this world has blinded the minds of the unbelievers, to keep them from seeing the light of the gospel of the glory of Christ, who is the image [*eikōn*] of God. . . . It is the God who said, 'Let light shine out of darkness,' who has shone in our hearts to give the light of the knowledge of the glory of God in the face of Jesus Christ. (2 Cor. 3:18; 4:4, 6)

The concluding references to Christ's face as the place where we see God's glory should already alert us to the fact that Paul speaks here not about Christ's inner-trinitarian existence as the image of God but, rather, about his incarnate form. Moreover, this observation is decidedly supported by Paul's use of *mirror* as a metaphor for the way in which Christ images God. A mirror is not of the same material or nature as that which it reflects. We may look in a mirror and see a reflection of ourselves; but whereas we exist as three-dimensional creatures made up of flesh and blood, the image we see is a two-dimensional reflection on a flat surface consisting of polished metal and glass. At the same time, the reflective character of the mirror allows us to see, and to learn about, the very entity it reflects. Mirroring language would not apply to the relationship between the trinitarian persons. On all accounts, each person is of the same exact nature and quality as the others. But in the case of the incarnate One, we are dealing with one whose nature and quality is indeed radically different from God's—a creature rather than the Creator, a man of flesh and blood. Nonetheless, the claim goes, in this creaturely nature we get to know the One who is on the other side of the ontological gap: the God of Israel, the Creator of the world. In this context, the notion of mirroring is not only appropriate but necessary. It fulfills the apostle's need to express simultaneously the radical ontological difference

---

Anthropology, 116). I argue for a third option: By its use of the *imago Dei* concept, the New Testament is advancing a theological claim identifying Jesus as the perfect human expression of what it means to be God.

between the Creator and the man of Nazareth and the fact that in this man we nonetheless behold the Creator, Godself.

In this passage, Paul makes use of imagery drawn from Exodus 33 and 34, according to which God communed with Moses—but nonetheless did not, as Moses wished, let Moses see God's face and glory. The rabbis have puzzled over the fact that Numbers 12:6–8a seems to be saying the opposite. There, God says, "With [Moses] I speak face to face—clearly, not in riddles; and he beholds the form of the LORD" (12:8a). One rabbinic exegetical tradition suggests that Moses had access to God by way of a mirror. Another suggests that what Moses really saw when he beheld the form of God was God's image. Either way, the Numbers text is read and harmonized with the Exodus material by suggesting that Moses saw God through an intermediary. This exegesis was also familiar to Philo, who rejected it. If it was familiar to Philo, it may also have been familiar to Paul. Therefore, some contemporary exegetes argue that Paul Christologically adapts this Jewish exegetical tradition when he claims that Christ is God's image. On such a reading, Paul may be taken to say that what Moses desired to see, and what he may (Num. 6:8) or may not (Exod. 33:20) have seen, was not the non-incarnate God but the incarnate Christ.[48]

And thus, again, it is a mistake to take this text as offering insight into the inner life of the Trinity and the nature of trinitarian self-differentiation. Rather, it expresses the economic self-communication of God in the human face of Jesus. And as such, this reading would fit well with a supralapsarian Christological hermeneutic according to which this economic self-communication goes to the core of God's intentions for the incarnation.

Hebrews 1:2–4

A final text in which I would like to explore the exegetical possibilities opened up by supralapsarian Christology for interpreting the New Testament's designation of Jesus as the image of God is Hebrews 1:2–4: "In these last days [God] has spoken to us by a Son, whom he appointed heir of all things, through whom he also created the worlds. He is the reflection [*apaugasma*] of God's glory and the exact imprint [*charaktēr*] of God's very being [*hypostasis*], and he sustains all things by his powerful word."

A traditional reading, adhered to by Thomas Aquinas, is to think about this as expressing inner-trinitarian relationships.[49] On this reading, *apaugasma*

---

48. On the rabbinic traditions, Philo, and this exegesis of Paul, see in particular M. David Litwa, "Transformation through a Mirror: Moses in 2 Cor. 3:18," *Journal for the Study of the New Testament* 34, no. 3 (2012): 286–97; and Kugler, *Paul and the Image of God*, 132–38.

49. See Thomas Aquinas, *Commentary on the Epistle to the Hebrews*, trans. Chrysostom Baer, O. Praem (St. Augustine's Press, 2006), 18–19. This interpretation is still defended by

is understood actively—as a radiance going forth from God's being, the way a beam goes forth from the sun. While many patristic readers understood the term in this way, many contemporary exegetes prefer its passive meaning: reflection. As such, *apaugasma* would read parallel to *charaktēr*.[50] The latter phrase stands for the imprint that a seal makes on a surface.[51] But such a surface is by definition different in nature from that which imprints it. On such a reading, *apaugasma* and *charaktēr* do not express an identity between the original (God) and the copy (the Son) but presuppose a difference; the Son reflects God's glory in something that is not God.[52]

An infralapsarian hermeneutic has difficulty making sense of this. After all, the text claims that the very one who reflects God's glory in what is not God is also the one through whom God created the world. On an infralapsarian understanding of the incarnation, this does not make sense—incarnation is supposed to logically follow creation, not the other way around. A supralapsarian hermeneutic, however, creates the logical space for exactly this claim. God's first intention is to be Jesus. Thus, through this One, God created the world; by this One, God has spoken "in these last days: (Heb. 1:2); and for this One, everything is destined.

The Incarnate One as Son (Adoption)

As I noted above, for Weinandy the central argument for the incarnability of only the second person of the Trinity hinges on the biblical imagery about the eschatological adoption of human beings as children of God. Ontologically, such adoption can be brought about only by the One who is naturally the Son, Weinandy claims. Further argument for this claim is not given, even

---

contemporary theologians. See, e.g., John Webster, *God Without Measure: Working Papers in Christian Theology*, vol. 1, *God and the Works of God* (T&T Clark, 2016), 59–80.

50. See Harold W. Attridge, *The Epistle to the Hebrews*, Hermeneia (Fortress Press, 1989), 42–43.

51. See Luke Timothy Johnson, *Hebrews: A Commentary*, New Testament Library (Westminster John Knox, 2006), 69.

52. This reading is already offered by Calvin. See John Calvin, *Commentaries on the Epistle of Paul the Apostle to the Hebrews*, trans. John Owen (Baker, 2005), 35–36:

> When, therefore, thou hearest that the Son is the brightness of the Father's glory, think thus with thyself, that the glory of the Father is invisible until it shines forth in Christ, and that he is called the impress of his substance, because the majesty of the Father is hidden until it shews itself impressed as it were on his image. . . . God is made known to us in no other way than in Christ: for as to the essence of God, so immense is the brightness that it dazzles our eyes, except it shines on us in Christ. It hence follows, that we are blind as to the light of God, until in Christ it beams on us, . . . for as God is in himself to us incomprehensible, his form appears to us only in the Son.

though *prima facie* it is not necessarily true. After all, the trinitarian Son receives his Sonship from one who is not naturally the Son. If the Father gives the Son Sonship without being a Son himself, what prevents the Father—or the Spirit—from being the trinitarian person through whose incarnation humanity's adoption is wrought?

For my purposes, however, it is most important to point out that what informs the notion of eschatological adoption is the Pauline stipulation that those "who are led by the Spirit of God are children of God" and "have received a Spirit of adoption" by which they cry "Abba! Father!" (Rom. 8:14–15). As such, they are "joint heirs with Christ" (8:17). This Christ is the Son Paul speaks of when he writes, "Those whom [God] foreknew he also predestined to be conformed to the image of his Son, in order that he might be the firstborn within a large family" (8:29). When Aquinas quotes these verses, it is clear that he interprets the Son, in whose likeness we are transformed, to be the second person of the Trinity, the person whose divine nature functions as the model for humans' eschatological transformation.[53]

However, this interpretation ignores the theological language fields in which Paul uses the terms *adoption* and *Sonship*. First, when Paul speaks of *adoption* he thereby underscores the qualitative difference, not the similarity, between God and creation. There is a long tradition in the Old Testament that speaks of Israel as sons and daughters of God (Exod. 4:22; Deut. 32:6; Isa. 43:6–7). Israel's king is even characterized as God's firstborn (Ps. 89:27). But as Israel's monotheistic understanding of God grew and the prophets emphasized the qualitative difference between God and all that is not God, any understanding of Israel as sons and daughters of God had to be severely qualified. In this context, the notion of adoption lies close at hand. Paul in turn uses the notion of adoption to show a theological opening for the inclusion of gentiles into the ever-expanding family. On the one hand, to Israel belongs the glory and the covenant (Rom. 9:4); but on the other hand, it belongs to them only adoptively, not naturally (9:4). Therefore, sonship is not an exclusive possession of Israel. God can take gentiles and, through them, widen God's adoptive family. In fact, Paul seems to say that this family is expanded so much that it includes even the nonhuman part of creation (Rom. 8:21).[54] This notion of adoptive sonship stands in contrast to the sonship of the One to whom Paul never applies any adoption language: Jesus. He is "the firstborn," the one after whose image the adopted family is being transformed eschatologically. However,

---

53. Aquinas, *Summa Theologiae* III.3.5 arg. 1–3. See "The Contingency of the Second Person's Incarnation," above, 177–78.
54. For a discussion of the ways exegetes come to this conclusion, see Van Driel, *Rethinking Paul: Protestant Theology and Pauline Exegesis* (Cambridge University Press, 2021), 345–46.

as I argued above, *firstborn* (*prōtotokos*) and *image* (*eikōn*) are phrases that include the notion of materiality. They are most naturally read as referring to the incarnate Christ. This is supported by the fact that Paul invokes the terms *Father* and *Son* to refer to the God who sends and the God who has been sent only in the context of God's relationship to and presence in creation through incarnation. It is in incarnational theology, not Trinitarian theology, that they are located. Paul employs these terms, though, to contrast the different ways in which two aspects of creation relate to God. On the one hand, Israel and the gentiles are only creatures and are therefore qualitatively different from God. When God graciously engages them, drawing them to Godself and making them even into family members, this can only be through something like adoption. The Son, on the other hand, is the one in whom Godself crosses the ontological divide between God and what is not God. His relationship to God is natural, as in his creaturely reality Godself is present. He is the image of God. In fact, as Paul says in the finale of Romans 8, human beings are adopted so that he, the Son, may have a large family. The transformation of human beings is entailed in their adoption; they are to be made like the incarnate Son, who is the blueprint for creation's eschatological life.[55]

It is exactly here that the exegetical difficulties arise for an infralapsarian reader like Aquinas. After all, Paul presents this transformation as an eschatological goal set from the beginning of creation. He conceives of peoples' determination as an expression of divine foreknowledge and election. These are divine intentions anchored in eternity rather than in time. But if humans are eternally elected to be with and like the Son, and the Son's incarnation itself is not part of the original blueprint for creation, then it is hard to see how God can intend other creatures to be modeled after the incarnate One. Paul then must be read as referring to the non-incarnate Son. But this demands that we ignore the nature of the argument from which Paul draws his conclusion, an argument for which Paul evokes imagery that circles around materiality. It is exactly here that a supralapsarian Christology offers a different way. On such a reading, we can recognize Paul's argument for what it is: an argument about the relationship between the firstborn and the rest of creation.

The Incarnate One as Word

As I noted above, two of the arguments for the fittingness of the second person's incarnation advanced by Aquinas circle around the biblical imagery

---

55. For a more expansive version of this reading of Rom. 8, see Van Driel, *Rethinking Paul*, 337–50.

of the Word. The first argument follows the familiar pattern of identifying a personal property that is essential to the second person as the result of divine self-differentiation and that makes it ultimately impossible for another divine person to become incarnate. The second argument follows another pattern. Focusing on the distribution of divinity within the act of divine self-differentiation, it argues that since the first trinitarian person is the font of divinity, he is also the source and font of creation; because the Father is the source and font through the Son, the Son becomes incarnate.

Regarding the second argument, Aquinas takes the idea that the Father is the font of divinity from the church fathers. Its ancient pedigree notwithstanding, I agree with John Calvin when he argues constructively that the fathers were wrong here.[56] They are importing philosophical ideas about emanation that do not fit a Christian understanding of God. If the Father is the source of divinity, the three trinitarian persons have divinity in different ways, which would mean that they are not equally God. If all three persons share in the same divine nature, they all have divinity *a se*, of themselves. They differ only in their interpersonal relationships; thus, what the Son receives from the Father is not divinity but sonship. Therefore, the fundamental premise supporting Aquinas's argument should be dismissed.

Aquinas's first argument holds that we should understand the procession of the Word from the Father as analogous to the way that, in an act of understanding, a concept of the object that is understood proceeds from the intellect. In knowing Godself, the Word proceeds from the Father, and in knowing Godself through the Word, God also knows all possibilities that are within God's power. These possibilities function as the exemplars for what God creates. When God creates, God therefore cannot create in any way other than through the Word. Without the Word, God would not know what lies within the realm of divine possibilities. And this act of creating through the Word makes it ultimately fitting that it is through the incarnating Word that God recreates creation.

It is striking how much this line of argument depends not on an exegesis of the biblical imagery of the Word but on a philosophical theory about cognition. There is a diverse range of exegetical lines of interpretation of the meaning of the Johannine Logos, ranging from Stoic thought to Jewish wisdom literature to the depiction of the Word of God in the Old Testament. None of these necessitates the theory of cognition Aquinas appeals to. However, the whole of Aquinas's theory about God being able to create only through

---

56. For an excellent recent discussion, see Brannon Ellis, *Calvin, Classical Trinitarianism, and the Aseity of the Son* (Oxford University Press, 2012).

the Word rests on this philosophical account, not on the biblical image that the theory appeals to.

One wonders whether more theological self-discipline is not needed here. Karen Kilby asks from whence theologians acquired "such a vivid feeling for the inner life of the deity."[57] She calls for some apophatic restraint on our pronouncements about God's inner-trinitarian reality. Kilby is writing here against social trinitarianism, but I believe a similar argument can be made regarding many theological accounts of inner-trinitarian self-differentiation. Bonaventure can write lovingly about the Son as the total expression of what the divine love is in itself and the ways in which the Father is open to the other in all its forms.[58] Jonathan Edwards can even report on inner-trinitarian dialogues between Father and Son.[59] And here, Aquinas can draw significant conclusions about the restraints upon and absolute fittingness of divine actions. In any of these instances, the theological account goes far beyond the sober words of Scripture.[60]

A call for theological conceptual reservation seems all the more appropriate when we take into account that for Aquinas the theory of cognition de facto functions as a way to *explain* the proceeding of the Son from the Father. This is different from how the church fathers account for the Son's generation. Take, for example, Gregory of Nazianzus who, while stipulating that the Son was begotten by the Father—as the biblical language invited him to confess—continues thus: "How was he begotten?—I repeat the question in indignation. The begetting of God must be honored by silence. It is a great thing for you to learn that he was begotten. But the manner of his generation we will not admit that even angels can conceive, much less you. Shall I tell

---

57. Karen Kilby, *God, Evil, and the Limits of Theology* (T&T Clark, 2020), 12.
58. See Zachary Hayes, "Incarnation and Creation in St. Bonaventure," 313–14.
59. See note 41, above.
60. It is interesting that in his book *The Knowledge of God the Father, and His Son Jesus Christ*, the seventeenth-century Puritan divine Thomas Goodwin first summarizes the theory of cognition to account for the proceeding of the Trinity but then observes, "Many of our reformed divines have been and are shy of [it], as too curious." Goodwin goes on to say that he nonetheless notices these very same writers who express reticence about the cognitive theory drawing on it in other places. See Thomas Goodwin, *The Works of Thomas Goodwin, D.D.*, vol. 4 (Edinburgh: 1862), 415. Goodwin references in particular "professors Leidenses," with which he probably means the *Synopsis Purioris Theologiae*. See, e.g., disputation 8: "They gathered this manner of production from an analogy to the mind of humans. . . . But because Holy Scripture does not make this claim so transparently and distinctly, we judge that an honest admission of ignorance is to be preferred to an all too daring assertion. And we prefer to wait eagerly that day when we shall see God face to face, and when we shall know perfectly and fully what we know only in part here." Dolf te Velde, ed., *Synopsis Purioris Theologiae / Synopsis of a Purer Theology: Latin Text and English Translation*, vol. 1, *Disputations 1–23* (Brill, 2015), 213–15.

you how it was? It was in a manner known to the Father who begot, and to the Son who was begotten. Anything more than this is hidden by a cloud and escapes your dim sight."[61] According to Gregory, we can say *that* the Son was begotten but not *how*. Aquinas however—and, again, he is not unique here, since the theory he put forth was shared widely by medieval scholastics—does venture to say how: The Word was generated in the Father's act of knowing himself and all *possibilia*.

If we juxtapose this more chastened understanding of John's Logos with a supralapsarian understanding of the incarnation, two interpretative possibilities open up. In chapter 7, I offered a supralapsarian reading of the prologue to John's Gospel.[62] John moves seamlessly between creation and incarnation, depicting the world as the home of the Word, the Word who sets foot on the world's threshold and thereby makes the invisible God visible. In this prologue, the incarnation is not a foreign element added to a previously designed plan; rather, the incarnation is the plan. The Word creates so that he might tabernacle among us. On this interpretation, creation is called into being through the Word because it is called into being for the Word.

A soft supralapsarian reading might take the designation of the one who becomes incarnate as Logos as expressing an inner-trinitarian reality while being apophatic about the exact nature of that reality. Read within a creedal context, one confesses that due to the unity in power any of the trinitarian persons could have been the one through whom God created and became incarnate. Given the personal properties of each person, each version of creation and incarnation might have looked slightly different. Had creation been through the Spirit, it might have been spirated rather than spoken into being. But God designated the Word to be the one through whom God created and became incarnate, and thus creation reflects the fact that it was the Logos for whom it was meant to be a home.

A hard supralapsarian reading might propose that the designation of the one through whom God created and incarnated as Logos is itself part of the divine economy. Contemporary exegetes tend to understand John's Logos against the background of the Old Testament notion of the "Word of God."[63] This phrase has a decidedly economic flavor. It is less concerned with a reality within God than with the notion of divine self-expression and speech. Unique to John is the claim that before God calls into being anything that is not God, there is already One with God, and identical to God, who is designated the

---

61. Gregory of Nazianzus, *The Theological Orations* 3.8, in *Christology of the Later Fathers*, ed. Edward R. Hardy (Westminster, 1954), 165.
62. See "Being With" in chap. 7, above, 139–40.
63. See, e.g., Andreas J. Köstenberger, *John* (Baker Academic, 2004), 25–27.

Logos. But if Logos is an economic term, John's claim could be read as saying that within the divine trinitarian self-differentiation, One was designated to be the Logos—the One through whom God was about to speak. This was also the One in whom God was to become incarnate and through whom God was to create the world. In other words, on such a reading, Logos is the economic but supralapsarian identity of one of the Trinity's persons, an identity out of which the rest of history unfolds.

Either way, the assumption of a supralapsarian understanding of the incarnation eases the pressure to anchor the theological claims of John's prologue deep in immanent, inner-trinitarian dynamics and identities. It allows us, rather, to read the text as the unfolding of a supralapsarian divine commitment to be a God with us—to be Jesus.

Conclusion

Could it be that creation is called into being through the Word—to reflect and image the Son and to be adopted as his family—not because of an essential personal property of the second person of the Trinity but because God freely intended for him to be the firstborn of all creation and, through him, to be with creation forever? Can we read the strong ties that the New Testament expresses between the One we call the second person of the Trinity and all of creation not as forcing us to make strong—and maybe impossibly strong—pronouncements about the inner life of the Trinity but simply as expressing God's economic design for how God wishes to commune with what is not God?

An infralapsarian Christology does not have the resources to respond to these questions positively. If the incarnation is contingent upon sin, any essential ties between Christ and creation cannot be contingent upon his incarnation but must be concerned with his divine person and its essential personal characteristics. A supralapsarian Christology, however, opens up new conceptual space to engage these questions differently.

At this point it might be important to underscore that answering these questions positively does not entail a denial of the immanent Trinity. It is true that many accounts of the immanent Trinity are shaped by characteristics drawn from biblical material that concerns the economic relationships between God and creation. If this material must be located in incarnational theology, rather than in the doctrine of the immanent Trinity, our understanding of the immanent Trinity will have to be construed differently.[64] But this does not deny

---

64. This chapter is not the place to explore this further, but I believe this would actually be a healthy consequence for Trinitarian theology. What gave rise to a Christian understanding of

the fact that in the dynamic of God's relating to what is not God we encounter differentiation, that there are three who are the one God of Israel.

However, the line of thought explored in this chapter allows us to say much more clearly that these three, because they are the one God of Israel, are truly and immanently one in power and divinity. And this in turn allows us to say, much more clearly, not that in the incarnate One we encounter *part* of the Godhead, but that "in him all the fullness of God was pleased to dwell."

God as Trinity was not that which has led to accounts of the essential personal characteristics of the persons but, rather, the fact that in their Scriptures Christians, though believers in the one God of Israel, nonetheless encountered three who all have the one Name. That is, it was not difference that led to trinitarian theology but oneness and sameness. A healthy exegetical basis for trinitarian theology therefore lies not in isolated texts that suggest difference but in the narrative identity of and relationships among the three who are all said to be YHWH.

10

"In Him All Things Hold Together"

Supralapsarian Christology and Astrotheology

The central intuition behind the explorations of this book is deceptively simple: In relation to what is not God, God intends from the first to be Jesus. The embodiment of God's commitment to be a God with others is the carpenter's son from Nazareth. All other things are called forth in the context of this divine intention. "All things have been created . . . for him," and "in him all things hold together" (Col. 1:16, 17). Jesus Christ is the linchpin of the cosmos.

The deceptive simplicity of this claim is belied when we try to unpack what "all things" actually means. Our planet is only one of eight planets circling the sun. According to current determinations, the sun is only one of one hundred billion stars in the Milky Way galaxy, which in turn is only one of about two hundred billion galaxies in the observable universe.[1] The size of the cosmos is unimaginable, comprising an inconceivable number of stars, planets, and moons. In the face of cosmic reality's immensity, does it make sense to say that "all things hold together" in Jesus?

For some theologians, it does not. Following the astronomer Carl Sagan, Andrew J. Burgess speaks of "earth chauvinism."[2] As he observes, "There does seem to be a kind of cosmic hubris in believing that the Creator of the

---

1. I take these numbers from Andrew Davison, *Astrobiology and Christian Doctrine: Exploring the Implications of Life in the Universe* (Cambridge University Press, 2023), 1, 4.
2. Andrew J. Burgess, "Earth Chauvinism," *Christian Century*, December 8, 1976, 1098–1102.

203

universe was incarnate on our own bit of interstellar debris and maintains a special relationship to the human species."[3] Willem B. Drees is concerned we may fall into "planetism," which he likens to racism or sexism.[4] He argues that we should not consider Bethlehem the center of the universe. And Douglas F. Ottati argues that, in the light of the sheer vastness of the cosmos, Christian theology should radically decenter humanity within God's intentions and concerns. In the "vast cosmic span of stars and planetary systems, billions of galaxies, black holes, and nebulae," humanity occupies only a small corner.[5] However we may experience things, human consciousness does not seem to be the center of it all, and it does not make sense to think about ourselves, as some theological designs do, as the high priests of creation.[6] Rather than taking this world to be the central stage within the vast cosmic drama, Ottati suggests we think about the cosmos as a constellation of many stages, each with their own particular dramas, some with intelligent life, others without it.[7] This multitude of cosmic stages, he holds, invites the thought that there may be "other manifestations and disclosures of the gratuitous dynamic of the Real within other scenarios, sequences, and lines of development."[8] To put it differently, among such an uncountable number of planets, some of which may be inhabited with intelligent lives, there might be other incarnations akin to God's incarnation in Jesus Christ.

This brings us back to supralapsarian Christology. For many participants in the conversation about Christian faith, astrobiology, and the possibility of extraterrestrial life, this approach creates the conceptual space for the idea of multiple incarnations. They hold that the very same arguments that lead one to embrace supralapsarian Christology could, or should, also lead one to embrace the idea of multiple incarnations.

In this chapter, I wish to scrutinize this position. I begin by clarifying the ontology of the incarnation, since there is an observable confusion about this in the literature that shapes this conversation. Then, engaging the astrotheologian Ted Peters, I map the various theological positions that are conceptually possible regarding supralapsarian Christology and multiple incarnations. I

---

3. Burgess, "Earth Chauvinism," 1098.
4. Willem B. Drees, "Bethlehem: Center of the Universe?," in *God for the 21st Century*, ed. Russell Stannard (Templeton Foundation, 2000), 69.
5. Douglas F. Ottati, *A Theology for the Twenty-First Century* (Eerdmans, 2020), 206.
6. Ottati, *Theology for the Twenty-First Century*, 233, 285.
7. Ottati, *Theology for the Twenty-First Century*, 209–10.
8. Ottati, *Theology for the Twenty-First Century*, 376. I offer an extensive analysis of these and other aspects of Ottati's Christology in Edwin Chr. van Driel, "The Firstborn of Creation and Redemption: A Response to Douglas F. Ottati's *A Theology for the Twenty-First Century*," *Journal of Reformed Theology* 19, nos. 1–2 (2025): 26–34.

argue that the ties between these two positions are significantly less strong than suggested. I then discuss the various arguments for a supralapsarian multi-incarnational account and argue that these fall short, especially in light of the Christological position I explore in this book. Finally, I argue for the opposite position. Following this book's central intuition, I argue that a single incarnation is the only defensible option. I explore how this position might respond to charges of planetism, earth chauvinism, and anthropocentrism. These latter discussions illustrate an observation made by Andrew Davison: Going on a journey into extraterrestrial territory may seem like an extravagant and maybe even fantastical enterprise, but it may allow us to return home with a fresh set of eyes that can help us see our own, earthly theological world anew.[9]

Ontology of the Incarnation

I take the creedal pronouncements of the ecumenical councils of the early church to be both confessionally normative for the Christian community and also the most creative theological starting point for further Christological reflection. Pivotal is the Chalcedonian stipulation that in Christ, there is one person with two natures. He is "the same perfect in divinity and perfect in humanity, the same truly God and truly man, of a rational soul and a body, consubstantial with the Father as regards his divinity, and the same consubstantial with us as regards his humanity, . . . acknowledged in two natures which undergo no confusion, no change, no division, no separation; at no point was the difference between the natures taken away from the union, but rather the property of both natures is preserved and comes together into a single person and a single subsistent being."[10]

Before the incarnation, the Word, the second person of the Trinity, already existed in one nature: divinity. In the incarnation, the Word assumes a second, human nature. Chalcedon does not further define the terms *person* or *nature*. In this context, a nature is best understood as a set of properties and powers by which the person can operate. I will refer to such a set of properties and powers as a *powerpack*.[11] Before the incarnation, the Word had only the divine powerpack. It includes properties and powers such as omnipotence, omniscience, omnipresence, and living in eternity. In the incarnation the Word gains an additional powerpack, consisting of created human properties and

---

9. Davison, *Astrobiology and Christian Doctrine*, 1.
10. Jaroslav Pelikan and Valerie Hotchkiss, eds., *Creeds and Confessions of Faith in the Christian Tradition*, vol. 1 (Yale University Press, 2003), 181.
11. I take this term from one of my teachers, the late Marilyn McCord Adams.

powers. The Word can now act through both powerpacks—no longer does he have only divine properties and powers, but with the human powerpack, he gains human powers such as physical action, growth in knowledge, and locomotion.

Chalcedon stipulates that the two powerpacks are neither confused nor changed nor divided nor separated. They are united in that both powerpacks are held by the same ontological owner, the second of person of the Trinity. They are, however, not fused or mixed; each powerpack exists in its own integrity. The Word thus can operate through both powerpacks simultaneously. As member of the Trinity, through the divine powerpack the Word lives in eternal bliss, ruling creation and upholding it from moment to moment. Through the human powerpack, the Word can—simultaneous to this bliss, ruling, and upholding—be a baby crying in a manger, a young man eating with his friends, or a prophetic teacher dying on a cross.

On the Chalcedonian logic, *person* and *nature* thus are best thought to relate as *who* relates to *what*. When we meet Jesus of Nazareth, *what* we encounter is a human nature, born from a human mother, living a human life, with a human body and soul. But the *who* we meet is the second person of the Trinity—that is, the Lord, the God of Israel and Creator of the world. We do not meet *divinity*, since the two natures are not mixed. The *what* we encounter is an integral human nature. Nonetheless, we do meet God, since the person whose nature this is, is not a human person, but Godself.

On the stipulations of other creedal formulations, and following the biblical narrative, incarnation is a permanent addition to the life of the Godhead. As the Nicene creed says, speaking of the incarnate Christ, "He ascended into heaven and is seated at the right hand of the Father. He will come again in glory to judge the living and the dead and his kingdom will have no end." Ascension does not mean that the human nature is shed and left behind; rather, the human nature is taken up into the center of power, the right hand of God, and he will return "in the same way" in which he left (Acts 1:11).

Given this ontological framework, the proposal of multiple incarnations should be understood as the idea that—in addition to adding a human set of properties and powers to the divine life, a powerpack through which God now lives and acts not only in divinity but also in humanity—God also adds additional created powerpacks to God's existence. Through those powerpacks God would not only live a fully human life on earth, and as such be seen and heard by humans, but also live fully extraterrestrial lives in other inhabitable parts of the cosmos, and as such be seen and heard by extraterrestrial creatures. As with the human powerpack, each extraterrestrial powerpack would exist without confusion, without change, without division, without

"In Him All Things Hold Together"   207

separation—with respect to the divine powerpack, with respect to the human powerpack that the Word has assumed on earth, and with respect to other extraterrestrial powerpacks. Each powerpack would exist in its full integrity, but in each case, if one were to encounter the powerpack, the *who* one would encounter would be the divine Word.

Given this account, I believe Andrew Davison rightly complains about the lack of precision regarding the assumed ontology of the incarnation in much of the literature about multiple incarnations.[12] It is not helpful to conceive of multiple incarnations as implying "a planet-hopping Christ," as some do.[13] The title *Christ*, a translation of the Greek word referring to the Jewish messiah, connotes the divine Word's human incarnation, not an incarnation in another context. The idea of multiple incarnations implies that the second person of the Trinity assumes multiple created natures, not that the Word as incarnate in a human nature (that is, *Christ*) would visit multiple planets after his ascension. Moreover, the image of "planet hopping" implies a temporal sequence of events in which Christ would subsequently appear on and disappear from a range of planets. On the contrary, the idea of multiple incarnations implies states of affairs that could obtain simultaneously. On the Chalcedonian logic, the divine Word could simultaneously assume a human nature on earth and one or more other created natures in extraterrestrial space. For the same reason, it is not correct to speak of "multiple incarnations of the one Christ."[14] The proposal concerns multiple incarnations of the one divine Word, one of which is Christ. It also makes no sense to argue that "Jesus became God-in-the-flesh only once."[15] Jesus *is* God in the flesh; the question at stake is whether God becomes incarnate also as something other than Jesus, taking on a different kind of flesh or other created reality.[16] Finally, it is wrong to say that "on the

---

12. Andrew Davison, "Christian Systematic Theology and Life Elsewhere in the Universe: A Study in Suitability," *Theology and Science* 16, no. 4 (2018): 452.

13. Ted Peters, "One Incarnation or Many?," in *Astrotheology: Science and Theology Meet Extraterrestrial Life*, ed. Ted Peters (Cascade Books, 2018), 272; Joshua M. Moritz, "One *Imago Dei* and the Incarnation of the Eschatological Adam," in *Astrotheology: Science and Theology Meet Extraterrestrial Life*, ed. Ted Peters (Cascade Books, 2018), 331.

14. Peter M. J. Hess, "Multiple Incarnations of the One Christ," in *Astrotheology: Science and Theology Meet Extraterrestrial Life*, ed. Ted Peters (Cascade Books, 2018), 317.

15. José G. Funes, "The Road Map to Other Earths: Lessons Learned and Challenges Ahead," in *Astrotheology: Science and Theology Meet Extraterrestrial Life*, ed. Ted Peters (Cascade Books, 2018), 69.

16. For this and other objections to conceptions of multiple incarnations that are based on insufficient understanding of the ontological implications of the creedal confessions about the incarnation, see Davison, *Astrobiology and Christian Doctrine*, 243–63. Davison and I mostly agree on the ontology of the incarnation. Davison also discusses extensively the objections to the possibility of multiple incarnations developed by Brian Hebblethwaite, especially in his "The Impossibility of Multiple Incarnations," *Theology* 104 (2001): 323–34. I believe

terrestrial level, Jesus Christ assumes a bodily nature by which all of creation
... is assumed into relationship with God."[17] Again, "Jesus Christ," refers to
the incarnate existence of the divine Word, born of Mary, and as such does not
assume but comes into existence in the act of assumption. Moreover, *assumption* means the act in which a part of created reality becomes the created extension of the Godhead. The claim that in the incarnation we have one person but
two natures expresses the fact that in the assumption this particular human
nature is not personified by a human person but, rather, by the second person
of the Trinity. As such, there is no ontological, interpersonal over-againstness
between this human nature and the divine Word: In him, the *what* is a human
nature, but the *who* is the person of the divine Word. But assumption is not
transitive. When the Word assumes (and thereby personifies) this nature, the
Word does not assume (and thereby personify) all natures. There continues
to be an interpersonal over-againstness between God and the rest of creation.
And therefore, it is not true that through the incarnation all of creation is assumed into relationship with God.

Mapping the Options

In several essays, Ted Peters maps a commitment to one or multiple incarnations against different kinds of Christology.[18] One distinction he introduces is
between "revelatory" and "atoning work" Christologies.[19] This distinction is
focused on the difference the incarnation makes. By "revelatory" Christologies
Peters means Christologies according to which "in Jesus we find a revelation
of a truth about God or an example as to how God's creatures should live."[20]
By "atoning work" Christologies Peters means Christologies that are focused
on Christ's work of salvation.[21] Peters seems to identity the first approach with
a low Christology and the second with a high Christology.[22] This in turn is

---

Hebblethwaite has been sufficiently responded to by Davison and by Timothy Pawl. See Timothy Pawl, "Brian Hebblethwaite's Arguments Against Multiple Incarnations," *Religious Studies* 52 (2016): 117–30. See also Timothy Pawl, "Thomistic Multiple Incarnations," *Heythrop Journal* 57, no. 2 (2016): 359–70.

    17. Ilia Delio, "Christ and Extraterrestrial Life," *Theology and Science* 5, no. 3 (2007): 257.

    18. Ted Peters, "Astrobiology and Astrochristology," *Zygon* 51, no. 2 (2016): 480–96. See also Peters, "One Incarnation or Many?"

    19. Peters, "Astrobiology and Astrochristology," 484. In "One Incarnation or Many?" he describes the same distinction as between "revelational or exemplary Christologies" and Christologies centered on "the idea that Jesus Christ performed the decisive work of atonement" (280).

    20. Peters, "One Incarnation or Many?," 280.

    21. Peters, "One Incarnation or Many?," 283–84.

    22. Peters, "One Incarnation or Many?," 280; Peters, "Astrobiology and Astrochristology," 485.

the basis for Peter's argument that a "revelatory" Christology finds it logical to affirm multiple incarnations, while an "atoning work" Christology would be drawn to a single incarnation. If Christ is only a means for divine revelation, he can be seen as one of many prophetic figures and historical events that reveal something about God. One could imagine these multiple ways of divine revelation on our earth and in our history to be multiplied throughout the cosmos. On the other hand, Peters says, an "atoning work" Christology will hold that the implications of Christ's work on the cross are cosmic and that therefore no other incarnation is needed.[23]

It is indeed a useful move to make a distinction between revelation and atonement as two aspects of Christ's work. The latter is contingent upon sin while the former is not necessarily. It is much more fanciful, though, to suggest that Christologies that focus on Christ's revelatory importance are necessarily low, while Christologies that focus on the atoning difference he makes are necessarily high—with a cosmic reach for Christ's atoning work. For example, a theological design that sees Christ as a form of divine self-revelation—because in Christ Godself becomes present in our history—might do so exactly because of a high, Chalcedonian understanding of who he is. Likewise, an "atoning work" Christology might hold that Christ's work on the cross has salvific effect only for those who embrace this work in faith (and since, unless mission trips were ventured to extraterrestrial space, it is very unlikely any possible extraterrestrial beings would ever have a chance to have faith in the Man of Nazareth, one might think his atoning work has only terrestrial effect).[24] In other words, Peters is right to call our attention to the correlation between one's understanding of the difference that Christ makes and the need for and possibility of multiple incarnations, but his proposed schema is far too limited to describe all the available theological options.

This is important, as the unnecessary conflation of several theological positions that characterizes Peter's distinction between "revelatory" and "atoning work" Christologies seems to shape Peters's subsequent distinction between infralapsarian and supralapsarian Christological approaches.[25] Peters

---

23. Peters, "One Incarnation or Many?," 280–86; Peters, "Astrobiology and Astrochristology," 483–85.

24. This is one reason why Robert John Russell protests Peterss's distinction. See Robert John Russell, "Many Incarnations or One?," in *Astrotheology: Science and Theology Meet Extraterrestrial Life*, ed. Ted Peters (Cascade Books, 2018), 306–8.

On the fanciful idea of expanding the frontiers of Christian mission to extraterrestrial space, see, e.g., Eugene A. Curry, "The Final (Missions) Frontier: Extraterrestrials, Evangelism, and the Wide Circle of Human Empathy," *Zygon* 54, no. 3 (2019): 588–601.

25. He calls these, respectively, the "fix-a-broken-creation model" and the "divine self-communication model." Ted Peters, "Astrobiology and Astrochristology," 489–92. Still another

points out that there are four logical positions with regard to the question of a single or multiple incarnations: infralapsarian Christologies that hold to a single incarnation, infralapsarian Christologies that hold to multiple incarnations, supralapsarian Christologies that hold to a single incarnation, and supralapsarian Christologies that hold to multiple incarnations.[26] Peters believes nevertheless that a supralapsarian Christology is most logically combined with the idea of multiple incarnations and is surprised that many supralapsarian Christological theologians do not seem to share this insight.[27] Peters never offers an argument for this. I believe his position here rests on his deficient understanding of revelatory Christology. Peters holds that "according to the divine self-communication model, the incarnation would happen anyway, whether the creation fell or not. According to this . . . model, God's incarnation in Christ is one more chapter in the story of God's self-giving love that began with creation."[28] According to this description, supralapsarian Christology is nothing but a subset of a low-Christological, revelatory understanding of the difference Christ makes.[29] Many kinds of supralapsarian Christology do not fit this mold. For example, Peters references Scotus's account, according to which the divine love for the human soul of Christ is the goal of creation, around which in turn all the universe is called into being as co-lovers.[30] According to Scotus, God expresses this love by assuming Christ's

---

name he uses for supralapsarian Christology is the "divine self-bestowal or incarnation anyway model." Peters, "One Incarnation or Many?," 287–90.

26. Peters, "Astrobiology and Astrochristology," 492–93.

27. Peters, "Astrobiology and Astrochristology," 491–93. As the sole example of these surprising dissenters, Peters names Wolfhart Pannenberg ("Astrobiology and Astrotheology," 490), citing Wolfhart Pannenberg, *Systematic Theology*, vol. 2 (Eerdmans, 1994), 64, 76.

28. Peters, "Astrobiology and Astrochristology," 492.

29. In this regard it should be noted that the prime examples Peters cites are Karl Rahner, Thomas F. O'Meara, and Ilia Delio. I discuss Delio's position below.

30. Peters, "Astrobiology and Astrochristology," 491; Peters, "One Incarnation or Many?," 288. It is odd that Peters, without any references, counts Bonaventure also among the supralapsarian Christological theologians—even calling him this position's "patron saint." Peters, "Astrobiology and Astrotheology," 490; Peters, "One Incarnation or Many?," 288. Bonaventure rejected supralapsarian Christology. See Bonaventure, *Commentaria in librum tertium sententiarum* 20.1.2, 5, 6. Bonaventure is an interesting case in the infralapsarian-supralapsarian debate. His theological emphasis on the primacy of Christ tends strongly toward supralapsarianism, and he concedes as much in his discussion of supralapsarian arguments. However, in the end he decides for infralapsarianism since he believes it inflames the faithful more than supralapsarianism. For discussions, see A. Gerken, "Bonaventuras Konvenienzgründe für die Inkarnation des Sohnes," *Wissenschaft und Weisheit* 23 (1960): 131–46; A. Gerken, *Theologie des Wortes: Das Verhältnis von Schöpfung und Inkarnation bei Bonaventura* (Patmos, 1963), 131–46; and Marilyn McCord Adams, *What Sort of Human Nature? Medieval Philosophy and the Systematics of Christology* (Marquette University Press, 1999), 24–28.

human nature into hypostatic union with the divine Word.[31] Such is a full Chalcedonian Christology.

Peters's discussion does illustrate that theologians have combined supralapsarian Christology both with accounts of a single incarnation and with accounts of multiple incarnations (which a particular theologian opts for often depends on the particular arguments that gave rise to their supralapsarian convictions). For this reason, in the next section I will assess three supralapsarian Christological arguments for multiple incarnations. Thereafter, I will argue that the account set forth in this book calls for a single incarnation that draws all of the cosmos together.

Supralapsarian Christological Arguments for Multiple Incarnations

In the literature at least three distinct, but related, supralapsarian Christological arguments are advanced to support the idea of multiple incarnations.

One line of argument holds that "God's omnibenevolence and desire for self-communication in light of an evolutionary worldview suggests that creation moves toward multiple beings that can respond to the divine self-gift in an otherwise free process of becoming."[32] This argument leads to an account of a multiplicity of kinds of spiritual beings throughout the cosmos, each potentially crowned by an incarnation of the divine. Oliver Putz claims that this argument swings on two theological hinges: a Scotistic doctrine of God and a Rahnerian embrace of an evolutionary worldview.[33] Putz interprets Scotus as holding that God "creates to communicate Godself and that creation exists to receive this loving and unowed divine self-gift."[34] God loves Godself perfectly and utterly rejoices in this self-love, but this perfect love "cannot but will perfection of this love" and, therefore, creates the world.[35] Creation is called into being so that God may have co-lovers.

When he wrote about co-lovers of the divine, Putz claims, Scotus could think of only one kind: humans. A contemporary Scotist, however, should "embrace an evolutionary worldview, according to which sentient beings emerge out of the free process of cosmic evolution that is transcendentally conditioned by divine action."[36] God is the transcendental cause of this process,

---

31. See chap. 1, above.
32. Oliver Putz, "God's Self-Communication in a Cosmos Bound for Life," in *Astrotheology: Science and Theology Meet Extraterrestrial Life*, ed. Ted Peters (Cascade Books, 2018), 162.
33. Putz, "God's Self-Communication," 161.
34. Putz, "God's Self-Communication," 161.
35. Putz, "God's Self-Communication," 164.
36. Putz, "God's Self-Communication," 164.

but not its determiner. The process tends toward the emergence of sentient creatures who are receptive to the transcendent, but it was never a given that those creatures would be humans. And even now that they are, they should not expect to be the only sentient and spiritual beings: "A God who wants to self-communicate, who predestines creation as recipients of this abundant love, and who by releasing creation into the free process of evolution (thus accepting the possibility of more than one co-lover to emerge) must want a multiplicity of spiritual beings."[37] The existence of extraterrestrial beings is thus likely, Putz holds. This in turn leads to the likelihood of multiple incarnations.[38]

Putz presents his argument as a variation on the principle of plenitude: the thought that all that is comes forth out of an unending source of generosity whose goodness cannot but share out of its own plenty.[39] Already medieval theologians like Robert Grosseteste took a Christian interpretation of this principle as the premise for a supralapsarian Christological account. As the most perfect and generous being, it is in God's nature to share of Godself to the fullest amount—first, by sharing of God's being in calling that which is not God into existence and, then, by sharing of Godself by becoming incarnate.[40] The problem with such an argumentative strategy is that it necessitates God's relating to what is not God. Creation and incarnation are the necessary outflow of who God is, rather than the contingent gift of God's free grace. What Putz does not notice is that Scotus, who was deeply familiar with the supralapsarian strategies of his predecessors, carefully avoids appealing to the principle of plenitude.[41] Rather, his argument starts from the otherwise contingent acts of divine election and incarnation *as they happened* and reflects on the logical ordering of these acts in the light of God's perfections. In this reflection, God's own self-love is not the necessary reason for creation or incarnation but is the reason for the incarnation and for creation's contingency. God does not need any co-lovers. God as Godself is enough. In precisely this way God is free to give Godself to what is not God as God wishes. This free wish takes the form of election. On this argument, incarnation is not the final step in an evolutionary process of divine

---

37. Putz, "God's Self-Communication," 165.
38. Putz, "God's Self-Communication," 168.
39. Putz, "God's Self-Communication," 161–62.
40. See "The Advantages of Scotus's Argumentative Strategy" in chap. 1, above, 19.
41. See "The Advantages of Scotus's Argumentative Strategy" in chap. 1, above, 20. For a further discussion of the history of the principle of plenitude in Christian theology, and Scotus's place therein, see Nico W. den Bok, "Eén ding is noodzakelijk: Duns Scotus en het volheidsbeginsel," in *Geloof geeft te denken: Opstellen over de theologie van Johannes Duns Scotus*, ed. A. J. Beck and H. Veldhuis (Van Gorcum: 2005), 225–81.

self-giving to transcendentally oriented sentient beings but, rather, the first step in which God decides to be a human being. God, from among many, elects human beings to be the recipients of divine self-communication. On Putz's line of argument, the particularity of Jesus, Israel, and humanity, as expressed in the notion of election, disappears in the mist of evolutionary development. On Scotus's argumentative strategy, this particularity is the basis for his thinking.

A second supralapsarian Christological argument advancing the idea of multiple incarnations seems at first glance much more interested in remaining anchored in the particularities of the biblical narrative. With reference to Colossians 1:16–17, Ilia Delio begins with the observation that "Christ is first in God's intention to love and hence to create. . . . Christ belongs to the very structure of the universe."[42] Delio then anchors this Christological principle in a trinitarian account of divine self-communication. According to this account, this self-communication is grounded in the Father, as "unbegotten self-communicative goodness."[43] The first result of this self-communication is the Son, who as such is also the expression of all that God can be in relation to what is not God. This "inner-Trinitarian speaking of the eternal Word is [therefore] the ontological basis for the possibility of creation."[44] From this trinitarian account Delio then concludes to what she calls the "Christophic Principle." Since the divine Word is the exemplar of creation, rooted in the inner-trinitarian act of self-communication that finds continuation in the economic trinitarian act of creation, "the universe is not simply fit, or even fine-tuned, for human life (anthropic principle) but is patterned on the divine Word of God and thus oriented toward Christ or the perfect union between God and created reality."[45]

Thus Delio lays the basis for a supralapsarian Christology. As she continues, however, she disconnects her understanding of "Christ" from its historic reference. Christ, Delio asserts, "is not simply the individual existent Jesus of Nazareth but the permanent openness of our humanity and hence to God's life in us. . . . Jesus is the Christ, . . . but Christ is more than the historical Jesus."[46] Christ is, says Delio, "the symbol of what is intended for created reality, that is, the divinization of creation which, on the level of human

---

42. Delio, "Christ and Extraterrestrial Life," 252.
43. Delio, "Christ and Extraterrestrial Life," 255.
44. Delio, "Christ and Extraterrestrial Life," 256. Delio offers this account as an exegesis of Bonaventure, but as I explored in chap. 9, in "Thomas Aquinas on the Incarnation's Contingency and Fittingness," 177n4, Bonaventure shares this account with Aquinas and other medieval theologians.
45. Delio, "Christ and Extraterrestrial Life," 257.
46. Delio, "Christ and Extraterrestrial Life," 259, 260.

experience, reaches its culmination in the person Jesus of Nazareth."[47] Because of this, Delio can now suggest "that every created life-bearing order is Christologically structured so that . . . there may be multiple incarnations but only one Christ. The reality of Christ, therefore, is the union of God and creation and, as symbol, mediates the divinization of every created order in its relationship to God."[48]

When Delio claims, based on the Colossians hymn, that "Christ" was first in God's intention to love and part of the very structure of the universe, she thus does not refer to Mary's son; she refers, rather, to a principle—the principle of divinization, in which all of creation is lifted up into union with God. This, however, is neither what the Colossians hymn means when it says that Christ is the firstborn of creation nor what the creeds mean when they confess that in Christ God became incarnate. The hymn does not reference a principle; it references a man of flesh and blood, who made the invisible God visible, whose blood was poured out on the cross, and who in the body of his flesh reconciled God and humanity. He can do all of these things, according to the creeds, not because he was divinized but because he was *God*. He does not represent a principle that will be true for everybody; he is a person whose life touches everyone and everything because he is the one for whom everything else was created.

A final argument for a supralapsarian Christological account of multiple incarnations is based on divine friendship. In contrast to the two previous lines of thought, Andrew Davison grounds his argument not in speculations about a divine principle but in the historical event of Christ's coming: in the "incarnation and redemption as we know them."[49] He also stipulates that, as nothing can necessitate God, his argument concerns suitability, not necessity; he explores what is fitting "given what God is doing with and for creatures."[50] Finally, in contrast to the previous argument, Davison works with a concept of incarnation that is firmly rooted in a Chalcedonian framework.[51] In all of this, Davison's premises overlap with the starting point of Scotus's supralapsarian Christological argument, as well as with the assumptions and strategies adopted in this book.

Grounded in these premises, Davison invites us to reflect on the nature of the incarnation and the difference it makes. Incarnation is aimed at establishing friendship, Davison argues: "Incarnation and redemption, as we know

---

47. Delio, "Christ and Extraterrestrial Life," 260.
48. Delio, "Christ and Extraterrestrial Life," 261.
49. Davison, *Astrobiology and Christian Doctrine*, 311.
50. Davison, *Astrobiology and Christian Doctrine*, 307.
51. Davison, *Astrobiology and Christian Doctrine*, 251, 257–62, 284–96.

them, are about God drawing close, indeed more than close: coming among us as one of us, drawing us into the mode of love known as friendship."[52] However, if extraterrestrial beings exist, it is hard to imagine that a divine incarnation in human form could draw those creatures into friendship with God in the same way that such an incarnation can engage human beings. Maybe extraterrestrial beings can understand what has happened to us and rejoice for us. But it would "not have the same texture or appeal" for them that it has for humans.[53] Moreover, if extraterrestrials have very different bodily forms and ways of life than we do, with very different kinds of cognition and thought (and it seems quite likely that they would), then the whole story of a human incarnation of God may completely fall outside of their conceptual framework. If God desires divine self-communication for the sake of friendship, then multiple incarnations, each one appropriate to the nature of the particular life that God wishes to engage, would therefore be entirely fitting.[54]

Davison places this line of thought in a supralapsarian Christological context. He agrees with Scotus's argument that in the incarnation the human soul of Christ was elected to the highest bliss—namely, hypostatic union—and that this election should be understood supralapsarianly.[55] He also thinks that much can be said for understanding creation's eschatological goal as bound up with incarnation—creatures, in need of redemption or not, are meant to be exalted by means of an incarnation.[56] As such, incarnation, "as a pattern of God coming to dwell with his people, wherever they are, hypostatically uniting their nature to himself," is the "central feature of the history and destiny of the cosmos."[57] However, given the fact that *all* God's creatures need to be able to experience this, Davison does not think that "incarnation" should be read here as "the incarnation"—that is, it is not an individual person, Jesus, who is the "central feature of the history and destiny of the cosmos" but, rather, "a full range of Incarnations."[58] Thus, while Davison begins with the historical incarnation as it happens, his argument ends in a place very similar to Delio: with a principle.

---

52. Davison, *Astrobiology and Christian Doctrine*, 311.
53. Davison, *Astrobiology and Christian Doctrine*, 312.
54. Davison, *Astrobiology and Christian Doctrine*, 312–16.
55. Davison, *Astrobiology and Christian Doctrine*, 325–27. See, e.g., Scotus, *Lectura* 1.41, in *Duns Scotus on Divine Love: Texts and Commentary on Goodness and Freedom, God and Humans*, ed. A. Vos, H. Veldhuis, E. Dekker, N. W. den Bok, A. J. Beck (Ashgate, 2003), 146–64. See "The Shape of the First Argument" in chap. 1, above, 18–19.
56. Davison, *Astrobiology and Christian Doctrine*, 322.
57. Davison, *Astrobiology and Christian Doctrine*, 327.
58. Davison, *Astrobiology and Christian Doctrine*, 327, 328.

The Primacy of Christ and Extraterrestrial Life

The Christological position I explore in this book starts from principles very similar to Davison. I too believe that "incarnation and redemption as we know them" should be the base and norm for our Christological reflections. I also believe incarnation is rooted in divine freedom, and that therefore no necessity governs God's actions. And I too believe that incarnation is centrally concerned with divine friendship.

My position differs from Davison's in that, for him, the incarnation as we know it is a means to a larger goal. Christ is not the center of history and the destiny of the cosmos; he is only the means by which part of history and part of the cosmos might reach this destiny. All things are not created for Christ; he is brought forth for the sake of creation. While this is a supralapsarian Christological position, it falls short, I believe, of the actual depth of the claims the New Testament makes about the incarnation. The Christological supralapsarian thread within the New Testament thinks about the incarnation not as a means to a goal but as itself the goal of all of creation. "All things have been created . . . for him" (Col. 1:16).

If all things have been created for Christ, the incarnate son of God and the carpenter from Nazareth, then the very first thing God intended was to be Jesus. That is, God first intended to be a human being, and God then created humanity as this human being's family and friends and the cosmos as the stage on which their friendship would unfold. It is in this way that "in him all things hold together" (Col. 1:17). This excludes the idea of any other divine incarnations in other parts of the cosmos as the means by which God draws other creatures to Godself. If this were the case, Jesus Christ would no longer be the linchpin of all of history and all of creation. The priority of Christ implies that God's project of creation knows only one incarnation.

In saying this I am not claiming that God could not become incarnate in a form other than human. Necessity does not govern God's intentions; but they do take the shape of election. From the unimaginable number of creaturely forms that God could call into being for the Son to assume, God freely chose humanity. It is therefore not strange that, as I will argue below, objections against this argument have taken a shape analogous to many of the objections against the idea of election.

If it is true that God becomes incarnate only as a human being, this may also have consequences for how we think about the existence of extraterrestrial life. As I outlined above, Davison's argument moves from assuming the existence of extraterrestrial beings to the fittingness of multiple incarnations, given the divine commitment to love and friendship. It is possible for him to direct the argument in this way since he ultimately considers the incarnation a means to a larger goal. Other assumptions, including the assumption of the existence of other creatures, can therefore take logical priority over the possible existence of created natures assumed by the divine. But if one's starting point is the absolute priority of Christ, the argument must be directed in the opposite way. If God first intends to be Jesus Christ, and if this intention is an expression of God's desire to be with what is not God, establishing creation as the recipient of divine love and friendship, this will have consequences for what one considers to be a fitting shape of this creation.

On this line of argument, two things can be said about the fittingness of extraterrestrial life. First, if God is after love and friendship, and these are given to creation in the incarnate Christ, then any creature drawn into this love and friendship must be able to receive him. Therefore, if there are any extraterrestrial beings, their existence, conceptual capacities, and way of life, must be such that they can be engaged by a God who relates to them in human flesh. This means that their existence must have significant similarities to human existence. Currently, all sentient creatures known to us that are not humans are nonetheless relatable for humans. Many animals have the capacity to receive human affection and instruction. Even those who do not can be cared for by humans. Angels are portrayed in the Scriptures as capable of interaction with human beings, communicating with them, and joining in humanity's relationship with the divine. Non-sentient creatures can be seen as the backdrop for the divine-human interaction.[59] On this line of argument, extraterrestrial beings, if they exist, would have to fall somewhere within these same conceptual categories. Second, if human beings are created to be the prime recipients of divine love and friendship as embodied in the person of Christ, the idea that somewhere in the cosmos, completely unknown to humankind—nowhere mentioned in God's relationships with and revelation to humans—exists a colony of extraterrestrial beings to whom God also relates in love and friendship is more unfitting than it is not. The Scriptures do, of course, speak of angels and suggest that God relates to them, and they to God and humans. Thus, if angels indeed exist, angelic existence should come as no surprise to humanity. But the Scriptures nowhere suggest that there might be another planet with another form of conscious existence, which God engages in ways similar to the ways God engages humanity. If there is such a planet, then God would be analogous to a father who, unbeknownst to spouse and children, has another family elsewhere

---

59. The story in Mark 1:12–13 is the perfect illustration of all this: Jesus was *with* the wild beasts, he was *in* the wilderness, and angels waited on him.

with whom he spends time as well. For God to have these completely hidden relationships, analogous to the self-giving and self-communicating ways in which God relates to humanity—without disclosing any of these until, presumably, the eschaton—seems to deny the very kind of self-giving and self-communicating relationship God draws us into in Jesus Christ. It would defeat the very premise on which our understanding of God's incarnation is built. It would suggest that God did *not* fully self-communicate Godself to humanity in Jesus Christ. Thus, if we believe God *did* fully communicate Godself in Jesus Christ, such an extraterrestrial community would seem incongruous with that belief.[60]

The Primacy of Christ and the Center of the Universe

At this point, however, one might surface an objection: Does not this line of argument imply a strong anthropocentric universe—anthropocentric to a level that is completely out of step with science, which has helped us see that the earth is only "a minor planet of a secondary star of an unimpressive galaxy somewhere out in space"?[61] Does this not indeed reek of some form of hubris, implying that Bethlehem is the center of the universe?

To suggest that the supralapsarian Christology laid out in this book is anthropocentric is to misunderstand fundamentally the theological shape of the argument. Rather than making humanity the key to the story, the proposed Christology radically decenters humanity. An infralapsarian Christology places humanity at the center. It suggests that the incarnation is focused on the restoration and well-being of humans and other creatures. Christ's existence stands solely in the service of creation's needs. Likewise, a supralapsarian Christology in which Christ is the completion of creation, or the means by which God draws creation to Godself, still takes what is not God as the cornerstone for its theological design. Only the notion of the primacy of Christ redirects this orientation. Here everything exists for Christ's sake, not the other way around.

The objections of "earth chauvinism," "planetism," and that it would be absurd to suppose that the Creator God would choose only this faraway corner of the cosmos in which to become incarnate invite a multilayered response.

---

60. I believe this observation holds not just for my form of supralapsarian Christology but also, for example, for Andrew Davison's. His argument too is built on the idea of incarnation as a form of divine self-giving and self-communicating friendship and love, which seems incongruent with the idea of a secret divine life engaging extraterrestrial parts of creation.

61. Burgess, "Earth Chauvinism," 1100.

First, theologically speaking, the objections are remarkably similar in structure to objections raised to the idea of election: Why would God choose a man from Ur as God's companion? From all the nations in the world, why would God choose a tiny, unremarkable, stiff-necked people as God's own? Among all the splendid cities built by ancient cultures, why would God choose to be born in backwater Bethlehem? Is there not something wrong with the relentless particularity in all these stories? If God is the Creator of all, why would God's concern with creation narrow down in an act of election?

The answers given to the objections concerning the cosmic centrality of the story of the humanly incarnate Christ will therefore also be similar to those offered in defense of the doctrine of election. The more intimately God is involved with creation, the more particular the shape of that involvement will be. Creation is by definition particular. As something that has no being in itself, it is contingent, limited, and bound up in time and space. If God decides not simply to call things into being but to bind Godself to what is not God, this therefore also involves taking on the particularities of whatever God commits Godself to. Moreover, we should not think about this as God first creating and then electing from among that which God has called into being (as many of the objections assume) but instead conceive of it the other way around. The logic of divine election does not presuppose the existence of that which God chooses; rather, God's choice calls forth that which it elects and establishes that which is not. Election is creative in its effect. God did not choose Israel from among many preexisting nations; God called Israel into being out of a woman who was barren and a man who, as Paul says, "was already as good as dead" (Rom. 4:19). God calls the Christian community into existence by making those who once were dead alive together with Christ (Eph. 2:5).[62] This is also the case here: God does not first create the earth and human beings only to choose thereafter to become incarnate on this planet as a human. Rather, God elects to become a human being and therefore creates the human nature of Christ and the rest of humanity as the recipients of this gift and this planet as the theater in which all of this plays out. And the fact that God did not choose to be born in Babylon, Alexandria, or Rome but in tiny Bethlehem, on a planet small and insignificant compared to the many splendid options that are out there, might very well reveal something about the character of God. Humility and condescending love characterize God's dealings with what is not God, not the desire for splendor.

---

62. On this part of the logic of election, see Edwin Chr. van Driel, "'To Be God to You and to Your Offspring After You': An Introduction to the Doctrine of Election," in *T&T Clark Handbook of Election*, ed. Edwin Chr. van Driel (T&T Clark, 2024), 6–8.

Second, spiritually speaking, the objections of "earth chauvinism" and "planetism" miss that the New Testament's proclamation about Christ and his work also implies a significant shift in the way the Christian community experiences the cosmos. While Christ's life may at first have unfolded on earth, in his ascension it continues in heaven. Jesus's ascension causes a shift in the spiritual mapping of the cosmos in the imagination of the church. As Jesus ascends, he is seated at the right hand of God—biblical language for the place of power. For the New Testament writers, Jesus's ascension does not signify departure, as if he were thereafter leaving his legacy for his followers to tend to. Rather, it means that he takes the reins over God's kingdom, leading creation to its final goal. But it also means that, for the first Christian communities, heaven is the center of the cosmos—not Bethlehem or Jerusalem, and certainly not Rome. Heaven is not a faraway place disconnected from earthly life but is instead a nearby place from which every aspect of earthly reality lies open to Christ's direction and presence. For this reason the Christian community is called to "seek the things that are above, where Christ is" (Col. 3:1). They are invited to discover a new spiritual geography, according to which the cosmos is much larger than ever imagined, and they are to await the eschatological joining of heaven and earth, when the curtain that now separates these two will tear, and the heavenly Jerusalem will join earth. In other words, rather than chauvinistically narrowing it, Christ's ascension expands and widens the ways the Christian church experiences cosmic reality.[63]

Unfortunately, in modern times Christ's ascension has dropped out of our theological imaginations. For the supralapsarian Christological argument I advance in this book, however, it is quite central. On completing his earthly career, Christ does not lay down his humanity but takes it up into his existence permanently, ascending as the incarnate One into heaven. And it is promised that he will return in the same way. This calls out for an explanation. On an infralapsarian understanding, there is no reason for Christ to hold on to his humanity. Once sin has been dealt with, the human powerpack has served its goal. The permanence of the incarnation points in a supralapsarian Christological direction.[64]

---

63. On the ways in which the ascension changes the spiritual geography, see for example Matthew Sleeman, *Geography and the Ascension Narrative in Acts* (Cambridge University Press, 2009).

64. For this argument, see Edwin Chr. van Driel, *Incarnation Anyway: Arguments for Supralapsarian Christology* (Oxford University Press, 2008), 149–55. Elsewhere I have teased out its ecclesial and practical implications. See Edwin Chr. Van Driel, "What Is Jesus Doing? Christological Thoughts for an Anxious Church and Tired Pastors," in *What Is Jesus Doing? God's Activity in the Life and Work of the Church*, ed. Edwin Chr. van Driel (IVP Academic, 2020), 1–23.

This invites a third, scientific response to the charges of "earth chauvinism" and "planetism." While understandable—in the light of general theological amnesia concerning Christ's ascension—it is nevertheless still surprising that the ascension plays no role whatsoever in the conversations about theology and astrobiology.[65] The New Testament, particularly Acts, suggests that, after his bodily ascension, every aspect of created reality lies open to Christ's engagement and that he will return from heaven in the same way he departed. This cries out not only for a theological justification but also for scientific modeling. If all this can be true, it suggests the cosmos is even vaster than our current scientific models imagine. It implies that beyond our awareness there is a space currently inhabited by Christ, having entered there in the mode of his resurrection body—a place from which he can suddenly appear to his disciples without visibly entering the room (John 20:19, 36) and to which he seems to disappear when he vanishes from people's sight (Luke 24:31).

Luco J. van den Brom's *Divine Presence in the World* is an example of the kind of scientific modeling that can help us imagine what these theological claims could mean for how we understand the world around us.[66] While discussing divine omnipresence, Van den Brom develops a mathematical account of how we could understand the space to which Christ ascended. Van den Brom uses the notion of *more dimensionality*. Mathematically, it is possible that reality contains more than the three dimensions we now know sensibly. There might be four, a five, or even a much higher number of dimensions; thus, our three-dimensional reality would be described as a subsystem of a larger system. We could think of the resurrected and ascended Christ as participating in a greater reality than our three-dimensional reality. But since our reality is a subsystem of Christ's reality, our reality is still directly accessible to Christ. He is no longer visibly present, but that does not mean he has left space altogether. Instead, as the firstborn of a new creation, he has entered a wider, *more-dimensional* reality, a reality into which he has gone to prepare a place for us and from which he will come again and take us to himself, so that where he is, there we may be also (John 14:3).

---

65. Andrew Davison, whose book is the most up-to-date, thoughtful contribution to the conversation, devotes only two pages to it, in which he mostly encourages his readers to take the ascension "as more than a spatial cosmic journey." Davison, *Astrobiology and Christian Doctrine*, 344.

66. Luco J. van den Brom, *Divine Presence in the World: A Critical Analysis of the Notion of Divine Omnipresence* (Kok Pharos, 1993), 266–316.

The Priority of Christ and the Vastness of the Cosmos

If human beings are called into existence to be the incarnate One's friends, why would God call this vast cosmos into existence? Why not limit creation to the earth, sun, moon, and maybe a few other planets for good measure? Why create this extraordinary universe, and what is this universe's relationship to the community of the incarnate One and his family, the goal of creation? This is where I started this chapter—with the earth as one of eight planets circling the sun, which in turn is only one of a hundred billion stars in our Milky Way galaxy, which in turn is only one of two hundred billion galaxies in the observable universe. If God is after friendship with little critters like human beings, if God has the humility to become one of these and move into their unassuming neighborhood, then why would God create this overwhelming universe, one that is far beyond anything we can observe or grasp?

In a well-known parable Søren Kierkegaard tells of a king who fell in love with a humble girl. He wanted to win the girl's heart but was bound by his own majesty. The chasm that existed between his royalty and her lowliness seemed just too deep. If he were to bring her into his palace, share the throne with her, make her his queen, she would be unable to resist him—after all, he was the king. But making her a queen would not win her heart. Maybe it would look like love. Maybe she would even imagine that she was starting to love him, overwhelmed as she would be by all he gave her. But how would either of them ever know that she loved the king for himself? So the king overcame the chasm not by bringing her into his palace and exposing her to his vast power and domain but by laying down his crown, giving up his power, becoming as poor as she was, and moving into her village to win her heart.[67]

A supralapsarian Christology resonates with Kierkegaard's tale. At the heart of the supralapsarian Christological narrative lies the claim that God is after a love relationship with God's creatures, and therefore God comes to us as close as God can, by becoming a human being. God comes, as it were, from behind God's majesty and awesomeness, from behind the invisible splendor of God's divinity, to assume a humble human nature through which God can be seen, heard, and touched.

But this is still God. God can come to us as close as God can, but it is still God who comes to us. And if the relationship God establishes is anything like real friendship and love, then part of that friendship and love must be that the friends know each other and love each other for what they are. That is, God knows and loves human beings as the little critters they are; but these

---

67. Søren Kierkegaard, *Philosophical Fragments: Johannes Climacus*, ed. and trans. Howard V. Hong and Edna H. Hong (Princeton University Press, 1985), 26–30.

humans, if they truly are to be God's friends, will have to be able to know and love God for who and what God is. That is, they must know and love God not just as a human being—not just as a crying baby in a manger, not just as the man from Nazareth, but as the numinous, omniscient, omnipotent, eternal, holy God of Israel, the Creator and sovereign of all things, the one who cannot be seen with human eyes or touched by human hands.

The king might win the girl's heart by clothing himself in rags and moving into the neighborhood. It might be true that now, indeed, he can know that she loves him not for his riches but for his heart. But does she really love him for who he is? Does she have a chance to love him for who he is? He is not just a raggedly dressed pauper; he is also the king. If she does not know this, and if she is not allowed to love him even as the king, one might question whether the king has indeed found what he was looking for. He can connect to the girl as the person she is—with the environment she comes from, the company she keeps, and the history that has shaped her. But she knows nothing about any of these things regarding him.

God reveals Godself in Jesus Christ. God discloses and communicates Godself fully in becoming incarnate. Thus God cannot just move among God's creatures as the unassuming rabbi from Nazareth. Exactly in this One, God also must reveal Godself in God's infinite awesomeness and power.

God cannot make us see God in God's divine glory. If we were to encounter God in God's divinity, we would, as God warns Moses, fall dead on our faces (Exod. 33:20). And thus, God reveals Godself to us, on the one hand, by taking on humanity, so God might personally come among us in order that we might see God, hear God, touch God, and be touched by God. But God also wants to reveal to us the awesomeness and glory of God's divinity. And it is of this that the vastness of the universe speaks. It is of this that Christ's ascension speaks. Here the one who comes so unspeakably close to us enters and governs a realm the size of which is simply unimaginable, overwhelming, beyond comprehension—exactly because it speaks of the overwhelming, infinite awesomeness of God's nature. Our solar system alone, with its majestic sun and planetary rhythms, is already impressive. Looking at the night sky, with its innumerable stars and their planets, is already overwhelming. Grasping the billions and billions of such galaxies is altogether beyond us—because it is the self-revelation of the Creator God, the baby of Bethlehem.[68]

---

68. This line of thought gives a supralapsarian Christological reading of what the Belgic Confession describes as one of the two books through which we know God:
> We know Him by two means: first, by the creation, preservation, and government of the universe; which is before our eyes as a most elegant book, wherein all creatures, great and small, are as so many characters leading us to contemplate the invisible things of

In Him All Things Hold Together

In Jesus Christ all things hold together, the Colossians hymn posits. He is the first in God's intentions *ad extra*, the one for whom all things have been created, and the one toward whom the arch of history bends. If this is the case, this will also have to determine our understanding of the meaning of the universe, the possibility of extraterrestrial life, and the thought of multiple incarnations.

God can become incarnate in as many varied creatures as God wishes. But if Christ is not a divine means to support a larger divine plan, but instead himself the goal of all things, multiple incarnations would not fit the divine intentions. Rather, all that exists, and that we assume to exist, should be understood in the light of the particular intentions that God has expressed in Jesus Christ: for humans to be drawn around him as a large family, for history to be shaped as the unfolding of this family's life of love and friendship, and for the universe to be the theater of this family's life.

For this reason, it is equally unfitting to hold that elsewhere in the universe there exists extraterrestrial life that could not find a place in this particular story. While such extraterrestrial life is certainly within the realm of God's creative capacities, it would seem to be incongruent with God's revealed intentions.

Positively, however, reading the book of the cosmos in the light of the supralapsarianly intended incarnation of the divine Word leads us to see our world and Christ differently. The resurrected Christ moves around sovereignly in space, appearing and disappearing from his disciples at will. He then ascends—in his resurrected, bodily form—withdrawing from his disciples to take up residence elsewhere; yet in this elsewhere, all the universe seems nonetheless open to his work and appearance. All of this suggests a much richer form of dimensional reality than we currently can experience with our senses. This, combined with the overwhelming awesomeness of the cosmic book itself, reveals to us the glory of the one who, as Mary's son, eats with us, drinks with us, and invites us into his circle of friends.

God, namely, His eternal power and divinity, as the apostle Paul saith (Rom. 1:20). All which things are sufficient to convince human beings, and leave them without excuse. Secondly, He makes Himself more clearly and fully known to us by His holy and divine Word; that is to say, as far as is necessary for us to know in this life, to His glory and our salvation. (The Belgic Confession II, in James T. Dennison Jr., comp., *Reformed Confessions of the 16th and 17th Centuries in English Translation*, vol. 2, 1552–1566 [Reformation Heritage Books, 2010], 425–26)

11

"By Making Peace Through the Blood of His Cross"

Supralapsarian Christology and Atonement

God comes to *be with* us, not just to *be for* us. The "not just" of the previous sentence is key to grasping the supralapsarian Christological position. The argument is not that God comes to be with us *instead of* being for us. Supralapsarian Christology does not deny that in Christ God reconciles with and atones for a sinful creation. The argument is, rather, that God's being for us needs to be understood in the context of a wider story. A Christological story focused on the cross is too narrow to do right by the narrative of Scripture. There is a wider arch that needs to be taken into account. And within this wider narrative arch, God's being for us in Jesus Christ is embedded in, and for the sake of, God's *being with* us. In saying that the incarnation is not contingent upon sin, the supralapsarian does not deny that in the incarnation God also deals with the sin problem. Rather, the supralapsarian theologian says, with the writer of Colossians, he through whom and for whom all things have been created, and who therefore is before all things, is now also the one through whom God reconciles all things, the firstborn from the dead and the head of the church, "so that he might come to have first place in everything" (Col. 1:18). It is because he is central to creation and eschatological consummation that the incarnate One is also central to reconciliation.

The question might now be raised whether a supralapsarian account of the incarnation also shapes one's understanding of *how* Christ deals with the sin problem—that is, whether what one believes about God's supra-lapsarian intentions shapes one's account of God's infra-lapsarian dealings.

In this chapter, I will explore the relationship between supralapsarian Christology and atonement theories in two directions. First, I will explore this relationship *from above*. That is, I will map how in the history of theology different commitments concerning God's supralapsarian intentions indeed have given rise to different accounts of God's infralapsarian dealings. But in this it will become clear that supralapsarian Christologies do not differ from their infralapsarian counterparts. Anselm of Canterbury's *Cur Deus Homo*, one of the central texts in Western atonement theories, argues that conceptually there were three possible ways for God to deal with human sin: God could simply forgive sin, God could punish sin, and God could ask for compensation for the damage done by sin. Each of these three possible avenues of divine action is reflected in a theological model of atonement. In each case, a theologian's attraction to a particular model is motivated by theological intuitions concerning God's supralapsarian intentions for and commitment to creation. What I will show, though, is that each of these sets of intuitions can take both an infralapsarian and a supralapsarian Christological shape. That is, there is an infralapsarian Christological account according to which in Christ God provides satisfaction for sin (Anselm's own position), but there is also a parallel supralapsarian Christological understanding of atonement (represented, for example, by John Duns Scotus). An influential infralapsarian Christological account holds that the incarnate One substitutes himself to receive the punishment for sin that should have been borne by humanity (John Calvin), but one might hold the same position on a supralapsarian Christological basis (Karl Barth). One might hold an infralapsarian Christological position according to which the cross is an expression of how God deals with sin by simply forgiving it and absorbing its consequences (as held by Gerhard Forde); one might also come to this understanding of the cross based on a supralapsarian Christological position (as Samuel Wells does, for example).[1] Second, I will ask which model of atonement is most fitting to the supralapsarian commitments that shape this book's Christological stance. In line with the hermeneutic of my supralapsarian argument—not speculating

---

1. This part of the argument should also lay to rest the suspicion that supralapsarian Christology is incompatible with penal substitutionary accounts of the atonement—a suspicion Thomas G. Doughty Jr. claims is pertinent among evangelical theologians. See Thomas G. Doughty Jr., *Christus Dominus: Supralapsarian Christology and the Progressive Work of Christ* (Lexington, 2024), 3–4.

about what God might have done but carefully reflecting on what God has done—this question has to be approached *from below*. I will ask, What do the Scriptures say about the nature of Christ's atoning work, and how does this map against both the supralapsarian commitments of this book and the various models of atonement discussed in the first part of the chapter?

Mapping the Options

Satisfaction: Anselm of Canterbury and John Duns Scotus

To map this relationship between supralapsarian Christologies and models of atonement, it may be best to start with the contrasting accounts of two medieval theologians, Anselm of Canterbury (1033–1109) and John Duns Scotus (1266–1308). Anselm's *Cur Deus Homo* has shaped much subsequent debate about atonement. The outline of his argument is well known. Because of human sin, history was derailed and God's gracious plans for creation could not be completed. Nevertheless, God, as the best possible being, cannot allow for lowly critters like us to thwart God's plans. God therefore has to take care of the sin problem and get history back on track.[2] In a carefully crafted road map, Anselm shows that there was only one way open if God wanted to accomplish this goal: the gift of life given by the God-man. All other possible avenues are, in the light of the perfection of God's character, dead-end streets. God could not just forgive sin because then order would not be restored, while disorder would be de facto sanctioned—which is not fitting for a perfect being.[3] Nor could God simply punish sinners because, while punishment may confirm God's righteousness, it would not accomplish God's goals. Punished sinners do not end up in eternal bliss but in eternal damnation.[4] Therefore, payment had to be made, a compensation that would

---

2. "The human race, clearly [God's] most precious piece of workmanship, had been completely ruined; it was not fitting that what God had planned for humankind should be utterly nullified." Anselm, *Cur Deus Homo*, in *Anselm of Canterbury: The Major Works*, ed. Brian Davies and G. R. Evans (Oxford University Press, 1998), 1.4.

3. Anselm, *Cur Deus Homo* 1.12. Anselm discusses here three arguments against "just forgiving" that all circle around the unfittingness of such action in the light of God's nature and character. To forgive without punishment, he argues, would be to leave imbalance in God's creation; to treat sinners and non-sinners equally; and to treat sinners as if they were not subject to the law, thereby making them resemble God.

4. As Anselm explains in *Cur Deus Homo* 1.14–15, to save God's honor, it does not really matter whether God punishes sinful creatures or receives compensation from them. Either way, God establishes God's authority over the creature, and authority leads to honor. It does however matter to the creature whether God punishes or whether compensation is provided: Given the weight of sin, punishment will be eternal, and therefore the creature will never reach

reconcile humans to their God and restore God's gracious order in the universe. But a sin committed against a best possible being is of immeasurable weight, and no creature has the infinite resources to make a payment that would compensate for such a sin.[5] Only one has such resources: God. The payment, however, must be made not by God but by Adam's family. Therefore, God becomes human to make available to the human family the infinite divine resources required to make the payment.

Such is Anselm's argument. What is not always taken into account is that Anselm's book is actually not concerned with giving an account of the atonement. As the title suggests, it is concerned with the question, *cur Deus homo?* ("Why did God become human?"). Anselm's book was meant to contribute to an ongoing debate between Jewish and Christian medieval theologians about the incarnation in which the Jewish rabbis argued that the incarnation was offensive to the dignity of God.[6] How could it be that God—who is, as Anselm himself puts it in his *Proslogion*, "that-than-which-a-greater-cannot-be-thought," the best possible being—would engage in this humiliating act of "descending into a human's womb, [being] born of a woman, growing up nurtured on milk and human food"?[7] This line of argument had hit home. It is for this reason that Anselm, while not challenging this fundamental premise, tried to show that, given the circumstances, God could not have done otherwise—there was no other way to solve the problem of sin.[8] It is exactly here that supralapsarians take a different route. They differ from Anselm in that they do not accept the premise of his conversation partners. Rather than seeing the incarnation as a humiliating act that God engages in only if no other possibility is open, supralapsarians see the condescending love that is embodied in the babe of Bethlehem as the ultimate expression of the very heart of God's character. It is here that we see what God's perfection actually looks like.

An example of this supralapsarian approach is the one put forth by the medieval theologian John Duns Scotus. Scotus embraces an Anselmian un-

---

the eternal bliss intended for them. Older interpretations that suggest Anselm's argument is fueled by medieval feudal notions of honor miss this eschatological motivation.

5. As Anselm argues in *Cur Deus Homo* 1.21, the weight of a sin is determined not just by the importance of the act of sinning but also by the importance of the one sinned against. Anselm takes God to be the best possible person, and therefore a person of immeasurable worth. Therefore, the weight of a sin against God is immeasurable.

6. See R. W. Southern, *Saint Anselm: A Portrait in a Landscape* (Cambridge University Press, 1990), 198–202.

7. Anselm, *Proslogion*, in *Anselm of Canterbury: The Major Works*, ed. Brian Davies and G. R. Evans (Oxford University Press, 1998), 1.3. See also Anselm, *Cur Deus Homo* 1.3.

8. This is the question Anselm seeks to answer: "By what necessity or logic did God, almighty as he is, take upon himself the humble standing and weakness of human nature with a view to that nature's restoration?" Anselm, *Cur Deus Homo* 1.1.

derstanding of the atonement, but he rewrites Anselm's proposal in a supralapsarian key. For Scotus the heart of the incarnation is love. In a theological reflection on the Pauline notion that everything is created "for him," for Christ (Col. 1:16), Scotus argues that the decision to become incarnate—that is, the decision to unite Godself with a human nature—logically precedes all other divine intentions. God wants to love, and God wants to share this love; therefore, God decides to become incarnate. Next, God decides to create all other things, humans and all the rest of creation, as the friends and companions of the incarnate One. But God also decides that, once humanity has rejected this love and turned against God, it is through the incarnate One that God will make payment for sin and draw us back again in reconciliation.[9] Scotus agrees to Anselm's analysis of the cross as a form of satisfactionary payment. In his discussion of redemption, he actually offers a detailed conceptual analysis of Anselm's argument, a unicum in Scotus's oeuvre.[10] He underscores the eschatological motivation of the argument.[11] With Anselm, he rejects the idea that God could just forgive.[12] He disagrees with Anselm on two points, though. First, he argues that Anselm makes a mistake by conceptualizing the weight of sin, and therefore the weight of the needed payment, as immeasurable. No finite being can commit a sin of infinite weight, even if it is against the infinitely worthy God. Therefore, the payment does not have to be infinite. But then, of course, we also do not need someone with infinite resources to supply the payment—and that means a simple creature would do. Why is it then God incarnate who does it? Here Scotus draws on the divine motivation he detected *supra* (before) God's intent to allow sin. Just as God does not

---

9. For a detailed analysis of Scotus's supralapsarian Christological argument, see chap. 1, above.

10. John Duns Scotus, *Lectura* 3.8–20. As far as modern-language translations go, the Latin text with a Dutch translation by Nico den Bok can be found in Nico den Bok and Guus H. Labooy, eds., *Wat God bewoog mens te worden: Gedachten over de incarnatie* (Boekencentrum, 2003), 59–75. Good introductions to Scotus's discussion include Richard Cross, *Duns Scotus* (Oxford University Press, 1999), 129–32; and Antonie Vos, *The Theology of John Duns Scotus* (Brill, 2018), 125–33. In the last few decades there has been a discussion about the exact nature of Scotus's account of voluntarism, satisfaction, and merit. The outcome of this debate is not very important for the few points I wish to make about Scotus's understanding of atonement, and thus I will sidestep it in this section. For an introduction to the debate, see Andrew S. Yang, "Scotus's Voluntarist Approach to the Atonement Reconsidered," *Scottish Journal of Theology* 62 (2009): 421–40; Andrew Rosato, "The Interpretation of Anselm's Teaching on Christ's Satisfaction in the Franciscan Tradition from Alexander of Hales to Duns Scotus," *Franciscan Studies* 71 (2013): 411–44; Thomas M. Ward, "Voluntarism, Atonement, and Duns Scotus," *Heythrop Journal* 58 (2017): 37–48; and Guus H. Labooy, *Christology and Atonement: A Scotistic Approach* (Lexington/Fortress, 2024), 107–24.

11. Scotus, *Lectura* 3.20.43.

12. Scotus, *Lectura* 3.20.18.

have to give Godself to creation in incarnation but *chooses* to do so out of love, similarly God does not have to step forward to make the payment for sin but, because of love, decides to do so. Second, while the incarnate One could have made the payment by a simple act of intense love, Scotus argues what is needed to outweigh an act of disobedience is simply an act of obedience that is of greater intensity than its negative counterpart. Thus he chooses to bring about atonement by an ultimate act of intense love, the giving of himself unto death. "And therefore he preferred to do it in this way, I believe: to draw us to a greater love to himself."[13]

Penal Substitution: John Calvin and Karl Barth

The comparison between Anselm and Scotus illustrates that what one believes about God's character and supra-lapsarian intentions does indeed have the potential to shape one's account of God's infra-lapsarian dealings. That insight, combined with Anselm's road map, can be used to further chart different understandings of the atonement. Anselm's decision to mark off "just forgiveness" and "punishment" as dead-end streets was motivated by his understanding of God's character and supra-lapsarian way of relating to the world. Given God's perfection, God could not "just forgive," and given God's eschatological intentions for the world, atonement could not be brought about by punishment. Once one perceives differently God's character and ultimate intentions, one may conceive of these different atoning acts more positively. The notions of "punishment" and "just forgiveness" both have prominent representatives in Western theology, and among these we can in turn distinguish between theologians with Christologically infralapsarian and supralapsarian intuitions. John Calvin, who, like Anselm, holds to an infralapsarian Christology, walked down a path Anselm had rejected as a dead-end street and understood the cross in terms of wrath and punishment. Human sin has evoked God's righteous anger, which will result in judgment upon and death for humanity. Wrath and anger are not, like Anselmian payment, quantifiable categories. If humanity is to be saved from God's judgment, the question is not, Who has enough resources to make a payment to satisfy God? Rather, the question is, Who has the adequate resources to withstand God's wrath and guide humanity through it to salvation? Like Anselm, Calvin believes only a Godman is adequate for this task. For Calvin, however, this is not because such a one can draw on infinite divine resources to pay what humanity cannot pay but because such a one, given his divinity, is life itself, and therefore can withstand the intensity of God's judgment and swallow up

---

13. Scotus, *Lectura* 3.20.20 (my trans.).

death: "It was his task to swallow up death. Who but the Life could do this? It was his task to conquer sin. Who but very Righteousness could do this?"[14] Given this understanding, Calvin therefore describes Christ's life, and more particularly his death, as a journey in which Christ receives God's punishment in our place.[15]

This understanding of atonement is driven by Calvin's intuitions about the nature of God. For Anselm, God has a choice: God can pursue punishment or payment. Both options establish God's authority and therefore uphold God's honor. For Calvin, God's character leaves God with only one option. A perfect God cannot allow God's law to be broken, he argues, and therefore, even if God wants to be gracious, God has to punish: "Since he is a righteous judge, he does not allow his law to be broken without punishment."[16] In his conception of things *infra* (after) the fall, Calvin ends up in a different place than Anselm because he starts in a different place when conceiving of things *supra* (before) the fall.

Calvin's twentieth-century heir Karl Barth, in turn, rethinks Calvin's account in Christologically supralapsarian terms. Barth holds on to the notion of penal substitution,[17] But he places this notion in the context of God's primordial determination to be a God for others. What precedes the history of human sin, or even the history of creation, is covenant. The covenant has a face: Jesus Christ. In Jesus, God elects Godself to be a God who will not be without humanity; but God also determines every human being as existing only within the context of Jesus Christ.[18] For Barth, the covenant is

---

14. John Calvin, *Institutes of the Christian Religion*, ed. John T. McNeill, trans. Ford Lewis Battles, 2 vols. (Westminster, 1960), 2.15.2.

15. Good introductions to Calvin's understanding of atonement can be found in Paul Dafydd Jones, "The Fury of Love: Calvin on the Atonement," in *T&T Clark Companion to Atonement*, ed. Adam J. Johnson (Bloomsbury, 2017), 213–36; Stephen Edmondson, *Calvin's Christology* (Cambridge University Press, 2004), 89–115; and Paul van Buren, *Christ in Our Place: The Substitutionary Character of Calvin's Doctrine of Reconciliation* (Oliver and Boyd, 1957).

16. Calvin, *Institutes* 2.16.1.

17. Barth writes, e.g., "The very heart of the atonement is the overcoming of sin: sin in its character as the rebellion of man against God, and in its character as the ground of man's hopeless destiny in death. It was to fulfil this judgment on sin that the Son of God as man took our place as sinners. . . . We can say indeed that he fulfils this judgment by suffering the punishment which we have all brought on ourselves." Karl Barth, *Church Dogmatics* IV/1, trans. G. W. Bromiley (T&T Clark, 1956), 253. And he continues: "Everything depends upon the fact that the Lord who became a servant, the Son of God who went into the far country, and came to us, was and did all this for us; that he fulfilled, and fulfilled in this way, the divine judgment laid upon him." Barth, *Church Dogmatics* IV/1, 273.

18. "The beginning of all things, of the being of all men and of the whole world, even the divine willing of creation, is preceded by God's covenant with man as its basis and purpose." Barth, *Church Dogmatics* IV/1, 53. And since the content and form of this covenant is Jesus, "in the history of Jesus, we have to do with the reality which underlies and precedes all other

the ontological determination of the being and history of everyone created within its context—and therefore, each person's history is included in the history of Jesus Christ.[19] This supralapsarian ontology allows Barth to deal with a question that has always haunted Calvin's take on atonement: How is God ethically justified in punishing one in the place of others? On Barth's account, human beings are not really others: When, in the incarnate One, God assumes humanity, God assumes all of humanity. The history of Jesus includes the history of all. His history is not, as on an infralapsarian Christological account, one person's innocent history added to an already created and fallen human history; his history precedes and encompasses everyone's history. It is for this reason that, according to Barth, Jesus can be both our substitute and our representative. Thus, on the one hand, since our histories are included in his, what happens to him really happens to us.[20] While, on the other hand, since our histories are included in his, what befalls him no longer has to befall us.[21]

Just Forgiving: Gerhard Forde and Samuel Wells

Anselm names as a last conceivable path for dealing with sin that God could "just forgive" the sin committed. Anselm rejects such a path as inconsistent with God's perfect character. Other theologians, though, consider such a path the very expression of God's perfect character. And again, while one might hold such an understanding within an infralapsarian Christology, it also finds expression in supralapsarian Christological frameworks.

---

reality as the first and eternal Word of God. . . . In this history we have actually to do with the ground and sphere, the atmosphere of the being of every man, whether they lived thousands of years before or after Jesus." Barth, *Church Dogmatics* IV/1, 53.

19. I have analyzed Barth's supralapsarian ontology in Edwin Chr. van Driel, *Incarnation Anyway: Arguments for Supralapsarian Christology* (Oxford University Press, 2008), 83–124.

20. See Barth, *Church Dogmatics* IV/1, 295:

That Jesus Christ died for us does not mean . . . that we do not have to die, but that we have died in and with him, that as the people we were we have been done away with, that we are no longer there and have no more future. . . . We died. This has to be understood quite concretely and literally. In his dying, the dying which awaits us in the near or distant future was already comprehended and completed, so that we no longer die to ourselves. . . . We died: the totality of all sinful men, those living, those dead, and those still to be born, Christians who necessarily know and proclaim it; but also Jews and heathen, whether they hear and receive the news or whether they try and still try to escape it.

21. See Barth, *Church Dogmatics* IV/1, 93: "In his place Jesus Christ has suffered the death of a malefactor. The sentence on him as a sinner has been caried out. It cannot be reversed. It does not need to be repeated. It has fallen instead on Jesus Christ." A good introduction to Barth's doctrine of atonement is Adam J. Johnson, "Barth on Atonement," in *The Wiley Blackwell Companion to Karl Barth*, ed. George Hunsinger and Keith L. Johnson (Wiley Blackwell, 2020), 147–58.

The twentieth-century Lutheran theologian Gerhard Forde holds that, rather than being the place where God pays for our sin or carries out the punishment for our sin, the cross is the place where God bears our sin. Forde starts with an important observation: Many atonement theories, including Anselm's and Calvin's, move away from the historical and messy nature of the actual events of Christ's death, speaking about them on a detached, transcendental level. For the church fathers, the story of Good Friday is a story about cosmic tyrants being overcome. For Calvin, it is a story about God's wrath finding an outlet so that thereafter God might forgive us. For the medieval theologian Abelard, as well as much early-twentieth-century liberal theology, it is a story of extreme dedication and moral example. But if we face up to the actual events as they unfolded in history, we see something that is quite different from lofty transcendental or moral constructions: We see a murder, a "cruel, bitter, excruciatingly painful, and utterly shameful execution."[22]

Forde combines this observation with a second, theological one: In approaching the cross from a detached, transcendental or moral level, we are "obscuring the cross by theological roses."[23] After all, all these theological theories amount to a position according to which, however things might appear on the surface, on a higher level Christ's death was a *good* thing—here the devil was tricked, or our debt was satisfied, or God's wrath was met. Moreover, on each of these theories, because Christ's death was a *good* thing, it is construed as the result of divine providence: Jesus *had* to die because it was in this way, and only in this way, that God's plan of atonement could be carried out. In construing our theologies in this way, however, Forde holds that we are "attempt[ing] to exonerate ourselves from the terrible nature" of our act.[24] Because if we look at the actual events, God did not kill Jesus—we did.

Forde's observation is rooted in a fundamental intuition of Lutheran theology: On their own accord, sinful human beings will never face up to the reality of the human condition. They will go to extraordinary lengths to cover up who they really are, and religious piety is their favorite way of doing this covering up. Left to themselves, they will never own up to who they are; rather, they need to be told who they are. In Lutheran theology, this is the work of the law. It exposes humans as sinners because they cannot do what it commands. But they resist this exposition; further, they attempt to use the law as a means to justify themselves, as a set of ethical obligations that they pretend they can follow. Something similar happens here, Forde charges: God

---

22. Gerhard O. Forde, "The Work of Christ," in *Christian Dogmatics*, ed. Carl E. Braaten and Robert W. Jenson, 2 vols. (Fortress, 1984), 2:84.
23. Forde, "Work of Christ," 2:80.
24. Forde, "Work of Christ," 2:82.

did not kill Jesus; humans did. But since they cannot own up to the fact that they killed him, they cover their tracks with religious theories that give his death meaning in a grand divine plan.

So, why did humans kill Jesus? Precisely because he showed them who they are, Forde charges.[25] In showing them mercy, in preaching God's forgiveness, Jesus treated them as the kind of people who need mercy and forgiveness—and they could not stand it. Therefore, they silenced him. And in allowing them to kill him, while staying true to the end to his expression of divine forgiveness, Jesus died *for us*. He died vicariously for us—that is, he died *on our behalf*. But he did not die *instead of us*. His death was not a form of substitution.[26] To put it differently, Christ's sacrifice was not something offered by humans to God but, rather, something offered by God to humans. In fact, in speaking about atonement as if *humans* need and have something to offer to God, we are still seeking a certain religious standing before God.[27] On Calvin's understanding of atonement, Christ offers something to God in our name. But on a Fordian understanding, Christ offers us something in God's name: forgiveness. God is not in need of anything; we are.[28]

In dying on our behalf, Forde holds, Christ "bears our sin," not as "an abstract affair, [not as] a strange metaphysical transference; it is actual and public fact. We beat him, spit on him, mock him as a 'king,' crown him with thorns, torture him, forsake him, kill him. He bears our sins in his body—actually. The real event occurs. It is not a rehearsal or a cultic substitution." He just does not bear it "in our stead."[29]

On Forde's proposal, God does not need anything in order to be able to forgive; God comes *in forgiveness*, and it is precisely because we reject this forgiveness that we kill Jesus. However, God does not allow us to thwart God's offer of forgiveness. Sin is overcome, atonement is made, because God does not allow our rejection to derail God's forgiving act. For Forde, the resurrection is the expression of this. On resurrection morning we see God's ultimate commitment to being reconciled to us. Where we caused nothing but death, God brings life. And, to use a term that Forde himself does not use but that nonetheless seems fitting, this makes the cross the place where God *absorbs* our sin and thereby brings about reconciliation.

25. Forde, "Work of Christ," 2:81.
26. Forde, "Work of Christ," 2:88.
27. Forde, "Work of Christ," 2:82–84.
28. See also Gerhard O. Forde, "Jesus Died for You," in *A More Radical Gospel: Essays on Eschatology, Authority, Atonement, and Ecumenism* (Eerdmans, 2004), 220–22.
29. Forde, "Work of Christ," 2:90.

The notion that God does not demand payment or punishment so that sin may be atoned but absorbs sin, not passing back the rejection embedded in it, and thereby *just forgives* can also arise from a supralapsarian Christological narrative. An example of this is Samuel Wells's recent book *Constructing an Incarnational Christology*.[30] For Wells, what we call atonement is simply God's utter commitment to *being with* God's creatures. Wells roots this account of *being with* in a social doctrine of the Trinity. The trinitarian persons are imagined as existing themselves in community and communion, embodying an inner-trinitarian *being with*.[31] Such community is characterized by "constant engagement, awareness, alertness, consciousness, appreciation."[32] In other words, all the things one might find in God's *being with* creation through incarnation, for Wells, are first of all found within the immanent life of the Trinity. The purpose of the incarnation is rather "to extend to creation the quality of being with that belongs to its inner-Trinitarian relationships."[33] Jesus embodies in his own existence what it means to be drawn into a *being with* that crosses the ontological divide between God and creation. Through his humanity, he is fully with creatures; through his divinity, he is fully with the Trinity.

The question is, What happens when "God's purpose to be with us now and forever meets with a refusal"?[34] This is what Gethsemane and Golgotha are about. Jesus does not come to die. His death is not the expression of a divine plan or need, but of the human resistance to being drawn into community with the Trinity. In quite a unique understanding of the cross, Wells insists this resistance means that the Son is forced to choose whom he will be with: the Father or humanity. Abandoning humanity would mean abandoning the very goal of creation—for God to *be with* what is not God. Abandoning the Father would, Wells writes, be even more catastrophic: It would mean that the Trinity is no longer the Trinity.

The cross is the breaking point. Jesus's cry of dereliction expresses that the Son, the second person of the Trinity, is no longer with the first person. The *being with*, "the very essence of God," no longer is.[35] This takes the Trinity

---

30. Samuel Wells, *Constructing an Incarnational Theology* (Cambridge University Press, 2024). See also his earlier *Nazareth Manifesto: Being with God* (Wiley Blackwell, 2015), 79–83, 239–44. For a discussion of Wells's argument, see "Samuel Wells: Grace Communicated Through Christ's Person" in chap. 5, above, 96–99; and "*Being With*" in chap. 7, above, 138.

31. Wells, *Constructing an Incarnational Theology*, 173.

32. Wells, *Constructing an Incarnational Theology*, 175–76.

33. Wells, *Constructing an Incarnational Theology*, 247. Or, as he says elsewhere, in the incarnation, "God repeats a relationship proper to itself in the inner-Trinitarian relationships." Wells, *Constructing an Incarnational Theology*, 167–68.

34. Wells, *Constructing an Incarnational Theology*, 244.

35. Wells, *Constructing an Incarnational Theology*, 252.

into unknown territory. The Father is still with the Spirit; so is the Son. "But the Father and the Son are not with each other."[36] For Wells, what is at stake here is more than the question, Does the Son suffer? Or, through the Son's suffering, does the Father also suffer? The question is how creation can continue when the Trinity is ruptured, and how the Trinity might possibly be repaired following such an unimaginable event.[37] It seems that sin, evil, nonexistence can step through the rupture at any moment.[38]

The chasm within the Trinity has come about because sin forces Jesus to make a choice that opposes what the incarnation is about. Jesus embodies God's *being with* us, but Jesus has to choose between being with us or being with God. In this, Jesus "undergoes the opposite of being with—complete separation and non-being—yet thereby affirms and demonstrates God's unbreakable commitment to being with us—whatever befall. He loves us to the end (John 13:1)."[39]

Likewise, the Father has a choice: Let the Son be with us, or insist on the integrity of the Trinity. Rather than choosing for the Trinity and against us, the Father also chooses to be who he is: "Being with is the very soul of the Trinity: it knows no other way. It is not, in the end, a choice. It is God being God. God being God means with. Here God stands: God can do no other."[40]

In this, God's means and end are identical. God's end is to be with us in Jesus Christ. God's means to bring this about is, again, to be with us in Jesus Christ. Even when that brings about a fissure within the Trinity, it does not change the Trinity's character.[41]

Given the examples of these various theologians, proponents of a penal substitutionary model of atonement—or any kind of atonement model—need not worry: A supralapsarian understanding of the incarnation does not bind one to a particular understanding of the cross. To embrace a supralapsarian Christological stance does not imply one denies that, in Christ, God takes care of the sin problem, nor does it commit one to a particular stance on the logic of atonement. How one construes Christ's reconciling work will depend on other underlying theological commitments, which also will shape which *particular* supralapsarian Christological model one is drawn to. This leads however to the next question: What understanding of atonement makes the most sense given the particular supralapsarian approach advanced in this book?

---

36. Wells, *Constructing an Incarnational Theology*, 254.
37. Wells, *Constructing an Incarnational Theology*, 255.
38. Wells, *Constructing an Incarnational Theology*, 256.
39. Wells, *Constructing an Incarnational Theology*, 257.
40. Wells, *Constructing an Incarnational Theology*, 259–60.
41. Wells, *Constructing an Incarnational Theology*, 263.

The Primacy of Christ and the Atoning Work on the Cross

I have argued that God's very first intention *ad extra* is for God to be Jesus Christ and that everything else is called into existence in the context of this intention. God determines to be a God-with-others, and human beings are called into existence as the recipients of this gift. But what happens when human beings do not want to receive this gift—when they do not want to *be with* God the way God intends to be with them? How will God draw them back to the goal for which they were created? How will God restore the relationship between God and what is not God? More specifically, what model of atonement arises from the supralapsarian commitments that shape this book's supralapsarian stance?

The last question seems to be a logical one to ask. However, to set up such a deductive theological argument would be inconsistent with a key characteristic of the hermeneutic embedded in my supralapsarian Christological approach. My Christological proposal does not arise from a deduction based on supralapsarian theological principles. Rather, I have argued that my proposal arises from careful reflection on history—that is, on the incarnation as it happened, on the Christ as he comes to us in the narrative of Scripture. My argument has been that the history of the incarnate One simply cannot be understood on an infralapsarian Christological account, that the logic of this history is supralapsarian in nature. In other words, my Christological argument comes about inductively rather than deductively.

If this is true, a similar approach will be needed when it comes to understanding the atoning work of Christ. It will have to be drawn from the theological logic embedded in the very ways in which Scripture accounts for the atonement as it happened, and then this theological logic will have to be read against the background of the supralapsarian Christological logic embedded in the same theological narrative.

This book offers explorations in supralapsarian Christology, not a full Christological design. Likewise, this section offers only an initial exploration of two aspects of the New Testament's speaking about the work of the cross. By all accounts, these two aspects are significant, if not decisive, for the ways in which the Christian community has spoken about the atoning difference Christ makes.[42] First, many New Testament writers draw on the

---

42. For example, John Calvin draws his account of atonement from his understanding of Israel's sacrificial cult, Isaiah's suffering servant, and the ways in which Paul seems to apply these notions to interpret the salvific meaning of Jesus's death. I have offered a critical discussion of Calvin's position and its exegetical underpinning in Edwin Chr. van Driel, *Rethinking Paul: Protestant Theology and Pauline Exegesis* (Cambridge University Press, 2021), 135–60. As

cult in Israel's sanctuary, and especially the liturgy of Yom Kippur, to make sense of Jesus's death. Second, throughout the New Testament, and probably going back to Jesus himself, Jesus's role is likened to that of Isaiah's suffering servant. My goal is to identify the theological logic embedded in both biblical figures and to see how this maps against both the supralapsarian commitments of this book and the various models of atonement that I just discussed.

Israel's Cult

Israel's cult consists of a range of carefully described rites and practices focused initially on the tabernacle and, later, the temple. The Old Testament narrative presents the erection of the sanctuary itself as the completion of the story of creation.[43] The story of the making of the tabernacle (Exod. 39–40) is shot through with vocabulary borrowed from Genesis 1 and 2. Patterns shaped by the number seven permeate the text. The rabbis, noting these parallels, expound on this in a comment on Solomon's completion of the temple (1 Kings 7:51) in Pesiqta Rabbati 6:6: "Only when Solomon came and built the Temple would the Holy One, blessed be He, say that the work of creating heaven and earth was now finished: 'Thus *all* the work . . . was finished.' Indeed, he was called Solomon (Hebrew: *Shlomo*, from the root *sh-l-m* meaning 'to bring to completion, finish') because it was through the work of his hands that the Holy One, blessed be He, completed the work of the six days of creation."[44] The work of creation is completed only once God has built Godself a home at creation's center. Creation finds it culmination in divine *being with*.[45]

God's living in the midst of the people is celebrated and supported by a range of sacrifices, which can broadly be divided into four categories. There are the daily burnt offerings, which are to be sustained "throughout your

---

I will document in the footnotes, in what follows in this chapter I draw in significant ways on the research for and arguments made about atonement in that book.

43. For an overview, with literature references, see Gary A. Anderson, *That I May Dwell Among Them: Incarnation and Atonement in the Tabernacle Narrative* (Eerdmans, 2023), 19–48.

44. William G. Braude, *Pesiqta Rabbati: Discourses for Feasts, Fasts, and Special Sabbaths* (Yale University Press, 1968), 126, quoted in Anderson, *That I May Dwell Among Them*, 22.

45. As Gary A. Anderson points out, this very logic drives the prologue of John's Gospel, in which "the world was created (vs. 1) . . . for the purpose of revealing the glory of the Word (vs. 14) [who] . . . 'tabernacled among us'" (Anderson, *That I May Dwell Among Them*, 24). In this context, it is also important to note that the parallels between the creation story in Genesis 1–2 and the tabernacle story in Exodus 39–40, which are both shaped by patterns focused on the number seven, find a repetition in the parallels between the Genesis chapters and the Colossians hymn (see chap. 7, above). Whereas for the Exodus writer the erection of the tabernacle is the completion of creation, for the Colossians hymn its completion is the incarnation.

generations" and that offer "a pleasing odor" to the Lord (Exod. 29:38–46; Num. 28:1–9), and to which are added similar sacrifices on the Sabbath, at the beginning of each month, and on feast days (Num. 28:9–29:6). These sacrifices seem to support the communion between God and God's people that takes place in the sanctuary.[46] There are the spontaneous sacrifices (Lev. 1–3), very similar in nature to the daily burnt offering, but rooted in people's personal desire to relate to the deity. Then there are the prescribed sacrifices (Lev. 4–7), which are to be brought when one unintentionally becomes ritually and morally impure, countering the effects that this impurity has on the relationship between God and the people. Finally, the rituals of Yom Kippur (Lev. 16) are ordered to deal with Israel's intentional sins.[47]

The New Testament writers repeatedly refer to elements of Israel's cult as metaphors to make sense of the salvific meaning of Jesus's death, even if they do not all refer to the same elements—or refer to them in the same way. At several places, Jesus is said to have become a purification offering, the central sacrifice made on the day of Yom Kippur (Rom. 8:3; 2 Cor. 5:21).[48] Elsewhere, Paul likens Jesus to the mercy seat, the cover of the arc and presumed place where God was enthroned in the midst of God's people, as well as the center of the atoning actions on Yom Kippur (Rom. 3:25).[49] The liturgy of Yom Kippur is the governing theme for the Christological argument of Hebrews, in which Christ is described as a new high priest, entering the original heavenly sanctuary of which the earthly temple is only a copy and enacting the high priestly work using his own life-giving resurrection blood. Here Jesus is thus identified as both priest and sacrifice.[50] Finally, Ephesians refers to Jesus as "a fragrant offering and sacrifice to God" (Eph. 5:2), thereby referencing the daily and spontaneous sacrifices, the only ones that are said to connect to God through a well-pleasing odor.

---

46. For helpful comments on the nature of these sacrifices, see Andrew Remington Rillera, *Lamb of the Free: Recovering the Varied Sacrificial Understandings of Jesus's Death* (Cascade Books, 2024), 30–35.

47. Good overviews of the scholarly conversation about the logic of Israel's sacrificial rites are Stephen B. Chapman, "God's Reconciling Work: Atonement in the Old Testament," in *T&T Clark Companion to Atonement*, ed. Adam J. Johnson (Bloomsbury, 2017), 95–113; and Christian A. Eberhart, *The Sacrifice of Jesus: Understanding Atonement* (Fortress, 2011), 13–101; as well as Gary A. Anderson, "Sacrifice and Sacrificial Offerings: Old Testament," in *The Anchor Bible Dictionary*, ed. David Noel Freedman, 6 vols. (Doubleday, 1992), 5:870–86.

48. I realize not all exegetes understand Paul's language in this way. For my reading, see Van Driel, *Rethinking Paul*, 150–54.

49. Van Driel, *Rethinking Paul*, 146–49.

50. See David M. Moffitt, *Atonement and the Logic of Resurrection in the Epistle to the Hebrews* (Brill, 2011); and David M. Moffitt, *Rethinking the Atonement: New Perspectives on Jesus's Death, Resurrection, and Ascension* (Baker Academic, 2022).

In drawing on these cultic metaphors, what interpretation do the New Testament writers give to Jesus's death? Theologians such as John Calvin interpret Israel's sacrifices through a substitutionary lens: the animals sacrificed die in the place of those who bring the sacrifice, thereby undergoing a form of punishment meant for others.[51] But Calvin here reads his own theological interpretation of Jesus's death into the New Testament's use of cultic metaphors and, from there, applies the same lens to understanding Israel's cult. Hermeneutically, the order should be the other way around: We should try to understand how first-century Jews thought about the meaning of the cult and use this to understand what the New Testament writers took themselves to be doing when they drew on the cult to interpret Jesus's death, which then can give rise to our own theological conceptualization.

If we follow this latter order, another picture arises. According to contemporary scholarship, the animal sacrifice embedded in the cult was not governed by the logic of substitution. It was also not focused on obtaining forgiveness for sin. Offerings do not ameliorate sin; this can be achieved only through "a broken and a contrite heart."[52] As Jacob Milgrom has argued in great detail, part of the cult was designed to counter the effect of sin on the sanctuary and, thereby, on God's presence. Sin results in impurity; and impurity, whether ritual or moral, causes pollution that enters the sanctuary and sticks to the liturgical furniture. God dwells among God's people in the temple but cannot abide in a defiled sanctuary. Pollution requires cleansing, and blood is a cleanser. Blood is holy because blood carries life. The goal of the sacrifice is, therefore, to cleanse the temple from pollution. The more severe the transgression, the more deeply pollution penetrates the sanctuary. When impurity is caused by an individual violation, only the horns of the altar in front of the steps to the sanctuary must be cleansed. In the case of a communal violation, blood must be applied also to the altar inside of the sanctuary and at the curtain separating the holy from the Holy of Holies. This is what happens on Yom Kippur. In all this, the central act of the sacrifice is not the killing of the offering but the application of the blood. The killing has a purely functional meaning: It gives access to the needed cleanser.[53]

---

51. See, e.g., Calvin, *Institutes* 2.16.6. See also Calvin, *Commentary on the Book of the Prophet Isaiah*, trans. William Pringle, 4 vols. (Baker, 2005), 4:124–25.

52. Anderson, *That I May Dwell Among Them*, 91.

53. See Jacob Milgrom's three volumes in the Anchor Bible Commentary: *Leviticus 1–16*, Anchor Bible 3 (Doubleday, 1991); *Leviticus 17–22*, Anchor Bible 3A (Doubleday, 2000); and *Leviticus 23–27*, Anchor Bible 3B (Doubleday, 2001); as well as his shorter *Leviticus: A Book of Ritual and Ethics*, A Continental Commentary (Fortress, 2004).

Read in this way, the cult is not about punishment for sin; rather, it is about avoiding punishment and other consequences for sin. Without the cleansing work of the sacrifices, God cannot stay with God's people and might withdraw. The cult stands in the service of God's continued presence among God's people.

The Suffering Servant

Nonetheless, Israel's sin can start to weigh so heavy, and the pollution of the sanctuary can become so severe, that it drives God away. This is how Israel experienced exile. Jerusalem could be burned down and the temple could be destroyed because God no longer was present with God's people. Exile was not just a political or economic crisis but a religious one as well. Exile was experienced as a curse—one that felt like the reverse of the exodus (see Deut. 27).[54]

How and when might God return to God's people? How might the curse be lifted, the judgment come to an end, and God live with God's people again? These are the questions that shape Deutero-Isaiah, in which Isaiah's songs about the suffering servant play a central role.

The songs suggest that the servant's life is instrumental in undoing Deuteronomy's curse. The exiled people were "as blind people grop[ing] in darkness" (Deut. 28:29). The servant will "open the eyes that are blind" (Isa. 42:7). Whereas the people had become "an object of horror, a proverb, and a byword among all the peoples" (Deut. 28:37), the exaltation of the servant will "startle many nations; kings shall shut their mouths because of him" (Isa. 52:15). Once "the pestilence clung" to the people (Deut. 28:21), but by the servant's bruises they were healed (Isa. 53:5).

However, Deutero-Isaiah does not give an account of *how* exactly the servant is instrumental to reversing the fate of Israel. This should give us pause in our reading of the texts. Broadly, there are four different ways in which scholars characterize the role the servant plays vis-à-vis the conflict between Israel and its God: substitute, sacrifice, representative, or mediator. I believe the text is open to each of these four lines of interpretation and that the matter is exegetically simply underdetermined.[55]

It is in this context that we should read the New Testament writers' identification of Jesus with the suffering servant. It is particularly Paul who, in doing

---

54. For the role of the Deuteronomy text in Israel's understanding of exile, see N. T. Wright, *Paul and the Faithfulness of God* (SPCK, 2013), 143–63.

55. I have backed up this position in an analysis of these lines of interpretation in Van Driel, *Rethinking Paul*, 122–27.

so, offers a highly original interpretation of the ways in which the servant's life and death reverse Israel's fate. In Philippians 2, Paul poetically reflects on Jesus's career by drawing directly on the description of the suffering servant in the fourth servant song.[56] Like the servant, Jesus poured himself out (Isa. 53:12; Phil. 2: 7). He humbled himself just as the servant was brought low (Isa. 53:7; Phil. 2:7), even to the point of death (Isa. 53:12; Phil. 2:7). He is also "exalted to the highest place," in the way that the servant is "exalted and lifted up, and shall be very high" (Isa. 52:13; Phil. 2:9). The vindication of Jesus in turn results in the inauguration of the eschatological *and* monotheistic vision of Isaiah 45:22–23: "Turn to me and be saved, all the ends of the earth! For I am God, and there is no other. . . . 'To me every knee shall bow, and every tongue shall swear'" (see also Phil. 2:10–11).[57] In Jesus's vindication, exile comes to an end, God will live among God's people again, and this will also be the moment when Israel's expectations about a creation-wide reign of Israel's God will be fulfilled.

Unique to Paul, though, is the claim that the inauguration of God's eschatological kingdom hinges on the acknowledgement of Jesus, the servant, as being identical to Israel's God. God's reign takes the shape of "every tongue . . . confess[ing] that Jesus Christ is Lord, to the glory of God the Father" (Phil. 2:11). In first-century Judaism, the word for Lord, *kyrios*, was used as a replacement term for the personal name of God, YHWH, as the latter was deemed too holy to be pronounced. To acknowledge Jesus as *kyrios* is therefore to acknowledge him as the bearer of the covenantal name, YHWH. That Jesus is given "the name that is above every name" (v. 9) confirms this. For a first-century Jew like Paul, there is no name above the name of Israel's God.[58] To confess Jesus as the bearer of this name is therefore not to glorify "God the Father" by honoring Jesus as someone who is different from God but rather to honor God in acknowledging Jesus as being identical to God.

In making this claim, Paul offers us a novel interpretation not only of the servant's identity but also of the role he plays in lifting the curse, bringing exile to an end, and paving the way for God's return. Within the flow of the Philippians hymn, the servant is not *instrumental* to God's return—as is implied in the models of substitution, sacrifice, and representation—but *identical* to it. In the life of the servant, God returns to God's people, and in

---

56. In what I say about the Pauline interpretation of the servant and Phil. 2 in the following paragraphs, I follow very closely what I have said about this in Van Driel, *Rethinking Paul*, 121–22, 128–30.

57. For this comparison, see Richard Bauckham, *Jesus and the God of Israel* (Eerdmans, 2008), 43, 201–2, 206–10.

58. Bauckham, *Jesus and the God of Israel*, 199.

doing so, God inaugurates God's eschatological reign. God does not return *after* the servant has played his role; rather, God's own self has taken the role of the servant, joined the people in their plight, and thereby brought it to an end. God has returned, and thereby, exile is over.[59]

The Logic of Atonement

With these accounts in hand, we can discern distinct but overlapping logics that shape the atoning effect of Israel's cult and Isaiah's suffering servant.

The sacrifices of the cult relate to divine presence, expiation, and dying for. The cult is aimed at preserving the continued divine presence in the midst of God's people. The cleansing of the sanctuary counters the pollution that sin causes and allows God to keep residence there. Cleansing happens through blood obtained by sacrifice. The blood obtained in the sacrifice has not a propitiatory aim but an expiatory one. It does not appease God's anger—such a notion is completely absent from the cult's logic—but removes the effect sin has on God's dwelling place. The deaths of those sacrificed have, in themselves, no atoning effect. These deaths are in the service of obtaining the needed cleansing. The animals do not die instead of those who sacrifice—the logic of substitution is as absent from the cult as propitiatory notions; at most, they might be said to die on behalf of those who offer the sacrifice.

The work of the suffering servant, in turn, is shaped by dying for, forgiveness, and divine presence. The servant undergoes the fate of Israel. He suffers with them in exile. He bears the people's infirmities, carries their diseases, is wounded for their transgressions (Isa. 53:4–5). He does not, however, do these things in the people's stead. They themselves already lived through the judgment of exile. Rather, he joins them in their plight, suffering on their behalf. In this *suffering with* lies healing. He is instrumental in bringing exile

---

59. See N. T. Wright, *Paul and the Faithfulness of God*, 682, speaking about Deutero-Isaiah's expectations:
> But of course the mysterious power of this prophetic tapestry is found in the strange, dark strand which is woven in at four key moments. These are the poems that speak of the vocation and accomplishment of the "servant," who at one level is 'Israel' and at another level stands over against "Israel," doing for the people what they cannot do for themselves. And the "servant," in the final climactic poem, is finally identified as "the arm of YHWH," albeit unrecognizable in his shameful and disfigured state (53:1). The prophet never resolves this puzzle. Somehow the work of the "servant," and specifically the redemptive achievement of his suffering and death, are the manifestations in action of the divine "righteousness," the accomplishment of the divine "salvation," and above all the full expression of what it means that YHWH, Israel's one God, has at last returned in glory to Zion. He has come back to be enthroned, not only as Israel's true king but as king of the world. This is, of course, a "Pauline" exegesis of Isaiah 40–55. So far as I know, the passage was not being read in this way before the public career of Jesus.

to an end. And, according to Paul, this happens exactly in God taking upon Godself the role of the servant. In joining Israel in exile, God undoes the judgment and embodies forgiveness.

If these are the interpretive lenses used by the New Testament to interpret the atoning effects of Jesus's life, death, and resurrection, and if this is the logic that governs them, then any twentieth-century understanding of atonement must be consistent with, and further explicate, the themes of this biblical material. If we, therefore, overlay the logic of the three atonement models discussed in the previous sections with the logic of these New Testament interpretative notions, one can make at least three observations.

First, any kind of theological understanding of the atoning effect of Jesus's death will have to consider that the New Testament material implies that Jesus dies on behalf of God's people but not in their stead. Neither the cult nor the figure of the suffering servant circles around the idea that one dies instead of the other. To read it in this way is to import theological ideas that do not arise from the text itself. This erases the exegetical basis for the account of penal substitution.

Second, in the accounts discussed above, God does not need to receive anything in order to be able to forgive human sin—God does not need to be propitiated. The logic of the cult turns not around forgiveness but around cleansing. The suffering of the servant does imply forgiveness, but, according to Paul's application of the servant figure to Jesus, it is an expression of forgiveness rather than a means to obtain it. God returns to God's people as the servant, and God's return implies that God *has* forgiven them. This also discounts a satisfaction theory.

Third, central to both New Testament approaches is the notion of divine presence. God wishes to *be with* God's people and therefore provides the cult through which Israel can counter the polluting effects of sin that might drive God away. And when, finally, God is indeed experienced as withdrawing, in the traumatic events of exile, the figure of the servant gives witness to the fact that even then God cannot give up on God's creatures and stays faithful to God's commitments, even at the cost of suffering and death.

The Primacy of Christ and the Logic of Atonement: On *Being With*

With these observations in hand, I return to the question of what understanding of the cross might flow forth from and be consistent with the primary intuitions that drive this book's supralapsarian account.

All of creation is called into being to be the recipient of God's gift of Godself in the incarnation. Humanity is created to be the incarnate One's family.

The goal of history is God's *being with* creation and creatures' *being with* God. This is the central intuition that shapes my supralapsarian Christological approach. In this light, sin is the refusal to accept the gift of divine self-giving. It is the rejection of the very goal for which God has created us. Rather than being gathered into Christ, sinful humanity draws away from him, refusing to be touched by his friendship and love. God's response in turn is to let the One in whom God comes to be with us to also be the one in whom God is for us. The firstborn of creation is also the one through whom God takes care of the sin problem—so that he might have the first place in everything. God atones for our sin, even if the act of atoning means God's death.

According to the logic of the New Testament's speaking about Christ's atoning death, we should not understand Christ's work as a form of penal substitution or as a satisfaction of God's demands through payment. Rather, Christ's work is characterized by divine presence, expiation, dying for, and forgiveness. God does not need anything in order to forgive us. But God forgives us exactly in dying for us, expiating us from our sin, with the very goal that God can be permanently present among us. As such, Christ's atoning work is not any different from Christ's work of *being with*; rather, it is the heightened, fully consequential embodiment of *being with*. On this reading, Christ's atoning work is what God's primary commitment—to be a God-with-others, to be Jesus Christ—looks like under the conditions of human sin and resistance.

This is the direction my exegetical reflections invite us to go, and it is congruent with Samuel Wells's account of Jesus's death. In general, among supralapsarian Christological approaches, his is most similar to what I attempt in this book. Like I do, he starts from the priority of Christ. God's intention to *be with* creation is the fundamental divine commitment in which everything that is not God is embedded, and the incarnation is both this commitment's means and its end.

Nonetheless, exactly at this point I have significant hesitations concerning Wells's proposal. To start, Wells's attempt to root his Christological move in a social trinitarian account reveals the deep theological problems embedded in an account of the Trinity anchored in the notion of divine self-differentiation. On the cross, Wells holds, a chasm occurs between the Father and the Son, so much so that the Trinity is no longer the Trinity. This leads us into uncharted territory, Wells acknowledges. "The question is how creation can continue when the Trinity is ruptured," when the Father has lost the Son and the Son has lost the Father.[60] It is telling that Wells never answers his own question.

60. Wells, *Constructing an Incarnational Theology*, 254.

Creation does not exist independently of the Godhead; it is upheld in its existence from moment to moment by God's sustaining power. On a classical understanding of the Trinity, all trinitarian persons act together through the one divine power of the Godhead. The unity of their power gives witness to the unity of the persons—that is, unity of power is intrinsically bound up with unity of persons.[61] If the unity of the persons is ruptured, so is the unity of the divine power and its enactment, and all that is sustained by this power would cease to exist. Wells's question lays bare the impossible task of accounting for trinitarian unity on a social trinitarian account. If the three persons share in one power, as the church fathers maintained, the events described in Wells's narration of Golgotha would have resulted in the dissolution of creation. But it did not. Thus, the trinitarian persons must each have their own power, and the combined power of Father and Spirit must be enough to sustain the universe. But then the question is this: What differentiates this picture from a polytheistic account of three gods?[62]

Wells might answer that what holds the Trinity together is not the unity of power but the trinitarian *being with*. After all, this is, according to his proposal, "the very essence of the Trinity."[63] However, Wells's understanding of what happens on the cross directly undermines this claim. The events of the cross lead the Son to be without the Father, and the Father to be without the Son.[64] If the Father and the Son can be without each other, *being with* is actually not essential to what it means to be God. *Being with* is an accident; it can be lost, given up as the Son decides to be without the Father. However, if *being with* is not essential to God but, rather, contingent upon the decisions of the trinitarian persons, then Wells's desire to root the incarnational *being with* in the very being of God fails. The trinitarian *being with* is just

---

61. See "The Contingency of the Second Person's Incarnation" in chap. 9, above, 178.

62. I am not even contemplating here the multitude of other questions that could now arise: If Father and Spirit can maintain creation together without the Son, could the Father or the Spirit maintain creation on their own? Does maybe one of these already maintain creation on its own—and which one? If Father and Spirit can maintain creation without the Son, is there any intrinsic relationship between the Son and creation (a negative answer, or even an inkling of a negative answer, would be devastating for the kind of supralapsarian Christological projects Wells and I are both committed to). And maybe the scariest question of all: If the three trinitarian persons can enact their powers independently, as the scenario under consideration seems to imply, what happens if they disagree? What if their powers turn against one another? The fact that the Son, according to Wells, can choose creation over the Father leaves the conceptual space for that possibility.

63. Wells, *Constructing an Incarnational Theology*, 252.

64. "This is being without the Father, and thus being not-God—being without the with that is the very essence of God. . . . The Father and the Son are not with each other." Wells, *Constructing an Incarnational Theology*, 252, 254.

as contingent as the divine *being with* creation that is the incarnation. Given the disastrous consequences of the kind of social trinitarian account needed to make sense of an immanent-trinitarian *being with*, we had better drop any attempts to base an incarnational *being with* on the Trinity in the first place.

Finally, even if one were to bracket these significant theological consequences, Wells's account of what actually causes the rupture in the Trinity itself is problematic. Wells holds that, as sinful humanity turns against God, the Son needs to choose between *being with* the Father and *being with* humanity. In choosing for humanity, the Son chooses to no longer be with the Father. The Son enters the realm of sin and experiences its devastation on the cross. However, this is not the only thing that happens. Wells reads Jesus's cry of dereliction as an expression of the fact that just as the Son has chosen not to be with the Father, so also the Father has withdrawn from the Son. The Father cannot reach the Son, and the Son cannot reach the Father.[65] However, why would this be? If *being with* is at the heart of the divine project of creation, and the Father lets the Son be with creation precisely because the Father wishes to save this very project, why would the Father simultaneously refuse to be with the Son as he ventures into the far country, choosing to be with the humanity that wishes to be without God? On Wells's own reasoning, humanity's rejection of God does not weaken the Father's commitment to *being with* humanity. But then, surely, it also does not weaken the Father's commitment to *being with* the Son.

For these reasons, I believe we need an account that offers an alternative to Wells's thesis. With him, I hold that *being with* is central to God's relationship to what is not God and that we should understand the events of Jesus's life, death, and resurrection as God's consistent commitment to *being with* creation. But there is no reason to anchor this trinitarianly. As I noted above, Wells's own attempt to understand God's *being with* as rooted in the immanent Trinity falters on his conceptualization of the cross. But maybe more importantly, everything that Wells wants to secure in his account—God's intention, embodied in the incarnation, to *be with* creation (the intention that is primary in God's relating to all that is not God) and the cross as God's ultimate commitment to this intention to *be with* creation—can be obtained in an account that is Christologically, not trinitarianly, grounded.

With Wells and Forde, I hold that God does not need the cross, Jesus's suffering, or his death. The cross is, rather, an expression of our resistance to Jesus's *being with* us. Human beings wished Jesus dead, not God. The

---

65. "A separation between Father and Son evacuates *presence*, because Jesus at this moment evidently finds himself utterly alone. This is a moment when Jesus cannot reach the Father, nor can the Father reach Jesus." Wells, *Constructing an Incarnational Theology*, 253.

cross does not reveal first of all who God is; it reveals first of all who we are. I therefore propose that we read the cross and atonement in the following way.

God's first decision is to be Jesus Christ. That is, everything that exists is created in the context of God's commitment to *be with* God's creatures, to draw all things to Christ, and, in Christ, to be the center of creation's life of love. To accomplish these goals, God creates Godself a family, forms out of them a people, and sets out for them a way of life so that through them God might take on human form, live a human life, and make them the first recipients of the gift of God's presence. But, as it turns out, sinful human beings have difficulty receiving this gift. They do not want to be bound together, they are ambivalent about a life of love, and they certainly find it difficult to be in the presence of God. And thus, the whole of God's history with God's people is shaped by a cycle of God coming near, of the people receiving God gratefully but then resisting God, of God covenanting with the people but then being rejected by them, of God's anger and judgment followed by the people recanting and regretting their choices, and of cries for forgiveness followed by reconciliation, only to be followed by more sin, more rejection, and renewed judgment.

It is this cycle that comes both to its head and to its end in the cross and resurrection. Here God comes once again, but this time fulfilling God's original intentions. No longer in a pillar of cloud or a blazing fire, no longer obscured from recognition through a burning bush or a gentle whisper—here God comes with a human face and a human voice, fully participating in the life of humanity. And for God's sinful people, it is just too much. It is too intimate. What he says and preaches is cutting too close. It is too revealing. And so they push him away, cast him out, silence his voice.

But this time, God does not let the cycle continue. God does not allow Godself to be pushed out, does not withdraw from God's people, and does not send anger and judgment upon them only to be met by remorse and pleas for forgiveness. God breaks the cycle. God absorbs the rejection and does not pass it back. God so fully absorbs the rejection that it leads to God's death. But even this cannot push God away. Even this cannot dispatch God's presence. Easter morning is the revelation that God is here to stay. It is the ultimate expression of God's *being with*. It is the end of the power of sin.

Read in this way, the logic of atonement is governed by the same commitment to *being with* that has shaped God's dealing with what is not God from the very beginning of creation. It is characterized by divine presence, expiation, dying for, and forgiveness. The very core of atonement is God's refusal to let God's intentions for creation be undermined by our constant wanderings, illusions, and sinful rejection. God follows through on the intention to be a

God-with-others. God even goes so far as to absorb a shameful death on a cross, refusing to pass our rejection back to us. Instead, God uses this moment to usher in the grand finale of creation's history, establishing eschatological life from within the open grave, and drawing us into this unending future of *being with* as in baptism we are united with Jesus in the death of our refusal and the new life of God's future. Death and resurrection thus become the means of our expiation. And in all this, God embodies the fact that sin does not determine who we are and who we might be. God *just forgives*.

12

"First Place in Everything"

Supralapsarian Christology and Eschatological Expectation

In *The Home of God*, Miroslav Volf and Ryan McAnnally-Linz argue that creation was called into being to be inhabited by God: "We argue that creation comes fully to itself when, indwelled by God, it becomes God's home and creatures' home in one."[1] They point out that home imagery imbues the whole of the biblical narrative. Focused particularly on Exodus, John, and Revelation, they argue that "the story of everything is the story of God coming to dwell in and with human beings and the world."[2] They point, for instance, at the correspondence between the creation story in Genesis and the chapters in Exodus focused on the building of the tabernacle: Creation is depicted as a macro-temple, while the tabernacle is portrayed as a microcosm of the ideal world, the world in which God intends to gather and dwell with the whole of creation.[3] They point at the Gospels' claim that "Christ's coming is the key step in God's mission of transforming the world—in sanctifying

---

1. Miroslav Volf and Ryan McAnnally-Linz, *The Home of God: A Brief Story of Everything* (Brazos, 2022), 2.
2. Volf and McAnnally-Linz, *Home of God*, 5.
3. Volf and McAnnally-Linz, *Home of God*, 5–6. See the observation made earlier in this book that the rabbis read the stories about the tabernacle and the establishment of the temple as the conclusion of the creation narrative ("Israel's Cult" in chap. 11, above, 238).

it—so that it can be a genuine home of God."[4] In this, as the Gospel of John puts it, Christ himself is the dwelling place of God, the One in whom God has tabernacled among us (John 1:14). And they point to John of Patmos's vision of the new Jerusalem, highlighting that as John saw the holy city come down out of heaven from God, he hears a voice saying, "See, the home of God is among mortals. He will dwell with them; they will be his peoples, and God himself will be with them" (Rev. 21:3).

For characterizing God's *being with* God's creatures, *home* is a far better metaphor than the available alternatives, Volf and McAnnally-Linz argue. For example, one might think of the temple, and the accompanying liturgical activities, as the focal point of divine dwelling. But, as Volf and McAnnally-Linz point out, in the new Jerusalem of the new creation there is no temple, nor is creation itself described as a temple. Rather, the temple "is the Lord God the Almighty and the Lamb" (Rev. 21:22). Likewise, the kingly strand of spheres of authority, terrestrial rulers, and subjects—running through the biblical story parallel to the priestly strand of divine presence, temple, priests, and worshipers—is ill-suited as a metaphor to govern the whole of the story. Not everything is politics; and in Revelation the eschatological outcome of history is portrayed as circling around a much more intimate form of divine dwelling with creation than political terms can describe.[5] Finally, throughout the history of Christian theology, theologians have taken Godself to be the final, determining goal of all creation. God has been said to be the ultimate end and final good for humans to enjoy. But Volf and McAnnally-Linz argue that such a metaphor has to "disregard the overwhelmingly worldly character of biblical eschatological hopes."[6] Not only does Scripture's narrative invite us to enjoy God's creation in addition to Godself; eschatologically speaking, God's presence will be enjoyed not in heaven but on earth, in the new Jerusalem, with God and the Lamb as its temple and center. God is not staying above but coming down, as God makes all things new.

Given Volf and McAnnally-Linz's focus on God's dwelling among God's people as the ultimate and essential focus and goal of creation—they sometimes characterize it as God's *being with*—it is striking that they do not seem to take creation to be essentially Christologically determined. Everything is directed at the coming of God, but the actual, embodied, most intimate form in which God comes is not recognized as the fulfillment of that goal. While they do characterize the incarnate One as key to God's mission to transform

---

4. Volf and McAnnally-Linz, *Home of God*, 8.
5. Volf and McAnnally-Linz, *Home of God*, 11.
6. Volf and McAnnally-Linz, *Home of God*, 13.

creation, they do not identify Christ as the one for whom all things have been created. History, they say, will end with the vision of God—but Jesus is absent from the description of that vision.[7] In a section explicitly devoted to the question *cur Deus homo?* ("Why did God become human?"), Volf and McAnnally-Linz argue that, particularly for the Gospel of John, it is not enough to say that the incarnation happens predominantly for the purpose of solving the problem of sin; it must be said, rather, that Christ comes to "bring God's intention for creation to fulfillment"—that is, for God to come to the world to dwell with and in human beings.[8] But they never go so far as to claim that Christ *is* the fulfillment of God's intentions for creation. For Volf and McAnnally-Linz, everything in the biblical narrative points toward the dwelling of God in creation, but their narration of the actual dwelling has a Jesus-shaped hole in it.

In this chapter, I wish to fill that hole in the narrative. With Volf and McAnnally-Linz, I hold that creation is called into being for God to *be with* creation. But I hold that this divine dwelling had from the beginning a particular intention, a specific face: the face of Jesus. Here I will explore what this means for our eschatological imagination—for our understanding of the eschatological interaction between God and humanity, the place of sin in history and the eschaton, eschatological remembering and forgetting, Jesus's wounds and our own, and the grand finale of human existence: the *visio Dei*, seeing God face-to-face.

Eschatological Eschatology: On *Being With*

The central intuition of this book is that God's first outward commitment is to be Jesus Christ. That is, God determines to become incarnate and to call what is not God into existence as the incarnate One's companions and friends. On this intuition, the goal of creation is *being with*—a gracious, embodied, unending community of friendship drawn around the incarnate Lord.

God's very first commitment is thus an eschatological one. In determining to become incarnate, God determines an eschatological future for Godself and for the recipients of divine self-giving. Creation is for the sake of realizing God's eschatological intentions; the eschaton is not for the sake of completing creation. As such, the supralapsarian Christological proposal I advance is different from many other supralapsarian Christological designs, according to which the incarnation may not be contingent upon sin but is nonetheless

---

7. Volf and McAnnally-Linz, *Home of God*, 222–26.
8. Volf and McAnnally-Linz, *Home of God*, 97.

contingent upon creation. On those proposals, the incarnation may be read as the completion of God's act of calling into being what is not God. The incarnation is seen as that which holds creation together and gives it coherence; the incarnate One is he who leads creation to its ultimate goal. On my read, it is exactly the other way around. The incarnate One is the firstborn of creation; all things have been called into being for him. He *is* the ultimate goal. Humanity was created so that he may have a large family; all of creation issues forth to be the stage on which this family's eschatological life of *being with* him and with one another may unfold.

For this reason, the incarnation determines the shape of creation's eschatological life. The world to come is participatory but not divinizing; a continued interpersonal interaction, rather than the preservation of the lived life; not elevated beyond space and time, but rather transformed and glorified—unending continuation and, as such, radically eschatological, as the eschaton is always pointing beyond the horizon.

In the incarnation, God gives Godself to what is not God. By calling forth and assuming a human nature as God's own, God creates the possibility of a life of *being with* God's creatures. That is, in the incarnation God steps outside of the realm of immanent divine existence and calls forth and condescends into what will become the realm of creation so that God may commune with what is not God. Incarnation is thus a form of participation. It is an act of radical self-giving in which God establishes and participates in what is not God, making God fully present to humanity and all of creation. But this participation does not—nor does it need to—include the opposite move: Humanity does not need to be drawn upward to participate in the divine life, attributes, energies, or glory.

The notion of deification as the eschatological goal of humanity, or even of all of creation, has become quite popular in the last couple of decades.[9] My supralapsarian Christological proposal steers clear of deification for three

---

9. There is a sprawling amount of, often inconsistent, definitions and accounts of deification in the literature. A good working definition is offered in a recent handbook on the doctrine:
> Deification is a process and goal by which the human being or church or in some way the whole of creation comes to participate in God, Christ, divine life, divine attributes, divine energies, or divine glory by growing into the likeness of God, while remaining a creature ontologically distinct from the Creator. This process is often also described as divine adoption, regeneration, glorification, sanctification, and union with God. Human deification is made possible by the incarnation of the divine Logos in Jesus Christ and is sustained by the Holy Spirit through the sacramental life of the church, prayer, ascetical discipline, and growth in virtue. (Paul L. Gavrilyuk, Andrew Hofer, and Matthew Levering, "Theses on Deification," introduction to *The Oxford Handbook of Deification*, eds. Paul L. Gavrilyuk, Andrew Hofer, and Matthew Levering [Oxford University Press, 2024], 5)

reasons: First, the idea of deification tends to be rooted in the presumed interaction between Christ's two natures. In the assumption of a human nature, it is this nature that is transformed and deified. Salvation for other human beings is a matter of being united to this nature.[10] I believe this line of thought is confessionally and ontologically problematic. According to the Chalcedonian definition, the two natures of Christ are united but not mixed. No seepage takes place from Christ's divinity into his humanity. It is not clear that the idea of deification can adhere to this creedal stipulation. Moreover, even if such seepage occurred and were creedally allowed, the question is how such deification of Christ's individual human nature would soteriologically effect the individual human natures of others, without having to assume a form of Platonic unity among all of humanity.[11] My approach sidesteps these difficulties. Nothing in my proposal hinges on the interaction between the two natures; rather, the act of the divine *person* who, in assuming a human nature, becomes present in creation is decisive.

Second, deification assumes an instrumentalized understanding of the incarnation. It holds that the incarnation itself does not accomplish God's eschatological intentions; rather, the incarnation serves a larger goal. As Athanasius says, "He [Christ] was made man that we might be made God."[12] If this were true, the incarnation would be an event that happens for the sake of creation; creation's deification would be the goal, and the incarnation would be a means of achieving it. On my account, however, the incarnation *is* the goal. Creation is called into being for the sake of the incarnation. In the incarnation, God is *with* creation, and creation is *with* God. Nothing else needs to be accomplished.[13]

And third, on my account deification is simply not needed. If participation, communion, *being with*, is the goal, this is accomplished in the incarnation. In the incarnation, the Creator becomes present as a creature; the invisible One becomes visible. And we are created to be what he is: human beings, members of his family. When, in sin, we wander away and reject God's company, God stays true to what God initially committed to be: God-with-us. History's eschatological finale is nothing but the full enjoyment of this condescending

---

10. See my discussion of Kathryn Tanner's Christology in "Kathryn Tanner: Grace Communicated Through Christ's Human Nature" in chap. 5, above, 92–96.
11. This is one of the difficulties with Tanner's account. See "Natures and Persons" in chap. 5, above, 101–4.
12. Athanasius, *On the Incarnation of the Word* 54, in *Christology of the Later Fathers*, ed. Edward R. Hardy (Westminster, 1954), 107.
13. In rejecting deification as the eschatological future of creation, my proposal aligns with the account of Volf and McAnnally-Linz (Volf and McAnnally-Linz, *Home of God*, 134–35).

love, given to us in the human face of Jesus: "When he is revealed, we will be like him, for we will see him as he is" (1 John 3:2).

The account of the incarnation I advance also has to part from a theological imagination according to which the eschaton is the preservation of the lived life. According to such an account, in the eschaton space and time will come to an end; history will have been completed, and creaturely life and agency will be no more. Nonetheless, all this will be preserved in God's hand—as that which has been. As Karl Barth, one of the prominent proponents of this approach, says,

> When the totality of everything that was and is and will be will only have been, then in the totality of its temporal duration it will still be open and present to him, and therefore preserved. . . . Everything will be present to him exactly as it was or is or will be, in all its reality, in the whole temporal course of its activity, in its strength or weakness, in its majesty or meanness. He will not allow anything to perish, but will hold it in the hollow of his hand as he has always done, and does, and will do.[14]

Eschatological *being with* presupposes interpersonal interaction, not just the preservation of what has been. It presupposes conversation, common work, and mutual joy and delight. This is indeed what is foreshadowed in the appearances of the resurrected Christ, who eats with his friends, sits down with them, and converses with them. If he is the model for the life to come—if we are "predestined to be conformed to the image of [the] Son, in order that he might be the firstborn within a large family" (Rom. 8:29)—then the eschaton is not the preservation of the lived life but, rather, its transformed and glorified continuation.[15]

---

14. Karl Barth, *Church Dogmatics* III/3, trans. G. W. Bromiley (T&T Clark, 1960), 89–90. See also Barth, *Church Dogmatics* III/3, 521: "Even in eternal life he [the creature] will still be in his time. For he will then be the one who, when there is no time but only God's eternity, and he is finally hidden in God, will have been in his time." For a wider analysis of Barth's account of time, eternity, and eschatological life, see Edwin Chr. van Driel, *Incarnation Anyway: Arguments for Supralapsarian Christology* (Oxford University Press, 2008), 111–17. Other proponents of an account of the eschaton as the preservation of the lived life include Eberhard Jüngel and Wolfhart Pannenberg. See Jüngel, *Death: The Riddle and the Mystery* (Westminster, 1974); and Pannenberg, *Systematic Theology*, vol. 3, trans. Geoffrey W. Bromiley (Eerdmans, 1998), 580–608.

15. In Van Driel, *Incarnation Anyway*, 150–55, I use this eschatological ongoing interaction between the incarnate and resurrected Lord and his people as the basis for a Christological supralapsarian argument. Here I move in the opposite direction: God's supralapsarianly intended *being with* has consequences for the ways in which we ought to imagine the eschaton. A full supralapsarian Christological proposal would need to contain both lines of thought.

Rather than the preservation of the lived life, the communion of friendship between God and humanity established in the incarnation is open-ended, always reaching beyond itself, never complete. As such, my proposal calls for an eschatology in which the horizon of history is never obtained since the active, interpersonal interaction between God and God's creatures never comes to an end. This kind of account is best anticipated in the eschatological theologies of Gregory of Nyssa and Jonathan Edwards. Gregory holds that we should expect an eschatological *epektasis*, a perpetual progress in which believers are infinitely changed for the better as they participate in the infinite goodness of God. Every stage obtained becomes a stepping stone to another phase of an unending journey, as more of God's glorious existence is experienced and absorbed. As Gregory says,

> [Created being is] ever changing for the better in its growth in perfection; along these lines no limit can be envisaged, nor can its progressive growth in perfection be limited by any term. In this way, its present state of perfection, no matter how great and perfect it might be, is merely the beginning of a greater and superior stage. Thus the words of the Apostle are verified: the stretching forth to the things that are before involves the forgetting of what has already been attained (Phil. 3:13). For at each stage the greater and superior good holds the attention of those who enjoy it and does not allow them to look at the past; their enjoyment of the superior perfection erases all memory of that which was inferior.[16]

Jonathan Edwards thinks of creation as a bride that God has prepared for Christ, the groom. The eschaton is like an unending wedding feast. As a feast, it is not a static experience but one of abundant movement. Where there is movement, Edwards argues, there is time, and where there is eternal time, it moves in an always upward, rising vector. In this eternal wedding feast God continually communicates God's infinite goodness, as divine self-communication is the core of God's act of creation. Thus the wedding feast takes the shape of an unending expansion of human knowledge of the glory and goodness of God.[17]

---

16. Gregory of Nyssa, *From Glory to Glory: Texts from Gregory of Nyssa's Mystical Writings*, ed. and trans. Herbert Musurillo (Scribner's Sons, 1961), 197. For Gregory's notion of perpetual perfecting, see Everett Ferguson, "God's Infinity and Man's Mutability: Perpetual Progress According to Gregory of Nyssa," *Greek Orthodox Theological Review* 18 (1973): 59–78; Lucas Francisco Mateo-Seco, "Epektasis," in *The Brill Dictionary of Gregory of Nyssa*, ed. Lucas Francisco Mateo-Seco and Giulio Maspero (Brill, 2009), 263–68; and Hans Boersma, *Seeing God: The Beatific Vision in Christian Tradition* (Eerdmans, 2018), 76–95.

17. See, e.g., Edwards's sermon "The Pure in Heart Blessed," in *The Works of Jonathan Edwards*, vol. 17, *Sermons and Discourses, 1730–1733*, ed. Mark Valeri (Yale University Press, 1999), 57–87; and Paul Ramsey, "Heaven is a Progressive State," in *The Works of Jonathan*

If the Christological vision set forth in this book is correct, Gregory's and Edwards's eschatological imaginations would have to be adapted. A *being with* relationship with God in Christ is not primarily focused on inner transformation and perfection or on an expansion of our knowledge of the divine; its core is, rather, the experience of interpersonal engagement and mutual delight. But Gregory and Edwards are right in saying that, as God's infinite goodness will infuse that relationship with new joy every day, there is always more to experience, more to enjoy, more to learn about God, even as the finitude of our own existence may make it impossible to retain the memory of the goodness previously received, as each new day adds goodness to goodness and delight to delight.

Being With—Without Sin

If the supralapsarian Christological proposal explored in this book invites us to think about the eschaton not as the end of the space-time continuum, not as the end of history, but as its unending fulfillment, this raises a host of questions about the relationship between this eschatological history and everything that precedes it. In this and the following three sections, I will explore a selected set of these questions, beginning with the place of sin and evil in this overall narrative. For this discussion, I will juxtapose my proposal with two other recent supralapsarian Christological designs.

In previous work, I have argued against supralapsarian Christologies like the one proposed by Friedrich Schleiermacher. Although he holds that the incarnation is not contingent upon sin, Schleiermacher nonetheless argues that God uses sin to bind us all to the incarnate One as our Redeemer. Schleiermacher's position is a variation on the *felix culpa* argument, according to which the evil of sin nonetheless ultimately brings about the good of being drawn closer to God. I have argued that his line of thinking devalues the goodness of God since it implies that God needs evil to bring about the good and could not have accomplished the good in ways that do not involve the suffering and destruction caused by sin and evil.[18] Supralapsarian Christology

---

Edwards, vol. 8, *Ethical Writings*, ed. Paul Ramsey (Yale University Press, 1989) 707–39; and Boersma, *Seeing God*, 376–83. On both Gregory and Edwards, cf. Patricia Wilson-Kastner, "God's Infinity and His Relationship to Creation in the Theologies of Gregory of Nyssa and Jonathan Edwards," *Foundations* 21 (1978): 305–21.

18. See Van Driel, *Incarnation Anyway*, 126–32, 165–66. I argued there, "Supralapsarians . . . should explore the meaning of the incarnation, the presence of God among us, as an excellent good in and of itself, and not take refuge in a doctrine of sin to beef up the incarnation's meaning. We do not need the bad to enjoy Christ" (131).

allows us to say that the best that has happened to creation—the incarnate presence of God in our midst—is in no way motivated or necessitated by evil but rests purely in the gracious, condescending love of God.

In response, Phillip A. Hussey worries that this approach will lead to the very "plan A–plan B" model that supralapsarian Christology left behind. For infralapsarian Christology, sin and incarnation do not belong to God's original intentions for creation. Christ is an emergency measure to counter what goes against God's will. The only way to counter the impression that sin is somehow able to undermine or redirect God's will is to incorporate sin into a larger intentional narrative. The *felix culpa* motive does exactly this: While sin and evil themselves may not be God's intentions, God weaves them into God's plan for this world by using them to bring about a greater good. Contrast this with supralapsarian Christology, in which the incarnation is always woven into God's original intentions. But if all forms of *felix culpa* are rejected, sin will remain a foreign element in God's history with creation, and God's subsequent plan of redemption will again be a plan B, Hussey charges. That which supralapsarian Christology seemed to offer—an integration of "nature and grace, creation and redemption around one unitive end"—is undone again.[19] For this reason, Hussey advocates an embrace of the *felix culpa* motive even within the context of a supralapsarian Christology. He agrees with Eleonore Stump, who writes, "the post-Fall world and the [individual] lives of those in grace in this world are somehow better, more glorious, more of triumph for the Creator, than the world and those lives would have been had there been no Fall."[20] This does not give any intrinsic value to the bad; rather, in the context of the bad human beings experience "the faithfulness and fullness of God's love for human creatures, even and especially in a world of sin and sinners." This allows them to be "brought in so as to plumb the infinite expanse" of divine love.[21]

Samuel Wells, on the other hand, rejects the *felix culpa* motive as morally untenable.[22] At the same time, he is also concerned about leaving sin and evil unexplained, as he believes that would be verging on the edge of a dualistic worldview.[23] He suggests we think about sin as "a false story": Just as the serpent told Adam and Eve a false story about God, sin tells falls stories

---

19. Phillip A. Hussey, *Supralapsarianism Reconsidered: Jonathan Edwards and the Reformed Tradition* (T&T Clark, 2024), 223–24.

20. Eleonore Stump, *The Image of God: The Problem of Evil and the Problem of Mourning* (Oxford University Press, 2022), 11, quoted in Hussey, *Supralapsarianism Reconsidered*, 224.

21. Hussey, *Supralapsarianism Reconsidered*, 225.

22. Samuel Wells, *Constructing an Incarnational Theology: A Christocentric View of God's Purpose* (Cambridge University Press, 2024), 271.

23. Wells, *Constructing an Incarnational Theology*, 272.

about God, ourselves, and others. The damage done by these false stories is not so much ontological but teleological. False stories have immense power: They "induce people to do brave, foolish, astounding or appalling things. Sometimes such stories are sinisterly crafted and intricately twisted, becoming part of an evil project to distort, misinform, discredit and destroy. Hence Jesus speaks of the devil as the 'father of lies' (John 8:44). At other times such stories arise from misunderstanding, lack of information, impatience, deficiency of imagination and self-centredness."[24]

Without further explanation, Wells seems to take these false stories to be inevitable by-products of the true story: "The point is, the channels that bring us revelation are the same channels that bring us false stories. So it is not that God 'allows' free will or 'plants' sin to enable a great redemption. It is that inextricable from the true story are a host of false stories, some harmless but many profoundly damaging and destructive: and sin and evil arise in and out of such false stories."[25] Therefore, "sin and evil will abide as long as creation, until the eschaton, because the cost of abolishing them would be the abolition of stories, and without stories, humanity would never learn the story of God."[26] This raises the question of how these false stories might be countered and overcome, and whether this implies that the eschaton does not know stories—since the eschaton will not know falsehood. To the first question, Wells answers that overcoming false stories does not come about by "substitutionary death, not by a triumphant resurrection, not by a transformative defeat." Rather, it is the church's calling to live, tell, witness to, and celebrate the true story—and that "every [such] telling, living, and celebrating of this story is the church's attempt to dispel sin and evil."[27] To the second question—whether it is possible to have stories without the possibility of false stories—Wells answers that this question must be left a mystery, even as he hopes that even our eschatological *being with* the Trinity will allow for narrative.[28]

With Wells, I am convinced that the *felix culpa* motive needs to be rejected. The very thing Hussey lifts up as its strength—that it allows us to weave sin and evil into the greater design of God because they allow humans to plumb the infinite love of God—strikes me as its theological weakness. It is indeed the case that in the current economy human beings tend to be more open to and aware of God's presence and love when the results of sin and evil invade

---

24. Wells, *Constructing an Incarnational Theology*, 276.
25. Wells, *Constructing an Incarnational Theology*, 276.
26. Wells, *Constructing an Incarnational Theology*, 277.
27. Wells, *Constructing an Incarnational Theology*, 276.
28. Wells, *Constructing an Incarnational Theology*, 277–78.

our lives. But this is, it strikes me, exactly the result of sin, which in good times whispers the lie that we can be happy and secure on our own. However, in the light of the infinity of both God's love and creation's eschatological future, it is theologically untenable that God would not be able to make us experience the same depths of divine presence and love without sin and evil marring creation's existence. This is the problem of *felix culpa*: It wants to say that sin is felicitous for us, that we are better off for it because our guilt allows us to experience aspects of God's love we would not otherwise experience. It thereby implies also that sin is felicitous for God, since it allows God to show us the depth of divine love in ways that God could not have otherwise. Theologically, this is deeply problematic.

In response to Hussey's worry that without *felix culpa* sin and redemption cause God to follow a plan B, I suggest we wield a distinction. I maintain that sin and evil are foreign elements in the divine economy. But whether redemption is to be understood as a plan B depends on one's theological account thereof. If sin causes God to make a payment that God originally was not to make (satisfaction theory), or to carry punishment for sin that God was originally not to carry (penal substitution theory), then God is indeed following a plan B in redemption. But not so if, as I argued in an earlier chapter, God redeems sin exactly by maintaining God's original intentions, *being with* creation, absorbing humanity's rejection, and not responding in kind. On my supralapsarian Christological design, God overcomes sin not by changing course, not by redirecting God's plans, but rather by sovereignly and lovingly continuing to lead creation to the future God always intended for it.

At the same time, the weight of sin is not fully measured by saying that sin is the result of a distorted story. It certainly is that, and the force of distorted stories is visible to us all on a daily basis. But sin is more than that, as evidenced by the fact that most of the time witnessing to and living into the true story is not enough to break the power of lies. Sin and evil operate not just on perception and narrative but also on the will, desires, and passions. One can witness to the truth, but those whose desires and passions are distorted cannot hear it. Therefore, to counter sin one needs more than a counter narrative; one needs *metanoia*, or conversion—the intervening, transforming, healing power of the Holy Spirit. One needs not just a new story but a new creation.

Moreover, the central intuition driving this book entails the promise that indeed it is and will be possible to tell a story without telling a false story. Stories narrate history. They express history's cohesion and meaning. The eschaton is still a history—an unending but nonetheless unfolding history of the *being with* relationship between God and God's people in which new things happen, surprises await, experiences are had. These make up a narrative.

In fact, in the exploration I offer here, there is a clear, coherent narrative that holds together the whole history of creation from its beginning to its unending eschaton. Unclear, and decidedly unclear, is the origin and role of sin and evil. They constitute foreign elements in this history—unexpected cancerous growth that threaten to undo it all, an "impossible possibility."[29] God's redemptive work is nothing but the consistency of God's *being with*, but sin and evil are not explained. This is, I believe, how it ought to be. There is clarity in God, in whom there is neither change nor darkness (James 1:17). Sin and evil, however, are without meaning or reason. They cannot be explained; they can only be overcome and left behind.

Being With—Without Memory

If sin is thus a foreign element—unexplained and, by God's grace, overcome and eschatologically left behind—what will be the legacy of sin in the eschaton? In particular, what will happen with our memories of sin and evil and the ways they have shaped us over time? If sin and evil are inexplicable things that are not able, by reason of their inexplicability, to be incorporated into a meaningful narrative but are to be named for what they are and ultimately overcome and cast out, would it not be incongruent with the overcoming of sin and evil for our memories of them to stay with us and to shape the realities of the eschaton? In that case, would sin and evil really be overcome? It is in the context of such questions that my sympathy arises for the proposal Miroslav Volf makes in his *The End of Memory*.[30]

While acknowledging the multiple ways in which remembrance is important in this life, Volf argues that in the world to come we will nonetheless receive the gift of forgetting all that was wrong. The Scriptures promise, Volf holds, that in the eschaton even God will no longer remember our sins.[31] If our sins will no longer come to God's mind, we may trust that they will no longer come to our minds either. This will not happen immediately once the trumpets sound and the eschaton arrives. That would not be right given the realities of sin and the need for judgment and reconciliation. Rather, Volf

---

29. Karl Barth, *Church Dogmatics* II/1, trans. G. W. Bromiley (T&T Clark, 1957), 505.

30. Miroslav Volf, *The End of Memory: Remembering Rightly in a Violent World*, 2nd ed. (Eerdmans, 2021). I first remarked on the alignment between supralapsarian Christology and Volf's account of the eschatological end of memory in an essay that became "*Theologia Crucis*: The Apocalyptic Argument" in chap. 2, above, 47.

31. As longed for by the psalmist ("Blot out all my iniquities," Ps. 51:9) and promised through the prophet Jeremiah ("I will forgive their iniquity, and remember their sin no more," Jer. 31:34). See Volf, *End of Memory*, 134.

imagines we will receive the gift of forgetting at the end of a long process. It will begin with the opposite of forgetting—that is, with remembering and remembering rightly. The Christian tradition holds that in the last judgment Christ will bring about justice for all who have been wronged. This means that the wrongs must come to mind. Since it is Christ who judges us, it is a judgment in grace. The goal is not wrath but reconciliation and salvation. This in turn involves a social process, Volf argues. As our sins are committed not only against God but also against one another, in order to enter the world to come we will have to reconcile both with God and with all others we have wronged. This involves truth telling, acknowledgement, and vindication—but also, ultimately, embrace.[32] But once all this happens, God will heal the wrongs committed and the evil experienced exactly by driving it out, by removing it, by giving us the gift of these things no longer coming to mind.[33]

I would like to make four observations about Volf's proposal: First, forgetting the bad is already something we experience in the here and now; thus, eschatological forgetting should not strike us as strange or uncomfortable. Many of us who remember loved ones who have died find that our memories hold onto the good things—the joyful memories, the admirable character traits—much more firmly than onto the bad things. *De mortuis nil nisi bonum dicendum est* ("Of the dead, nothing but good must be said") is not just an ethical admonition but a description of how our memories work. When we look back in love, we seem to retain the good and leave the bad behind. Admittedly, we have a much harder time doing so when it comes to those we did not or could not love. But this is why eschatological forgetting obtains only after reconciliation has taken place, and why it is not something we will enact ourselves but something given to us as a divine grace.

Second, on reflection, the opposite of eschatological forgetting seems simply not possible. We do not have the minds to remember all that would need to be remembered. Only God has the infinite capacity to hold all that is passed

---

32. Volf, *End of Memory*, 179–83. See also, esp., Miroslav Volf, "The Final Reconciliation: Reflections on a Social Dimension of the Eschatological Transition," *Modern Theology* 16 (2000): 91–113.

33. See Volf, *End of Memory*, 182–83:
  After Christ has completed the work of salvation and the eschatological transition has taken place, *after* the wrongdoers and the wronged have entered the world that cannot be undone—*after* the Last Judgment, *after* wrong committed and suffered has come to public light in God's judgment of grace, *after* the perpetrators have been accused and the victims vindicated, *after* they have embraced each other and recognized each other as belonging to the same community of perfect love, after all of these occurrences—the memories of wrongs suffered will be released. They will no longer come to mind to diminish the joy that each person will know in the presence of others and all will know in the presence of God.

before God's mind without being overwhelmed by it. Even if we were able to remember all the sins and evils in our own lives—both those we experience and those we commit—if eschatological remembrance were to take some communal form in which all sins and evils ever obtained would be rightly remembered, our emotional and cognitive faculties would be completely overwhelmed. Therefore, Gregory is right to suggest that, in the eternal living into the enjoyment of God, "at each stage the greater and superior good holds the attention of those who enjoy it and does not allow them to look at the past; their enjoyment of the superior perfection erases all memory of that which was inferior."[34]

Third, the alternative to eschatological forgetting—the idea that all past sins and evils will be remembered in a redeeming narrative—ignores the horrendousness of evil.[35] Concerned about Volf's proposal, Hussey prefers the idea, expressed by Robert Jenson, that eschatologically "our wounds will neither 'heal nor fester.' They will become icons of the Son's love."[36] Can we really expect this to be true of all evil? The two-year-old toddler who is raped by her father while her mother watches, the woman who is mentally and physically tortured by her captors, the trauma undergone by prisoners of war—can these become icons of the Son's love? Or is the Son's love expressed exactly in this: that once evil has been named and recognized, judgment has been pronounced, and justice has been done, he gives the victims—and even the perpetrators!—the gift of forgetting, so that these wounds simply cannot determine their lives and identities forever?

And fourth, the proposal of eschatological forgetting assumes an understanding of identity different from one prevalent in modernity, in which identity is established by our own experiences and actions and held together by consciousness, narrative, and meaning making.[37] On Volf's proposal, our identities map onto a much more fragmentary history than modernity imagines; what holds our identities together are not our experiences and actions, but the ways in which God relates to us in creating us, redeeming us, and

---

34. Gregory of Nyssa, *Glory to Glory*, 197.
35. For the alternative, see Volf, *End of Memory*, 183.
36. Robert W. Jenson, *Systematic Theology*, vol. 1, *The Triune God* (Oxford University Press, 1997), 200, quoted in Hussey, *Supralapsarianism Reconsidered*, 225.
37. An example of such an understanding of identity can be found in Danielle Tumminio Hansen, "Remembering Rape in Heaven: A Constructive Proposal for Memory and the Eschatological Self," *Modern Theology* 37 (2021): 662–78. Tumminio Hansen argues that "the suggestion that we will forget our lives in the eschaton also poses problems for theological anthropology when read through the lens of sexual trauma because such an assertion challenges the ways in which our selves are constituted through the events and memories that emerge throughout life" (674). Tumminio Hansen would have been right had she said that this assertion challenges the ways in which *modernity* takes our selves to be constituted.

leading us into eschatological consummation.[38] In this, events, experiences, and actions that we now consider to be highly important and meaningful may, in the eschaton, turn out to be illusions, while almost forgotten events may be the ones that most express who we are. In fact, if Christian theology is to be believed, it is exactly God's choosing us before the foundation of the world and drawing us through the waters of baptism—events that, for most of us, lie completely outside our memory—that give more meaning to our lives than anything else.[39]

Being With—Without Wounds

If our wounds will eschatologically heal and disappear, the same must be said for Christ's wounds. This is a controversial statement, since there is a strong tradition that argues for the permanence of Christ's wounds.[40] On an infralapsarian Christological account, this makes sense. If the incarnation is contingent upon sin, and Christ is present in the eschaton as the incarnate One, then there must be an eschatological memory of sin to account for this particular form of divine *being with*. The wounds are the visible expression of Christ's atoning work. They invite the people of God into an ongoing eschatological celebration of the sacrifice of the Lamb. As Bede Venerabilis says, Christ retained the signs of his passion so that "all the elect who have been received into everlasting happiness . . . never stop thanking him, recognizing that it is by his death that they live."[41] One might question, though, whether

---

38. See here the proposals of Volf's Yale colleague David H. Kelsey in his *Eccentric Existence: A Theological Anthropology* (Westminster John Knox, 2009).

39. As a sidenote, this is where eschatological forgetting is the exact opposite of what we now call cancel culture. The latter remembers sin forever and, for that reason, removes the person from society. The former forgets sin so that persons can rejoin society and live in joy forever. Cancel culture illustrates that our culture actually does not know what to do with sin and, therefore, with forgiveness. The Christian story deals with sin within the context of friendship and grace. Supralapsarian Christology is an expression of the conviction that grace is the ultimate foundation of nature. But grace is here not an abstract philosophical or theological point; it has a particular human face: that of the incarnate One.

40. For a recent example, see Laura Cerbus, "The Beauty of the Body and the Ascension: A Reclamation and Subversion of Physical Beauty," *Scottish Journal of Theology* 77 (2024): 138–48.

41. Bede Venerabilis, *Homilies on the Gospel* 2.9, quoted in Peter Widdicombe, "The Wounds and the Ascended Body: The Marks of Crucifixion in the Glorified Christ from Justin Martyr to John Calvin," *Laval théologique et philosophique* 59 (2003): 137–54. Widdicombe's essay offers a rich collection of texts from the church fathers that show them all assuming that the ascended Christ retains his wounds. He also shows, however, that this assumption does not go without saying: Martin Luther and John Calvin assume the exact opposite, taking the ascension to also involve a healing and further glorification of Christ's resurrection body. Moreover, the patristic

on such an account sin has not won, by making an indelible impression on the shape of the eschaton.

A supralapsarian Christology, however, has a wider Christological imagination. It knows of a Christological reality that arises long before the notion of sin sticks to created reality. It sees a Christologically shaped eschatological life far beyond sin's history and memory. It knows of a time when sin, guilt, and the cross will have been erased from human identity. And therefore, it can also reach to a time when Christ's own human reality will no longer be marred by the wounds of human rejection.

This does assume that Christ's resurrection body has not yet attained full glory. But this is in line with everything the Scriptures witness about his current reality. Christ may have ascended, but this does not mean his work is done. He may be seated at the right hand of God, but every knee does not yet bend to acknowledge him as Lord. He is still persecuted by the Sauls of this world. He is still hungry and receives nothing to eat. He is still thirsty but receives nothing to drink. He is still sick and imprisoned with no one looking after him. His reign may have been inaugurated, but it has not yet been consummated. If this is all true, then there is no reason to think his bodily reality would not reflect the same tensions. Just as all of creation simultaneously lives in the overlapping realities of old and new age, so does he. And just as human beings may already participate in the eschatological realities of his new creation—as, through baptism, they have died and been resurrected with him—likewise his glorified resurrection life still bears the scars of his participation in the old age. The promise of supralapsarian Christology is, however, that his existence was simply never rooted in this old age; therefore, both he and we reach for the time when our existence will be fully made new—as was intended from the very beginning.[42]

Being With—The Heritage of the Past

If sin and evil and their memory do not make it into the world to come, if our identities are being held together not by our own capacities of narration and meaning making but by the ways in which the triune God relates to us in creation, reconciliation, and consummation, if we look for the wounds of the

---

material that Widdicombe presents refers mostly to Christ in his current, ascended state. This material does not say anything about a possible further glorification following the last judgment and recreation. I name this because this means the fathers do not necessarily contradict the proposal I am making. I propose that the ascended Christ retains his wounds, but that following the final reconciliation, Christ's wounds will be healed just as our memories will be.

42. Miroslav Volf is thinking in the same direction. See Volf, *End of Memory*, 190–91.

old age to be eschatologically healed and their scars to disappear, how then do the old and the new age relate? How might we expect our lives in the here and now to have continuity and give shape to the world to come?

Every eschatological design must wrestle with this question. For a design shaped by infralapsarian intuitions, the most pressing issues concern how it could be that what has no plan in God's original intentions for creation—in fact, what is opposed to God's intentions and aims to undermine and undo them—has such everlasting consequences for the shape of eschatological life. According to Scriptural witness, the eschaton is centered upon and modeled after the incarnate One. It entails the everlasting presence of God in Christ, because of whom the new Jerusalem has no temple, as God and the Lamb are its temple and light (Rev. 21:22–23). But, on an infralapsarian Christological account, none of this would have been true had sin never interrupted creation's history. How does one make theological sense of this?[43] For a design that holds on to eschatological remembrance of all that happens in the present age, as that which gives rise to and shapes our identities, the most pressing issues circle around why things done and experienced in the threescore years and ten of our lives would determine who we are until all eternity. If, indeed, the eschaton is not the preservation of the lived life but the transformation and glorified continuation of the life we live, our existence in the here and now will finally be but a blip within an ever new, ever surprising eschatological life with God. Would it even be possible for the memory of the old age to everlastingly determine our identity? And if it does, and given the fact that for all of us the old identity is shaped by the dynamic of sin and forgiveness, why would the history and scars of sin determine eschatological reality forever? Would that not mean that, perversely, sin actually wins?

For an eschatological design that embraces supralapsarian Christology and embraces the eschatological forgetting of sin and evil, the pressures are different. The question is, What place does the heritage of the old age have in the new age? There is, of course, continuity. In fact, all of my proposals circle around such continuity. It is the Son of Mary, born of the flesh of Abraham, a first-century Jew, for whom creation is meant and who everlastingly is its center.[44] And just as there is continuity for the incarnate and resurrected Christ, there likewise is for us and for all of creation. The kings of the earth will bring the treasure of their nations into the heavenly city (Rev. 21:24). But

---

43. Elsewhere I have argued that this is exactly the kind of fissure in the infralapsarian Christological narrative that gives rise to a supralapsarian argument (see Van Driel, *Incarnation Anyway*, 150–55).

44. I say more about the continuity in the resurrection in Van Driel, *Incarnation Anyway*, 145–49.

at the same time, this city clearly does not function as the result of the kings' building projects; it comes from heaven, a gift from God, and not the climax of creatures' endeavors. And if my proposals are right, the treasures that the kings bring in are piecemeal and carefully selected and cleansed, healed, transformed, lifted up, and cleared of any residues of sin and evil.

A suggestion made by N. T. Wright comes to mind. He seizes on the words of the apostle Paul, "Therefore, my beloved, be steadfast, immovable, always excelling in the work of the Lord, because you know that in the Lord your labor is not in vain" (1 Cor. 15:58). Paul's words come at the end of an argument about the resurrection. Paul has just argued that in the eschatological transformation our perishable bodies will put on imperishability and our mortal bodies, immortality. And just as the physical realities of our bodies will be used as building blocks for the eschaton, he seems to say, God will likewise include the works of our hands. This is how Wright takes it: "What you *do* in the present—by painting, preaching, singing, sewing, praying, teaching, building hospitals, digging wells, campaigning for justice, writing poems, caring for the needy, loving your neighbor as yourself—*will last into God's future*. . . . They are part of what we may call *building for God's kingdom*."[45] In other words, the world to come will be a place where God is *with* human beings and all of creation. The new Jerusalem will be a home for God and God's people. But the home will not be beautified just by God. What makes it a place where God and the people can live together is exactly that God will draw on the building blocks of history to fashion a place where God's family can dwell. Not all of history will make it into this home—some, maybe much, must be left behind. God is like an artist who sorts through the rubble of stones and broken glass pieces and makes out of it a new artifact of beauty, evoking joy and delight. From the pieces of our histories, God may fit together a place that will feel both new and familiar, both old and surprising, but above all a place where we will finally find the destiny for which we were created.

---

45. N. T. Wright, *Surprised by Hope: Rethinking Heaven, the Resurrection, and the Mission of the Church* (HarperCollins, 2008), 193. Later, he adds,

Every act of love, gratitude, and kindness; every work of art or music inspired by the love of God and delight in the beauty of his creation; every minute spent teaching a severely handicapped child to read or to walk; every act of care and nurture, of comfort and support, for one's fellow human beings and for that matter for one's fellow nonhuman creatures; and of course every prayer, all Spirit-led teaching, every deed that spreads the Gospel, builds up the church, embraces and embodies holiness rather than corruption, and makes the name of Jesus honored in the world—all of this will find its way, through the resurrection power of God, into the new creation that God will one day make. (208)

And he concludes, "I have no idea what precisely this will mean in practice. I am putting up a signpost, not offering a photograph of what we will find once we get to where the signpost is pointing" (209).

Being With and Seeing God

Once evil has been overcome, people have been reconciled with God and with one another, wounds have been healed, and the memory of all that is bad has faded, creation will come to its own: the home of God, called into being for the incarnate One, in which God in Christ will be with human beings and all that is created forever. Human beings will be changed for the better—recreated, remodeled after Christ—and enjoy "seeing the glory of God in the face of Jesus Christ" (2 Cor. 4:6). Following biblical parlance, the Christian tradition usually speaks about the core of this eschatological life as the *visio Dei*, the seeing of God, the fulfillment of Moses's plea to see God's face (Exod. 33:18–20).

The ways Western theology has imagined the *visio Dei* are very much shaped by the account of it given by Thomas Aquinas. He takes the eschatological seeing of God to be an exclusively intellectual activity. For Aquinas, the *visio Dei* is to give human beings their highest joy; the intellect is humans' highest faculty, and the invisible God is not available to the senses, therefore the *visio dei* has to be an act of the intellect. God is not a natural object to the intellect, but in heaven (and in the eschaton) God graces the intellect with the capacity to immediately and intuitively grasp the essence of God, and thereby the blessed receive their eternal bliss.[46]

In recent years, theologians have raised several objections against the fittingness of Aquinas's account of the eschatological seeing of God.[47] Three problems in particular stand out. First, resurrection and eschatological embodiment do not figure in his account. The blessed, those who have died in

---

46. For his account of the beatific vision, see Aquinas, *Summa Theologiae* I.12; and I-II.3.8.

47. This has led to a number of publications, with rejoinders from a Thomistic perspective: Suzanne McDonald, "Beholding the Glory of God in the Face of Jesus Christ: John Owen and the 'Reforming' of the Beatific Vision," in *The Ashgate Research Companion to John Owen's Theology*, ed. Kelly M. Kapic and Mark Jones (Ashgate, 2012), 141–58; Simon Francis Gaine, "Thomas Aquinas and John Owen on the Beatific Vision: A Reply to Suzanne McDonald," *New Blackfriars* 97 (2016): 432–46; Hans Boersma, "The 'Grand Medium': An Edwardsean Modification of Thomas Aquinas on the Beatific Vision," *Modern Theology* 33 (2017): 187–212; Simon Francis Gaine, "The Beatific Vision and the Heavenly Mediation of Christ," *TheoLogica* 2 (2018): 116–28; Hans Boersma, "Thomas Aquinas on the Beatific Vision: A Christological Deficit," *TheoLogica* 2 (2018): 129–47; Simon Francis Gaine, "Thomas Aquinas, the Beatific Vision and the Role of Christ," *TheoLogica* 2 (2018): 148–67. An analysis of a commentary on the conversation is offered in Marc Cortez, "The Body and the Beatific Vision," in *Being Saved: Explorations in Human Salvation*, ed. Marc Cortez, Joshua R. Farris, and S. Mark Hamilton (SCM, 2018), 326–43. The analysis given by Gavin Ortlund offers no further insight and mainly repeats the position of Gaine. See Ortlund, "Will We See God's Essence? A Defence of a Thomistic Account of the Beatific Vision," *Scottish Journal of Theology* 74 (2021): 323–32.

Christ, already have the complete *visio Dei* in the intermediate, heavenly state between death and eschatological consummation.[48] Aquinas holds that it is solely the intellect that sees God; the senses do not participate in the vision. If the *visio Dei* is the very core of human fulfillment and happiness, this makes one wonder what contribution embodiment makes to eschatological bliss.[49] Second, the account seems to leave Christ behind. Aquinas does say that Christ's mediatory work is the reason for the blessed's *visio Dei*.[50] He also says that the blessed are aware of Christ by way of the *visio Dei*: In seeing the essence of God, they also see in God's essence everything God does, and this includes the work of incarnation.[51] Nonetheless, both positions make Christ only accidental to the beatific vision. The mediatory work of Christ is contingent upon sin, not essential to the eschaton. Likewise, Christ is only a *mediate* object of those who receive the vision, not a direct object. This seems to fall short of biblical accounts that suggest that at least part of the eschatological communing with God is an embodied communing with the resurrected Christ. Aquinas does agree that the blessed in their resurrection will see Christ with bodily eyes, but this seeing is not part of the *visio Dei*.[52] Finally, Aquinas's account of the beatific vision as the enjoyment of the divine essence, already obtained upon death, seems to leave little space for variance and development. Aquinas holds that, while the blessed cannot see all of God, what they see they see all at once.[53] This suggest the *visio Dei* is a static occurrence, rather than an eschatological life moving from delight to delight.[54]

To expand our eschatological imagination, the same theologians who object to Aquinas's account recommend the positions of two Reformed divines: the puritans John Owen and John Edwards. According to Owen, without incarnation God would remain essentially invisible, both now and in the future. The essence of God is beyond our comprehension. The object of the *visio Dei*, according to Owen, is the glory of Christ, both in his humanity and his divinity. In the eschaton, we will see the human face of Christ; and in contemplating his humanity, we will behold his divinity also.[55] Jonathan

---

48. Aquinas, *Summa Theologiae* I.12.1 s.c.
49. This worry is expressed in McDonald, "Beholding the Glory," 154–56; Boersma, "Grand Medium," 198–99; and Boersma, "Aquinas on the Beatific Vision," 144.
50. See the discussion in Gaine, "Thomas Aquinas and John Owen," 438–39.
51. Gaine, "Thomas Aquinas and John Owen," 436.
52. Aquinas, *In Sent.* 4.48.2.1. See the discussion in Gaine, "Thomas Aquinas and John Owen," 437–38.
53. Aquinas, *Summa Theologiae* I.12.10 s.c.: "What is seen in the Word is not seen successively, but at the same time."
54. For a quick summary of all three objections, see Boersma, "Grand Medium," 187.
55. On Owen, see particularly McDonald, "Beholding the Glory," with references to Owen's *Meditations and Discourses on the Glory of Christ in His Person, Office, and Grace*, which can

Edwards, similarly, holds that human beings will never have an immediate vision of God or the divine essence. Only Christ, as the only begotten Son of the Father, has such vision. For human beings, the *visio Dei* always remains mediated. Edwards agrees with Aquinas that the *visio Dei* happens through the eyes of the soul, although his understanding of this seeing expands far beyond the intellectual, involving the affections as much as the intellect. However, the vision comes about by the blessed being united with Christ, whom in the eschaton we will see with physical eyes. As we contemplate his glory, seeing his humanity with bodily eyes, we will see his divinity also; and in seeing his divinity, we will contemplate his works.[56] All this constitutes, for Edwards, the beatific vision. As such, he is open to a much more dynamic understanding of what the vision entails. I noted above that, for Edwards, the eschaton is an ongoing wedding feast, an upward vector in which believers continuously grow in their enjoyment of God. For Edwards, this begins already in the intermediate state, where believers are aware of the ongoing rule of Christ, contemplate the unfolding of salvation history, and rejoice in Christ's victories.[57] On Aquinas's model too, the believer is aware of the actions of God, since in seeing God's essence, the believer also sees everything God does and brings forth. However, since Aquinas interprets the *visio Dei* as an intuitive grasping of all things at once, it is hard to see how this equilibrium of life would be combined with contemplating the ups and downs of history. Edwards's model, however, is open to such changing experience.

The recommendation to embrace a model like Owen's or Edwards's has not gone without pushback from defenders of a Thomistic account of the *visio Dei*. In particular, it has been asked how, exactly, on the accounts of the Reformed divines, the blessed will move from contemplating Christ's humanity to contemplating his divinity; how the resurrection body is supposed to make a contribution to the eschatological seeing of God if it is admitted that even in the intermediate state we already receive the *visio Dei*; and whether it is not a problem that, on the accounts of these divines, the content of Christ's own *visio* is remarkably different from that of the blessed (that Christ sees directly into the divine life while the blessed do not).

---

be found in John Owen, *The Works of John Owen*, ed. William H. Goold, 16 vols. (Banner of Truth, 1965), 1:274–415. Boersma holds that Owen, schooled in Thomistic theology, consciously applies characteristics like "immediate," "direct," and "intuitive"—which in Aquinas are applied to the seeing of the divine essence—to the seeing of the glory of Christ (Boersma, "Aquinas on the Beatific Vision," 139).

56. On Edwards, see Boersma, "Grand Medium."

57. See Jonathan Edwards, "Happiness of Heaven is Progressive," in *The Works of Jonathan Edwards*, vol. 18, *The "Miscellanies," 501–832*, ed. Ava Chamberlain (Yale University Press, 2000), 431–32.

The central dilemma in the dispute is thus Christological: Is the incarnate One integral to the beatific vision, or not? And if so, how is the *visio Dei* Christologically shaped? For Aquinas, Christ is accidental to the vision—because, Aquinas argues, the beatific vision is the essential goal of human existence, but the incarnate One belongs to human history only contingently. For Owen, Edwards, and their contemporary defenders, Christ is indeed integral to the *visio Dei*—but, so it is charged, they do not clearly integrate Christology into the eschatological vision. The supralapsarian account I am exploring in this book can make a contribution toward solving this dilemma.[58]

God's first intention *ad extra* is to be Jesus. That is, God's fundamental determination is to *be with* what is not God, to give Godself to what is not God. And thus the invisible becomes visible; the One who is divine self-expresses in humanity, becoming a human being and creating human beings as the recipients of this gift. God's incarnation is not a means in the service of a larger goal. In the incarnation, goal and means are the same. In becoming an embodied human being and calling forth other human beings as this One's family, God gives shape to the goal of creation: a life of God with God's people, at home in creation.

If, as the Scriptures suggest, the *visio Dei* is the eschatological goal of humanity, and if, as a supralapsarian Christological reading of the Scriptures propose, *being with* Jesus is the goal of humanity's existence, then the content of the *visio Dei* is the life of this family; it is the enjoyment of embodied life with Jesus.

On this account, the *visio Dei* entails the seeing of God, but there is no reason to expect that it entails the seeing of divinity. A Chalcedonian understanding of the incarnation clarifies how this can be so. Whoever sees Jesus, sees God—even though they see God not in divine existence but in human existence. When we encounter Jesus, we encounter a human nature—but it is the human nature of God. As I said previously, the *what* we see in Jesus of

---

58. Cortez holds that the driving concern in the conversation is that, for Aquinas, the resurrection body is extraneous to the beatific vision. However, he observes, everyone "who affirms even the possibility of an intermediate state in which human persons exist in conscious relationship with God and other human beings must maintain that the body is nonessential for performing at least fundamentally important human activities." Cortez, "The Body and the Beatific Vision," 333. On my analysis of the debate, the main concern is not the use of our bodies (which would suggest an anthropological deficit on the part of the traditional, Thomistic understanding of the *visio Dei*) but the role of Christ's body and humanity (which implies a Christological deficit on the part of the traditional view). The point is that the incarnation does not play an essential role in Aquinas's understanding of the *visio Dei*. This is confirmed by the observation that Aquinas works on the assumption that the *visio Dei* could also have been obtained in a world without incarnation (Gaine, "Thomas Aquinas, the Beatific Vision and the Role of Christ," 156–57).

Nazareth, that which we behold with our senses, is humanity; but the *who* we see is God, the second person of the Trinity.

On this account, it also makes little sense to speak of the *visio Dei* of Jesus, or to expect or need Jesus's experience of the eschatological life to be the same as ours. Jesus's eschatological joy is not the seeing of God; it is the seeing of and *being with* human beings. His life is the embodiment of God's attention directed toward us; he is God's desire to *be with* humanity expressed in the flesh.[59]

Also, on this line of thought, there is no reason to think that those who have died will not see Jesus in the intermediate state. But there is also no reason to speak about this seeing of Jesus as the *visio Dei*. If the vision of God is the eschatological fulfillment of the creature's life, those in the intermediate state have not arrived yet. Their lives are still scarred by sin and evil. Death still has a hold on them. According to John the Seer, they are aware that history has not yet come to its completion. The souls under the altar cry out, "Sovereign Lord, holy and true, how long will it be before you judge and avenge our blood on the inhabitants of the earth?" And they are told "to rest a little longer" (Rev. 6:10–11). They are aware of the struggle and pain on earth; how then would it make sense to suggest that they are completely at rest? In fact, Jesus's own life is not yet characterized by rest and enjoyment; he is still at work to draw all things to himself. If he does not experience the eternal joy, there is no reason to suggest those who have died experience it. At the same time, the image from Revelation suggests that they do not just see the struggle on earth; they also see Jesus. They are in his presence and are aware of him. *How* they are aware of him—and of earthly events—without having bodies, the text does not explain. But in either case, what they are aware of are not spiritual realities—such as the divine essence—but embodied realities: They are aware of salvation history as it continues to play out on earth and of the rule of the embodied, ascended Christ in heaven.

Pulling these threads together, on the supralapsarian Christological account I explore here, there is no reason to drop the intermediate stage from our theological imaginations, even if we have no account for how

---

59. Whatever this does to Jesus's own self-consciousness is another matter. But one certainly should not expect it to be akin to ours. Even while it is a completely human self-consciousness, it is nonetheless *God's* human self-consciousness. There is a human *I* in Jesus, but it is the *I* of the Godhead. What it does to the self-consciousness, self-awareness, and even awareness of God for a human nature to be personified, not by a human person, but by a divine person, we do not know—there exists only one example of it in our history. But one should certainly not expect that it amounts to a *visio Dei* that is similar to ours. I reflect more about Jesus's self-consciousness in Edwin Chr. van Driel, "The Logic of Assumption," in *Exploring Kenotic Christology*, ed. C. Stephen Evans (Oxford University Press, 2006), 286–90.

the disembodied souls in heaven are aware of embodied realities. There is also no reason to deny that embodiment is part of the way in which we will enjoy the seeing of God. What should be dropped, however, is the idea that the *visio Dei* is the seeing of the divine essence. Once we make that move, all the other pieces fall into place. The *visio Dei* is the eschatological enjoyment of communion with God—a communion for which we were created, as we and all of creation are embedded in God's very first decision *ad extra*, God's decision to be Jesus Christ. It is this decision, the divine commitment to incarnation, that makes the *visio Dei* possible. It is as the invisible, omnipresent God becomes visible and localized that God can be seen, enjoyed, and engaged with by people, whom God makes as embodied and sensory creatures. The seeing of God is made up of this embodied, sensory experience of God.

Dropping the theological assumption that the *visio Dei* concerns gazing God's essence with the intellect and embracing the idea, instead, that it concerns the sensory experience of the incarnate One would in fact be supported by the biblical materials that gave rise to the doctrine of the *visio Dei* in the first place. Given the entrenchment of the idea that eschatologically we will see the essence of God, it is remarkable how at odds such a notion is with the ways in which the Scriptures speak about our eschatological enjoyment of God. None of these suggest a spiritual seeing of the unseeable God. Rather, the small amount of biblical material on which the notion is based has a definitively embodied character to it. The notion of the *visio Dei* goes back to two forms of expression: those having to do with *seeing* God (Matt. 5:8; Heb. 12:14; 1 John 3:2) and those that speak of meeting God "face to face" (1 Cor. 13:12; see also Rev. 22:4). Both forms of expression have their roots in the Hebrew Bible. Jacob, Moses, and Gideon are all said to have met God "face to face" (Gen. 32:30; Exod. 33:11; Judg. 6:22), while the faithful go up to the temple to see God's face (Pss. 11:4–7; 42:2). All these concern sensory, not intellectual, experiences. The point of Moses's desire to see God is that he longs for his experience of God to be more than just the hearing of a voice of one otherwise hidden by a pillar of cloud; he wants to see God with his eyes. Gideon meets God face to face by engaging an angel sitting under the oak at Ophrah (Judg. 6:11–24). The faithful in the Psalms go to the temple not to enjoy God by their intellect but to participate in a very sensory temple ritual.

At the same time, the Old Testament strongly emphasizes that God cannot be seen. God denies Moses's request because "no one shall see [God] and live" (Exod. 33:20). Gideon does not see God directly; rather, he deals with an embodied messenger from God. In the temple one might meet God, but the

Holy of Holies, where God is enthroned above the ark, is still hidden from the people by a curtain.⁶⁰

In the New Testament, the incarnation is presented as God's way of overcoming this chasm. Now the invisible God can be seen. Jesus's coming is God's answer to Moses's longing. Whereas God once tabernacled among God's people in a pillar of cloud, now God tabernacles among us in God's own flesh and blood (John 1:14). In the incarnate One, God overcomes the ontological gap that separates divinity from humanity. The *visio Dei* now becomes a reality. The eschaton is breaking into creation's history.

Conclusion: Being at Home

Creation is called into existence to be God's home, as Volf and McAnnally-Linz convincingly argue. God does not just relate to what is not God as its cause and sustainer; God brings forth the universe as a dwelling place where God will live in love and friendship with God's people in the eschaton.

But what makes a place a home? Volf and McAnnally-Linz list four characteristics that distinguish homes from mere places: Homes are places where people find resonance, where relationships of attachment to others and things are developed and fostered, where one receives welcome and knows one belongs, and where the web of relationships is shaped by mutuality.⁶¹ Embedded in these characteristics, I believe, are the notions of boundedness and presence: For finite human beings, whose sensory experience reaches only so far, homes need to stay within the limits of a certain size, otherwise they become cold, uncomfortable, too big to attach to; in other words, homes need to be bounded. Further, homes need to be places where people actually live, spend time together, commune together; in other words, homes require presence.

Homes can deteriorate into mere places. Negative or traumatic experiences can undo the resonance, attachment, and relationships that make a place a home. Malformation by insiders, harm done by outsiders, destructive acts and experiences, painful memories—these can all lead to the unraveling of the sense of home.⁶²

Creation is called into existence to be a home for God and God's family. It is the place where God will tabernacle among God's people. But for this to happen, humans must be able to experience God's presence in a way that is fitting to their own existence. It requires that God be somewhere specific,

---

60. For further discussion, see Van Driel, *Incarnation Anyway*, 157–60.
61. Volf and McAnnally-Linz, *Home of God*, 14.
62. Volf and McAnnally-Linz, *Home of God*, 15–18.

rather than just everywhere, and that people be able to engage God as the embodied, sensory creatures they are. Throughout the Old Testament, this is the tension that surrounds God's dwelling places in Israel. God is enthroned among God's people in tabernacle and temple, but God's presence stretches also far beyond this, beyond even the boundaries of what is already, seemingly, an unending universe. God is present and can be engaged, but at the same time, such engagement is shrouded in mystery, surrounded by danger. Pillars of cloud and fire, burning bushes, and thick temple curtains shroud God from the people's vision. This makes God's homemaking tangential at best.

Moreover, that which God has called into being to be God's home has, in many respects, lost the character of a home. Creation is the recipient of many blessings, but it is also a place of deep damage and trauma, enslaved to decay, drenched with the blood of its inhabitants, torn apart by acts of sin and experiences of evil.

In this chapter, I have shown how supralapsarian Christology offers building blocks for a renewed exploration of how, nonetheless, creation can be the eschatological home for God and God's people. It offers a vision of a God whose first act of homemaking is to step outside of the realm of divine existence, to commit, as it were, to human size, becoming visible and present in such a way that God can be seen, touched, heard, and engaged. Creation is designed to be Jesus's home. And because this act of participating in human history is not contingent upon sin but, rather, precedes and establishes this history, this in turn creates the conceptual framework for an eschaton in which this history continues but the history of sin does not. In such an eschaton, creation is cleansed, renewed, transformed, recreated, and lives toward a never-ending eschatological horizon of eternal love and delight, leaving behind even the memories of what once threatened to undo God's handiwork.

13

On *Being With* and Resonance

Supralapsarian Christology for a New Missional Era

Supralapsarian Christology is an alternative way of telling the large story of God and creation. It offers a fresh perspective on the ways in which the Christian faith thinks about meaning making, community, the role and importance of all that is wrong and evil, and the nature of Christian hope for creation's future. As such, I argued above in chapter 6—in the historical section of this book—that supralapsarian Christology can make an important contribution to the search for a soteriological narrative that meets the needs of a new missional era.

In this final chapter, I am returning to that claim. In chapter 6, I made my case by way of offering a novel reading of Lesslie Newbigin's ecumenical and missional project. Here, I will test my argument for the missional fruitfulness of supralapsarian Christology by engaging the work of the contemporary American practical theologian Andrew Root and, through him, that of the German sociologist and philosopher Hartmut Rosa.

In recent years, practical theologian Andrew Root has drawn significant attention with a series of books about Christian ministry in a secular age.[1] His

---

1. Andrew Root, *Faith Formation in a Secular Age* (Baker Academic, 2017); *The Pastor in a Secular Age: Ministry to People Who No Longer Need a God* (Baker Academic, 2019); *The Congregation in a Secular Age: Keeping Sacred Time Against the Speed of Modern Life* (Baker Academic, 2021); *Churches and the Crisis of Decline: A Hopeful, Practical Ecclesiology for a Secular Age* (Baker Academic, 2022); *The Church After Innovation: Questioning Our Obsession with Work, Creativity, and Entrepreneurship* (Baker Academic, 2022); and *The Church in an*

project aims to empower churches in this new missional era by helping them focus ministry on the presence and work of God. Fearing that churches are captive to the same modern impulses that inaugurated secularism in the first place, Root tries to draw the church in the West away from missional methods that put the onus of the future of the church on human shoulders, which he considers to be another form of functional atheism. He thus redirects the church's attention to its source and hope: God's encountering presence. Root in turn draws heavily on two conversation partners, both to analyze modern secularization and to express the ways in which, in his view, the church might expect God to once again show up: Canadian philosopher Charles Taylor and German sociologist and political scientist Hartmut Rosa. Charles Taylor's *A Secular Age* gives Root categories to interpret modernity's secular experience of space; Hartmut Rosa's *Social Acceleration: A New Theory of Modernity* and his *Resonance: A Sociology of Our Relationship to the World* help Root to interpret modernity's secular experience of time.[2] Moreover, and critically, the combined categories offered by these two thinkers also shape the way in which Root subsequently recommends a new theology of the cross to prepare the Christian congregation for a renewed encounter with God even in the midst of secularity.

It is the latter move in particular that I wish to critically engage in this chapter. While I am deeply sympathetic to Root's focus on divine agency and find his use of Taylor and Rosa to interpret our own cultural moment quite helpful, I do not believe that either his theological arguments or his sociological and philosophical analyses support the theological lens Root recommends. In fact, I will argue that his analyses call out for a very different theological story about God and God's relationship with the church and the world. Embedded in Root's work are two different stories about God. The first, the one he explicitly advances, is a story focused on the cross. The second is implicit, but better supported by his arguments: It is a story about divine resonance. The first is focused on God's being *for us*; the second is focused on God's being *with us*. I will argue that the second story calls out for a supralapsarian Christological grounding and, as such, is more fruitful for empowering the Christian community as it finds its way in this new missional era.

Age of Secular Mysticisms: Why Spiritualities Without God Fail to Transform Us (Baker Academic, 2023). The books are presented as volumes of a series entitled Ministry in a Secular Age.

2. Charles Taylor, *A Secular Age* (Harvard University Press, 2007); Hartmut Rosa, *Social Acceleration: A New Theory of Modernity*, trans. Jonathan Trejo-Mathys (Columbia University Press, 2013); Hartmut Rosa, *Resonance: A Sociology of Our Relationship to the World*, trans. James C. Wagner (Polity, 2019).

I will develop my argument in four steps. First, I will set out the ways that Root uses Taylor and Rosa to understand the secularization of modern space and time. Second, I will trace the story Root sets forth to help congregations recognize God's presence even in the confines of a secularized space-time. Third, I will show how Root's arguments actually call for an alternative story. And fourth, I will tease out some of the contours of that alternative story and its consequences for our ecclesial and missional practices.

A Secularized Space and Time

Charles Taylor and the Secularization of Space

Many narratives of modernity take the shape of what Charles Taylor calls "subtraction stories."[3] They are premised on the idea that all of humanity shares in an essential form of rationality and morality. Modernity and its accompanying secularizing tendencies develop when, over time, humanity sheds illusory, misleading ideas so that, in the end, only those features of rationality and meaning making common to all are left. On such a view, modernity lays bare the most natural and essential features of what it means to be human. Anything else—such as religion—is an unnatural, and often harmful, addition.[4]

Taylor argues that, on the contrary, modernity is the result not of subtraction but of invention. It is a way of looking at the world that results in a new, constructed understanding of the self, of the practices that the self meaningfully engages in, and of the spaces in which modern selves move and have their being.

This newly invented understanding of space develops over time. In premodern eras, people lived in spaces with porous boundaries. Reality was laid bare for the transcendent to make itself present. Daily practices were imbued with sacred meaning. The self was open for the presence of the divine. But as people started to look at reality with modern eyes, their experience of space changed. The transcendent and the secular became different planes of existence, finally separated by the immanent frame. By this phrase, "immanent frame," Taylor refers to "the sense of . . . living in impersonal orders, cosmic, social, and ethical orders which can be fully explained in their own

---

3. Taylor, *Secular Age*, 26–29. See also Charles Taylor, "Apologia pro Libro suo," afterword to *Varieties of Secularism in a Secular Age*, by Michael Warner, Jonathan VanAntwerpen, and Craig Calhoun (Harvard University Press, 2010), 301–2.
4. For a similar analysis, see Nicholas Wolterstorff, *John Locke and the Ethics of Belief* (Cambridge University Press, 1996).

terms and don't need to be conceived as dependent on anything outside, on the 'supernatural' or the 'transcendent.'"[5]

Taylor distinguishes three stages of the development of secular space and the immanent frame. In the first stage, the modern logic of subtraction is for the first time applied to notions of the sacred. The communal space is declared secular, stripped of references to God or religion. It is not that people do not believe in God or have no sense of the sacred. In fact, in this phase the majority of a population may very well be religious. But religion is declared to belong in the private space and not the public. Religious expressions are not wrong, but they should not spill over into the public arena. The public space and its institutions are shaped by what everyone is thought to have in common. Religion and its institutions are relegated to their own spaces, where their practices may be enacted.[6]

In the second stage, the religious institutions start to crumble. Fewer people have a sense of the transcendent, even in their private lives. The "buffered self" gets in the way, the autonomous self that is no longer automatically open to experiences of and direction from beyond its own horizon.[7] Participation in the life of the church and other religious institutions decreases. These institutions are therefore also less and less visible in the space inhabited by modern people.[8]

As the sacred fades away, in the third stage, the transcendent and divine action become implausible and irrelevant. Space is enclosed by the immanent frame. The door to the transcendent cannot be found. It is not that people who occupy this space have no space at all for spirituality, but their spirituality is self-created, rooted in their own interests. It is no longer experienced as a response to a divine action that comes from the outside. But even these kinds of spiritualities are only one option among many forms of secular meaning making that are devoid of any reference to what might be outside the immanent frame.[9]

The three stages of secularism should not be imagined as unfolding in a determined tempo and order. Within the Western world, different countries

---

5. Taylor, "Apologia," 306–7.
6. Taylor, *Secular Age*, 2–3.
7. See Taylor, *Secular Age*, 38–39:
> For the modern, buffered self, the possibility exists of taking a distance from, disengaging from everything outside the mind. . . . For the porous self, the source of its most powerful and important emotions are outside the "mind"; or better put, the very notion that there is a clear boundary, allowing us to define an inner base area, grounded in which we can disengage from the rest, has no sense. . . . The buffered self can form the ambition of disengaging from whatever is beyond the boundary, and of giving its own autonomous order to its life.

8. Taylor, *Secular Age*, 2–3, 12–15, 423–25.
9. Taylor, *Secular Age*, 2–3, 12–15, 18–21.

and cultures have moved into each stage in their own way.[10] And even within a culture shaped by the immanent frame there will always be subcultures that are rooted in one of the earlier stages, or for whom the transcendent is still an experienced reality. But even so, whereas in a pre-secular era religious faith is axiomatic, in a culture caught within the confines of the immanent, unbelief is the default option.

Hartmut Rosa and the Secularization of Time

Whereas Taylor can be read as describing the secularization of modern space, Rosa focuses on the secularization of modern time. As Root reminds us, time was once kept by the church: The days were framed by the prayers of the hours, the rhythm of the week was marked by the celebration of Christ's resurrection, and the times of the year moved from saints' days to holy feasts.[11] In modernity, this is no longer the case. Time has freed itself from the slow and steady pace of the liturgy and the church year. The defining feature of a modern society is acceleration. As Rosa argues, modern time is shaped by dynamic stabilization: Just *maintaining* the socioeconomic and institutional status quo requires constantly accelerating growth and innovation. The central motor of this is capitalism, but dynamic stabilization extends well beyond the economic sphere. The welfare state and the system of democratic politics, as well as modern concepts of science and knowledge, depend on it. So does art, with its onus on innovation and originality. Society can maintain its course only as it produces more every year.[12]

To maintain constantly accelerating growth, modern society needs constantly expanding amounts of resources. It is here that the negative implications

---

10. See Root, *Congregation in a Secular Age*, 140–42.
11. Root, *Congregation in a Secular Age*, 49–55.
12. This is a central thesis in Rosa's *Social Acceleration*. For a short summary of Rosa's account of acceleration and dynamic stabilization, see Rosa, *The Uncontrollability of the World*, trans. James C. Wagner (Polity, 2020), 9–14. In "Two Versions of the Good Life & Two Forms of Fear: Dynamic Stabilization and the Resonance Conception of the Good Life," paper presented to the Yale Center for Faith & Culture, "Joy, Security, and Fear," November 8–9, 2017, https://faith.yale.edu/media/two-versions-of-the-good-life-two-forms-of-fear, Rosa illustrates his thesis with a simple, widely relatable observation:
> One very curious but consistent fact about late modern life is that almost irrespective of their values, status and moral commitments, subjects feel notoriously short on time and tirelessly pressed to hurry. Individuals from Rio to New York, from Los Angeles to Moscow and Tokyo feel caught in a rat-race of daily routines. They are possessed by the fear of losing out, of being left behind, of not being able to catch up with all the requirements they feel obliged to meet. No matter how fast they run, they close their days as subjects of guilt: they almost never succeed in working off their to do lists. Thus, even and especially if they have enough money and wealth, they are indebted temporally.

of accelerated growth become visible. To acquire these resources, society is organized around competition and aggression. The world needs to be known, mastered, conquered, and made useful in order to guarantee that humanity will have access to the resources to sustain this growth. But as humans try to grasp this greater and greater knowledge and mastery, they find the resources withdrawing themselves from human control. The environmental crisis, the crisis of democracy, the psychological crisis, and numerous other social and political crises are expressions of this withdrawal. But further, the more humans try to use their environments as resources for their endless expansion, the more alienated they find themselves from these very same environments. They use their environments, but they do not live with them. They have causal and instrumental connections and interactions with their surroundings, but the world no longer speaks to them. The world seems shallow and silent. It is no wonder that so many in our society are suffering from burnout, says Rosa, because the experience of burnout is exactly this: no longer feeling any meaningful inner connection to what surrounds us. The faster we are forced to live, the faster we silence the world and veer toward alienation.

God's Presence in Secularized Space and Time

A Cross-Shaped Divine Presence

In a world enclosed by the immanent frame, how can we nonetheless expect God to show up? How might we experience God, and how might we witness to others about divine presence and agency? Root responds to these questions with a theology of the cross, which offers a twofold cruciform description of reality.

First, for people caught in the immanent frame, a religious experience takes the shape of an experiential layer put on top of a generally shared humanity. Secularization is not the result of subtraction. It is the result of a differently constructed self and space. An encounter with the transcendent will therefore be experienced as resulting in what Taylor calls *cross pressure*: The self is pressed "between the closed system of the immanent frame and the echoes of transcendence that seem realer than real."[13] If one takes this experience of

---

13. Root, *Faith Formation*, 114. According to Charles Taylor, "The whole culture experiences cross pressures, between the draw of the narratives of closed immanence on one side, and the sense of their inadequacy on the other, strengthened by encounter with existing milieu of religious practice, or just by some intimations of the transcendent. The cross pressures are experienced more acutely by some people ... than others, but over the whole culture, we can see them reflected in a number of middle positions, which have drawn from both sides." Taylor, *Secular Age*, 595.

the transcendent seriously, it will result in a form of death. Such an experience cannot be added to one's own construction of self and space; it will lead to the death of that construct and the resurrection of something new.

Second, Root combines this phenomenological description of the religious experience with a theological claim about divine agency and the faith that responds to it. Theologically speaking, Root argues, it is exactly in the experiences of negation and death, of despair and divine absence—in the places where reality seems to fall apart and humans can no longer see a way forward—that we can expect God to show up. Throughout his Ministry in a Secular Age series, Root claims that "God meets us primarily in suffering."[14] He portrays God as one who "chooses to identify with (to locate himself in) events of God's absence."[15] In fact, Root holds, God can be experienced only *after* God's absence.[16] The experience of God is therefore always and only cruciform—"and this is so because the very shape of the experience that takes you into Christ, leading to faith, is the experience of death."[17] Faith is "a transcendent experience born out of negation (death, brokenness, and longing). Faith is to experience the encounter of Christ through the negation of the cross."[18]

To illustrate and support this point, in several of his books Root appeals to the biblical descriptions of the ways in which the apostle Paul and the patriarch Abraham experienced God. Root focuses on Paul's encounter with Christ on the road to Damascus. He takes this to be a uniquely formative experience for all of Paul's subsequent writings about faith, interpreting this encounter as a cross-pressured experience. While it is not an experience in which Paul is caught between a closed, immanent social imaginary and an encounter with the transcendent, nonetheless, it is an experience of death followed by an experience of the risen Christ giving him new life. The kind of religious righteousness Paul once pursued dies in the encounter with the risen Christ. In its place, Paul finds that real life comes from, and remains, outside of himself, as from this moment onward he is "in Christ."[19]

---

14. Root, *Congregation in a Secular Age*, 202n22.
15. Root, *Pastor in a Secular Age*, 203.
16. Root, *Pastor in a Secular Age*, 203.
17. Root, *Faith Formation in a Secular Age*, 136. As examples of such experiences of death, Root names "encounters with rejection, loss, and fear" (136), "marital turmoil or a child's illness" (137), and the discovery of marital unfaithfulness, cancer, and a child's addiction (Root, *Pastor in a Secular Age*, 206–7). Roots writes, "When we confess these experiences, we find the risen Christ coming near us, giving us new life out of death, ministering to us out of God's own experience of death on the cross" (Root, *Faith Formation in a Secular Age*, 136).
18. Root, *Faith Formation in a Secular Age*, 119.
19. Root, *Faith Formation in a Secular Age*, 123–24, 131–51. See also Root, *Pastor in a Secular Age*, 174. To support his reading of Paul, Root appeals to the work of Pauline scholar

Root sees a similar dynamic in the stories about Abraham and, by extension, the stories about Sarah. They too, Root believes, are people whose lives are shaken up by cross-pressured experiences. Here is Abraham, having "a good life in his father's household; he has position, privilege, a legacy, safety, and sure identity." God's appearance to him undoes all of this. Abraham leaves it all behind, "emptying himself of position, privilege, and safety."[20] He responds to God's call in faithfulness, but in the end all that is left is Sarah's barrenness. Sarah herself comes to think of herself as "nothing but a god-cursed woman with no future."[21] Root portrays her as awfully burdened with sin and guilt.[22] But God makes this very reality of death and nothingness the stage of God's arrival.[23] Likewise, in faith Abraham awaits this arrival, "seeking God in what is impossible, in and through the negation (the crucifixion) of his experience."[24]

The call of the Christian community in a culture shaped by the closed doors of the immanent frame as well as by acceleration's alienation, Root believes, is to witness to the surprising arrival of this cruciform God. To do so, the community must place itself at the sites of death and negation in the expectation that at these very sites they may be able to call people's attention to the God who is about to show up. As Root says, speaking of the pastor, but meaning to include anyone who is called upon to give witness to the living God:

> The pastor enters into time and space where the event of your nothingness happens, meeting you at the site of a crash or in a hospital room. The pastor,

---

Michael J. Gorman on the cruciformity of Paul's gospel (see Root, *Faith Formation in a Secular Age*, 158–80). Gorman actually holds that, for Paul, God is essentially cruciform (see, e.g., Gorman, *Inhabiting the Cruciform God: Kenosis, Justification, and Theosis in Paul's Narrative Soteriology* [Eerdmans, 2009], 27–28). If this is the position Root wishes to embrace, it would be a third plank to his proposed theology of the cross, as it would anchor it in the doctrine of God. From Root's own prose and arguments, it is not clear he fully mines Gorman's position. When Root reports on Gorman's arguments, he has him say that "the cross is the revelation of God's own being." Root, *Faith Formation in a Secular Age*, 163. One could say this, though, without saying that God is essentially cruciform. The cross can be the revelation of God's own being and still be a contingent event. In such a case, one would hold that the cross is the way in which God reveals who God is under the contingent circumstances of human sin and rejection. To say that God is essentially cruciform, though, excludes this contingency. It implies that there is only one possible reality: the one in which God suffers on the cross. This would make reality as it is, including the reality of sin, necessary—which is highly problematic theologically. Since it is unclear, however, what theological position Root is committed to at this point, I will bracket this from my discussion of his *theologia crucis*. I have critically engaged Gorman's reading of Paul in Edwin Chr. van Driel, *Rethinking Paul: Protestant Theology and Pauline Exegesis* (Cambridge University Press, 2021), 270–74.

20. Root, *Faith Formation in a Secular Age*, 125.
21. Root, *Pastor in a Secular Age*, 205.
22. He quotes T. F. Torrance to this effect (Root, *Pastor in a Secular Age*, 205n37).
23. Root, *Pastor in a Secular Age*, 205.
24. Root, *Faith Formation in a Secular Age*, 125.

present as this event now presses its weight into your being, witnesses to a central chapter in the story you tell, or refuse to. The pastor's just showing up becomes powerful; it witnesses that in nothingness comes arrival. Up against nothingness, the pastor arrives to be present, witnessing with this presence that God too can and will arrive with ministry in just such times and places. The pastor's showing up to share in these events is a powerful testimony to divine action.[25]

Alienation and Resonance

While drawing on the experiences of Abraham and Paul to account for the presence of God in secularized space, to account for God's presence in secularized time, Root returns to Rosa.

Alienated from the surrounding world, in modernity humanity is alienated also from the transcendent. If time is used simply to gain more resources and things are used simply to support accelerated growth, we lose any relationships that are meaningful. The voices of things around us have been silenced—including the voice of God. Now that we find ourselves in this situation, simply slowing down is not adequate to cure the ills of modernity. As long as dynamic stabilization shapes the practices through which we engage reality, engaging in these practices more slowly will not restore our relationships with those we have alienated.[26]

For Rosa, the medicine for acceleration comes in encounters of resonance.[27] Whereas acceleration leaves the world dull and dead, as our lack of time and increasing speed leave us without connections, resonance does the opposite: It gives us the experience of a real encounter. Resonance is a mode of relating in which a person is truly affected by something and in which they develop an intrinsic interest in that part of reality affecting them. The person feels touched, moved, or addressed by the people, places, or objects they encounter. The capacity for resonance is, according to Rosa, "the 'essence' not only of human existence but of all possible manners of relating to the world."[28]

Take the experience of dear friends meeting for lunch. It may be that so much is exchanged, so many stories shared, that, as the saying goes, time flies. While several hours later, the friends may be surprised at how late it is, it would be wrong to describe their experience of time as an experience of time either accelerating or slowing down. Rather, they experience time as *full*—so full that the encounter, not time, shapes their experience. One can

25. Root, *Pastor in a Secular Age*, 207.
26. Root, *Congregation in a Secular Age*, 174–76, 194.
27. In the words of the famous opening sentence of Rosa's *Resonance*, "If acceleration is the problem, then resonance may well be the solution." Rosa, *Resonance*, 1.
28. Rosa, *Uncontrollability of the World*, 31.

have such experiences in interpersonal encounters, but such experiences can come also in one's relationships to objects, events, art, and nature. Music can speak to us, a book can draw us in, and nature can render us speechless. When we long to escape the dullness and deadness of modernity's alienation, we are not so much longing for time to slow down as we are longing for these kinds of experiences.

Rosa describes resonance as a mode of relating that can be defined by two pairs of characteristics. It exists, first of all, in a sense of being affected. When we resonate with something, we find that it calls to us and becomes important to us for its own sake. This sense of being affected by something external to us corresponds, secondly, with a subsequent act of response. It includes the awareness that we have the capacity to reach out and affect others and that we can respond to what engages us.[29] As Rosa points out, in this, resonance is the opposite of, and an antidote to, alienated depression. It is symptomatic of depression that nothing touches or moves the depressed person anymore,[30] but resonance "synchronizes our own action with the world itself."[31] Rosa tries to visualize this first pair of characteristics by using arrows: Resonance involves experiences of "af←fection" and "e→motion"; there is something that touches us by moving toward us, and we find ourselves responding with a movement in the opposite direction, toward that which touches us.[32]

A third characteristic of resonance is that experiencing resonance changes us—most often subtlety, but sometimes radically. Because of this, a person may say that an encounter of resonance—the meeting of a particular person, the reading of a special book, the listening to some specific music—renders them a different person. In this way, resonance is life-giving. This third characteristic forms a pair with the fourth: Resonance, as such, is uncontrollable. It cannot be manufactured or engineered. That makes it very different from the methods that support dynamic stabilization. Resonance demands that we await the arrival of the other.[33]

---

29. "The simplest version of such a resonant relationship consists in an exchange of glances, or in a dialogue in which the two speakers both listen and respond to each other. Our eyes are windows of resonance. To look into someone's eyes and feel them looking back is to resonate with them." Rosa, *Uncontrollability of the World*, 33.
30. Rosa, *Uncontrollability of the World*, 34.
31. Root, *Congregation in a Secular Age*, 207.
32. Rosa, *Resonance*, 174; Rosa, "Two Versions of the Good Life & Two Forms of Fear," 18.
33. In addition to *Resonance*, one of Rosa's large books, very helpful shorter introductions to his understanding of resonance can be found in Rosa, *Uncontrollability of the World*, chap. 4; Rosa, "Two Versions of the Good Life & Two Forms of Fear"; and Harmut Rosa, "Acceleration and Resonance: An Interview with Hartmut Rosa," interview by Bjørn Schiermer, *Acta Sociologica*, E-Special: Four Generations of Critical Theory in *Acta Sociologica* (2018), https://journals.sagepub.com/pb-assets/cmscontent/ASJ/Acceleration_and_Resonance.pdf.

Root uses these four characteristics of resonance to think about the calling of the congregation in a time of the secularization of space and time.[34] Congregations themselves experience and generate alienation because they have lost faith in real transformation—denying the possibility of becoming different people through real encounters with the divine.[35] Assuming real transformation is impossible, they think the best they can do is innovation—that is, changes that play by the rules of dynamic stabilization, aiming to expand the congregations' reach and resources in order to survive. But once congregations get into this groove, the world becomes mute and God is silenced.[36] Root worries that many methods of faith formation, missional redevelopment, and innovation are thus beholden to the same practically atheist principles that erected the immanent frame and lead only to congregational alienation and depression.

If congregations want to rediscover God, they will therefore have to attend to resonance rather than to innovation. And resonance, Root argues—and this, once again, is the theological element in Root's analysis I wish to call attention to—is found in the way of the cross. "Suffering awakens to otherness," and experiencing otherness lies at the heart of the experience of resonance.[37] "Sharing in death—in the brokenness of persons' narratives, ministering to one another . . . —awakens . . . to life itself."[38] To experience resonance, we therefore ought to be rooted in kenosis, to begin with humility, to have "the willingness to see our own and our neighbor's death experience."[39] It is through this stance, when I realize that "I'm the kind of creature who needs to

---

34. Rosa's analysis of alienation and resonance in modernity has drawn significant attention from theologians and religious scholars. See, e.g., Martin Laube, "'Eine bessere Welt is möglich,': Theologische Überlegungen zur Resonanztheorie Hartmut Rosas," *Pastoraltheologie* 107 (2018): 356–70; Roland Rosenstock, "'Etwas, was nicht ist und doch nicht nur nicht ist': Konturen einer resonanzsensiblen Theologie im Gespräch mit Hartmut Rosa," *Pastoraltheologie* 107 (2018): 401–7; Darío Montero and Felipe Torres, "Acceleration, Alienation, and Resonance: Reconstructing Hartmut Rosa's Theory of Modernity," *Pléyade* 25 (2020): 155–81; Jörg Hübner, "Reich-Gottes-Hoffnung als Auferstehungs-Resonanz: Hartmut Rosas Resonanzkonzept ins Gespräch gebracht—ein theologisches Experiment," *Evangelische Theologie* 81, no. 3 (2021): 223–36; Bojan Žalec, "Rosa's Theory of Resonance: Its Importance for (the Science of) Religion and Hope," *Religions* 12, no. 10 (2021): 797, https://doi.org/10.3390/rel12100797; Oriol Quintana and Xavier Casanovas Combalia, "Resonance: The Final Dissolution of Religions or the Last Stage of Secularization," *Religions* 14, no. 6 (2023): 689, https://doi.org/10.3390/rel14060689. As may be apparent, all these studies come from Europe. One of the merits of Root's work is that he has introduced Rosa's work into the North American conversation about church and secularization.
35. Root, *Congregation in a Secular Age*, 209.
36. Root, *Congregation in a Secular Age*, 209.
37. Root, *Congregation in a Secular Age*, 202n22.
38. Root, *Congregation in a Secular Age*, 223.
39. Root, *Congregation in a Secular Age*, 236.

find resonance with otherness" and that "I'm a person who *is* in and through relationship," that I may find resonance and, thereby, transformation.[40] And the same is true on the level of the congregation.

Finding God

Is it true, though, that God is to be found particularly, or even exclusively, in experiences of brokenness? Is Root correct that God first must be absent in order to be present? Is faith, indeed, born only out of an experience of negation—of longing and death?

It is certainly deeply ingrained in all kinds of religious experiences that God can be trusted to be present when life falls apart. Psalms, ancient and contemporary, sing of how God has come through in times of crisis, of how God comes near when nothing else can be relied on. Calling attention to experiences of life out of death, of God's presence being found there, where there seems to be no future and no hope, can be particularly encouraging for congregations that ask, bewildered, whether their current experience of decline really is the future that God has in mind for them.

It is also likely to be true that, for good or ill, human beings are more open to divine presence in times when it seems that nothing else can be relied on, when nothing else seems to count anymore, when our own agency has come to its end.

Nevertheless, none of this suggests that God can be present and experienced *only* in times of crises. In fact, I contend that the very building blocks Root uses for a new theology of the cross actually point in a different direction. The stories of Abraham and Paul and the notion of resonance call out for a narrative of divine presence that is much more expansive than the one Root offers, in which encounters with the divine are limited to moments of nothingness and despair. In fact, they call out for one in which God *causes*, rather than responds to, an experience of cross pressure.

Divine Presence and Cross Pressure

As I've noted, Root's theology of the cross comes as a twofold cruciform description of reality: the cross pressure one experiences when the transcendent knocks on the door of the immanent frame and the experience of divine presence at times of negation and death. Root does not actually give us an account of how these different cruciform layers of reality connect, though

---

40. Root, *Congregation in a Secular Age*, 238.

the flow of his argument suggests he identifies the two kinds of experience. However, on closer inspection, the experience of cross pressure and the experience of God's showing up in times of negation and death actually follow a very different logic.

Cross pressure obtains when one's socially constructed narratives of the immanent frame lose plausibility in the face of experienced reality. One has an experience of the divine that simply does not fit one's social imagination. Embracing that experience as real will therefore lead to a crumbling of one's meaning-making narrative, forcing one to adopt a new narrative. What dies is one's construction of meaning; and it dies in the light of one's encounter with an abundance of transcendent life that cannot be contained by the narrow confinement of the immanent frame. But when God shows up in the cruciform experiences of life, what dies is not one's (social) construct of meaning and life but life itself. Life diminishes in experiences of brokenness, or tragedy, or despair. The hospital room or the deathbed seem to be signs of the end, but God turns them around so they can be sites of consolation and new hope. Such experiences can be occasions for significant encounters with God. However, divine action in the cruciform experiences of life works differently than divine action in cross pressure.

In the former case, of God's showing up in times of negation and death, God's presence *follows* the experience of cruciformity; in the latter case, of cross pressure, God's presence *precedes* and *causes* the experience of death. In the former, human beings find themselves already in crisis: death already has entered their existence, life as they know it is already crumbling, and then God comes to be near them. But in the latter, God's knocking at the door of the immanent frame causes the crisis. Before that moment, there is no reason to think anything is wrong. The entrance of God into one's life reveals that everything one has lived by previously has been a lie, and this precipitates an existential crisis. This difference between divine action in the cruciform experiences of life and divine action in cross pressure is important to keep in mind as we engage the biblical stories of Paul and Abraham that Root cites. These narratives have a logic akin to the logic that governs experiences of cross pressure, not one similar to the logic that governs God's showing up in times of death and despair. The biblical texts do not mention any personal experiences of crisis either in Abraham's case or in Paul's prior to God's showing up. As far as the texts indicate, neither were aware of anything in particular having gone wrong with their lives. There is no word about negation, crisis, or despair. God doesn't show up in their lives in moments of crisis; rather, God's showing up precipitates crises. Once God enters their lives, everything they thought they knew has to be radically reevaluated, and a whole different kind of existence is opened up to them.

Admittedly, there is a plurality of readings of these texts within the Christian tradition. Protestant theology has tried to turn both Abraham and Paul into proto-Protestant believers whose encounters with God were something akin to Luther's search for a gracious God. Such readings portray Paul against the background of a first-century Judaism that supposedly aimed to curry God's favors through strict adherence to the law, a striving Paul experienced himself to be failing in as much as the sixteenth-century Luther knew himself to be failing in living up to the expectations of divine righteousness. This hermeneutic portrays Abraham as a desolate sinner, looking for forgiveness and grace, who comes to God "bringing nothing of his own, except a confession of his misery, which is a solicitation of mercy," and who finds that salvation is faithfully accepting the grace of God.[41] However, the biblical texts bear out none of this. First-century Judaism knew as much as Luther did that grace was a gift and not something to be earned. The Saul who is on his way to Damascus experienced no troubled conscience; in fact, he considered himself "as to righteousness under the law, blameless" (Phil. 3:6).[42] Nowhere is Abraham described as wrestling with sin. He does struggle with whether God will keep God's promises (Exod. 15); but this struggle is, again, caused by God's appearance and promises to Abraham (Gen. 12). God causes, rather than resolves, this struggle.[43]

With the exception of his portrayal of Sarah, who is characterized as a woman wrestling with a sense of divine rejection—for which there is no basis in the biblical narrative whatsoever—Root does not fall into the trap of portraying these biblical figures as proto-Protestant believers. But his exegesis does continue the Protestant hermeneutic of reading their stories as moving from crisis into divine presence, even though, in the texts, their lives seem to cohere just fine *until* they are turned upside down by the call of God.

This is good news, however, for Christian congregations wrestling with the reality of the immanent frame. It means that God does not have to wait until the stories we tell about ourselves fracture; God's presence is not contingent upon felt crises in our lives. According to the biblical stories, God's voice sovereignly breaks through any kind of frame, whether it is the polytheistic frame

---

41. John Calvin, *Commentaries on the Epistle of Paul the Apostle to the Romans*, trans. and ed. John Owen (Baker, 2005), 155.

42. The now-classic takedown of Paul as a proto-Lutheran is Krister Stendahl's "The Apostle Paul and the Introspective Conscience of the West," in *Paul Among Jews and Gentiles and Other Essays* (Fortress, 1971), 60–78.

43. For a discussion of the ways Protestant theology has traditionally misread the Abraham figure, and the theological consequences thereof, see Van Driel, *Rethinking Paul*, 38–68.

of Abraham's day, the inability of Jewish leaders in Jesus's day to recognize the Christ in their midst, or our culture's difficulty in finding the door to the transcendent. God does not need death or despair to get a hearing; God creates a hearing if and when God wills. But if this is true, we need a different story about divine presence and agency.

Resonance and Divine Presence

Building blocks for such a narrative, I believe, can come from Root's second source of inspiration: Rosa's account of resonance. Root suggests congregations find resonance in the way of the cross. He does not offer much of an argument for this other than that suffering awakens us to otherness. Rosa's own discussion of resonance, however, suggests both a much more expansive understanding and a different focus.

Rosa maps experiences of resonance along three axes. There are horizontal, or social, experiences of resonance in encounters of love, friendship, and family relationships, as well as in wider social life, including politics. There are diagonal, or material, experiences of resonance in encounters with objects— the wood of the carpenter, the board of the surfer, the ball of the soccer player. There are also vertical, or existential, experiences of resonance that connect us with life, or the universe, as such. For some, such experiences may come in hiking the mountains or otherwise communing with the natural world. For others, they may come in reading a book, listening to music, or engaging a piece of visual art. For still others, they may come in the practice of religion.

A sense of delight is characteristic of these experiences of resonance.[44] In resonance we come to enjoy something, as Rosa says, "for its own sake."[45] When friends spend a lunch together and experience, therein, resonance, they discover something deeper in each other's company than any benefit they might obtain, more significant than any end for which their lunch together might be a means. Rather, they find joy, delight, in simply being with each other.

For Rosa, the promise of this kind of encounter penetrates to the heart of the Christian faith. Religion concerns "a relationship, one which promises the categories of *love* and *meaning* as a guarantee that the basic, primal form of existence is a relationship not of alienation but of resonance."[46] The Bible, Rosa holds, can be interpreted as a plea for resonance—a plea responded to

---

44. Interestingly, Root notices this (see Root, *Congregation in a Secular Age*, 196–98); however, nowhere in his use of Rosa's account of resonance does he observe that delight and cruciform experiences do not easily sit together.

45. Rosa, *Uncontrollability of the World*, 32.

46. Rosa, *Resonance*, 258.

with a promise: "There is one who hears you, who understands you, who can find ways and means of reaching you and responding to you."[47] Religious rites, such as the Eucharist or blessings, are ways in which "the experience of deep vertical resonance is connected both to horizontal axes of resonance between the faithful . . . and to diagonal resonant relationships, inasmuch as things and artifacts such as the bread, chalice, wine, and cross . . . are here 'charged' with resonance."[48] From the perspective of resonance theory, sin then "is to be understood as a state of resonancelessness, or rather *resistance to resonance*, in which the subject is neither ready, willing nor able to hear any voice but its own."[49] Nonetheless, Rosa holds, "religion is then a promise that the world or the universe or God still speaks (or *sings*) to us *even when we are incapable of hearing it, when all our axes of resonance have fallen mute*."[50]

An Alternative Story About Divine Presence

Embedded in the work of Root and Rosa are thus two stories about divine presence in a secular world. Both emphasize divine agency: Communion with God is not in our hands but is dependent on God's free decision to become present in our midst. Root emphasizes this repeatedly as he urges the church not to rely on its own agency in innovating its own future but instead to be present faithfully at the moments of cross pressure in human experience, to wait for God to show up. A similar emphasis is embedded in Rosa's notion of resonance, as he underscores that this experience is uncontrollable and cannot be fabricated or manipulated.

However, Root and Rosa differ in their accounts of what kind of relationship is established when God does appear. In earlier chapters, I reflected on the difference between relationships characterized by *being with* and relationships characterized by *being for*. *Being for* describes attitudes and relationships built on a perceived need. It assumes a deficit that can be remedied, a problem that needs to be solved. It describes relationships that do not demand that the relating parties engage one another for their own sakes. The relationships are functional, constituted by and focused on the work that must be done. The very core of *being with* is different. It describes a relationship in which the partners enjoy each other for their own sakes. It is not based on a deficiency that needs to be met or a problem that needs to be solved. It is not a relationship contingent upon a larger goal; rather, *the relationship is the goal*.

---

47. Rosa, *Resonance*, 261.
48. Rosa, *Resonance*, 263.
49. Rosa, *Resonance*, 265.
50. Rosa, *Resonance*, 265.

The account of divine presence that is driving Root's narrative is shaped by *being for*. God shows up when things are falling apart and is *for* us—directing us toward a future, creating new life, providing resurrection. The account of divine presence to which Rosa's notion of resonance points, on the other hand, is shaped by *being with*: It is about the voice who was present before all else, about a God who, in offering us an experience of resonance with the divine, offers us an experience in which we enjoy God not for what God can to offer or for the difference God can make but simply for God's own sake. And, if resonance is what Rosa claims that it is, this experience is also one in which God enjoys us for our own sakes. On Root's account, God's presence is ultimately in the service of something else: God comes in order to deal with a problem. As such, the relationship created by this divine presence is functional. But on Rosa's account, the relationship itself is the goal.

The Story of Divine Resonance

A theology of the cross does not do right by the intuitions embedded in the idea that the core proclamation of the Scriptures is about divine resonance. A theology that holds, with Rosa, that resonance is the "primal form of existence" would do well to unpack this vision in terms of a theology shaped by a divine *being with*, rather than a divine *being for*.[51] Supralapsarian Christology, determined in particular by the notion of the primacy of Christ, offers the building blocks to tell such a theological story of divine resonance.

On the account that fuels the argument of this book, everything that exists is embedded in, shaped by, and directed toward the divine commitment to *be with* us. God's very first decision *ad extra* is to be Jesus Christ; the human family is called into existence "in order that he might be the firstborn within a large family" (Rom. 8:29), and all of creation is standing on tiptoe awaiting "the revealing of the children of God" (Rom. 8:19). Creation is to be the home of God and God's family, the theater stage on which the life of friendship and love will unfold.

On this account, the story of God and creation is not a story driven by what is lacking or by what went wrong. Rather, it is a story driven by abundance and what has always been right. It is driven not by brokenness but by wholesomeness. It is shaped not by death but by life. It reverberates not with cruciformity but with experiences of delight.

This is not to deny the ways in which sin, evil, and death are at work to undermine the goodness of creation; to turn abundance into scarcity; to break

---

51. Rosa, *Resonance*, 258.

that which God made whole; to reject the very love, friendship, and community for which we were created. Supralapsarian Christology does not take the realities of sin and evil any less seriously than a theology of the cross. But it holds that these realities are discovered only in the light of the goodness of God's *being with*, not the other way around. I discover myself to be a sinner only in the light of the revelation of Jesus Christ, a revelation that resonates with the very reason for which I exist. If this is true, supralapsarian Christology offers many more paths to await, discern, and evoke the presence of God in our lives than a cruciform theology does. God does not enter our world only at the places where it is crushed. God is not recognized only in that which goes wrong. It is not only at the places where sin, death, and evil are experienced that God must be proclaimed. Every aspect of a creature's life exists for the sake of divine *being with* and can become a place of community with God and with other creatures.

Rosa's account of resonance, I propose, ought to be read as the sociological account of the theological claim that all of creation is meant to be God's home. And the kind of supralapsarian Christology explored in this book narrates the story in which such a theological claim makes sense.

An Ecclesiological Expression

If all of existence is created for resonance, this invites new thinking about the identity of the church and its mission. If from the beginning God intended all of creation to be gathered into Christ, if the incarnation is the expression of the divine intention to be with human beings and for human beings to be with God, then community formation is at the heart of the *missio Dei*. God wants to be with humans, and God enacts this intention in a very concrete, embodied form by taking on flesh, living in a specific place and time, and drawing a group of friends around him. The proclamation of the New Testament is that this gathering has never ended, that the resurrected and ascended Christ continues to knit people into this community, expanding and widening it until all of creation has been gathered into him (Eph. 1:10).

There is a tendency in missional ecclesiology to think about the church as only a witness to the missional work of God, a means to a larger goal. God is thought to be focused fundamentally on the establishment of God's reign, not on the establishment of the church. The church should consider itself as existing for the sake of the world. However, a theological vision focused on divine resonance as the keynote of creation and on the incarnation as focused on establishing a community of God being with God's people and God's people being with one another will have to reject this tendency. This is because, on this vision, the church itself is the expression of Christ's gathering work; the church is the community in which God's gift of *being with* is already experienced.[52]

Moreover, North American Christians tend to think about the church as an expression of our response to God's being *with us* or *for us*—that is, they tend to think about the church as a voluntary community in which those who respond to the gospel positively flock together, responding in faithfulness to God's gift of salvation. Seen through that lens, the reality of the church of the secular age, with its aging membership, its decreasing numbers, and its disappearing resources, can only lead to depression and alienation. But if the church itself is an expression of Christ's gathering work, as the reality of his forging of a new community around himself, then the church is itself the sign of his continued presence. Every Sunday morning when the pastor stands in front of her flock, however small, however aging, she may know that the very reason that both they and she are there is that Christ is with them—as the very reason they *are* is that Christ drew them to himself.

Finally, this vision leads us to the same place that Lesslie Newbigin was led in his postcolonial response to traditional Protestant ecclesiology.[53] As I noted in a previous chapter, in reaction to the Roman Catholic understanding of the church as mediator of salvation, Protestants tend to hold that the church is not necessary for obtaining salvation. Salvation, on this view, is one's own getting into the right with God, which is something obtained by grace through the faith of the individual believer. Against this, Newbigin advocates an account in which ecclesiology and soteriology are essentially intertwined. Similarly, in an ecclesiology shaped by the idea of *being with* and *resonance*, salvation is about community formation. To "be saved" is to be reached by Christ's gathering work, to be knitted into this new, concrete, embodied community around the incarnate One.

Being With, *Being Silent, and Resonance*

Finally, such a theological vision has both the need and the potential to develop a richly nuanced, multilayered understanding of divine *being with* and resonance. *Being with* and resonance are not the same thing. As Rosa observes,

---

52. As Lesslie Newbigin continued to emphasize, the church is not just the instrument and sign but also the first fruits of salvation (see chap. 6, above). This is a dimension absent from Root's work, as Root tends to speak about the church as only the witness to God's arrival. This tendency is strengthened by his interest in the work of the younger Karl Barth, for whom the church is an event rather than an established reality. See Root, *Churches and the Crisis of Decline*.

53. See "Church and Mission" in chap. 6, above, 119–20.

resonance is uncontrollable. It cannot be manufactured or engineered. It is, therefore, not a given. Friends can be together without experiencing resonance. They may catch each other's eye, but nothing is exchanged. Human beings can exist in a state of resonancelessness, or resistance to resonance, and not be willing or hear one another, whether the other is another creature or God. But this does not mean that one is not held in a relationship of *being with*. One can be with one's friend even if one does not experience resonance with them. God can still be with us—in fact, Rosa claims, God promises still to speak—even when we cannot hear or experience God. In other words, on this vision we can see even our culture, locked up in the immanent frame as it is, as held within in the presence of God's *being with*.

Reflecting on both the relationship and the distinction between *being with* and resonance will help us think through questions about divine agency, presence, and absence with regard to secularization and post-Christian cultural realities. Since resonance is uncontrollable, the absence of resonance with God in a culture caught within the immanent frame may be not only a reflection of a cultural inability to listen but also the result of a divine decision not to speak. Rosa's claim that God promises to continue to make God known even when we have become deaf to God's voice may be too optimistic.

First Samuel 3 tells the famous story from Samuel's apprenticeship at the sanctuary at Shiloh in which Samuel receives a nighttime visitation as the Lord calls him into divine service. The story starts by telling us, "The word of the LORD was rare in those days; visions were not widespread" (1 Sam. 3:1). This is not a thing we hear about very often in the Scriptures. Usually, the God of the Bible is a speaking God, a revealing God, an active God. But maybe this is a somewhat misleading picture. Yes, the Scriptures dwell on the mighty events of God's intervention and presence. But this may cause us to miss the fact that there were vast stretches of time in between these events, stretches of time in which God's voice was not heard and God's presence was not sensed. There are the centuries that Israel is said to have lived in Egypt before God finally appeared to Moses. There is the time of the judges. And there are the centuries between the end of the Old Testament and the beginning of the New. These are all times from which we hear hardly anything about divine speech. Seen in this light, divine speech, visions from the Lord, or resonance with God may be much rarer and fragmentary than we might usually think or want.

As theologians, we do not reflect often on this kind of divine silence. But I think we neglect this aspect of God's dealing with God's people in the Scriptures to our peril. I wonder whether such a silent period is not the very kind of thing we, the church in the West, are experiencing right now.

We tend to speak about this time of secularization as a time in which our culture has grown hard of hearing, as one in which the culture at large is unwilling to listen. Many of us also see this time, in which so many institutional structures are crumbling and disappearing, as a chance to renew our listening to God—as an opportunity to, like missional theologians like to say, discern where God is present and how we can get in on it.

But all this still assumes God is speaking. It still assumes God is doing things that can be seen. But what if the problem actually lies deeper than our inability to hear? What if God has been silent? What if, as in the time of Samuel, the word of the Lord is rare, and visions are not widespread? What if God is withholding divine resonance rather than granting it?

There is, however, also another side to the setting of the story of Samuel's call. Judges makes clear that the sanctuary at Shiloh, and the leadership in charge of it, were deeply compromised. Eli's sons, who were to follow him as priests, were completely unsuitable for the job. Eli himself was turning a blind eye. The complaints of the people were ignored. The sanctuary had become a corrupt institution, and maybe it is therefore no wonder that the word of the LORD had become rare and visions were not widespread. But even with all of that being the case, "the lamp of God had not yet gone out, and Samuel was lying down in the temple of the LORD, where the ark of God was" (1 Sam. 3:3). The lamp of God is the lamp that was to burn in the temple day and night as a sign of the presence of God. The ark was the artifact that God had told Moses and Aaron to build and put in the holiest part of the tabernacle. It was a box with two golden angels on it who held their wings so as to form a seat, and on this seat God was thought to sit, enthroned in the midst of Israel. Even in this corrupt institution, served by unsuitable priests, in a time when the Lord's word was rare, the lamp of the Lord still had not gone out, and the ark, the place of God's presence, was still there.

As it turns out, God may withhold resonance, but this does not mean that God also withholds God's presence. God's word was rare, but God was not absent. God was not experienced, but God had not withdrawn. God was still *with* the people. *Being with* denotes more than only resonance. In this lies consolation for a church living in the immanent frame. From the many examples and experiences Root has gathered in his books, we may know and trust that God will show up in times of cruciformity, when all that we have relied on breaks apart and we feel that we have reached the end of our rope. Yet, from the analyses of resonance that Rosa offers in his studies, we may infer that it is not just moments of cruciformity that open the door to the coming of the Lord; God also reveals Godself and is known and experienced in moments of delight, of joy, of abundance. But, as the Samuel story illustrates, even when God is not experienced, when God is not seen, when God's voice is not heard, God can still be trusted to be there. God's presence is more abundant, wider in reach, and richer in texture than that which is experienced even in resonance and cruciformity. And supralapsarian Christology has a way of telling us why: because divine *being with* is the grain of the universe; because everything is called into existence for the sake of the firstborn; because the very first thing that God decides is to be Jesus Christ.

Conclusion

The Promise of Supralapsarian Christology

In the introduction to this collection of explorations of supralapsarian Christology, I raised the question, What would it look like to rethink our understanding of the biblical narratives, and of the theological *loci* that are built on these, in the light of the intuition that the very first thing that God decides is to be Jesus Christ? What would it look like to think about the whole story of creation through to the eschaton as an unfolding of God's commitment to give Godself to what is not God, to be a God-with-others? What would it be like to rethink all major doctrines of the church in the light of the absolute priority of Jesus Christ? The arguments of this book offer tentative responses to these questions.

As I look back at these explorations and imagine what might be the way ahead, I recall the four characteristics I named in the conclusion to chapter 7 as shaping a supralapsarian Christological doctrine of election. These four, it turns out, aptly describe the general contours of the theological approach taken in this book as a whole. Together, they also indicate what a fully-fleshed-out supralapsarian Christological dogmatics might look like. In opposite order, these characteristics are as follows.

The story told in this book concerns a divine movement that is *participatory but not divinizing*. God's first commitment *ad extra* is not simply to create what is not God but to establish what is not God as the recipient of God's very own presence, friendship, and love. Everything that exists is embedded in and determined by this fundamental act of divine self-giving. Every aspect of creation is participated in by the incarnate One. Therefore, there is no need for the divinization of creatures, for human participation in the divine powers, energies, or life. Creation already participates in the life of God because creatures are created to be the company of Jesus.

God's act of participation creates relationships, therefore, that are *both highly communal and deeply personal*. Community formation is essential to the incarnation. God comes to *be with*. The goal of all things is to be drawn into Christ. This implies that all things are also drawn to one another, as expressed by the notions of family, friendship, and covenant. At the same time, as these notions express, the relationships thus forged are deeply personal. They are all embedded in a *being with* the incarnate One. This way of telling the story challenges the centrifugal movements in Christian spirituality and ecclesiology that draw apart individual piety and common life and that divide forms of Christian community along the lines of personal preferences or theological or liturgical commitments. If Christ is drawing all things into himself, one always finds him in the company of all, but this company in turn is held together only by his personal presence.

Therefore, this kind of supralapsarian Christological narrative also has the potential to resolve deeply felt tensions between *the particular and the universal*. In becoming a human being, a creature of flesh and blood, God becomes a particular creature, located in a particular space, shaped by a particular time, bound through ties of nature and culture to a particular family and tribe. At the same time, it is this one, in his particularity, who draws *all* things into himself. Embedded in God's supralapsarian commitment to be Jesus is thus also a supralapsarian commitment to Israel, as well as to the universal reach God's covenant with Abraham will have. Israel is not a plan B, nor is the church a plan C. Supersessionism is cut off from the beginning, but so is the thought that Jews and gentiles have their own respective paths to the God of Israel, the Creator of all.

Finally, in all of this, the narrative expresses a form of divine relating in Jesus Christ that is *supralapsarian but not instrumental*. The incarnation does not serve a greater good; it is the good. Christ is not the means to a larger goal; the means is the goal. The goal of incarnation is to *be with*, and this goal is embodied in and accomplished by the very person of Jesus Christ himself. Because of this, supralapsarian Christology offers a uniform story in which Christ's *being with* is central to each of the three major ways in which God relates to what is not God: All that is not God depends for its existence on God's work of creation. God draws this creation toward eschatological consummation. And when creation wanders away, God draws it back in reconciliation.

In the narrative explored in this book, each of these acts of divine relating circles around the very same thing. Creation is called into existence to be the recipient of the gift of incarnation. We are human beings because Christ is a human being, not the other way around. We have eyes so that we may see him, hands so we may touch him, bodies so that we may sit down and eat with him. The goal of our lives is to be his friends and family; the goal of the cosmos to be the theater of God's *being with*. Eschatological consummation is the unending celebration of this *being with*: It is the realization of the *visio Dei*, in which our eyes will finally and permanently behold the incarnate God. It is the messianic meal, the heavenly banquet, the wedding feast. It is the exploration, new every day, of the goodness of what it means to be in the presence of the incarnate One and one another. Finally, reconciliation takes the shape of the persistence of God's commitment to *being with*. When we wander away from God, resist God's presence, reject God's incarnation, God persists, refusing to return our rejection in kind. Rather, God absorbs our rejection and is *with* us even if that means death and the grave. God overcomes sin exactly by staying true to God's first and ultimate determination: to be a God who is with us. In all this, the incarnation does not become a means for a larger goal, an instrument to obtain a larger good. The incarnation continues to be a divine *being with*, the center of the universe, the goal for which everything exists, the firstborn of creation.

CREDITS

An earlier version of chapter 1 was published as "God and God's Beloved: A Constructive Re-Reading of Scotus' Supralapsarian Christological Argument," *Heythrop Journal* 63 (2022): 995–1006. Reprinted with permission of John Wiley & Sons.

An earlier version of chapter 2 was published as "'To Know Nothing Except Jesus Christ, and Him Crucified': Supralapsarian Christology and a Theology of the Cross," in *The Wisdom and Foolishness of God: First Corinthians 1–2 in Theological Exploration*, ed. Christophe Chalamet and Hans-Christoph Askani (Fortress, 2015). Reprinted with permission of Fortress Press.

An earlier version of chapter 3 was published as "'Too Lowly to Reach God Without a Mediator': John Calvin's Supralapsarian Eschatological Narrative," *Modern Theology* 33, no. 2 (2017): 275–92. Reprinted with permission of John Wiley & Sons.

An earlier version of chapter 4 was published as "'His Death Manifested Its Power and Efficacy in Us': The Role of Christ's Resurrection in John Calvin's Theology," *Journal of Reformed Theology* 12 (2018): 217–34. Reprinted with permission.

An earlier version of chapter 5 was published as "Sharing in Nature or Encountering a Person: A Tale of Two Different Supralapsarian Strategies," *Scottish Journal of Theology* 75, no. 3 (2022): 193–206. © Cambridge University Press, reproduced with permission.

An earlier version of chapter 6 was published as "All Things Summed Up into Christ: On a Particular Christological Impetus of Lesslie Newbigin's Missional-Ecumenical Project," *Ecclesiology* 21 (2024): 191–211. Reprinted with permission.

An earlier version of chapter 7 was published as "'All Things Have Been Created For Him': On Christ, Election, and Creation," in *T&T Clark Handbook to Election*, ed. Edwin Chr. van Driel (Bloomsbury, 2023). Reprinted with permission.

An earlier version of chapter 8 was published as "Incarnation and Israel: A Supralapsarian Account of Israel's Chosenness," *Modern Theology* 39 (2023): 3–18. Reprinted with permission of John Wiley & Sons.

Part of chapter 11 reuses sections of "Supra/infralapsarianism," in *T&T Clark Companion to Atonement*, ed. Adam J. Johnson (Bloomsbury T&T Clark, 2017). Used with permission.

INDEX

Abraham, call of, 146–47, 170n57
Adams, Marilyn McCord, 27–28, 159, 205n11, 210n30
adoption to sonship, 183, 195–97
Albert the Great, 7, 20n7
Anderson, Gary A., 238n43, 238n44, 238n45, 239n47, 240n52
Anselm of Canterbury, 48, 227–29
Aquinas, Thomas
  on assumability, 102, 175n2
  on metaphysics of the incarnation, 26n22
  on supralapsarian Christology, 4n2
  on trinitarian theology, 177–84
  on the *visio Dei*, 269–75
ascension, Jesus's, 220
assumption of human nature, 93–94, 104–5, 178–79, 208
astrotheology and supralapsarian Christology, 203–21
Ateek, Naim Stifan, 154
Athanasius, 141n26, 255n12
atonement
  Anselm of Canterbury, 227–28
  Barth, Karl, 231–32
  Calvin, John, 230–31, 237n42, 240
  Forde, Gerhard O., 233–39, 247
  and Israel's cult, 238–41, 243
  Scotus, John Duns, 228–30
  and the suffering servant, 241–44
  and supralapsarian Christology, 35, 225–49
  Tanner, Kathryn, 95–96
  Wells, Samuel, 99, 235–36, 245–47
  and Yom Kippur, 239, 243

Attridge, Harold W., 195n50
Augustine, 18, 36, 131–33, 187n37
Ayers, Lewis, 178n7

Balic, Karl M., 24n18
Balke, W., 60n28
Barclay, John M. G., 42n15
Barnes, Corey L., 180n10
Barnes, Michel, 178n7
Barth, Karl, 30n31, 30n33, 43–44, 105n51, 118n27, 125n49, 132–33, 140n22, 141, 150n44, 166, 256, 262
  on atonement, 231–32
  on supralapsarian Christology, 5
Barth, Markus, 134n9, 135n10, 136n16, 192,46
Battaglia, Vincent, 187n35
Bauckham, Richard, 135, 242n57, 242n58
Bauerschmidt, Frederick Christian, 180n10
Bavinck, Herman, 141n24, 142
Bede Venerabilis, 265
being with, 96–98, 103–4, 137–40, 299–301
  and atonement, 244–49
  and creation, 142–43
  and eschatology, 105, 150, 253–76
  and resonance, 292–301
Billings, J. Todd, 65
Blanke, Helmut, 134n9, 135n10, 136n16, 192n46
Boersma, Hans, 257n16, 269n27, 270n49, 270n54, 270n55, 270n56
Bolt, John, 60n28
Bonaventure, 20n8
  on supralapsarian Christology, 210n30
  on the Trinity, 175, 180n10, 182n18, 199

305

Bonnefoy, Jean-François, 17n1, 21n12, 23n15, 24n17
Bosch, David, 121n37
Bradbury, Rosalene, 34n2, 34n3
Brown, David, 180n10
Burgess, Andrew J., 203, 218n61

Calvin, John, 21, 51–89, 195n52, 198, 265n41, 290n41, 384n8
  on atonement, 230–31, 237n42, 240
  on eschatology, 59–72, 81–87
  on infralapsarian and supralapsarian eschatology, 60–62
  on resurrection, 73–89
  on supralapsarian Christology, 51–59
Campbell, Douglas A., 5n2, 136n16
Canlis, Julie, 52, 57–59, 65n49
Carol, Juniper B., 17n1, 20n8, 21n12, 23n15
Case, Brendan, 20n7, 20n8
Cerbus, Laura, 265n40
Chapman, Stephen B., 239n47
Colossians hymn, 6, 8, 21–22, 133–37, 142–43, 163, 191–93
Combalia, Xavier Casanovas, 287n34
Congdon, David W., 34n1
Cortez, Marc, 150n46, 191n42, 192n47, 269n47, 272n58
counterfactuals and supralapsarian Christology, 21
creation
  and *capax Dei*, 175
  as play, 143
  and supralapsarian Christology, 94–95, 98, 140–43
  Tanner, Kathryn, 94–95
  and the Trinity, 178n7, 180–84
  Wells, Samuel, 98, 142n30
Crisp, Oliver D., 52, 100n41
  on John Calvin and supralapsarian Christology, 53–57
  on supralapsarian Christology, 5n2, 6
cross pressure, 282–85, 288–91
Curry, Eugene A., 209n24

Davis, Joshua B., 44n22
Davison, Andrew, 205, 207, 214–16, 218n60
Dean, Maximilian Mary, 19n4, 21n12
deification, 152, 254–56, 299
Delio, Ilia, 17n1, 28n28, 208n17, 210n29, 213–14
den Bok, Nico, 20n8, 23n16, 26n24, 30n32, 212n41

divinization. *See* deification
Dorner, Isaak, 5
Doughty, Thomas G., Jr., 226n1
Drees, Willem B., 204

Eberhart, Christian A., 239n47
Edmondson, Stephen, 52n5, 58n25, 73n1, 231n15
Edwards, Jonathan
  on the eschaton, 257–58, 270–71
  on the Trinity, 189–90, 199
election
  of Israel, 153–71
  and love, 163–64
  and supralapsarian Christology, 18–19, 29, 117–18, 131–52, 153–71, 219
Ellis, Brannon, 198n56
Emery, Gilles, 180n11
Emmen, E., 64n47, 73n1
Ephesians and supralapsarian Christology, 8, 111–12, 123–26, 139
eschatology
  and *being with*, 253–76
  and deification, 254–56
  Edwards, Jonathan, 257, 258, 270
  and forgetting, 262–65
  Gregory of Nyssa, 257–58
  and preservation of the lived life, 256–58
  and supralapsarian Christology, 36, 46–47, 249–50, 251–76
  Barth, Karl, 105n51, 256
  Tanner, Kathryn, 95–96, 104–5
  Wells, Samuel, 99
  and the *visio Dei*, 269–75

felix culpa, 126n50, 168–69, 258–61
Ferguson, Everett, 257n16
fittingness, argument from, 180
Forde, Gerhard O., 39n10, 233–34, 247
forgetting, eschatological, 42, 47, 262–65
Funes, José G., 207n15

Gaine, Simon Francis, 269n47, 270n50, 270n51, 270n52, 272n58
Gavrilyuk, Paul L., 254n9
Gerken, A., 210n30
Ginther, James R., 20n7
Goheen, Michael W., 110n1, 110n3, 121n37, 125n48, 144n34, 156–57
Goodwin, Thomas, 199n60
Gorman, Michael J., 283n19
Gregory of Nazianzus, 199–200

Index 307

Gregory of Nyssa, 99, 150, 257, 264
Grosseteste, Robert, 19–21, 136n17, 212

Hansen, Danielle Tumminio, 264n37
Harink, Douglas, 44n22
Hart, David Bentley, 5n3
Hayes, Zachary, 177n4, 180n10, 182n18, 199n58
Hebblethwaite, Brian, 207n16
Heidelberg Disputation, 39–41
Herberg, Will, 153n1
Hess, Peter M. J., 207n14
Hitchcock, Nathan, 105n51, 150n44
Hoekendijk, J. C., 121–23
Hofer, Andrew, 254n9
Holmes, Stephen R., 178n7
Horan, Daniel P., 20n8
Hübner, Jörg, 287n34
Hunsberger, George R., 110n3, 112n4, 118n27
Hunter, Justus H., 5n3, 19n5, 20n7, 20n8
Hussey, Phillip A., 5n3, 259–62, 264

Iammarrone, Giovanni, 25n20
image of God, 189–95
　Jesus as the, 190–95
incarnability of the trinitarian persons, 174–75, 177–84
incarnation
　end of, 62–65, 169
　metaphysics of the, 25–26, 100–104, 205–7, 255, 272–73
　multiple, 206–18
intention, divine, 2–4
Israel, election of, 143–46, 153–72

Jansen, J. F., 64n47
Jenson, Robert W., 264
Johnson, Adam J., 232n21
Johnson, Luke Timothy, 195n51
Jones, Beth Felker, 79–80
Jones, Paul Dafydd, 231n15
Jowers, Dennis, 187n35
Jüngel, Eberhard, 256n14

Kaminski, Joel S., 146n37, 146n38
Kandler, Agathon, 25n20
Kelsey, David H., 44n22, 140n22, 191n42, 265n38
Kerr, Nathan R., 44n22
Kierkegaard, Søren, 222–23
Kilby, Karen, 199
knowledge, trinitarian, 181–82

Köstenberger, Andreas J., 200n63
Kugler, Chris, 191n44

Labooy, Guus H., 229n10
Laing, Mark T. B., 110n3, 120n95
Laube, Martin, 287n34
Lee, Yang-Ho, 65n49, 66n52
Legge, Dominic, 180n11
Levenson, Jon D., 158–59, 166n44
Levering, Matthew, 254n9
Lindholm, Stefan, 72n65
Lombard, Peter, 174
Louth, Andrew, 38n7
Lovejoy, Arthur, 19n6
Luther, Martin, 39–41, 265n41, 290

MacIntyre, Alasdair, 143n31
Marshall, Bruce D., 170n57
Martyn, J. Louis, 44–47
Mateo-Seco, Lucas Francisco, 257n16
Maximus the Confessor, 38n7
McAnnally-Linz, Ryan, 251–53, 255n13, 275–76
McCormack, Bruce L., 65, 66n50, 67–68
McDonald, Suzanne, 269n47, 270n49, 270n55
McEvoy, James, 20n7
McFarland, Ian A., 5n3
McKnight, Scot, 134n9, 192n46
means, goal, and incarnation, 118n27, 216–17, 255, 300
　and the election of Israel, 162–63
Meilach, Michael D., 17n1, 21n12
messianic intermezzo, 169
Milgrom, Jacob, 240
missional hermeneutics, 156–57
missional theology, 109–27, 156–57, 277–301
Moberly, R. W. L., 146n38, 158–59, 166n44
Moffit, David M., 239n50
Molinist Christology, 28n30
Moltmann, Jürgen, 35n4, 64n47, 76n6, 142n27
Montero, Darío, 287n34
Moritz, Joshua M., 207n13
Mosser, Carl, 65n49
Muller, Richard A., 64n47

natures and persons, 100–104, 205–8
Newbigin, Lesslie, 109–27, 295
　on the church's mission, 118–20
　on election, 117–18
　on salvation, 115–17
　and supralapsarian Christology, 124–26
Nikolajsen, Jeppe Bach, 110n3

Ollerton, A. J., 65n49
O'Meara, Thomas F., 210n29
Ortlund, Gavin, 269n47
Osiander, Andreas, 51, 55n13, 69n62
Ottati, Douglas F., 204
Owen, John, 270–71

Paas, Stefan, 126n51
Pancheri, Francis Xavier, 17n1, 20n8, 24n17, 30n32
Pannenberg, Wolfhart, 76n6, 210n27, 256n14
participation, 6, 66–71, 94–95, 106, 152, 254, 255, 299–300
particularity and universality, 12, 115, 144, 161–63, 300
Pawl, Timothy, 208n16
persons and natures, 100–104, 205–8
Peters, Ted, 207n13, 208–11
Plato, 141
primacy of Christ, 6–7, 21–22, 136–37, 210–11, 300–301
principle of plenitude, 19, 20n8, 212–13
processiones and *missiones*, trinitarian, 175, 179, 184–87
prologue to the Gospel of John
  and supralapsarian Christology, 9, 139–140, 238n45
Putz, Oliver, 211–13

Quintana, Oriol, 287n34
Quistorp, Heinrich, 64n47, 79–80, 83n46

Rahner, Karl, 2n1, 16, 185–87, 188n22, 210n29
Ramsey, Paul, 257n17
Rauser, Randal, 187n35
resonance, 285–88, 291–98
Rillera, Andrew Remington, 239n46
Rogers, Eugene F., Jr, 5n3
Root, Andrew, 277–98
Rosa, Hartmut, 278, 281–82, 285–88, 291–98
Rosato, Andrew, 229n10
Rosenstock, Roland, 287n34
Rupert of Deutz, 15, 19
Russell, Robert John, 209n24

Schaeffer, Hans, 126n51
Schiermer, Bjørn, 286n33
Schlageter, Johannes, 25n20
Schleiermacher, Friedrich, 155, 166, 168, 258
  and the absolute priority of Christ, 6–7, 9, 21
  and supralapsarian Christology, 6, 106, 107n57, 137n18

Schrader, Dylan, 5n3
Schuster, Jürgen, 110n3, 125n48
Scotus, John Duns, 17–32, 52n6, 202, 132–33, 137n19, 140, 161n31, 210, 215, 228–30
self-communication, divine, 185–87
self-differentiation of trinitarian persons, 175–76, 180–81, 184–89
self-love, divine, 29–30
Shenk, Wilbert, 121n37
Sheridan, Timothy M., 110n1, 121n37
Sherman, M. Scot, 110n3, 121n35
Slater, Jonathan, 65n49, 66
Sleeman, Matthew, 220n63
Sohn, Seock-Tae, 145n35, 145n36
Soulen, R. Kendall, 164–70
Southern, R. J., 48n3, 228n6
Stancaro, Francesco, 58–59
Stendahl, Krister, 290n42
Stoppels, Sake, 126n51
Stump, Eleonore, 259
substance, primary and secondary, 100–101
supersessionism, 164–70
supralapsarian Christology, 2
  and apocalyptic theology, 44–47
  and the argument from counterfactuals, 21
  and the argument from the principle of plenitude, 19–20, 212–13
  and the ascension, 220–21
  and astrotheology, 203–24
  and atonement, 35, 225–49
  and *being with*, 137–40
  and the church, 146–49
  and creation, 94–95, 98, 140–43
  and divine self-differentiation, 187–89
  and election, 18–19, 29, 117–18, 131–71
  and the election of Israel, 143–46
  and eschatological forgetting, 42, 47
  and the eschaton, 36, 46–47, 149–50, 251–76
  and extraterrestrial life, 217–18
  and friendship, 37–38
  and the *missio Dei*, 127
  and missional theology, 109–27, 277–301
  and multiple incarnations, 211–18
  and the primacy of Christ, 6–7, 21–22, 136–37, 210–11, 300–301
  and sin, 41–42
  and supersessionism, 164–70
  and *theologia crucis*, 33–50
  and trinitarian theology, 174–202
  and the *visio Dei*, 36–37, 150n46, 269–75

Index

Tanner, Kathryn, 5n3, 93–127, 255n10, 255n11
Taylor, Charles, 278–82
Tertullian, 142
te Velde, Dolf, 19n3
theologia crucis, 33–50
theology of glory, 39–40
Torrance, T. F., 84n47, 99, 284n22
Torres, Felipe, 287n34
trinitarian theology
   Aquinas, Thomas, 175, 177–84
   Bonaventure, 175, 177n4
   and creation, 180–84
   and divine self-differentiation, 175–76, 180–81, 184–87
   and divine unity and power, 178n7
   Edwards, Jonathan, 175
   Hegel, G. W. F., 175
   and social trinitarianism, 28, 175–76, 199, 235–37, 246–47
   and supralapsarian Christology, 173–203
Turretin, Francis, 72

Unger, Dominic, 27n25

Van Buren, Paul, 73n1, 231n15
Van den Brom, Luco J., 221
Van Gelder, Craig, 110n1
Van Ruler, A. A., 143n32, 169
Veldhuis, Henri, 25n20
Vidu, Adonis, 26n24, 178n7, 187n37, 188n39
visio Dei, 36–37, 269–75

Volf, Miroslav, 47, 251–53, 255n13, 262–66, 275–76
Vos, Antonie, 23n15, 23n16, 229n10

Wainwright, Geoffrey, 110n2, 122n42
Ward, Thomas M., 229n10
Webster, John, 195n49
Weinandy, Thomas G., 184–85, 189, 195
Wells, Samuel, 96–106, 149n43
   on atonement, 99, 235–36, 245–47
   on *being with*, 96–97, 138–39
   on creation, 142n30
   on eschatology, 99, 105
   on the *felix culpa* and sin, 259–60
Weston, Paul, 110n3, 123n47
Widdicombe, Peter, 265n41
Williams, Rowan, 7
Willis, E. David, 52n5, 64n47
Wilson-Kastner, Patricia, 258n17
Wolterstorff, Nicholas, 279n4
Word, trinitarian, 181–83, 185
Wright, Christopher J. H., 144n34, 156–57
Wright, N. T., 5n3, 76n6, 78n14, 136n16, 144n34, 155, 157n18, 162–63, 268
Wyschogrod, Michael, 153, 158, 166n44

Žalec, Bojan, 287n34
Zanchi, Jerome, 71–72
Zscheile, Dwight H., 110n1
Zwijze-Koning, Karen, 126n51